The Poetry of Thought in Late Antiquity
Essays in imagination and religion

PATRICIA COX MILLER
Syracuse University, USA

Routledge
Taylor & Francis Group
LONDON AND NEW YORK

First published 2001 by Ashgate Publishing

Reissued 2019 by Routledge
2 Park Square, Milton Park, Abingdon, Oxon, OX14 4RN
52 Vanderbilt Avenue, New York, NY 10017

Routledge is an imprint of the Taylor & Francis Group, an informa business

© Patricia Cox Miller 2001

Graham Roberts-Phelps has asserted his right under the Copyright, Designs and Patents Act 1988 to be identified as the author of this work.

All rights reserved. No part of this book may be reprinted or reproduced or utilised in any form or by any electronic, mechanical, or other means, now known or hereafter invented, including photocopying and recording, or in any information storage or retrieval system, without permission in writing from the publishers.

Notice:
Product or corporate names may be trademarks or registered trademarks, and are used only for identification and explanation without intent to infringe.

Publisher's Note
The publisher has gone to great lengths to ensure the quality of this reprint but points out that some imperfections in the original copies may be apparent.

Disclaimer
The publisher has made every effort to trace copyright holders and welcomes correspondence from those they have been unable to contact.

A Library of Congress record exists under LC control number:

ISBN 13: 978-1-138-71199-0 (hbk)
ISBN 13: 978-1-138-71195-2 (pbk)
ISBN 13: 978-1-315-19953-5 (ebk)

THE POETRY OF THOUGHT IN LATE ANTIQUITY

Representing a different voice in the study of late ancient religion, these collected essays by Patricia Cox Miller identify new possibilities of meaning in the study of religion in late antiquity. The book addresses the topic of the imaginative mindset of late ancient authors from a variety of Greco-Roman religious traditions. Attending to the play of language, as well as to the late ancient sensitivity to image, metaphor, and paradox, Cox Miller's work highlights the poetizing sensibility that marked many of the texts of this period and draws on methods of interpretation from a variety of contemporary literary-critical theories.

This book will appeal to scholars of late antiquity, religious literature, and literary critical theory more widely, illustrating how fruitful dialogue across the centuries can be - not only in eliciting aspects of late ancient texts that have gone unnoticed but also in showing that many 'modern' ideas, such as Roland Barthes', were actually already alive and well in ancient texts.

Patricia Cox Miller is Professor of Religion at Syracuse University, USA and author of books which include: *Dreams in Late Antiquity* (Princeton University Press) and *Biography in Late Antiquity* (University of California Press).

For David, with love and a chrysanthemum

Contents

Acknowledgements vii
List of Abbreviations ix

INTRODUCTION 1

PART I: POETIC IMAGES AND NATURE

Preface 15

1   "Adam Ate From the Animal Tree": A Bestial Poetry of Soul 19

2   Origen on the Bestial Soul: A Poetics of Nature 35

3   The *Physiologus*: A Poiēsis of Nature 61

4   Jerome's Centaur: A Hyper-icon of the Desert 75

PART II: POETIC IMAGES AND THE BODY

Preface 103

5   "Plenty Sleeps There": The Myth of Eros and Psyche in Plotinus and Gnosticism 107

6   "Pleasure of the Text, Text of Pleasure": Eros and Language in Origen's *Commentary on the Song of Songs* 123

7	The Blazing Body: Ascetic Desire in Jerome's *Letter to Eustochium*	135
8	Desert Asceticism and "The Body from Nowhere"	159

PART III: POETIC IMAGES AND THEOLOGY

Preface		177
9	"In My Father's House Are Many Dwelling Places": κτίσμα in Origen's *De principiis*	181
10	Origen and the Witch of Endor: Toward an Iconoclastic Typology	199
11	Poetic Words, Abysmal Words: Reflections on Origen's Hermeneutics	211
12	In Praise of Nonsense: A Piety of the Alphabet in Ancient Magic	221
13	"Words With An Alien Voice": Gnostics, Scripture, and Canon	247

Bibliography   *271*

Acknowledgements

The articles collected in this volume were written over the course of twenty years and appeared in a variety of publications. I gratefully acknowledge and thank all those who gave permission to reprint these essays. Credit lines are listed in the order in which the essays appear in this volume. Cox, Patricia. "'Adam Ate From the Animal Tree': A Bestial Poetry of Soul", *Dionysius* V (1981), 165-80. With permission of the Editors of *Dionysius*; Cox, Patricia. "Origen on the Bestial Soul: A Poetics of Nature", *Vigiliae Christianae* 36. Copyright 1982 by Brill Academic Publishers. Reproduced with permission of Brill Academic Publishers via Copyright Clearance Center; Cox, Patricia. "The *Physiologus*: A Poiesis of Nature", *Church History* 52 (1983), 433-43. By permission of the Executive Secretary of the American Society of Church History; Miller, Patricia Cox. "Jerome's Centaur: A Hyper-Icon of the Desert", *Journal of Early Christian Studies* 4:2 (1996), 209-233. © The Johns Hopkins University Press. Miller, Patricia Cox. "'Plenty Sleeps There': The Myth of Eros and Psyche in Plotinus and Gnosticism", In Richard T. Wallis and Jay Bregman (eds), *Neoplatonism and Gnosticism*, Studies in Neoplatonism, vol. 6, 223-38. © State University of New York Press, 1992; Miller, Patricia Cox. "'Pleasure of the Text, Text of Pleasure': Eros and Language in Origen's *Commentary on the Song of Songs*", *Journal of the American Academy of Religion* LIV/2 (1986), 241-53; Miller, Patricia Cox. "The Blazing Body: Ascetic Desire in Jerome's *Letter to Eustochium*", *Journal of Early Christian Studies* 1:1 (1993), 21-45. ©The Johns Hopkins University Press; Miller, Patricia Cox. "Desert Asceticism and 'The Body From Nowhere'", *Journal of Early Christian Studies* 2:2 (1994), 137-53. © The Johns Hopkins University Press. Cox, Patricia. "'In My Father's House Are Many Dwelling Places': κτίσμα in Origen's *De principiis*", *Anglican Theological Review* LXII:4 (1980), 322-37; "Origen and the Witch of Endor: Toward an Iconoclastic Typology", *Anglican Theological Review*

LXVI:2 (1984), 137-47; Miller, Patricia Cox. "Poetic Words, Abysmal Words: Reflections on Origen's Hermeneutics", In Charles Kannengiesser and William L. Petersen (eds), *Origen of Alexandria: His World and Legacy*. © University of Notre Dame Press, 1988. Miller, Patricia Cox. "In Praise of Nonsense", In A. H. Armstrong (ed), *Classical Mediterranean Spirituality*, World Spirituality, vol. 15, 481-505. © Crossroad Publishing Company, 1986. Miller, Patricia Cox. "'Words With An Alien Voice': Gnostics, Scripture, and Canon", *Journal of the American Academy of Religion* LVII/3 (1989), 459-83.

There are three people to whom I offer special thanks for their contributions to the making of this volume. First, I thank Sarah Lloyd, commissioning editor at Ashgate Publishing, for her initial interest in and enthusiasm for the project; I am very appreciative of her support. Second, I am deeply indebted to Deborah Pratt, an outstanding member of the staff that keeps the Religion Department at Syracuse University operative. Without her generous devotion of time, technological wizardry, and keen eye for detail, I would not have been able to manage the volume in a timely fashion, if at all. Finally, I thank my husband and colleague, David L. Miller. He suggested the idea of a collection of essays (and gently persisted until I came to believe in the idea myself) and, more than anyone else, he has taught me to understand that "there is no wing like meaning" (Stevens, *Opus Posthumous*, p. 162). I dedicate this book to him with love and admiration.

Abbreviations

ACW	*Ancient Christian Writers* (Newman Press, New York, 1946—)
ANF	*Ante-Nicene Fathers* (Christian Literature Company, New York; Eerdmans, Grand Rapids, 1867—)
AP	*Apophthegmata patrum*
CCL	*Corpus Christianorum*, Series Latina (Brepols, Turnhout, Belgium, 1953—)
Comm.	*Commentarius, Commentarii*
CSEL	*Corpus Scriptorum Ecclesiasticorum Latinorum*, C. Gerodi et al., Vienna, 1866—)
Enn.	Plotinus, *Enneads*
Ep.	*Epistula*
GCS	*Die Griechischen Christlichen Schriftsteller der ersten drei Jahrhunderte*, J. C. Hinrichs, Leipzig, 1899—)
Haer.	Irenaeus, *Adversus Haereses*
HL	Palladius, *Historia Lausiaca*
HM	*Historia monachorum in Aegypto*
Hom.	*Homilia, Homiliae*
NHC	*Nag Hammadi Corpus*
NPNF	*A Select Library of Nicene and Post-Nicene Fathers*, 2nd series (Christian Literature Company, New York, 1887-1902)
PG	*Patrologia Graeca*, ed. J. P. Migne (Migne, Paris, 1857-66)
PGM	*Papyrae Graecae Magicae*
PL	*Patrologia Latina*, ed. J. P. Migne (Migne, Paris, 1844-65)
RSV	Revised Standard Version, *The Holy Bible* (Thomas Nelson and Sons, New York, 1952)
TDNT	*Theological Dictionary of the New Testament*
VA	Athanasius, *De vita Antonii*
VP	Jerome, *De vita sancti Pauli*

Introduction

"God was not dead in the Roman Empire", as Averil Cameron has observed in a recent study. "Religion became, and continued to be, a main focus for discourse, and the more so as traditional political discourse closed off".[1] Not only was God not dead, neither was the human imagination. Many of those who produced the discourse of religion referred to by Cameron were deeply engaged by the creative possibilities of language and drew on a wide variety of images to give shape and texture to the beliefs and practices that structured their world and themselves. Almost anything—flocks of sheep, a bride munching apples, even the letters of the alphabet—could be subjected to the metaphorizing process that turned the ordinary into an extraordinary vehicle of meaning. As Mark C. Taylor has remarked in another context, "religion often is most effective where it is least obvious".[2]

In the essays that comprise this volume, "religion" is constituted by literary texts from the Christianities, Gnosticisms, Neoplatonisms (and in one case, magical traditions) that claimed allegiance in the late ancient world. Despite the very real differences that mark the ways in which these texts characterize their gods and reflect on their own practices as adherents of these traditions and communities, they all share what I claim is a "poetic" apprehension, that is, a sensitivity to the allusive, shifting qualities of human attempts to state what is most fundamental to their lives. I often use the term *poiēsis* and its derivatives in English in the basic sense of "creation", a "making" that is consonant with the line of the poet Wallace Stevens that "reality is an activity of the most august imagination".[3] By using these terms, I wish to call attention to the late ancient sensitivity to image, metaphor, and sign and so to highlight the figurative sensibility that is a distinctive feature of many of the texts of this period.

Of course, as Jonathan Z. Smith has argued, the student of religion must be aware of her own "poetic" apprehension, that is, her own stance as interpreter and maker of meaning. Noting the modernity of the term "religion", Smith observes that, "If we have understood the archeological and textual record correctly, man has had his entire history in which to imagine deities and modes of interaction with them. But man, more precisely western man, has had only the last few centuries in which to imagine religion. It is this act of second order, reflective imagination which must be the central preoccupation of any student of religion".[4] Thus in what follows, I will be focusing not only on the late ancient imagination but my own practices as an interpreter as well.

In her study of the role of memory in medieval culture, Mary Carruthers remarks that, "when we [in Western culture] think of our highest creative power, we think invariably of the imagination. 'Great imagination, profound intuition,' we say: this is our highest accolade for intellectual achievement, even in the sciences".[5] She goes on to make the following observations about the role of imagination in medieval culture that are relevant to late ancient culture as well.

> We make such judgments (even those of us who are hard scientists) because we have been formed in a post-Romantic, post-Freudian world, in which imagination has been identified with a mental unconscious of great, even dangerous, creative power. Consequently, when they look at the Middle Ages, modern scholars are often disappointed by the apparently lowly, working-day status accorded to imagination in medieval psychology—a sort of draught-horse of the sensitive soul, not even given intellectual status. Ancient and medieval people reserved *their* awe for memory ... Because of this great change in the relative status of imagination and memory, many moderns have concluded that medieval people did not value originality or creativity. We are simply looking in the wrong place.[6]

The relevance of Carruthers' observations for late antiquity is twofold. On the one hand, "imagination", insofar as it stands as an adequate translation of the Greek φαντασία and the Latin *imaginatio*, did not generally carry the high estimation of creativity with which it is endowed today, especially since both terms could point in the direction either of unreality or mere fancy.[7] On the other hand, the statement that "we are simply looking in the wrong place" opens up other possibilities for finding resources in late antiquity for a sense of what is now termed "imagination".

Carruthers' study of memory provides one body of literature for locating a "right" place to look in order to recuperate ancient and medieval ways of valuing originality and creativity. And there were other pedagogies of the imagination as well. One might, for example, look to certain techniques of rhetorical training such as the *ethopoiia*, an exercise in composition defined as "a speech giving the imagined words of an historical, mythological, or biblical character",[8] or the *ekphrasis*, an exercise that trained students to compose speeches that brought a particular subject—whether it be a person, place, artistic object, or event—so vividly before the eyes of the listener, and with such emotional affect, that the listener was transformed into a spectator.[9]

My own quest for the late ancient imagination has focused on theories of interpretation and language as well as on texts that, whether implicitly or explicitly, use images not as mere reflections of reality but as vehicles that generate meaning and, in so doing, transform the reader's perception at the same time as they alter the conditions of meaning. The authors of the texts considered here did not use images simply as ornaments or rhetorical embellishments that could be discarded as secondary to their arguments. Rather, images were constitutive of the insights of such texts. As a contemporary literary theorist has put it, "Some metaphors enable us to see aspects of reality that the metaphor's production helps to constitute".[10]

In a word, figuration has been the locus of my explorations of late ancient imagination. Figuration, however, is a complex affair, no less in antiquity than today. Ancient writers had at their disposal a large vocabulary of figurational terms, as the following catalogue shows: "*eikōn, eidōlon, morphē, mimēma, tūpos,* and *graphē*—image/likeness, image/simulacrum, shape/form, imitation/copy, stamp/impression, and painting/drawing".[11] Such a generous range of terms suggests that the question, "What is an image?", drew as broad a spectrum of answers in antiquity as it does now, and it suggests further that one way to engage the figurative qualities of ancient texts is to affirm what a contemporary literary theorist has called "the value of recognizing the equivocal richness of apparently obvious or univocal language".[12]

Some of the texts in discussed in this volume were explicit about their own status as figural discourse. The *Gospel of Philip*, for example, states that "[t]ruth did not come into the world naked, but it came in types and images. The world will not receive truth in any other way".[13] True to its own axiom, this text argues by means of several enigmatic images such as the well-known "mirrored bridal chamber".[14] Further, its revisionary metaphorizing both of early Christian ritual (for example, its view of baptism as a process of being tinted by God the "dyer") and of central Biblical texts (as in its alternative view of the trees in Eden as bearing human beings and animals) demonstrates how figural discourse can create hitherto unimagined perceptions of familiar texts and experiences.[15]

This kind of imaginal consciousness, that is, the propensity to think in images rather than in discursive, propositional language, can be seen in the work of the Neoplatonist philosopher Plotinus as well. Plotinus was distrustful of discursive reasoning because it sets up a subject-object dualism, an unbridgeable gap between perceiver and what is perceived.[16] As Sara Rappe has explained, for Plotinus "[t]ruth cannot be ascertained by means of linguistic or conceptual representations; it can be apprehended only when there is an identity between the knower and the known ... Metaphor enters as one of the ways in which Plotinus, holding to this theory of truth, tries to bring the possibility of the identity of the knower and the known into the sphere of experience".[17] One of his best-known spiritual exercises, in which the reader is asked to imagine the earth as a diaphanous sphere,[18] is illustrative of what Rappe calls his method of proof by metaphor; rather than using images for revisionary or iconoclastic purposes like the author of the *Gospel of Philip*, Plotinus used metaphor to achieve a "rhetoric of immediacy".[19]

Aside from such intentional uses of figures to subvert the binarisms of discursive prose, however, Plotinus was wary of the tendency of all language toward fixity or referential closure. Knowing that "every act of naming delimits",[20] Plotinus resorted, on the one hand, to the technique of *apophasis*, un-saying or negating positive statements, and, on the other, to explicit statements about the figural quality of language *per se*, insisting that all language about ultimate reality be glossed with a metaphorical "so to speak".[21] Thus displaced from any direct reference to what Plotinus called "real being", language was paradoxically both fragmenting and evocative of the realities that Plotinus pursued in writing.

This view of language itself as a system of signs was shared by Plotinus's older contemporary, Origen of Alexandria. Origen, however, was more positive about the signifying possibilities of religious language, which for him was above all the language of Scripture. Given his view, as a Christian, that the Holy Spirit had authored the Bible, Origen viewed all of its words as icons, images virtually bursting with a plenitude of meaning.[22] Such linguistic polysemy was understood by Origen to be an invitation for interpretation; as Martin Irvine has observed, "Scripture was seen to be a vast field of continuing signification productive of a limitless play of meanings. Exegesis unfolds the continuous productivity which is the Text".[23] Origen used an agrarian trope to express the generative aspects of both text and interpreter: "I think each word of divine scripture is like a seed whose nature is to multiply diffusely ... Its increase is proportionate to the diligent labor of the skillful farmer or the fertility of the earth".[24]

Such effervescence concerning the richness of linguistic play, however, is only one side of Origen's theorizing about figural discourse. For allegory, the interpretive method that Origen privileged when dealing with language as a system of signs, can not only uncover meaning, it can also scatter it. This problematic aspect of textual semiosis was well expressed by the philosopher Gaston Bachelard when he wrote that, "to grasp the imagining role of language, we must patiently search out for every word its inclinations toward ambiguity and double meanings".[25] Interpretation is thus virtually endless, and agonistic as well since, however polysemous their potential, words were for Origen like "gates of brass" that must continually be broken open by active interpretation.[26] Because words were further understood by Origen to be riddling, they actually worked to decenter or defer meaning. Finally, like Plotinus, Origen had to confront the dispersive tendencies of human attempts to articulate religious truths.[27]

In these samples of late ancient views of figuration, it is clear that speculation about images leads ineluctably to theories of—and anxieties about—interpretation. As Irvine has observed, ancient interpreters like Origen "acknowledge the necessity for multiple interpretations but are disturbed by the multiplying of texts which forever seek to reveal the unity of the Logos over against the multiplicity of discourse. This multiplying of discourse includes the possibility of heretical interpretation: signs require interpretation, but according to which ideologically encoded discourse?".[28]

Such troubling questions about how meaning is produced in and by language have also been characteristic of contemporary theorists who inquire into the nature of images. Since "iconology"—the discourse that people produce about images—has recently been explored primarily in the area of literary theory rather than in religion,[29] the problematic aspects of the relations among image, text, and ideology have not been construed in terms of heresy, nor do god-terms usually function as the ground of signification. Nonetheless, among those today who ask the question, "What is an image?", many of the issues seen above in ancient authors regarding referentiality, immediacy and deferral, and the enigmatic play of language are once again central to their discussions.

In his book *Iconology*, which is a sustained analysis of historical and contemporary understandings of the nature and function of images, W.J.T. Mitchell has observed that for Enlightenment philosophers and critics, language and imagery were "perfect, transparent media through which reality may be represented to the understanding".[30] Today, however, "the situation is precisely the reverse". "For modern criticism, language and imagery have become enigmas, problems to be explained, prison-houses which lock the understanding away from the world".[31] What Mitchell is describing is the "linguistic turn"[32] in contemporary critical theory, succinctly defined by the literary critic J. Hillis Miller as "the moment of criticism which hovers in a prolonged interrogation of language as such".[33]

As Miller elaborates elsewhere when discussing what he calls "the linguistic moment", this new turn in criticism is marked by "a return to the explicit study of rhetoric" understood as "the investigation of figures of speech rather than the study of the art of persuasion".[34] Viewing literary works as heterogeneous and dialogical rather than homogeneous and monological, such critical analysis, again in Miller's summary, "involves an interrogation of the notion of the self-enclosed literary work and of the idea that any work has a fixed, identifiable meaning". And, in terms that are remarkably consonant with those of Origen, Miller characterizes the linguistic moment's perspective on texts as "open and unpredictably productive. The reading of a poem is part of the poem. This reading is productive in its turn. It produces multiple interpretations, further language about the poem's language, in an interminable activity without necessary closure".[35] While this form of criticism does not typically petition "the imagination"—a concept viewed as hopelessly entangled with Romantic idealism—still its insistence on the problematic, subversive but nonetheless productive character of language in general, and of the "inherence in one another of figure, concept and narrative"[36] in particular, has revolutionized practices of reading writing for a whole generation.[37]

The "linguistic turn" is a phrase that encompasses a wide variety of critical practices over the past thirty years. Variously called "postmodern", "poststructuralist", and "deconstructive", these are the literary-critical contexts in which my own practices as an interpreter of late ancient texts have been formed. Any historian is, of course, nourished by her own intellectual culture. Further, as Elizabeth Clark, following Hayden White, has pointed out, "history has no distinctively historical method, but borrows its models from a variety of other disciplines".[38] Long dominated by the model of "decline and fall" associated with the work of Edward Gibbon, the study of religion in the late Roman empire has been through a series of "sea changes" in recent decades.[39] Methods drawn from psychoanalysis, cultural anthropology, sociology, and feminist theory have dramatically altered the way in which the history of late antiquity, once dominated by positivism and by theological motivations, is written.

My own contribution to "redrawing the map" of late ancient religious culture has been to initiate a dialogue across the centuries between "postmodern" theorists and late ancient writers. In drawing on an eclectic range of contemporary literary criticism, what I have found most valuable is the performative view of textuality that underlies how many of these interpreters view the function of a text's images. "Performative" in this case means "generative": the principle that I have followed, in the concise formulation of Hillis Miller, is that there is "no such thing as an innocent image or myth ... No metaphor or myth is a mere 'symbolic convenience', separable from the thought it embodies. It is the body of that thought, the secret generator of the concepts it incarnates".[40] In all of the essays in this volume, I have begun by asking what might claim attention if a text were approached through a striking or discordant image or group of images. By thus following the logic of a text's figuration, new dimensions of the text can be disclosed.

In other words, texts often "speak otherwise" when one is attentive to what might be called the storytelling function of the specifically *poetic* image, that is, the image that deforms or changes how one apprehends a text's meaning rather than conforming to habituated modes of understanding.[41] The poet Ezra Pound defined images as "clusters of fused ideas endowed with energy". It is that "energy"[42] that I have tried to tap. In reflecting on his own experience as a writer, Italo Calvino gives a good description of the energy that is activated by the storytelling image:

> [T]here was a visual image at the source of all my stories ... In devising a story, therefore, the first thing that comes to my mind is an image that for some reason strikes me as charged with meaning, even if I cannot formulate this meaning in discursive or conceptual terms. As soon as the image has become sufficiently clear in my mind, I set about developing it into a story; or better yet, it is the images themselves that develop their own implicit potentialities, the story they carry within them.[43]

As for Calvino, there has usually been such an image at the source of the essays in this volume. Adam eating from an animal tree, Christ imagined as a lunar panther, a witch, a centaur, an ascetic body ablaze with desire or angelic radiance: these are some of the poetic images whose narratives I have followed in my own "stories".

Some of these figures seemed, at the beginning, to be marginal to the interests of a given text; Jerome's *Life of Saint Paul* is not, after all, "about" a centaur. Yet such textual details have what Roland Barthes, writing about arresting details in photographs, calls "a power of expansion". Such a *punctum* or detail is paradoxical: "while remaining a detail, it fills the whole picture".[44] Following the associative movements of such "details" can, however, reveal aspects of a text's interpretive thrust that an author may (or may not) have intended or been conscious of. In the case of Jerome's biography, taking his image of the centaur seriously—that is, allowing it to become the *punctum* of his text—led to an understanding of how animal "wildness" was fundamental to his theory of ascetic identity. Whether consciously or not, Jerome constructed a strongly transgressive image of the ascetic life, and it is an image that virtually "pictures" his theory of asceticism.[45]

The interpretive approach of many of these essays has been influenced by Roland Barthes' argument that an author is not "the subject with the book as predicate".[46] That is, the explicit intentions of an author cannot always control or limit the meanings that arise from the configurations of his text's tropes. Texts can articulate perspectives and bear significations that are quite different from the announced goals of the author. For example, Origen of Alexandria would probably be surprised to read Chapter Two of this volume, which argues that he composed a virtual bestiary of the soul in the course of his allegorizations of beasts that are mentioned in various biblical passages. Yet, once alerted to his animal metaphors, one can see that they are not mere details; they "fill the whole picture" of his profound grasp of human psychology.

Privileging the poetic image does not lead only to the so-called "death of the author", however. It can also clear up certain conundrums in ancient texts as well as enable the development of new paradigms for interpretation. For example, when I began studying the literature of desert asceticism, I was at first startled, even repulsed by the way in which observers of desert ascetics could view ascetics' sometimes mutilated and emaciated bodies as angelic bodies. By staying with such images instead of dismissing them as fanciful (or pathological), I was led to see that theological explanations of the phenomenon of asceticism, while helpful, could not account for these unusual observations. Turning to contemporary theories of perception and ritual (which I would not have done had it not been for these perplexing images) not only enabled me to "see" these images as meaningful constructs, it also aided in the development of a paradigm for the study of ascetic behavior that brings forth its ritualized, performative aspects. Finally, privileging the poetic image can also lead to the recuperation of the integrity of texts that have been negatively valued in the scholarly tradition, as I found when dealing with such controversial texts as those from Gnostic and magical traditions. "Metaphors are risky," as the critic Stanley Hopper once remarked.[47] They have a habit of unsettling one's tidy interpretive structures.

The fact that these studies have constituted a dialogue across the centuries, as I indicated earlier, rather than a monological "application" of contemporary theory to late ancient texts, is clearest in Chapter Six, which is structured as contrapuntal exchange between Roland Barthes and Origen of Alexandria on the topic of an erotics of textuality, and Chapter Thirteen, in which certain contemporary theories of textual semiosis are shown to have been already formulated, although with a different vocabulary and mythos, in Gnostic texts from the Valentinian tradition. In all of the essays in this volume, however, there is a certain concordance of image and perspective between the ancient and modern texts that I have considered. This is not only because I have chosen my reading companions carefully (although I have); it is also because "it can always be demonstrated that the apparent novelty of any new development in criticism is the *renewal* of an insight which has been found and lost and found again repeatedly through all the centuries of literary study since the first Homeric and Biblical commentaries. The novelty of any 'new criticism' is not in its intrinsic insights or techniques but rather in the 'accident' of its expression ...".[48]

I therefore offer this volume of my own "accidents" in the spirit of the poet Wallace Stevens, who wrote about

> Thinkers without final thoughts
> In an always incipient cosmos,
> The way, when we climb a mountain,
> Vermont throws itself together[49]

and in the spirit of my husband and colleague, David Miller, who wrote that to begin and end one of his books with a poem was "not only to indicate that things are better said poetically, though that of course is true, but rather to express the view that some things can be said, if at all, only in image, metaphor, and likeness ...".[50]

Notes

1. *Christianity and the Rhetoric of Empire*, p. 44.
2. "Introduction", in Taylor (ed), *Critical Terms for Religious Studies*, p. 4.
3. Stevens, "Reality is an Activity of the Most August Imagination", *Opus Posthumous*, p. 110.
4. *Imagining Religion*, xi.
5. *The Book of Memory*, p. 1.
6. Ibid.
7. It should be noted, however, that in Stoicism and Neoplatonism, *phantasia* was an important faculty of the soul, crucial to consciousness and intellectual comprehension. See Warren, "Imagination in Plotinus", pp. 277-85, and Goldhill, "The naïve and knowing eye", pp. 208-9.
8. James and Webb, "'To Understand Ultimate Things and Enter Secret Places'", p. 4.
9. Ibid., pp. 4-7, 9-10.
10. Black, "More About Metaphor", pp. 431-57, quoted in Rappe, "Metaphor in Plotinus' *Enneads* v8.9", p. 160, n. 15.

11 Zeitlin, "The artful eye", in Goldhill and Osborne (eds), *Art and text in ancient Greek culture*, p. 138.
12 Miller, "The Critic as Host", in Bloom, DeMan, and Derrida, et.al., *Deconstruction and Criticism*, p. 223.
13 *NHC* II, 3.67 (Robinson, p. 140).
14 *NHC* II, 3.65 (Robinson, p. 139).
15 *NHC* II, 3.61 (Robinson, p. 137: God as dyer); *NHC* II, 3.71 (Robinson, p. 143) (the two trees).
16 See the discussion by sells, *Mystical Languages of Unsaying*, pp. 22-25.
17 Rappe, "Metaphor in Plotinus", pp. 156-57.
18 See *Enn.* 5.8.9.
19 Rappe, "Metaphor in Plotinus", pp. 157-61, 169.
20 Sells, *Mystical Languages of Unsaying*, p. 15.
21 On *apophasis* in Plotinus, see Sells, *Mystical Languages of Unsaying*, pp. 14-33; for Plotinus's statement, "Everywhere we must read 'so to speak'", see *Enn.* 6.8.13 (MacKenna).
22 See, for example, Origen, *De Engastrimutho* 2, 4: *Hom. in Jer.* 50.11.2 (Nautin and Husson, vol. 2, p. 343): "The Holy Scriptures have not a single dot which is empty of the wisdom of God ... The holy books breathe the spirit of plenitude".
23 Irvine, *The Making of Textual Culture*, p. 245.
24 Origen, *Hom. in Ex.*, 1.1 (Heine, p. 227).
25 Bachelard, *Air and Dreams*, p. 3.
26 Origen, *De prin.* 4.3.11 (Butterworth, p. 306).
27 See Irvine, *The Making of Textual Culture*, p. 266: "The unity of the Logos is fragmented into a multiplicity of temporal discourses which simultaneously attempt and fail to return to its unity; no repetition or multiplication of *logoi* is Logos. The transcendental signified remains beyond the reach of all temporal sign relations yet is immanently manifest in all of them".
28 Irvine, *The Making of Textual Culture*, p. 266.
29 Notable exceptions include the development of a "theologia imaginalis" by D. L. Miller in a series of books beginning with *Christs*; Funk, *Language, Hermeneutic, and Word of God*; and Taylor, *Erring*. I have borrowed the term "iconology" from Mitchell's book *Iconology*.
30 Mitchell, *Iconology*, p. 8.
31 Ibid.
32 This phrase was coined by Rorty (ed), *The Linguistic Turn*.
33 Miller, "Deconstructing the Deconstructers", p. 29.
34 Miller, "Stevens' Rock and Criticism as Cure, II", p. 333.
35 Ibid.
36 Ibid., "The Critic as Host", p. 252.
37 See Taylor, *Erring*, p. 13, for a characterization of deconstruction as "a revolutionary reading of writing".
38 Clark, "The Lady Vanishes", p. 1.

39	Recent surveys of some of these changes include the *Journal of Early Christian Studies*, vol. 6, no. 3 (Fall, 1998), which is devoted to a reassessment of the influence of Peter Brown's landmark study of the holy man; *Symbolae Osloenses*, vol. 72 (1997), pp. 5-90, entitled "The World of Late Antiquity Revisited", which contains a variety of analyses of developments in the field subsequent to the publication (in 1971) of Peter Brown's *The World of Late Antiquity*; Cameron, "Redrawing the Map: Early Christian Territory After Foucault"; and Clark, "The Lady Vanishes", pp. 1-14.
40	Miller, "Tradition and Difference", p. 10.
41	Here I am borrowing from Bachelard's definition of imagination: "We always think of the imagination as the faculty that *forms* images. On the contrary, it *deforms* what we perceive; it is, above all, the faculty that frees us from immediate iamges and *changes* them. If there is no change, or unexpected fusion of images, there is no imagination; there is no *imaginative act*. If the image that is *present* does not make us think of one that is *absent*, if an image does not determine an abundance—an explosion—of unusual images, then there is no imagination. There is only perception ..." (*Air and Dreams*, p. 1 [emphasis in original]).
42	*Ezra Pound: A Critical Anthology*, p. 57.
43	*Six Memos for the Next Millenium*, pp. 88-89.
44	*Camera Lucida*, p. 45.
45	For a discussion of such images, see Mitchell, *Picture Theory*, pp. 35-82.
46	"The Death of the Author", in idem, *Image, Music, Text*, p. 145. See also Foucault, "What Is An Author?".
47	"The Bucket As It Is", p. 15.
48	Miller, "Stevens' Rock and Criticism as Cure, II", p. 332 (emphasis added).
49	"July Mountain", *Opus Posthumous*, p. 115.
50	*Christs*, xv.

PART I

POETIC IMAGES AND NATURE

PART I

POETIC IMAGES AND NATURE

Preface

Nature engaged late ancient authors in a variety of ways. It produced sheer wonder at its strange beauty, but it also provoked complex readings that treated it as a cache of riddles that needed to be deciphered. Beginning with the Hellenistic *Physika* (literary compendia of the elements of nature often arranged alphabetically) and continuing through the late ancient Christian genre of the *Hexaemeron* (commentaries on the six days of creation in the book of Genesis), interpreters surveyed the natural world for the wisdom it had to offer.

Although the *Physika* and the *Hexaemera* included plants and other natural phenomena like rocks and planets within their purview, it was nature's animals that were most compelling. Whether real or imagined—scowling lions, an animal tree, frugal ants and playful partridges, as well as such hybrid monsters as centaurs and satyrs—animals claimed the attention of writers who meditated on nature in late antiquity. Generally, animals claimed attention in this period not as objective specimens to be classified scientifically but rather as indicators of a dynamic process that was defined both theologically and psychologically. What I have thus called the "bestial imagination" is the focus of the essays included in this section.

For the late ancient interpreters presented here, animals were "good to think with." Although authors like Marcus Aurelius sometimes seemed to portray nature, and especially nature's beasts, as a discreet "real" world valuable in its own right, there was typically another, specifically religious perspective at work that transformed "real" animals into images bearing meanings quite different from those of naturalism or zoology. For example, when Marcus included "the drip of foam from a wild boar's jaw" in one of his lists of the signs of nature's grace and fascination (*Meditations* 3.1), he not only conjured up a "real" animal; he also poetized it by making it an image of that vast providential order whose intricate workings thus manifested themselves.

This penchant for theologizing "nature" by turning its elements into tropes of the spirit, whether in Stoicism, Gnosticism, or Christianity, is the main theme of the essays that follow. Natural phenomena were used as the vehicles through which to explain religious conceptions of reality. Animals, in particular, were not the subject-matter to be explained; instead, animals became part of a "language" of divine images and patterns that could be "read" in such a way as to disclose stark truths about human life in a world thought to be shot through with riddles and enigmas of the divine.

The key to the theological art of meditation on nature in late antiquity is the beast-as-metaphor. This zoological rhetoric was wielded for different purposes: in some texts, animals images were used to explore the very process of figuration of which they were a part, while in other texts, animals were metaphors of the irrational aspects of the human soul whose "wildness" expressed one aspect of the multiplicity of the self. In still other texts, animals figured the cunning presence of God in the world. Despite the tendency among modern interpreters to slight these "textual" animals as naïve or romantic fabrications, bestial images were not the product of an ancient credulity. On the contrary, they formed part of an imaginal sign-system in which nature was infused with religious and emotional sensibilities.

Whenever bestial metaphors appear in the texts studied here, they are agonistic images; they carry the violence, discord, and dissonance that attend the breaking of habituated modes of consciousness and structures of thought. The violence of many of these images is understandable, since the bestial imagination tended to expose areas of human life that were unsettling, as the following examples from the chapters in this section demonstrate.

Drawing on Scripture for the veritable menagerie of animals that appear in his theological writings, Origen of Alexandria used beasts as figures for unexplored dimensions of the human soul that must be dragged into consciousness, wrestled with, and tamed. Serpentine, horse-like, and piggish, these psychic fantasies represented for Origen both the pitfalls and the opportunities for ethical and spiritual development. Jerome likewise used an animal to picture human identity. Paradoxically using as figure for the celibate ascetic the sexually-aggressive centaur—a half-human, half-bestial monster from mythology—Jerome portrayed the radical but ambivalent self-consciousness demanded of the Christian ascetic as he experimented with physical and psychological transformation.

In such texts, animal were metaphors used to evoke and contemplate the often discordant complexity of the human soul. Religious psychology, however, was not the only haunt of the beasts. Theology was also subject to the violent insights associated with these images. The most stunning presentation of the "animalization" of the divine realm studied here can be found in the *Physiologus*, a text whose bestial images of Christ as stealthy lion and savage panther complicate simplistic definitions of divine beneficence. With its use of animal stories to provide connections between passages from the Old and New Testaments that are often quite disparate, this text also introduces a jarring note into the allegorical tradition of interpretation to which it is indebted. Even sacred texts were subject to bestial dissonance.

I have emphasized the violent quality of so many of these bestial images because, at least in the case of the texts presented in this section, there is an underlying realization that to see with the eye of the beast—that is, to accept metaphor as the foundation of human language and consciousness—is itself violent. It is violent because its premise is that meaning is not single, simple, or literal, but multiple, allusive, paradoxical, and riddling. The bestial imagination of late antiquity offers a view of reality that is as uncomfortable as it is rich.

Chapter One

"Adam Ate From the Animal Tree": A Bestial Poetry of Soul

> The person has a mould. But not
> Its animal. The angelic ones
> Speak of the soul, the mind. It is
> An animal. The blue guitar –
> On that its claws propound, its fangs
> Articulate its desert days.
> The blue guitar a mould? That shell?
> Well, after all, the north wind blows
> A horn, on which its victory
> Is a worm composing on a straw.[1]

In these lines from a modern poet, one is confronted by a remarkable example of the use of bestial metaphors to give image to the play of language. This "modern" idea that language plays like an animal is to be found in a surprising way already in Late Antiquity in the thinking of such authors as Origen and Plotinus. Across the centuries, poets and philosophers, critics and theologians have entertained the uncomfortable thought that speaking is a bestial music.

Wallace Stevens' "The Man with the Blue Guitar" pictures the mould of a man—his shape, his shell—as an animal. Further, it is angelic ones who speak thus of man, as though the beast were our angelic name. Yet the beast has claws and fangs, which pick a desert tune on the blue guitar.

In these verses there is an abysmal figuration of meaning. It is impossible to tell what is what. Is the blue guitar the animal, the music of our bestial mould? Do we play the blue guitar, or does it play us? There is a play here, which one critic has likened to "a snake almost succeeding in getting its tail in its mouth".[2]

Stevens was fascinated by this "almost", by absurd, bestial dissonance.[3] Earlier in "The Man with the Blue Guitar", he had written:

> It is the chord ~~that~~ falsifies . . .
> The fields entrap the children, brick
> Is a weed and all the flies are caught,
> Wingless and withered, but living alive.
> The discord merely magnifies.[4]

In a letter on this passage, Stevens remarked that "the chord destroys its elements by uniting them in the chord. They then cease to exist separately. On the other hand, discord exaggerates the separation between its elements ".[5]

The point is that, for Stevens, bestial music is a figure for language. Playing the guitar is a kind of speaking, and a poet finds himself drawn especially to the magnifying discordant notes. "Personally, I like words to sound wrong", Stevens once wrote.[6] Perhaps he was thinking of the dissonant quality of words themselves, where words are images that coil about our thoughts snake-like, succeeding—almost—in biting the tail of meaning.

The Bestial Play of Words

There is something insidiously serpentine about words. If the beast is a metaphor of poetic language, it is so abysmally. As one ancient literary critic, Plutarch, noted, words tell the truth while lying. Naked truth wounds, and is too harsh; thus the Gods speak in poetic circumlocution, that is, in metaphor.[7] Divine language is equivocal, supremely indirect, a beast almost as discordant as the truth that it reveals while hiding it.

Other poets, and literary critics as well, have been drawn to the beast as image for the play of language through us. A gentle example is the poet Howard Nemerov, who found it fitting to open an essay on the nature of metaphor by comparing purple finches to sparrows dipped in raspberry juice.[8] Marianne Moore likened poetry to imaginary gardens—with real toads in them.[9]

Somewhat darker is the image offered by the theologian and literary critic, Stanley Romaine Hopper. In one of his essays,[10] he discusses metaphor as a kind of thinking and speaking that creates space for being to come to presence. That is, metaphoric consciousness violates or breaks through those frameworks of interpretation that we absolutize to such an extent that they become the unconscious presupposition of all our thinking. Metaphor places us forcefully in what has been called, variously, the "between", the "gap", the "rift", the "boundary", the "abyss"—in Hopper's words, a gap between the perceiver and that which is perceived, between identity and difference, between self-identity and openness.

Of course, to speak about metaphor abstractly is to perpetuate the very kind of thinking that radical metaphor militates against. To speak about figure without figures is to miss the point. Professor Hopper knows this, and turns to the beast. The setting is a conversation among certain Zen masters.

> Goso said: "It's like a buffalo passing through a window. His head, horns, and four legs have all passed through. Why is it that its tail cannot"? Master Dogen says: "The tail is the mind which knows neither passing nor not passing. This world is but the tail of a buffalo passing through a window". Master Hoen says: "The tail is nothing else than the formless form of reality". Master Hakuin writes: "Always the same is the moon before the window. Yet, if there is only a plum branch, it is no longer the same". Comment: "If to this tail anything at all is added, its true form of no-form is lost". Hakuin adds: "Goso likes the tail that cannot pass through. As for me, I like the tail that can pass through".[11]

Professor Hopper remarks: "Metaphor is perpetually running the buffalo through windows".[12]

A still more violent play on the violent play of language is offered by the literary critic J. Hillis Miller. In an essay on Wallace Stevens' poem "The Rock", Miller remarks that, in a poem, even the most innocent-looking words can become "momentarily nodes, at once fixed rock and treacherous abyss of doubled and redoubled meanings, around or over which the thought of the poet momentarily swirls or weaves its web".[13] He says further that such words "may not be translated, and thereby made transparent, dispensed with, evaporated, sublimated".[14] He then offers *his* beast, which is, miraculously, *both* man *and* beast at the same time.

Miller conjures up a cartoon in *The New Yorker* magazine by Charles Addams that shows "the receding reflections in doubled mirrors of a man in a barber chair, facing frontwards, then backwards, then frontwards again, in endless recession. One figure in the midst of the sequence, five images back into the mirror's depths, is a wolfman with fangs and a hairy face. The wolfman is the terrifying item that is part of the series but does not fit it, though he is neither its beginning, nor its end, nor its base".[15] The wolfman shatters the hypnotic repetition of the mirror's reflections. He refuses to allow for neat symmetry—or perhaps he makes it possible to see the pattern at all. In either case, reflecting seems to be a fearful process. It is not quite canny. There is a wolfman lurking within our efforts to structure experience.

But, in the cartoon's reflections, the wolfman's face is one of *our* faces. Does this mean that there is something irrational about our reflecting? Or do the images of reflection sometimes *seem* irrational because we resist their equivocal character, covering them over with propositions and neat assertions, shaving the hairy face?

The play of language is beginning to seem less playful than sparrows dipped in raspberry juice. Perhaps the darkest image of all is offered by Maxine Hong Kingston in her book, *The Woman Warrior: Memoirs of a Girlhood Among Ghosts*. The passage quoted below is a figure for memory itself, which Plato said was the truest kind of knowing.[16] In Kingston's novel about ghosts, the following ghost figures all the ghostly images that haunt our thinking, and it is very bestial indeed.

Kingston begins this extended image by noting that her mother was capable of eating ghosts. Then, she says, at certain moments,

> I would hear my mother's monkey story. I'd take my fingers out of my ears and let her monkey words enter my brain. I did not always listen voluntarily, though. She would begin telling the story, perhaps repeating it to a homesick villager, and I'd overhear before I had a chance to protect myself. Then the monkey words would unsettle me; a curtain flapped loose inside my brain. I have wanted to say, "Stop it. Stop it", but not once did I say, "Stop it".
>
> "Do you know what people in China eat when they have the money"? my mother began. "They buy into a monkey feast. The eaters sit around a thick wood table with a hole in the middle. Boys bring in the monkey at the end of a pole. Its neck is in a collar at the end of the pole, and it is screaming. Its hands are tied behind it. They clamp the monkey into the table; the whole table fits like another collar around its neck. Using a surgeon's saw, the cooks cut a clean line in a circle at the top of its head. To loosen the bone, they tap with a tiny hammer and wedge here and there with a silver pick. Then an old woman reaches out her hand to the monkey's face and up to its scalp, where she tufts some hairs and lifts off the lid of the skull. The eaters spoon out the brains".
>
> Did she say, "You should have seen the faces the monkey made"? Did she say, "The people laughed at the monkey screaming"? It was alive? The curtain flaps inside my brain closed like merciful black wings.[17]

This is a dangerous ghost, difficult to eat. Were one to imagine that this is what thinking and speaking are like, it would truly give pause. Perhaps it would even provoke a shaving of the wolfish face in the mirror and a closing of the black curtains in the mind. This is the danger of the beast ... yet this beast has a beauty, too. Encountering an image like this, the reader falls into the text, and the words begin to show their animal faces, taking on a writhing, twisting life of their own. Such word-images become an indelible part of imagining—or perhaps they are imagining itself.

Adam's Beasts, The Imagination, and Soul

The French poet Valéry once said that "language is the beautiful chains which entangle the distracted God in the flesh".[18] Who is this distracted God, entangled in the flesh of his speaking? For some ancient authors in the Western tradition, this entangled God was Adam, and I would like to turn now not only to the book of Genesis, where Adam plays out his dramatic bestial role, but also to certain Greek interpreters of Adam, who have let the sensuous force of Adam's story play through themselves in remarkable variations on the animal theme.

As Genesis says, in Eden Adam named the beasts, and was tempted into knowledge by the wiliest beast of them all.[19] In the Hebrew original, God gave Adam the beasts, to see what he would call them, and whatever he called the beasts, that was their name. The Greek translation of Genesis in the Septuagint gave this story an interesting twist. There God gave Adam the beast, as in the Hebrew. But what Adam named was "the living soul".[20] What was Adam doing when he named the living soul, the beasts? Was he, as Howard Nemerov has suggested, pointing to the "gorgeous or powerful or merely odd emanations of our as yet undivided selves"?[21] Further, what was *God* doing when he made "coats of skins" for this living soul now endowed with bestial names? It seems to have been the Biblical intuition that we are involved with the beast, and that this involvement is a knowledge as intimate as a name, a knowledge that finally casts us out into the "cursed ground" of our living selves, sheathed by the animal.

Such questions—what was Adam doing, what was God doing—were precisely the kind of questions that were asked by Origen of Alexandria, the third-century Platonizing Christian who flirted with Gnostic thinking. Origen seems to have known what Rilke later wrote in the *Notebooks of Malta Laurids Brigge*, that "before one can write a single verse, one must get to know the animals".[22] For, running through his always imaginative, often phantasmal, metaphoric glosses on Scripture is an intrigue with the animals that writhe and twist there.

For Origen, animals are "chimeras and fantastic monsters of the mind".[23] Theologically, their gruntings and brayings and hissings and howlings give voice to aspects of soul—in particular, to the abysmally diverse nature, the *pathos*, the instinctual existence of the soul that is not one, but many. Origen describes Scriptural animals variously as our "unreasoning instincts"; as daimons that "stir up" our bestial imaginings; as bodily affections; as "dispositions of the soul and the thought of the heart".[24] Rarely does he speak about animals from the objective stance of an Aristotelian naturalist. For him the world of the beasts is an interior geography of the human soul. It is the ark of our covenant with the serpent, but also the firmament of our heavenly gifts from the Creator.[25] Animals are the bestial clothing of the soul, the almost innumerable "coats of skins" whose layers give shape to an inner cosmos: "Understand that you have within yourself herds of cattle ... flocks of sheep and flocks of goats ... and that the birds of the air are also within you ... You see that you have all those things which the world has".[26]

So, for Origen, the beasts form a zoological garden of the soul, the swarming, creeping, slithering chaos of the mind made in the image of God that has not yet achieved his likeness. But animals are not merely faces of the soul; they are also figures for the working of the human imagination. Often in Origen's writings, animal figures are parabolic.[27] They are ways of expressing the soul's roaming, its quest for its true nature. Animal images, then, have a place in the tropical density of Origen's interpretative theories, which have to do not only with *how* we look at texts, but also with *what* we are doing when we look.

Bestial images are phantasms—"chimeras and fantastic monsters of the mind"—but it is precisely in that realm of *phantasia* that soul begins to move toward self-knowledge. Beasts are the tropes of our imaginative looking; they are metaphors for thinking about thinking.

For Origen, soul is mind embodied. There are several kinds of "bodies" in which minds find themselves—ethereal, aerial, earthy, demonic, and so on—that represent the character of the mind's thoughts.[28] "Body" is a metaphor for a way of thinking, so that the variety of embodied minds that one finds in Origen's writings form the pleroma of the soul's dispositions.[29] Body and mind come together as soul, and soul is the carrier of our perceptions about the nature of things, including ourselves.

The most basic character of soul is imaginative.[30] We perceive through fantasies, whose images Origen describes as "bodily affections".[31] These bodily affections are the beasts, the *pathēmata* of soul that can either devour or nourish, depending upon how we interact with them.[32] Thinking, then, is an act of imagining, and the beasts form the "body" of our untamed thoughts. It is in the imaginal realm of soul that we learn how to wear our animal skins. The ways in which we wear them give shape to that "immense, monstrous animal",[33] the universe of our soulful quest for understanding. What Adam named, God clothed and set free: the ravening longings of the soul to know itself.

Clement of Alexandria said that Adam "uttered prophecies" when he named the animals,[34] and Origen seems to have been following in that tradition when he suggested that the "breath of God" that made man "a living soul" may have been the (prophetic) Spirit of God, "in view of the fact that Adam is found to have uttered certain prophecies".[35] If Origen means, like Clement, the prophecies regarding the bestial names, he has linked the animal imagination with the Spirit in us. We are spirited by the beasts, whose passionate nature is the life of soul.

Origen knew that the passions are divine blessings, bestial food given to man by the grace of God.[36] But he also knew that these divine beasts have a monstrous side. We have a tendency to make the animal more divine than the human, turning our irrational thoughts into concrete actions, making the trope literal.[37] We forget to think. We lose the scent of the spirit's breath in the beast's panting. The kingdom of the Spirit within is the hunting ground of beasts, but we need not fall prey to its chimeras. As Jesus says in the *Gospel of Thomas,* "Blessed is the lion that the man will devour, and the lion will become man. And loathsome is the man that the lion will devour, and the lion will become man".[38] The man who devours the lion, who "reduces the Monster to himself",[39] knows like Origen that his bestial names figure the passionate realities of being human in the world.

Within and through the animal, Adam turns the world to trope—or so Origen seems to have thought. But certainly the bestial Adam turning within Origen provoked a poetry of interpretative vision and even what one might call a subversive love for the creative possibilities of the word.

From an Origenist perspective, seeing through the animal names seems to involve a creation, and a *poiēsis.* One of Origen's loves, Plato, had described the dream as the place where the beastly and savage part of the soul gambols.[40] Having already described the soul as a "many-headed beast",[41] Plato now suggests that what the dream holds is a lawless brood of desires. Dream-images are beasts glutted with food and blood. Origen, we might say, was glutted with the food and blood of the Scriptural texts, which he treats as though they were dreams, lawless broods of images within which he turned, spinning intricate webs of meaning. Like Adam, Origen was a distracted God, entangled in the fleshy insides of words, the "beautiful chains" of language.[42]

Pathos and the Bestial Image

Perhaps Norman O. Brown was thinking in this Origenist fashion about the interior spaces of the beast when he wrote the following aphorism:

> Turning and turning in the animal belly... The way out: the poem.[43]

Turning with this aphorism, we find ourselves in the belly of the beast. We are placed, and find our place, according to Brown, in a bestial vessel, and it is a vessel defined not by its exterior but by the movement that happens in its inner spaces. The animal belly is a void, an abyss in which a turning takes place. The turnings in this bestial emptiness give shape to the void—coils, labyrinths, serpentine tracings.

This turning that shapes by its sensuous indirection is the way out, the poem, which is, curiously, another way in. For the poem is itself a beast, harboring within its bestial body vast empty spaces where its images writhe and twist together, marking and remarking the traces of the deep. As the poem is an animal belly, so the animal belly is the poem—if only we will turn in the right way, turning not to escape, but to dwell more deeply in the inner spaces, where the turning is.

To say "bestial" is to suggest "pathological", as Origen knew. Bestial images, like Brown's animal belly, are pathologized images. They are, for thinkers like Origen, Plotinus, and certain Gnostic authors, the body of our *pathos,* where *pathos* is considered to be a profound interior bond to soul's experience. In traditional philosophical terms, the word *pathos* is defined as affection.[44] As it is used by these ancient thinkers, pathetic affection is an embrace of those moods, emotions, and thoughts that stir the soul deeply.

Fundamental to strenuously pathologized images—the shining fireface of the *Apocryphon of John,* for example[45]–is a prodding of the soul lost in its literal perspectives on life's meaning. Animal images are pathologized images that provoke movement in the soul stuck in the coagulations of physical, merely material realities. They skin this perspective alive, releasing the soul into other ways of seeing. As one scholar has suggested, pathetic images "express the decomposition of the natural: they are images which do not and cannot take place in the natural world ".[46]

Rufinus' translation of a passage in Origen's *De principiis* makes this bestial point with an appropriately bestial vocabulary. "Images drag the soul", says the text.[47] The Latin verb that Rufinus has chosen for the action of images on the soul is *rapio,* which carries the following meanings: "seize and carry off", "snatch", "tear", "drag", "ravish", "ravage", "plunder", "take by assault".[48] Lurking behind the Latin is the Greek *harpē:* the bird of prey (also elephant-goad and hippopotamus' tooth!).[49] Images are the mind's harpies, pecking and tearing at our material, merely natural obsessions, forcing us to let go our grasping ways.

Such images are pathetic beasts. They are both coarse and subtle bodies: coarse in their violent provocations, subtle in their poetic bearing of inner worlds where the whispers and echoes of the soul's presence to itself can be heard. What they bear are perspectives on *how* the soul is present to itself–and for one ancient author, this presence is the presencing of God, the man-eater, in the human soul.[50]

The same author who pictures God as a monstrous man-eater has an unusual vision of Paradise. "There are two trees growing in Paradise", says the *Gospel of Philip*. "The one bears animals, the other bears men. Adam ate from the tree which bore animals. He became an animal and brought forth animals. For this reason the children of Adam worship animals".[51] The eating from the animal tree was Adam's fall. What Adam beheld when he woke from his Paradisal innocence were monstrous images and bestial forms, including, perhaps, the man-eating nature of God himself.

Truth, according to the *Gospel of Philip*, does not come naked; it comes in "types and images".[52] What is the resurrection? "The image must rise again through the image".[53] The coarse body must become a subtle body. Adam's real sin was not that he brought forth animals, for the animals are his children, and his children are described as his "accomplishments". "They originate in a moment of ease". "You will find", says this author, "that this applies directly to the image. Here is the man made after the image accomplishing things with his physical strength, but producing his children with ease".[54]

Adam's real sin was not his bestial imagination; it was, rather, his failure to let go of the images once they appeared. He worshipped them, and they became opaque idols. Adam forgot that, lying latent, ready to pounce within the comfort of our material sleep, is the bestial violence of insight, the prowling animal of imagination, the raw insides of words that, finally, insist upon the lack of innocence that characterizes every attempt to fix meaning. There is always an abyss lurking within our efforts to structure experience. "If you become horse or ass or bull or dog or sheep or another of the animals which are outside or below, then neither human being nor spirit nor thought nor light will be able to love you. Neither those who belong above nor those who belong within will be able to rest in you, and you have no part in them".[55]

Adam's goal, for the *Gospel of Philip*, is to eat from the human tree. It is "to make the things below like the things above, and the things outside like those inside".[56] His task is not to turn away from the bestial bodies, but to turn within them. What Adam must suffer, pathetically, is that "truth is a life-eater";[57] it is a "law of shadowing"[58] that makes of every image a luminous body of reflections within reflections, of "visions envisioning the soul itself".[59] The truth eats life by depriving our reflections of safe resting-places; it devours all of our efforts to secure what is present by noting what is absent; finally, it shatters even those pathetic images that bore it into consciousness. For just as the abysmal truth of our reality is the secret generator of the images that embody it, so also is it their secret destroyer. Perhaps the *Gospel of Philip* describes truth as a life-eater because truth seems destructive and subversive. Its call is not to see images, but to see through them; it dwells in the moment when the world disappears into meaning; and it loves nothing so much as the twists and turns of a paradoxical figure: the luminous body, the invisible image, the silent word.

Traces of a Bestial God in Image, Imagination, and Serpentine Speech

Twisting and turning—what was on that animal tree from which Adam ate? The *Gospel of Philip* does not say. Its author was concerned with the first step of establishing the bestial fruit of the tree and Adam's involvement with it.

Mircea Eliade and C.G. Jung, however, both remarked that philosophical or world trees are almost always associated with animals, and, with surprising frequency, with particular animals, serpents and dragons.[60] As in Genesis, trees of wisdom are laced about by serpents, who guard the words of life.

One of the *Gospel of Philip's* Gnostic predecessors, a teacher named Justinus, suggested that the serpent in Eden *was* the tree of knowledge.[61] Yet another twisting of the serpentine image has been offered by the poet Robert Duncan in his "Narrative Bridges for *Adam's Way*". Envisioning Adam before the tree in Paradise, Duncan writes about the tree's inhabitant: ". . . the Serpent, the hydra Wisdom in the Tree of Knowledge of Good and Evil, that multiplies, rising until his snakey heads brood in all the lights and centers of our being, and to certain sleights of hand and meaning therein".[62] Duncan goes on to suggest that Adam's encounter with the serpent is his "awakening" to the "depths and distances" within himself. Adam awakens to his bestial self, the "snakey heads" that brood within. It is a rude awakening, this coming face-to-face with serpentine wisdom:

> Perhaps, before the betrayal of the Creator's secrets, Adam was no more than a reflection of his maker, having within no inkling of depths or distances. But now, toucht by the dragon's cold, the lingering knowledge of old orders in their extinction, he must reflect himself upon that which he is a reflection of. Creature of the creative angst, he is drawn into the magic of (the anxiety of), the creation of—his Self.[63]

In Eden, Adam was touched by "the dragon's cold", by the fierce power of that primal serpent that, for Duncan, gives image to the coiling shape of our knowing.

Perhaps the brooding that Adam's encounter with the primal serpent brings is a bestial music, like Stevens' "worm composing upon a straw". Such was the thought of Hermes Trismegistus in the *Poimandres*. In this Hermetic treatise, an initiate seeking wisdom receives a vision "without limit, all becoming light". Within this light, however, a darkness "winds towards the depths", a darkness wound round in "tortuous spirals like a serpent", breathing a vapor of fire. From this frightening apparition there issues "a voice of fire", described as a "loud cry", "an inarticulate sound". This vision, says Hermes Trismegistus, is a vision of Mind (*nous*), and the resounding cry that issues from the dark serpent is the "luminous Word, the son of God".[64]

As with Stevens' bestial music, so here there is an abysmal figuration of meaning. The inarticulate sound of the beast, the divine son, the winding monster, all give light and fire to the *Poimandres*' thought about thought itself. When Mind speaks, it is serpentine music. The luminous word that is the child of God proceeds from the mouth of the dragon primeval.

According to the *Poimandres*, then, when Mind shows itself, it is a winding serpent. The endless "reflections within reflections" that characterize our knowing are imaged here by that most ancient of abysmal images, the dragon, whose way with man is dark, tortured, spiraling—and divine.

Hermes Trismegistus was not the only thinker in his time to imagine an intimate connection between God, wisdom, and the dragon. Origen, for example, was interested in the Biblical dragon, Leviathan. With Psalm 103 in mind, he says: "The Jewish scriptures, with a hidden meaning in mind, said that this Leviathan was formed by God as a plaything".[65] The dragon, it would seem, is God's play in the world; or, God's play in the creation is serpentine. But this is not all, for Origen suggests that the Psalmist had a hidden meaning in mind, and, in a curious passage in his long meditation on John 1:1, "In the beginning", Origen may be suggesting one way of imagining that meaning.

In his *Commentary on John*, Origen, following Job 40.19 (LXX), says that the dragon is "the beginning of the creation of the Lord, made for the sport of the angels".[66] After a brief discussion, he quotes another Old Testament passage about the beginning, this one from Proverbs 8:22, where Lady Wisdom says: "The Lord made me as the beginning of his ways for his works". Like Hermes Trismegistus and Robert Duncan, Origen has brought the dragon and wisdom face-to-face. Although he has not made their connection explicit, these two images, Sophia and the dragon, jostle one another in rather close quarters in his discussion. It is tempting to imagine that here too the play of divine wisdom in the world is serpentine.

A final spiraling image from Greek antiquity will bring this discussion back to its beginning, to that metaphoric play of wisdom in the word that was likened to "a snake almost succeeding in getting its tail in its mouth".[67] The thinker to whom I now turn is Plotinus, who knew like Origen that there is something truly pathetic—ravishing and ravaging—about the word-images that bear human reflections on the nature of things.

Speaking in *Ennead 5* about that groundless ground, the primal no-thing that he calls "The One", Plotinus finds himself in "agony for a true expression".[68] Speaking is an agony; the *topos* of language is an *agōn*. Yet Plotinus wrestles with his interpretative expressions anyway, in spite of his agony. He suggests that perhaps the phrase "beyond being" is the best name for that abysmal reality that he says "coils" around us.[69] Primal reality is serpentine, and "beyond being" is the best name for it because such a name "assigns no character, makes no assertion, allots no name, carries only the denial of particular being; and in this there is no attempt to circumscribe it; to seek to throw a line about that illimitable nature would be folly, and anyone thinking to do so cuts himself off from any slightest and most momentary approach to its least vestige".[70] Our inclination, of course, is to think positively of this primal nothing, but Plotinus says that "there would be more truth in silence.... For this is a principle not to be conveyed by any sound; it cannot be known on any hearing but, if at all, by vision; and to hope in that vision to see a form is to fail of even that".[71]

How, then, can we speak, and what do we know? According to Plotinus, "outflowings" from The One "break into speech".[72] Like Hillis Miller, Plotinus knew that language plays through man. It is, however, a violent play, for what comes to him are the "strikes and stings" of being that give the "impress" *(pathēma)* of reality.[73] Plotinus had a bestial word for these strikes and stings that bear the real: it is *ichnos*, the "footprint" or "trace" that a beast leaves behind. Existence itself, he says, is a "trace" of The One.[74] Thus what we know and speak are the traces of the coiling abyss.

When this bestial word appears in Plotinus' writings, it is generally used metaphorically, as in Wisdom of Sirach 50:29: "The light of God is his *ichnos*". This trace is not a vestige or remnant of some higher form of ontological reality, nor is it a way, a form, that one can imitate. It is not a loop around the abyss, which Plotinus called folly. Rather, the traces are like what Rilke called "A breath for nothing. A wafting in the God. A wind".[75] To be stung by a trace entails a willingness to listen to the word of fire proceeding from the dragon, or, like Wallace Stevens, to like words to sound wrong.[76] This kind of knowing is a learning of what is unspoken, a being touched by the presence of what is absent. As Plotinus would say, it is giving a name to the nameless, a face to what is fundamentally faceless—and to *know* that that is what one is doing. The traces are images, momentary lightbearers that fade, leaving however the shadow of presence, a meaningful phantom, a coiling serpent.

All of the thinkers who have spoken in this essay seem to agree that there is a wise serpent in every Adam, and that listening to that beast involves an agonizing fall into a particular perspective on language.

> The original mistake in every sentence: metaphor. Metaphor consists in giving the thing a name that belongs to something else ... The original sentence, the original metaphor: Thou art that ... Metaphor is mistake or impropriety; a faux pas, a slip of the tongue; a little madness; *petit mal;* a little seizure or inspiration.[77]

The chord that falsifies, magnifies, such that when Adam wakes to the dragons in his speaking, there is angelic play.

Notes

1 Wallace Stevens, "The Man With the Blue Guitar", XVII, in *Collected Poems*, p. 74.
2 Miller, "Stevens' Rock and Criticism as Cure", p. 14.
3 Ibid., pp. 9-13.
4 Stevens, "The Man With the Blue Guitar", XI, in *Collected Poems*, p. 171.
5 Wallace Stevens to Hi Simons, August 10, 1940, in *Letters of Wallace Stevens*, p. 363.
6 Wallace Stevens to Henry Church, June 1, 1939, in *Letters of Wallace Stevens*, p. 340.
7 Plutarch *De pyth. orac.* 26, 407e (Babbitt), (and see the discussion of Plutarch's position on this issue in Pépin, *Mythe et Allégorie*, p.180).
8 Nemerov, "On Metaphor", p. 33.
9 Marianne Moore, "Poetry", p. 325.
10 Hopper, "The Bucket As It Is", pp. 5-47.
11 Ibid., pp. 40-41.
12 Ibid., p. 41.
13 Miller, "Stevens' Rock and Criticism as Cure", p. 7.
14 Ibid.
15 Ibid., p. 15.
16 See, for example, *Phaedo* 73-76; *Meno* 81c-85b.
17 Kingston, *The Woman Warrior*, pp. 107-8.
18 Quoted by Norman O. Brown, *Life Against Death*, p. 73.
19 Gen. 2:19-20; 3:1-7.
20 *psūche zōsa.*
21 Nemerov, "On Metaphor," p. 36.
22 Rilke, *Notebooks of Malte Laurids Brigge*, p. 26.
23 The phrase is Montaigne's, in *Essays* 1:26.

32   The Poetry of Thought in Late Antiquity

24   Origen, *Contra Celsum* 4.81 (Chadwick, pp. 248-49) and *De prin*. 3.1.2 (Crouzel and Simonetti, vol. 3, pp. 18-20); *Contra Celsum* 4.92-93 (Chadwick, pp. 257-58); *Hom. in Gen*. 1. 17 (Doutreleau, p. 73); *Hom. in Gen*. 1. 16 (Doutreleau, p. 69).
25   *Hom. in Gen*. 1.8; 2.6 (Doutreleau, pp. 44-46, 112).
26   *Hom. in Lev*. 5.2 (PG 12, 450).
27   *Contra Celsum* 4.87 (Chadwick, pp. 252-53).
28   See *De prin*.1. 8.4 (Crouzel and Simonetti, vol. 2, pp. 119-23).
29   For an extended discussion, see Cox, "'In My Father's House Are Many Dwelling Places'", pp. 322-37.
30   *De prin*. 3.1.2-3 (Crouzel and Simonetti, vol. 3, pp. 19-26).
31   *Hom. in Gen*. 1.17 (Doutreleau, p. 73).
32   *De prin*. 1.8.4 (Crouzel and Simonetti, vol. 2, pp. 119-23); 2.9.2 (Crouzel and Simonetti, vol. 1, pp. 355-57); 4.4.10 (Crouzel and Simonetti, vol. 3, pp. 427-29).
33   Ibid., 2.1.3 (Crouzel and Simonetti, vol. 1, pp. 239-41).
34   *Stromata* 1.135.3 (Stählin, vol. 2, p. 84).
35   *De prin*. 1.3.6 (Crouzel and Simonetti, vol. 1, p. 156).
36   *Hom. in Gen*. 1.17 (Doutreleau, p. 73).
37   *Contra Celsum* 4.92-93 (Chadwick, p. 258).
38   *Gospel of Thomas*, logion 7 (Robinson, p. 118).
39   The phrase is from Wallace Stevens, "The Man With The Blue Guitar", XIX, in *Collected Poems*, p.175.
40   Plato *Republic* IX, 571c.
41   Ibid., 588c.
42   See n. 18 above.
43   Brown, *Love's Body*, p. 56.
44   Liddell, Scott, and Jones, *A Greek-English Lexicon*, s.v. *pathos*.
45   *Apocryphon of John* 11, in Robinson (ed), *Nag Hammadi Library*, p. 105.
46   Hillman, *Re-Visioning Psychology*, p. 91.
47   Origen, *De prin*. 3.4.4 (Crouzel and Simonetti, vol. 3, p. 210).
48   Lewis and Short, *A Latin Dictionary*, s.v. *rapio*.
49   Liddell, Scott, and Jones, *A Greek-English Lexicon*, s.v. *harpē*.
50   *Gospel of Philip* 63 (Robinson, p.138).
51   Ibid., 71 (Robinson, p. 143).
52   Ibid., 67 (Robinson, p. 140).
53   Ibid.
54   Ibid., 72 (Robinson, p. 143).
55   Ibid., 79 (Robinson, p. 147).
56   Ibid., 67 (Robinson, p. 141).
57   Ibid., 73 (Robinson, p. 144).
58   For a discussion of the "law of shadowing", see Miller, "The Critic as Host", pp. 217-53.
59   The phrase is from Heidegger, *What is Called Thinking?*, p. 140, where Heidegger is referring to the "wealth of images" that the soul "pours forth".
60   See Eliade, *Patterns in Comparative Religion*, pp. 265-330, and various passages in his *Shamanism*. Jung's discussion is in *Alchemical Studies*, pp. 251-349.
61   Hippolytus, *Refutation of All Heresies* 5.21.
62   Robert Duncan, "Narrative Bridges for *Adam's Way*", p. 106.
63   Duncan, "Narrative Bridges for *Adam's Way*", p. 108.
64   *Poimandres*1-6, in *Corpus Hermeticum* (Nock and Festugière, vol. 1, pp. 7-8).
65   Origen, *Contra Celsum* 6.25 (Chadwick, p. 340).
66   Origen, *Comm. in Ioh*. 1.17 (Blanc, vol. 1, p. 110).

67 See n. 2 above.
68 Plotinus, *Enn.* 5.5.6 (MacKenna).
69 Ibid., 5.5.9 (MacKenna).
70 Ibid., 5.5.6 (MacKenna).
71 Ibid.
72 Ibid., 5.5.5 (MacKenna).
73 Ibid., 6.6.12 (MacKenna).
74 Ibid., 5.5.5 (MacKenna).
75 Rilke, *Sonnets to Orpheus* 1.3.
76 See n. 6 above.
77 Brown, *Love's Body*, p. 244.

Chapter Two

Origen on the Bestial Soul: A Poetics of Nature

Wisdom, wrote Origen, "not only mixes her wine in the bowl; she also supplies fragrant apples in plenty, so sweet that they not only yield their luscious taste to mouth and lips but keep their sweetness also when they reach the inner throat".[1]

This remark will come as something of a shock to lovers of the austere Origen, denigrator of the flesh and devotee of realities solely spiritual. For here is a statement of obvious sensuous delight, rivaling New Testament images of the simple splendors of the natural world. Why this shock? That is, why has the aesthetic sensibility of Origen been passed over and his supposed spiritual flight away from the realm of the senses emphasized instead?

That the interpretive tradition has not favored the aesthetic dimension of Origen's thinking can be seen as early as the fourth century. Objecting to Origen's ideas about the soul's bestial bodies, Jerome says:

> At the end of the book [Book I of *De principiis*], he argues at great length that an angel, a human soul, or a demon—he affirms that they share the same nature, but are diverse in will—can become a beast through its great negligence or its folly, and that, rather than suffer the torments of punishments and the intense heat of fire, it may prefer to be an animal which lives in the sea or some other species of beast: thus we have to fear receiving not only the body of a quadruped but of a fish as well![2]

Jerome offers his reading of Origen's suggestions concerning the bestial potential of the soul as proof of Origen's belief in "Pythagorean metempsychosis".[3] Yet his comments also reveal his own horror at the thought that nature, the realm of the beasts, might be ensouled. The idea that a soul might be "fishy" strikes Jerome as quite disgusting. Further, his rendition of the "bestial body" is thoroughly literal: like Origen, Jerome equated the beast with the irrational (*alogos*); unlike Origen, however, Jerome rejects the idea that metempsychosis might be an *imaginal* journey through the depths of *pathos*, a seeing with the eyes of the beast, and not a literal brutish fall.[4]

As I will suggest, Origen subscribed to a *poiēsis* of nature that enabled him, like the modern poet, to "turn the world to glass".[5] Origen, one might say, saw "the flowing or metamorphosis" by "following with his eyes the life" and using "the forms which express that life, and so his speech flows with the flowing of nature".[6] One of Origen's real concerns was what Emerson called "the passage of the world into the soul of man",[7] and this concern enabled him to imagine the reality, if not the beauty, of a fishy soul with a perspective rather different from that expressed by Jerome in his letter.

Jerome's literal reading of Origen's comments on the bestial bodies, which understood connections between soul and nature to be distasteful and heretical, has found its way into modern readings of the fate of the sensuous world at the hands of Late Antiquity's thinkers. E. R. Dodds, for example, situated Origen squarely within the "madness" of physical torment that he found to be endemic in Late Antiquity. And the madness of self-abuse is itself placed within the context of gross devaluation and denigration of the natural world.[8] Working out of the perspective for which Jerome is emblem here, Dodds has carried forward a supposed Late Antique hostility to the created world as an opaque prison.

In its modern guise, this perspective presents us, not with an heretical Origen, but rather with an Origen made in the image of his old antagonist: a self-castrator, a proponent of the sinful origins of the cosmos. But what of the Origen who could find Wisdom herself in the sweetness of an apple? What of the man who could use as figure for the entire cosmos an ensouled beast, immense and enormous?[9]

If Dodds has continued the tradition of the unrelenting dislike of the sensuous, Charles Singer has maintained the literalist perspective, especially concerning the relation of Late Antique thinkers to the world of the beasts. "With edification always in view", he wrote about Patristic authors, they "produce moralized and sometimes illustrated animal stories which exhibit no intelligent observation and are often childish to the verge of imbecility".[10] So much for the Fathers and the animals! Yet a thinker like Origen could imagine with ease how Wisdom lurks within "the natures of animals and the rages of beasts".[11] Origen, who was probably not an imbecile, knew an aesthetic that is entirely at odds with Singer's approach, and it enabled him to write about the bestial world—indeed, the entire sensuous realm—as a living text, an explosive constellation of divine designs, a record of mysteries like holy scriptures themselves. As Origen himself says in his *Commentary on the Song of Songs*, the bodily senses (which include scripture) are the "windows" through which the Word of God enters the soul.[12]

Perhaps part of this interpretative dilemma stems from a modern misappropriation of the ancient term "nature" (*phūsis*). For example, in a book entitled *The Greek Patristic View of Nature*, D. S. Wallace-Hadrill sets out to defend early Christian thinking against charges like those advanced by Singer. In a "designedly one-sided book", he works "to counteract the idea that Christianity necessarily ignores this world in favor of the next; that it necessarily involves denigration of the world and the flesh, and inevitably completes the Satanic triad by associating them with the devil".[13] What follows in his study is a picaresque journey through Patristic comments on plants, animals, and other natural phenomena, all assembled to show that the Fathers not only studied but appreciated "nature". Even though he has amassed convincing evidence against Singer's "fools for Christ" argument, however, Wallace-Hadrill has remained as distant from ancient senses of *phūsis* as his adversary. For both authors have used the term "nature" as though it referred to a monolithic reality "out there". But to speak about nature in this way not only reduces the immense variety of the world of living things to a single entity; it also sees "nature" as a world both separate from and inferior to the world of man, fit only for our powers of scientific observation and appreciation (correct or otherwise).

Contrary to the tendency, whether ancient or modern, to restrict the referent of the word *phūsis* to the literal world of animals and plants, many ancient thinkers imagined *phūsis* as a dynamic process or power that showed itself *through* the lives of plants, animals—and human beings. Nature was a process of making, growing, arising, unfolding, and it was identified variously with cosmic sympathy, providence, soul, and God. From the Pre-Socratics through Aristotle to the later Stoics, *phūsis* was an experience of the coming-to-presence or the opening-out of that hidden reality to which every living thing gives expression. Paradoxically, the very movements of change and metamorphosis that seem to testify to discord and death were held to bear, however enigmatically, the mystery of order and life.[14]

Meditations on *phūsis*, then, could include not only looking out at the sensuous world, but also, and more basically, looking through that world to the "flowing" hidden within it. In the generation of thinkers just prior to Origen, it was this non-literal sense of *phūsis* that prevailed. No one gave more eloquent voice to that sense than Marcus Aurelius, who could find the whirling process of transformation that he called Nature in "the grinning jaws of real lions and tigers", "the drip of foam from a wild boar's jaws", and "the wrinkling skin when a lion scowls".[15] For Marcus, cultivating a "real intimacy" with Nature meant recognizing the cosmos as the "dear city of God", hung with the "intricate tapestry of the ordinances of Providence".[16]

Marcus' ability to find divine nature in a lion's grin is typical of the Stoic identification of God and nature; but the theologizing of the idea of nature, apart from such explicit identification, had a pervasive influence in the second and third centuries A.D., especially in the Platonic traditions.[17] Plutarch, for example, remarked that animals are "mirrors" of the enigma of the divine, although he cautioned that one must worship not the literal animal but rather what is reflected through it.[18] Similarly, Clement of Alexandria wrote about a *gnōstikē phūsiologia,* a gnostic art of nature that constitutes an initiation into divine mysteries by way of the things of the earth.[19] By seeing in nature a language of divine images and patterns, such thinkers had embraced meditation on *phūsis* as part of the theological task.

When Origen finds divine Wisdom herself in an apple's "luscious taste", he too is on the way toward a theological "semiotics of nature".[20] He too followed the Stoa in finding *phūsis* to be the expression of the divine word.[21] Yet, unlike Marcus Aurelius, Origen was uncomfortable with the term *phūsis,* as he remarks in the course of an argument with Celsus concerning miracles as divine acts "contrary to nature".[22] Perhaps his discomfort grew out of the apparent ease with which *phūsis* as a branch of divine philosophy could be confused with *phūsis* as mere observation, that is, a curiosity about the sensuous world that embroiled the observer in visible realities and thus blocked his ability to understand "the invisible likenesses and patterns".[23] Interestingly, even when he does address the study of divine *phūsis* by name, he immediately moves his discussion away from the abstract term to images that carry the sense of his thought. Thus the book of Ecclesiastes and Isaac "digging wells and searching out the roots of things" become Origen's figures for *phūsis,* as though *phūsis* as a mode of understanding were intimately tied to metaphoric interpreting.[24]

That metaphor is the key to *phūsis* as a theological art becomes clear in Origen's discussion of the branches of learning.[25] Having distinguished ethics, physics, and *theōria* (contemplative seeing) as the three standard branches,[26] he goes on to say that there is another, logic, which some consider a fourth branch. But Origen feels that logic "does not stand by itself", but is "mingled and interwoven with the other three".[27] For Origen, logic is the hermeneutic heart of these three "degrees of the spiritual life":[28] "it deals with the meanings and proper significances and their opposites, the classes and kinds of words and expressions, and gives information as to the form of each and every saying".[29] When the lifeblood of one's learning is logical, one is able "to grasp the shades of meaning in words" and to unfold "immense and perfect truths in short and pithy phrases".[30] Logic is a work of expanding enigmas, as Origen says. Grasping shades of meaning and shortening immense truths are metaphoric ways of knowing, and Origen remarks that *phūsis*, seen in this way, brings us to the point where "metaphors" will not cause us to "stumble".[31] Further, when this "stretching of words" happens, "the heart of a man is enlarged".[32]

When *phūsis* provides the body of one's meditations, the heart is enlarged with "figures": the "parables, dark speech and riddles" of the sensuous world.[33] For the wisdom of nature consists in a journey through the visible aspects of "each single thing" to "certain secret metaphors".[34] It is not a renunciation of the sensuous world, but rather an embrace of that world as an enigmatic bearer of the kingdom of heaven itself.[35] This passage is an important moment in the *Commentary on the Song of Songs*, for it is here that Origen says that natural images, as likenesses, are not merely bearers of "some heavenly pattern but of the kingdom of God itself". In other words, natural imagery is not merely a structure of analogies. Henri Crouzel has made a pertinent remark in this regard. Discussing the "divine sensibility" of Origen's doctrine of homonyms as natural metaphors, Crouzel says: "When the spiritual meaning is considered to be an analogy, there is a duality of subject and object. But the Origenist ideal goes further: this opposition must be overcome in order to achieve a union, a fusion, a mélange of knower and known, which become one without ceasing to be two".[36]

It is important to add here that in Origen's writings, the sensuous world is not singular, but plural; further, "the things on earth" with which he is concerned appear as images in Scriptural texts. Thus Origen is dealing at once with world as text and text as world, full of parables, dark speech, and riddles that pierce the one who "extends his thinking" like "wounds of love" and "chosen darts" of the Word itself.[37] The sensuous world is not singular, but plural: when Origen names these images that wound, the word he uses is not *phūsis*, but *aisthētos*. As Crouzel has pointed out, "this word occurs most often in the context of spiritual exegesis", and "it designates sensible realities seen as symbolic realities".[38] In other words, to call "each single thing" *aisthētos*, and to name the sensuous realm collectively *ta aisthēta*, as Origen typically does, is to treat those things and that realm as shadings of meaning in life. It is also to treat those things as occasions for exploring the shades of text, for *aisthētos* also designates the "letter" of scripture, the literal word that "wounds" when its "dark speech" is explored.[39]

What arises from Origen's sense of *phūsis* as an aesthetic perspective is an appeal for human transformation, a wounding that heals. This call for transformation—literally, for metamorphosis—in the context of aesthetic thinking comes most poignantly in his *Dialogue with Heraclides*. Here there is a discussion concerning how natural metaphors can be ways of imagining what "the creation in the image" means, and especially how we are to understand the *language of* creation—serpents, pigs, and so on—in scriptural texts. Such questions, Origen says, are "delicate", "disturbing", and "terribly distressing". Yet enduring the distress brings the power of metamorphosis, and metamorphosis "depends on us". Further, such discourse can be shaped "so as to heal the souls of the hearers". The whole process is one of transformation into the image of the Word, when one receives the eyes of God, the point being not to see God, but to see as God sees.[40]

The working of sensuous images as living texts is most essentially an interior journey of the soul, which Daniélou called a voyage through "the night of the senses".[41] This voyage is perhaps most fully described by Origen in his *Homilies on Numbers,* where again it is the painful process of aesthetic self-reflection that Origen details, here in terms of the soul's nomadic wandering through a desert of sensuous images that have to be lived in, wrestled, and uprooted. It is a voyage through the senses. What Origen means by "senses" is, of course, "the senses of the heart"—*ta aisthētēria tēs kardias*—which are pierced and transformed whenever the "outer man", the merely personal self, sees with the eyes of the "inner man", the iconic or imaginal self.[42]

This piercing process of aesthetic self-reflection is not dispensable since, as Origen says, mindful understandings, *ta noēta*, come through sensuous images, *ta aisthēta*.[43] The wisdom of Origen's apple is a sweetness in "the *inner* throat"; but that inner sweetness can be savored only by tasting the fruit. And this tasting, that is, seeing the sensuous aesthetically, is not always pleasant, as Origen would be the first to say. When the world passes into the soul, words are stretched and the heart is enlarged, but with parables, dark speech, and riddles that transform only as they are lived in and through.

Nowhere are the painful darts of this aesthetic journey more evident than in the bestial images that rage through many of Origen's reflections. For seeing with the eyes of the beasts is, as Jerome knew, disgusting and distasteful; yet, as Origen knew, to see with the eyes of the beasts is to redeem those monstrous riddles of the self, and to transform them into heavenly children.[44]

Partridges Playing in the Dust

In his *Homilies on the Song of Songs,* Origen remarks that the evangelists "did not write fables and narratives, but mysteries" *(non fabulas et narrationes, sed mysteria).*[45] The scriptural word is "mysterious", and not only in the New Testament but in the Old as well.[46] Sacred discourse lives in the closed flowers of its ambiguous or equivocal words,[47] which unfurl in the mind of the reader only when his reading is as ambiguous as the sacred words themselves. To dismiss such words as fanciful decoration *(fabula)* or to mire such words in literal history *(narratio)* is to read with a withering eye, mistaking the mysterious for the obvious.

Origen is particularly adamant about the importance of reading words as mysteries when he addresses scripture's beasts. "I am not concerned with the obvious sense of the words ... but I examine these words to find out their hidden meanings *(ainigmata)*", he says in his *Contra Celsum* in regard to the "ants, locusts, and lizards" of Proverbs 24 *(LXX).*[48] Mocking Celsus' literal zoological interpretations of these beasts, Origen brands such reading as "crude and illiterate".[49] Celsus has failed to see that such words are *ainigmata,* dark images that live most profoundly in the soul of the text, not in the natural world. "The ants who have no strength" are "wiser than the wise" when they "prepare their food in the summer", as Proverbs says. Yet whatever one might say about the frugal disposition of actual ants is merely *narratio* until one sees, as Origen says, that "it is not the literal ants who are even wiser than the wise, but those alluded to under a proverbial form".[50] Until one can see that it is precisely the "literal ants" *(aisthētoi murmēkes) in the text* that carry the proverbial figure, one will miss the aesthetic perspective of the text, refusing the *aisthēta* their metaphoric unfolding.

These ants prepare their food not only in the text of scripture, but also in the text of self. Speaking elsewhere about real animals "out there", Origen states that "the corporeal beasts are neither evil nor good, but neutral. These are the mute animals". But the scriptural animals are "spiritual", and they are not silent.[51] On the contrary, their "gruntings and brayings and hissings and howlings"[52] are the voices of soul itself. We shall see that, for Origen, the beasts are one dimension of the soul's speaking, and it is a language of creation, as was implied earlier.[53] Further, when the animal speaks, there is an aesthetic play, as the following bestial riddle from the *Acts of John* seems to suggest.

> Now one day as John was sitting there, a partridge flew by and came and played in the dust before him; and John was amazed as he saw it. But a certain priest, who was one of his hearers, came and went in to John and saw the partridge playing in the dust before him. And he was offended and said to himself, "Can such a man, at his age, take pleasure in a partridge playing in the dust"? But John knew in the spirit what he was thinking, and said to him, "it would be better for you, my son, to watch a partridge playing in the dust and not to foul yourself with shameful and impious practices ... For I have no need of a partridge playing in the dust; for the partridge is your own soul".[54]

In this text, the play of the literal animal is an offense, and watching it seems a frivolous pastime. But when that animal is seen with what Origen calls the eyes of the inner man,[55] it comes alive as an amazing play of soul. The one who is able to watch in this way is the one who "knows in the spirit", while the other is fouled with "impious practices".

Like John, Origen was able to see the beasts as sportive monsters of the soul. In his aesthetic vision, the "partridge playing in the dust" is an interior figure; it is a way of sensing, and making sense of, an inner world. The following passage speaks to the point of this world of inner sense:

> Understand that you have within yourself herds of cattle...flocks of sheep and flocks of goats ... and that the birds of the air are also within you. Do not be surprised if we say that these are within you, but understand that you are another little world.[56]

Origen says further in this passage that our task is to "discover" or "find a home" for these animals "in the soul" *(invenies eas intra animam tuam)*.

What is at stake in making a home in the deep self, the soul, for these beasts? Although it may seem a startling one, Origen's argument at this point is clear. The animals are part of that world that is, as the prophet Jeremiah says, filled with God.[57] That world is also filled with the son of God, and with the holy spirit of God.[58] When the beasts are placed in this context, they become vessels for the presence of God, but only when they shape an *inner* world. When we see that we have "all those things which the world has",[59] we see that divine indwelling is sometimes bestial. God is at home in the soul as "flocks of sheep and flocks of goats", or, to put it another way, beasts are one way in which God fills the inner world of the self.[60]

Of course, these bestial flocks are also at play in the inner world of the scriptural text, for the *mysteria* of the interior figures of soul are also the *ainigmata* of the sacred word. Origen asks that we discover the herds of cattle in the soul, but that home-making is intimately bound up with seeking the "soul" of textual images.[61] In the play of aesthetic seeing, the word of God is no longer an external image that has no connection with the life of the reader; rather, image becomes metaphor, a means for *sensing* the inner realm of soul's character. As Origen says, the corporeal beasts are mute. It is the spiritual beasts that speak in the heart of soul and text.

One of Origen's most pointed statements about aesthetic soul-work comes in his *Commentary on the Song of Songs*.[62] Here Origen suggests that "spiritual blessings" (the fruit of *theōria*) come by way of "the power of scent". The one who hunts the "difficulties" of the "meaning of the words of scripture" hunts successfully only by "the wise dog within". For without that dog, the hunter is misled by "hot trails" and "track-marks" and thus misses "the hidden lairs". The hard work of interpretation—hunting for the image's hidden lair—involves learning to scent rather than to see. While Origen is optimistic in this passage about the movement from tracking to scenting and finally to receiving the blessing, he is also aware that the play of *aisthēsis* (literally, "scent"[63]) in the inner worlds of soul and text can be dangerous. The wise dog is also a snarling hound. Aesthetic understanding involves discovering this beast in the soulful text of the self, for in Origen's work sensuous images give figure to the passionate realities of the quest for understanding. The beasts in particular are not only tropes for thinking about thinking; they are the very scent of the dispositions of our inner selves.

The Wrestling of the Beasts

In Genesis 1:28, the Lord God says to Adam: "Have dominion over the fish of the sea and the birds of the sky, over the beasts of burden and all the animals on the earth and the reptiles that crawl on the earth". When Origen treats this statement in his *Homilies on Genesis,* he imagines that it describes a kind of zoological garden of the self:

> These animals indicate either that which proceeds from the dispositions of the soul *(de sensu animae)* and the thought of the heart *(de cordis cogitatione)*, or that which issues from bodily desires *(ex desideriis corporalibus)* and from the movements of the flesh *(ex carnis motibus)*.[64]

These interior beasts are what "embellish this little world which is man".[65] And they are man's bestial *insides*, for as Origen says in his discussion of creation, the man made in the image of God is "our interior man" *(interior homo noster)*, and it is *his* qualities that the creation narratives address.[66]

Further, these beasts are a *"theological* menagerie", as Crouzel has remarked.[67] That is, they are divine gifts, blessed by God.[68] However, like the "piercing darts" of the scriptural texts, these bestial blessings are ambiguous gifts. When the language of creation speaks in the soul, it is equivocal, as Origen says when he comments on Genesis 1:20-21.[69] In this passage, God creates the great sea monsters and the winged birds: for Origen, these are the soul's "good and bad thoughts made known" *(cogitationes bonas vel malas proferre in medium)*. These animals are the soul's conscious reflections, and *all* of them carry divine possibilities. "By the word and order of God", says Origen, we are to "bring all these forward for the inspection and judgment of God so that, illumined by him, we might be able to distinguish the bad from the good". Making the bestial ambiguity conscious is thus that part of the dynamic of divine illumination which entails a profound probing of the full range of soul's reflections.

Origen is not unaware that his argument on this issue might seem a bit odd. After all, he has imagined the human heart as the chaotic waters in which the sea monsters romp, including the primordial dragon; he has also imagined the heart as the "heaven" through which the birds fly; *and* he has said that even the "nefarious" beasts are graceful gifts.[70] Thus he remarks, "One might well wonder why the sea monsters and the animals which swarm play host to evil, and the birds to good, since it is said of all of them together, 'And God saw that they were good'".[71]

Invoking Job, Origen offers the following explanation:

> It is because, for the saints, the beasts which oppose them are good, because the saints are able to conquer them and that victory brings them greater glory before God. After all, when the devil demanded that he be given power against Job, the attacks of the enemy were for Job the occasion for a glory twice as great following the victory ... Thus the Apostle said that "no one is crowned unless he contends according to the rules.[72]

Origen carries this statement on with a series of rhetorical questions: how to struggle without an adversary? how to see the glitter of the sun without the obscurity of the night?, and so on. The good strikes more forcefully through encounter with its opposite; in the present context, it is the monstrous aspects of the beasts that must be wrestled so that their celestial potential can be released to fly. True self-reflection is a contest of the beasts within, and it is a divine struggle, for as Origen says, God saw its "utility and reason", and blessed it.[73]

When Origen speaks in this way about the soul as a repository of ambiguous thoughts that can either fly or swarm in the depths, depending upon how we engage them, he is relying on what Peter Brown has called the Greek gift to Late Antiquity: "a sense of the multiplicity of the self".[74] As Brown points out, the "sense" of this multiplicity for a thinker like Origen is an awareness that the soul plays host to a whole array of transpersonal presences—angels and demons—that "preside over the weaving of his thoughts".[75] For Origen, consciousness is multiple; it has "secret recesses" (*arcana conscientiae*)[76] and, as he says, "the soul of man can admit different energies (*diversas energias*), that is, controlling influences of spirits either good or bad".[77]

Origen has an intriguing figure for this receptive character of the soul. The term that conveys his idea concerning how an individual soul provides space for the play of diverse energies comes at the conclusion of his lengthy discussion of the soul's entertaining of spirits, where he calls the soul an *hospitium*, a "guest-chamber".[78] As one scholar has indicated, *hospitium* is an uncanny word, uncanny because it turns into its opposite. *Hospitium* is a place of hospitality—for strangers. It derives from *hospes*, which means *both* host *and* guest. Thus the host "contains in himself the double antithetical relation of host and guest, guest in the bifold sense of friendly presence and alien invader".[79] The soul is a guest-chamber. It is, for Origen, host to the influx of daimonic hordes that fill the mind's secret recesses; but it is also guest, recipient of the favors, whether good or ill, of those invading spirits that twine our thoughts.

What these daimons speak in the soul is a language of creation, for they are images, phantasies that come on their own, and they provide occasion for the soul to become conscious of its own possibilities. Speaking in *De principiis* about his idea that the soul's reflections are not merely subjective delusions, Origen refers to "the book of the Shepherd", which teaches that "two angels attend each human being, and whenever good thoughts arise in our heart they are suggested by the good angel, and whenever thoughts of the opposite kind they are the inspiration of the bad angel".[80] The angelic "suggestions to our heart", Origen goes on to say, are not finally determinative in any way. They are rather the "commotion" and "incitements" produced by the mind's daimonic inhabitants.[81] It is up to the soul, the hospitable guest that feasts on all this commotion, to decide how to work with and understand the agitations of its invaders.

That soul's inhabitants are phantasmal creatures is clear in Origen's discussion of the psychological dimensions of free will, again in *De principiis*. Here Origen asserts that it would be a mistake to imagine that actual people, events, or objects *(to exōthen)* determine our thoughts.[82] To this point he often quotes Eph. 6:12: "For our wrestling is not against flesh and blood, but against principalities, against powers, against the rulers of the darkness of this world, against spiritual hosts of wickedness in the heavenly places".[83] Our actions and thoughts are not simply reactions to sensory impressions. We wrestle, not with flesh and blood, but with those beings that occupy the "places" in our minds.[84] Further, that interior wrestling forms our perception of the world, and not the other way round.[85]

Like Jacob, then, our struggle is with angels. We do not summon them; they come to us. They are the vessels of the soul's movement toward conscious reflection, its imagination. As Origen argues, animate beings *(ta empsūcha)* are moved or impelled from within themselves *(aph' eautōn)* "when there arises within them an image *(phantasia)* which calls forth an impulse *(hormē)*". When such phantasies arise, the "imaginative nature" *(phūsis phantastikē)* sets the impulse "in ordered motion". Origen's example for this process is a spider weaving its web: a weaving image arises, and prompts an impulse to weave; the web results from the incitements of the spider's imaginative nature.[86] When Origen speaks about "order" in this context, he does not mean to imply that imagining is an irenic process. The real situation is, if anything, the reverse, for the "impulses" that phantasies summon are frenzied. This is what the word *hormē* suggests: "rapid motion forwards", "assault", "attack", "invasion", all associated with such images as "the rage of fire", "the shock of a wave", "a spear's cast", "the spring of the knee".[87] The phantasies of soul are truly piercing darts.

The spider is a captive of its phantasies, since it has only an imaginative nature. We human beings, however, are not only guests of these raging phantasies, but also hosts. Each of us is a "reasoning being" *(logikon zōon)*. We are moved not only from *within* ourselves, but also *through* ourselves *(di'autōn)*. Along with our phantasies we have reason *(logos)*, which gives us the ability to distinguish and so interpret the mind's commotions.[88] The spider has no "seeds of wisdom within",[89] and it does not reflect; for it, the phantasy is occasion for immediate, unmeditated action, and its meaning is univocal and literal. But we do have "seeds of wisdom". We have possibilities for profound reflection, whose call is not only to recognize the phantasies, but also to wrestle them. When we struggle with the sensuous clamorings of soul's inner voices, we are released from the dilemma of the spider. That is, we are freed from the "outer man" for whom phantasies are what Origen calls "specious attractions",[90] agitations that are taken personally, and acted out literally.

Of course, as Origen says, even the "inner man" cannot evade the soul's monstrous riddles: "the sensations and incitements are there",[91] and they are God-given, as we have seen. The point is to understand soul's monsters as "embellishments", ways of sensing—or scenting—the mysterious depths of soul's character. But this way of understanding is a struggle, for while we are always moved "from within" by the very nature of soul as *hospitium,* we are not always moved "through ourselves". As Origen says, it is easy for the reader of scripture to see the obvious meaning of words, just as it is easy to mistake the impulse that phantasy provokes as a call for actual behavior, thus miring the phantasy in *narratio,* literal history. The easy way sees no ambiguity, expands no enigmas, grasps no shades of meaning in text or self.

The "movement through ourselves" is the difficult way that Origen recommends, a way that requires much "instruction and discipline".[92] It is a difficult way, because it involves finding a home for those raging daimons of the mind. It involves understanding even the most monstrous phantasy as a divine vessel, an occasion for meditating *consciously* on the "hidden treasures" of our nature as images of God. In the context of scriptural interpretation, Origen remarks that when one brings a metaphoric understanding to the text, there is a "bursting of iron bars" as the literal image is shattered and one is carried through to multiple hidden meanings.[93] So also in the present psychological context: the difficult way, which I have called the way of aesthetic understanding, takes its place precisely in the moment when the literal sense of phantasy is shattered. When the angels are wrestled, they become perspectives that carry us through to "invisible patterns and likenesses". To contemplate phantasies thoroughly, then, is to come to see them as metaphors of the self. This is the "rule" by which we, like Job, must contend.

Origen does not often give abstract discussions of the dynamic of this movement from the personal to the imaginal self. Rather, his aesthetic understanding is most often expressed, appropriately enough, through his own wrestlings with sensuous imagery, especially as it appears in scriptural texts. I now turn in detail to one of those sensuous languages, with which Origen was most intrigued, the language of the beasts.

Serpents in the Soul

When soul becomes conscious of its possibilities, there is a bestial awakening. Origen makes this bestial point with a bestial vocabulary. In *De principiis*, he says that images *drag* the soul.[94] Here is a case where Rufinus' translation has not softened the force of Origen's thought. The verb used in this statement is *rapio*: "seize and carry off", "snatch", "tear", "drag", "ravish", "ravage", "plunder", "take by assault".[95] Lurking behind the Latin is the Greek *harpē:* the bird of prey. Phantasies are the mind's harpies, and they peck and tear.

Origen's handling of the sensuous world of the animals that populate scripture finds its context precisely in the soul's engagement with its phantasmal ravishers. That is, the perspective that Origen generally brings to animal images is a psychological perspective.[96] For, just as an aesthetic interpretation of scripture's people, events, and places can yield "mindful understandings" of theological and cosmological realities, so also such interpretation can reveal the hidden workings of the self. As Origen says again and again, the characters and happenings of scripture are *already images* (whatever their historical value might be) by virtue of their very presence in the text;[97] for him, the world has passed into the book. Our task as interpreters is to "put on" that book, since it is the living mask through which the hidden faces of God are revealed. As with scripture's historical figures, so also with its natural figures: the beasts, too, are already images, and when they are "worn" they confront the interpreters with the passionate depths of the soul.

When Origen interprets the text, he is also interpreting the self. In the case of the text's animals, this kind of interpreting can be a truly unpleasant, if not horrifying, journey to the interior. It is unpleasant because "tasting the fruit" of animal images seen as psychological realities entails recognizing and confronting not simply the soul's "fishes", but also its "wild beasts". Commenting on Jer. 12:8, "My heritage has become to me like a lion in the forest", Origen suggests that the soul that does not "repent and acknowledge its false steps" *is* that lion, lost in the forest of its blunders".[98] The companion verse, "Go, assemble all the wild beasts and bring them to devour" (Jer. 12:9), is taken to show that such souls are "devoured by opposing powers".[99] Similarly, when Origen discusses the "ark" of the soul in his *Homilies on Genesis,* he imagines that the lower niches of this structure contain the violent and savage beasts.[100] The lower region is a psychic hell of impure animals that provoke lustful and angry behavior.[101]

In each of these examples, the aesthetic beast in the text clearly carries the "night of the senses" in the soul. Yet there is light concealed in these dark figures. As Origen says in the Jeremiah commentary above, the wild beasts that devour the heart are sent by Christ. The suggestion seems to be that when these "opposing powers" are acknowledged, then the "nurturing angels" are released, as if knowing the beast brings the angel.[102] So also with the ark. It has stages, the lowest holding the "ferocious beasts and serpents" and the intermediate containing "the more tranquil animals" (i.e., the pure animals: memory, intellect, discernment, and so on). At the summit is man.[103]

When, at a later point in the homily, Origen discusses these three stages as degrees of spiritual attainment, the man at the summit is shown to be the man who lives his life in accord with reason and understanding.[104] He is the "higher" man in every soul, whose kingdom comes when "the wolf and the lamb, the leopard and the kid, the lion and the steer will be together in pasture".[105] As Origen remarks elsewhere, the man who is truly man—*homo-homo*—is the one no longer imprisoned by the "serpent-man" and the "horse-man".[106] He has explored every nook and cranny of his ark, and the pure and impure animals lie together. Like the beast and the angel, the pure and the impure animals form a pair. The light in such dark figures as lust and anger is that they are natural, even necessary, to all souls.[107] Accepting this paradox is the key to aesthetic understanding.

Although in his *Homilies on Genesis* Origen distinguishes between good and bad animals, his usual way of proceeding with animal imagery is like his treatment of Jeremiah's lion. The beasts are the mind's demons.[108] They are those pecking and tearing phantasies that form the shadow-side of angels, for, as Origen says, animals are not rational.[109] Just as an actual animal can never become a *logikon,* so bestial images are soul's phantasies. These demons carry the deep *pathos* of the soul struggling with riddling "movements from within", and that *pathos* is the place where the "outer man" is pierced and wounded by glimpses of the "inner man".[110] The beasts are the sensuous embodiments of the unexplored spaces of the self, and grappling with them brings an awareness of soul's "deeper frontiers". As Peter Brown has remarked, "self-awareness and awareness of the demonic form a pair".[111]

Origen expresses this perspective on the demonic forcefully in his *Homilies on Joshua*. In Book VIII, Origen is interpreting the confrontation between the Israelites and the inhabitants of Ai in the promised land (Josh. 7). Because this is a particularly "difficult and arduous" passage if taken historically,[112] Origen treats it as a drama of the soul. Ai is chaos.[113] When soul dwells in this place, it is ripe to the bursting point with demonic hosts, which Origen calls "inhabitants of chaos and masters of the abyss".[114] The soul agape with such abysmal impulses burns with an eternal fire, a fire sent by Christ as a "remedy for deliverance".[115] The fire of Wisdom moves us through our demonic selves.[116] Like the Israelites killing their enemies of Ai, each of us has to "kill" the demons. But, as Origen says, this has nothing to do with being blood-thirsty, and besides, killing the demons "does not deprive them of their existence".[117] Rather, "killing" involves "guarding the heart" so that no *cogitationes malae* proceed out of it. The soul is not only guest, but host: it must contain its phantasies, not letting "a single fugitive escape".[118] The soul that contains its phantasmal fugitives knows that self-awareness comes only through experiencing the burning fire that such containment entails. We have "serpents in the soul"; yet those beasts are the turning points for the transformation of the "outer man" into the "inner man".[119]

God's Bestial Play

Clement of Alexandria said that Adam "uttered prophecies" when he named the animals.[120] Origen, working out of the traditional link between prophecy and the Holy Spirit, seems to be following in Clement's line when he suggests that the "breath of God" that made man "a living soul" may have been the Spirit of God, "in view of the fact that Adam is found to have uttered prophecies".[121] If Origen means, like Clement, the prophecies regarding the bestial names, he has linked the animal imagination with the Spirit in man. We are spirited by the beasts, whose passionate nature goads the soul to explore its depths.

As we have seen, Origen knows that the passions are divine blessings, bestial food given to man by the grace of God.[122] But he also knows that these divine beasts have a monstrous side. We have a tendency to make the animal more divine than the human, turning our irrational thoughts into concrete actions, making the trope literal.[123] We forget to think. We lose the scent of the Spirit's breath in the beast's panting. The kingdom of the

Spirit within is the hunting ground of beasts, but we need not fall prey to its chimeras. As Jesus says in the *Gospel of Thomas*:

> Blessed is the lion that the man will devour, and the lion will become man. And loathsome is the man that the lion will devour, and the lion will become man.[124]

In our context, "devouring the lion" is that journey through the night of the senses that constitutes an aesthetic self-understanding.

Integral to an aesthetic perspective on the self is an aesthetic understanding of scripture. For the words of scripture's "magicians" (Moses, Jesus, the prophets) play the role of serpent-charmer to the serpents in the soul.[125] Even when these words seem obscure or merely literal to the outer man (the ego or personal self), they speak powerfully to soul's interior figures, feeding the angelic and starving the demonic with their incantatory food.[126] As Crouzel has remarked in this regard, Origen is speaking of an "evangelization of our being" that "must not be limited to univocal [*claire*] consciousness but extends itself also to those unconscious psychic depths, the mark of our animality, which contemporary psychology is discovering more and more".[127] Scripture, it would seem, speaks directly to the angel in the beast.

When scripture speaks in this way, there is a metamorphosis in the soul. One of Origen's most striking figures for this metamorphic process, which consists in the transformative turning from *homo-animal* to *homo-homo*, is the metaphor of the mask. As Origen points out frequently, the soul of every man was created "according to the image". But it was Adam's mistake, which we replicate, to "clothe" the heavenly image with the terrestrial image, literally, with the image of clay *(tēn eikona tou choikou).*[128] Our mistake, it would seem, lies in making the inner, luminous self into an opaque (clay-like) exterior. Mistaking the earthly for the heavenly, we turn the angel into a beast. Thus Origen remarks that in place of Christic images, "we wear the mask *(persona)* of the lion, the dragon, the fox ... and the pig".[129] The animals are masks! They are the personifications of our earthy selves and, as scriptural images, they make visible the unconscious depths of the soul. It is because these images can be masks that they function as points of metamorphosis.

One of Origen's most urgent and eloquent pleas for psychic transformation comes precisely in the context of a lengthy excursus on the soul's bestial "shapes" *(morphoi)*. It is just when we are thoroughly molded by the beast that the resolve to be transformed is awakened.[130] He goes on to suggest that "if we are willing to understand that in us there is the power to be transformed from being serpents, swine, and dogs, let us learn from the apostle that the transformation depends on us. For he says this: 'We all, when with unveiled face we reflect the glory of the Lord, are transformed into the same image'".[131] We must not only wear the animal mask, but see through it as well, thereby unveiling the inner reflective self.

As one modern scholar has remarked, "the mask conceals, the mask terrifies, but most of all, it creates a relation between him who wears it and the being it is made to represent".[132] Further, the mask is "an instrument of unifying transformation" because it brings about the revelation of something hidden".[133] These comments have a direct bearing on our interest in exploring Origen's aesthetic as a "poetics" of nature. For Origen, the transformative turn comes when the bestial image can be seen as a mask, that is, as a metaphor, a poetic figure whose allusive indirection both conceals and reveals. He suggests that when an image functions in this way, it creates a relation between the sensuous world *(ta aisthēta)* and the Christic power *(ta noēta)* hidden within that world.[134] As he says, "everything awaits discovery" for the one whose knowing is aesthetic.[135] This is because "all of the *aisthēta*" are "white fields, ready for harvest"; and, although his examples of "sensible realities" here are the savage beasts of Genesis, in fact these bestial images figure the terrifyingly "masked" quality of all images.[136]

The "harvest" that aesthetic thinking brings is a godlike vision that sees the beauty in all things, a beauty that Origen names *logos*.[137] For, as he insists, it is the *word* that transforms from wild beast to man; it is the *word* that "touches the soul" and empowers the metamorphosis.[138] I have already remarked that, for Origen, the world has passed into the scriptural word. But that word is itself informed by a Word, the Christ, whose iconoclastic force breaks through the "iron bars" of all our literalisms and releases a "healing power".[139] That healing power is the discovery of Christic perspectives in the soul, and this discovery is intimately tied to aesthetic interpretations of scripture's image-masks. In Origen's words, "the one who possesses aesthetic understanding *(tōn aisthētōn logos)* is governed by the Christic word".[140]

In Origen's aesthetic vision, the sensuous world of scripture's images serves as an *agent provocateur* whose words provide striking personifications of the mysterious depths of human character. Most provocative of all are the beasts, since they carry starkly that "dark speech" by which the Christic word wounds the soul with its loving revelations. As Origen himself remarks, Christ rides on the beast! The Word is carried even by our bestial selves, and its Christic power is released when we interpret that word aesthetically, thus cutting the animal loose from merely personal attachments.[141] The point seems to be that the Christic treasures of the word are revealed when the beasts are seen as personifications, perspectives with which the inner man must wrestle.

Only when one journeys through the night of the senses aesthetically will one understand the angelic aspect of God's bestial play, his scriptural poetry of sensuous images. As we saw earlier, the beasts provide one way of imagining how God fills the soul. Perhaps the idea that God is present in the soul as a bestial play explains Origen's apparent fascination with two Biblical verses, Job 40:19 (LXX) and Ps. 103:24-26, both of which state that Leviathan, the greatest beast of them all, had a premier role in God's creative plan.[142] These passages say that Leviathan was formed by God as a plaything for himself and the angels.[143] God also made this beast for the laughter or mockery of the angels.[144] Even the monstrous Leviathan is God's plaything in the world. Further, this beast carries angelic laughter. All this is a mystery, as Origen says.[145] Perhaps the key to understanding the secret of God's bestial play in the worlds of soul and text is *aisthēsis*. When the phantasies of soul and the images of text can be seen as metaphors, the angels laugh at these beasts, and we are released into a kind of understanding that takes all the *aisthēta* as perspectives, occasions for discovering the divine *logos* that fills the self and the word. The "poetry" of Origen's view of the sensuous world is based in the aesthetic play of God's word, which, while it does not shrink from the pathos of the beast, yet hears the angelic laughter as well.

Notes

1 Origen, *Comm. in Cant.* 3.5 (*GCS* 8, 180-81). I have followed the English translation of Lawson, *Origen: The Song of Songs, Commentary and Homilies*, p. 181.
2 Jerome, *Ep. ad Avitum* 4.
3 Ibid.
4 On the beasts and the irrational, see, for example, Origen, *De prin.* 1.8.4; *Contra Cels.* 4.85-89. See also the sources cited by Crouzel, "Images bestiales", in *Théologie de l'Image de Dieu chez Origène*, pp. 197-206. The connection between *pathos* and the beasts is explored in the main body of this essay.
5 The phrase is from Emerson, "The Poet", in *Essays*, 2nd series, *The Complete Works of Ralph Waldo Emerson*, vol. 3, p. 20.
6 Ibid., pp. 20-21.
7 Ibid., p. 21 (italics mine). On the passage of the world into the soul of man in Origen, see *Comm. in Cant.* 3.12 (*GCS* 8, 208-10; Lawson, pp. 218-21). See also the discussion by Crouzel, *Connaissance Mystique*, pp. 50-54.
8 Dodds, *Pagan and Christian in an Age of Anxiety*, pp. 10-17, 32-33.

9 Origen, *De prin.* 2.1.3 (Crouzel and Simonetti, 1:238): "The universe is as it were an immense, monstrous animal, held together by the power and reason of God as by one soul".
10 Singer, *History of Biology*, p. 62, quoted by Wallace-Hadrill, *The Greek Patristic View of Nature*, p. 3.
11 Origen, *Comm. in Cant.* 3.12 (GCS 8, 211; Lawson, p. 222).
12 See ibid., 3.13 (GCS8, 219-20; Lawson, pp. 233-34) and 3.14 (*GCS* 8, 223; Lawson, p. 239), where Origen speaks about the bodily senses as "windows" through which the Word of God enters, and compares scripture to those senses.
13 Wallace-Hadrill, *The Greek Patristic View of Nature*, vii.
14 For an excellent summary of the voluminous scholarship on *phūsis*, see Grant, *Miracle and Natural Law in Graeco-Roman and Early Christian Thought*, pp. 1-18.
15 Marcus Aurelius, *Med.* 3.1-2; for passages that give his sense of the "whirl" of Nature, see *Med.* 4.36; 6.15; 7.23; 7.25, and so on.
16 Ibid., 3.2; 4.23; 2.3.
17 See Grant, *Miracle and Natural Law*, p. 10, and Curley (trans), *Physiologus*, xii-xiii.
18 Plutarch, *De Isis et Osiris* 382B-C. For a brief discussion of Plutarch's thoughts on the mythic aspects of nature, see Pépin, *Mythe et Allégorie*, pp. 184f.
19 Clement of Alexandria, *Strom.* 4.1.3.
20 The phrase is from Curley, *Physiologus*, xiv.
21 See Grant, *Miracle and Natural Law*, pp. 16, 198-208.
22 See *Contra Cels.* 5.23, where Origen agrees to speak about "nature" only "if we are *forced* to use this terminology" (italics mine).
23 Origen uses this phrase in *Comm. in Cant.* 3.12 (GCS 8, 210; Lawson, p. 220). This entire section of the commentary is devoted to a discussion of things manifest and hidden. For a useful discussion, and voluminous citations, concerning Origen's thoughts on *phūsis*, see Crouzel, *Connaissance Mystique*, pp. 50-54.
24 Origen *Comm. in Cant.*, prologue, 3 (GCS 8, 75-79; Lawson, pp. 39-46).
25 Ibid.
26 It is difficult to render the sense of the name of the third branch of learning in English. Origen's word here is "enoptics", but elsewhere he calls this branch simply "theology" (*Comm. in Gen.* 3) or "mystical inspection" (*Comm. in Lam.*, frag. 14). In the notes to his translation, Lawson remarks that "enoptic" is commonly called in English either "contemplative" or "theoretic". "Neither of these terms is wholly satisfactory; for 'contemplative' suggests looking at God, as far as may be without intervening images, and 'theoretic' has lost its original idea of 'beholding,' and carries an almost wholly intellectual meaning. But what Origen here calls the enoptic science is concerned with the unseen realities behind the seen". Lawson goes on to translate "enoptic" as "inspective", pp. 318-19. Crouzel also uses both "enoptic" and "inspective", in *Connaissance Mystique*, p. 52, n. 2 and pp. 62-63, while in *Origène*, p. 298, Jean Daniélou uses "unitive". Both of the French translators place the enoptic branch in the context of spiritual love and mysticism. It is important to note that both Crouzel (ibid., p. 231) and Daniélou (ibid.) have shown how closely physics and enoptics are tied together in Origen's discussion of them, especially in the *Comm. in Cant.* Daniélou remarks about *phūsis* (which he translates as the "illuminative" branch): "Elle consiste a se former un jugement vrai sur les choses, c'est-à-dire a comprendre le néant des choses temporelles et que seul le monde spirituel est réel. Il s'agit donc ici de se déprendre de l'illusion du monde et de s'attacher aux réalités véritables. Une fois cette conviction établie dans l'âme, elle peut entrer dans les voies de la contemplation des choses divines".

27 Origen *Comm. in Cant.*, prologue, 3 (*GCS* 8, 75; Lawson, p. 40).
28 Daniélou, *Origène*, p. 297.
29 Origen *Comm. in Cant.*, prologue, 3 (*GCS* 8, 75; Lawson, p. 40).
30 Ibid. (*GCS* 8, 76-77; Lawson, pp. 42-43).
31 Ibid. (*GCS* 8, 77-78; Lawson, pp. 43-44).
32 Ibid. (*GCS* 8, 77; Lawson, p. 43).
33 Ibid. (*GCS* 8, 77; Lawson, p. 42). In this passage, Origen says that parables, riddles, and so on are the "different modes of expression and sundry forms of speech in the divine words whereby the order of living has been transmitted by the prophets to the human race".
34 Ibid. (*GCS* 8, 75, 78; Lawson, pp. 40, 44).
35 Ibid., 3.12 (*GCS* 8, 208; Lawson, p. 219).
36 Crouzel, *Connaissance Mytique*, pp. 506-7.
37 Origen *Comm. in Cant.*, prologue, 2 (*GCS* 8, 67; Lawson, p. 29).
38 Crouzel, *Connaissance Mystique*, p. 230.
39 See ibid., p. 231, for discussion and references.
40 Origen, *Dialogue with Heraclides* 13. Cf. Origen *Comm. in Ioh.* 13.42.
41 Daniélou, *Origène*, p. 296.
42 For the phrase "senses of the heart", see Origen, *Dialogue with Heraclides* 21. A bit later in the same passage, Origen says: "The inner man has a heart. But when a man has neglected to cultivate his ability to understand *(hexeōs noētikes)*, and because of idleness the principle of thinking *(dianoētikon)* has atrophied, he has lost his heart" (ibid., 22). Origen often links heart and mind; see, for example, *De prin.* 1.1.9 (Crouzel and Simonetti, vol. 1, pp. 108-10). See also Crouzel and Simonetti, vol. 4, p. 63 (n. 29), for Origen's use of *kardia, nous,* and *hēgemonikon* as synonyms.
43 Origen, *De prin.* 4.3.6 (Crouzel and Simonetti, vol. 3, p. 366).
44 In *Comm. in Ioh.* 13.42 (Blanc, vol. 3, p. 181), Origen remarks that for those who see in the way described here, all of the *aisthēta* are "white fields, ready for harvest".
45 Origen, *Hom. in Cant.* 1.4.
46 For Origen's theory of scriptural interpretation, see *De prin.* 4, especially sections 2 and 3.
47 On the term *mūsterion* in Origen, see Crouzel, *Connaissance Mystique,* passim. Note that *mūsterion* comes ultimately from the verb *mūo,* which means "to close" or "to be shut" as in "closed eyes" and "closed flowers". Cf. Liddell, Scott, and Jones, *A Greek-English Lexicon,* s.v. *mūo.*
48 Prov. 30:24-28 (RSV). This statement comes from *Contra Cels.* 4.87. For "enigma" as a technical term in Origen's writings, see Crouzel, *Connaissance Mystique,* pp. 228-29.
49 Origen, *Contra Cels.* 4.87.
50 Ibid.
51 Origen, *Hom. in Lev.* 16.6 (*GCS* 6, 502).
52 For this wonderful litany of animal sounds, as well as some pertinent remarks on the beasts in Paradise as "odd emanations of our as yet undivided selves", see Nemerov, "On Metaphor", p. 36.
53 See n. 42 above.
54 *Acts of John* 56.
55 For Origen's comments on "all the parts of the visible body in the inner man", see *Dialogue with Heraclides* 16-25 (Scherer, 89-103).

56 Origen, *Hom. in Lev.* 5.2 (*PG* 12, 449-50). In this passage, Origen is interpreting the sin and guilt offerings of Lev. 6 and 7. He uses the animals in question as emblems for a world filled with God, and goes on to discuss them as spiritual sacrifices.
57 Origen quotes Jer. 23:24 and 2 Cor. 6:16-18.
58 Origen quotes Ps. 32:6; Sap. 1:7; Mt. 28:20; and Joel 2:28.
59 Origen, *Hom. in Lev.* 5.2 (*PG* 12, 450).
60 This is one way in which Origen imagines what Daniélou has called "cette psychologie spirituelle de l'action des divers esprits" (*Origène*, p. 239).
61 See *Comm. in Cant.* 3.12 (*GCS* 8, 21217f; Lawson, pp. 223ff), where Origen brings together numerous Biblical passages in order to elucidate the "spiritual" nature of the hart referred to in Song of Songs 2:9.
62 Origen, *Comm. in Cant.* 3.13 (*GCS* 8, 216; Lawson, pp. 229-30). Origen also refers to the hunting dog "whose work comes close to reason" in *De prin.* 3.1.3 (Crouzel and Simonetti, vol. 3, pp. 22-24). As Crouzel and Simonetti point out, this is a typical Stoic example of the diverse manifestations of a single *pneuma* in the world (vol. 4, p. 19, n. 14).
63 Liddell, Scott, and Jones, *A Greek-English Lexicon*, s.v. *aisthēsis*, which, as a hunting term, means "scent".
64 Origen, *Hom. in Gen.* 1.16 (Doutreleau, p. 69).
65 Ibid., 1.11 (Doutreleau, p. 53).
66 Ibid., 1.13 (Doutreleau, p. 57).
67 Crouzel, *Théologie de l'Image*, p. 197 (emphasis mine).
68 Origen, *Hom. in Gen.* 1.10 (Doutreleau, p. 48).
69 Ibid., 1.8-10 (Doutreleau, pp. 44-50).
70 Ibid., 1.8 (Doutreleau, pp. 44-46); 1.9 (p. 48).
71 Ibid., 1.10 (Doutreleau, p. 48). It should be noted that when Origen says that these animals "play host to" good and evil, the verb used is *accipio*. When that verb is translated by the French "représenter", as in Doutreleau's edition, Origen's metaphoric argument is moved to an argument by analogy. This is misleading, since Origen is arguing in this section that the beasts *are in* the soul, and do not merely "represent" various virtues and vices.
72 Origen, *Hom. in Gen.* 1.10 (Doutreleau, pp. 48-50). The scriptural quotation is from 2 Tim. 2:5.
73 Ibid. (Doutreleau, p. 50). See Daniélou, *Origène*, p. 239, for further passages in Origen's works where the place of demons in salvific contexts is discussed.
74 Peter Brown, *The Making of Late Antiquity*, p. 68.
75 Ibid., p. 70. Brown's quotation is from *Hom. in Num.* 20.3. See the many references, and discussions, in Daniélou, *Origène*, pp. 235ff., and Crouzel and Simonetti, *Origène*, vol. 4, pp. 64-65 (n. 34), where the classical origin of such thinking is emphasized.
76 Origen, *De prin.* 3.3.4 (Crouzel and Simonetti, vol. 3, p. 192).
77 Ibid.
78 Ibid., 3.3.6 (Crouzel and Simonetti, vol. 3, p. 198).
79 Miller, "The Critic as Host", pp. 220-21. Miller is not, of course, commenting on Origen's use of *hospitium*. However, when he discusses the critic's relation to a text in terms of the host/guest paradox, and remarks that his argument is "for the value of recognizing the equivocal richness of apparently obvious or univocal language" (p. 223), he is giving a "modern" rendition of Origen's thoughts on the relation between the soul and its bestial phantasies, as well as the relation between scriptural images and their hidden splendors.

80 Origen, *De prin.* 3.2.4 (Crouzel and Simonetti, vol. 3, p. 170). See Daniélou, *Origène*, pp. 236-37, for further references.
81 Origen, *De prin.* 3.2.4. (Crouzel and Simonetti, vol. 3, p. 170).
82 Ibid., 3.1.4-5 (Crouzel and Simonetti, vol. 3, pp. 26-32). Here Origen says flatly that to blame external things for what happens to us is to "declare that we are like stocks and stones", simply dragged about helter-skelter. His example to the contrary is the situation of a man confronted by an alluring woman: if he succumbs to her charms, she is not to blame, for he was seeing with the eyes of pleasure anyway, and had simply found occasion to act on what was coloring his world.
83 Origen, *De prin.* 3.2.1 (Crouzel and Simonetti, vol. 3, p. 516). See also 3.2.2; 3.2.4; 3.2.5; 1.5.2.
84 See ibid., 3.2.2 and 3.2.4 (Crouzel and Simonetti, vol. 3, pp. 162, 172). In the latter passage, Origen quotes Eph. 4:27 and says: "When he says, 'Give not place to the devil,' he shows that by a certain kind of action or a certain kind of inaction a place in the mind is given to the devil ...". The case of Jacob is particularly interesting since, as Origen suggests in *De prin.* 3.2.5 (Crouzel and Simonetti, vol. 33, pp. 176-78), Jacob provided the battleground for the struggle of two angels, one good and one bad.
85 See *De prin.* 3.2.2 (Crouzel and Simonetti, vol. 3, pp. 158-62).
86 Ibid., 3.1.2 (Crouzel and Simonetti, vol. 3, pp. 18-20).
87 Liddell, Scott, and Jones, *A Greek-English Lexicon*, s.v. hormē.
88 Origen, *De prin.* 3.1.3 (Crouzel and Simonetti, vol. 3, p. 22). See also *De orat.* 6.1. For the Stoic provenance of Origen's comments on free will, see Crouzel and Simonetti, *Origène*, vol. 4, pp. 16-28.
89 For "seeds of wisdom", see Origen, *De prin.* 1.3.6 and 4.4.9 (Crouzel and Simonetti, vol. 1, pp. 154; vol. 3, p. 426).
90 Origen, *De prin.* 3.1.4 (Crouzel and Simonetti, vol. 3, p. 26).
91 Ibid., 3.1.4 (Crouzel and Simonetti, vol. 3, p. 26). In *Origène*, p. 238, Daniélou quotes Origen's *Hom. in Jos.* 15.5: "God permits the contrary spirits to fight against us so that we might conquer them".
92 Origen, *De prin.* 3.1.4 (Crouzel and Simonetti, vol. 3, p. 28).
93 Ibid., 4.3.11 (Crouzel and Simonetti, vol. 3, p. 384). For a discussion of this issue, see Cox, "'In My Father's House Are Many Dwelling Places'", p. 335.
94 Origen, *De prin.* 3.4.4 (Crouzel and Simonetti, vol. 3, p. 210): "It is in no way surprising that if two images *(verisimilitudines)* occur to a man in turn and suggest contrary modes of action, they should drag the mind in different directions *(in diversas partes animum rapiunt)*."
95 Lewis and Short, *A Latin Dictionary*, s.v. *rapio*.
96 When the term "psychological" is used in this essay, it refers to issues pertaining to the soul, and does not have reference to any modern academic system.
97 Origen, *De prin.* 4.3.5 (Crouzel and Simonetti, vol. 3, pp. 362-64).
98 Origen, *Hom. in Jer.* 10.8 (Nautin, p. 414).
99 Ibid.
100 Origen, *Hom. in Gen.* 2.3. (Doutreleau, pp. 90-92).
101 Ibid., 2.6 (Doutreleau, p. 112) for the attributes of the animals; 2.5 (p. 104) for the heavenly, earthly, and demonic stages of the ark. See *De orat.* 26.5, where Origen makes a similar interpretative move, by seeing "earth" and "heaven" as psychic dispositions.
102 Origen, *Hom. in Jer.* 10.8 (Nautin, p. 414).
103 Origen, *Hom. in Gen.* 2.1 (Doutreleau, pp. 80-82).

104 Ibid., 2.3 (Doutreleau, pp. 90-92).
105 Ibid., 2.5 (Doutreleau, p. 106). This is also a vision of the church.
106 Origen, *Hom. in Ezek.* 3.8 (*GCS* 8, 355-57). Cf. also Origen's *Hom. in Num.* 24.2 (*GCS* 7, 228).
107 Origen, *Hom. in Gen.* 2.6 (Doutreleau, p. 112). Cf. Dodds, *The Greeks and the Irrational*, pp. 213-14, for remarks on the irrational beast and the controlling *daimon* as two aspects of one natural force which belong together.
108 See Origen's discussions of demons and animals in *Contra Celsum* 4.93 and *Comm. in Cant.* 3 (4).15 (*GCS* 8, 235-41; Lawlor, pp. 255-60). See also the discussion by Crouzel, *Théologie de l'Image*, pp. 198-99.
109 Origen, *Contra Cels.* 4.83-85 and *De prin.* 1.8.4 (Crouzel and Simonetti, vol. 2, pp. 119-23).
110 On animals as *pathēmata*, see Origen, *Hom. in Luc.* 8.3. See also the discussion and references in Crouzel, *Théologie de l'Image*, p. 209. Note that, in Koetschau's fragment 17a, included in his edition of the *De principiis* as part of 1.8.4 and taken from Gregory of Nyssa, *De Hom. Opificio* 28, Origen is quoted as saying that "passion in a human soul is a likening to the irrational". See Butterworth, *Origen: On First Principles*, p. 73.
111 Brown, *Making of Late Antiquity*, p. 90.
112 Origen, *Hom. in Jesu Nave* 8.2 (Jaubert, p. 220). See also 8.5 (p. 230).
113 Ibid., 8.2 (Jaubert, p. 220).
114 Ibid., 8.7 (Jaubert, p. 234).
115 Ibid., 8.5 (Jaubert, p. 230).
116 To this point see also Origen, *De prin.* 2.10.4 (Crouzel and Simonetti, vol. 1, p. 384): "When the soul has gathered within itself a multitude of evil deeds and an abundance of sins, at the proper time the whole mass of evil boils up into punishment, and is kindled into penalties; at this time also the mind or conscience, bringing to memory through divine power all the things whose signs and forms it had impressed upon itself at the moment of sinning, will see exposed before its eyes a kind of history of its evil deeds ... Then the conscience is harassed and pricked by its own stings, and becomes an accuser and witness against itself".
117 Origen, *Hom. in Jesu Nave* 8.7 (Jaubert, p. 234).
118 Ibid., (Jaubert, p. 236).
119 On serpents in the soul, see Origen, *Hom. in Luc.* 8.3 and *Dialogue with Heraclides* 14 (Scherer, p. 85).
120 Clement of Alexandria, *Strom.* 1.135.3.
121 Origen, *De prin.* 1.3.6 (Crouzel and Simonetti, vol. 1, p. 156). Note that in 1.3.5 (p. 154), Origen remarks that the spirit dwells only in those who are "turning".
122 See Origen, *Philocalia* 27.9 (Junod, pp. 298-300), for a particularly strong statement of Origen's doctrine of "divine therapy".
123 Origen, *Contra Cels.* 4.92-93. One of Origen's major complaints against Celsus here is his divinizing of the animal.
124 *Gospel of Thomas*, logion 7, in Robinson, ed., *The Nag Hammadi Library*, p. 118.
125 See Origen, *Hom. in Jesu Nave* 20.2 (Jaubert, pp. 412-16), for Origen's remarks on the efficacy of obscurity, and Crouzel, *Théologie de l'Image*, p. 206, for discussion of scripture as serpent-charmer.
126 Origen, *Hom. in Jesu Nave* 20.2 (Jaubert, p. 412) as well as the quotation from *Philocalia* 12 (Jaubert, p. 415), and Jaubert's n. 2, p. 410.
127 Crouzel, *Théologie de l'Image*, p. 206.

128 Origen, *Hom. in Jer.* 2.1 (Nautin, pp. 238-40); *Hom. in Luc.* 39.5 (Crouzel et al., pp. 454-46).
129 Origen, *Hom. in Luc.* 8.3 (Crouzel et al., pp. 166-68).
130 Origen, *Dialogue with Heraclides* 13-14 (Scherer, p. 84).
131 Ibid., 14 (Scherer, p. 84).
132 Kerenyi, "Man and Mask", p. 153.
133 Ibid., pp. 153, 155.
134 Origen, *Comm. in Ioh.* 13.42 (Blanc, pp. 180-84).
135 Ibid. (Blanc, p. 184).
136 Ibid. (Blanc, pp. 180-82).
137 Ibid.
138 Origen, *Dialogue with Heraclides* 13 (Scherer, p. 84).
139 Origen, *Hom. in Jer.* 2.2 (Nautin, p. 242).
140 Origen, *Comm. in Ioh.* 1.28 (Blanc, p. 158).
141 Origen, *Hom. in Luc.* 37.1-4 (Crouzel et al., pp. 436-40). In this section, Origen is explaining Lk. 19:29-40, in which Jesus directs his disciples to untie an ass.
142 See Origen, *Contra Cels.* 6.25; *Comm. in Ioh.* 1. 17 (Blanc, p. 110); and *De orat.* 26.5.
143 Origen, *Contra Cels.* 6.25: Leviathan as God's plaything; *De orat.* 26.5: Leviathan as the plaything of the angels.
144 Origen, *Comm. in Ioh.* 1. 17 (Blanc, p. 110).
145 Origen, *Contra Cels.* 6.25.

Chapter Three

The *Physiologus*: A Poiēsis of Nature

In August 1940, the poet Wallace Stevens wrote a series of letters to Hi Simons, a Chicago literary critic who had sent Stevens a list of questions concerning various images in his poems. Wary of explanations of poetry that betray the poetic voice, Stevens composed notes that intensified his images, rendering them, if anything, stranger rather than more common. In the course of one letter, he was moved to comment on the nature of poetry itself.

> Poetry is a passion, not a habit. This passion nourishes itself on reality. Imagination has no source except in reality, and ceases to have any value when it departs from reality. Here is a fundamental principle about the imagination: It does not create except as it transforms.[1]

If we were to adopt the standard scholarly perspective on the *Physiologus*—a book in which the devil is a fox, Christ is a panther, and believers are exhorted to abandon their hedgehoggish ways—we would have to say that, while it is unusually transformative, it is not very good poetry. For, in the traditional view, the imagination of the *Physiologus* has its base precisely not in reality but in embarrassing flights of zoological fancy. A.-J. Festugière, for example, characterized the *Phusika* literature, literature that meditated on nature, as a "museum of the weird" and contrasted its "disconcerting credulity" with Aristotle's program of establishing fixed natural laws. In a similar vein, B. E. Perry remarked that the *Physiologus* was written by "a simple man for simple people". Naive and unartistic, fantastical, romantic, and magical, the *Physiologus* was responsible virtually singlehandedly for blotting out the bright light of Aristotelian science for nearly a thousand years. Finally, there is the statement by Max Wellmann, who studied the *Phusika* literature more thoroughly than anyone: "It is surprising that the *Physiologus* played such a remarkable role in world literature, given its trivial contents which clearly reflect the decline of the intellect".[2]

These scholars obviously have a clear and distinct idea about what constitutes the "reality" to which the *Physiologus* was so woefully unresponsive. It is the reality of Aristotelian scientific observation, which catalogues, classifies, orders, and arranges the natural world, placing its bewildering superabundance of forms into a manageable system. From this biological perspective, a document like the *Physiologus* has no art and no specialty, or at best the negative specialty of a "capricious distortion of stories about natural science".[3]

Yet, as Stevens remarked in the last year of his life to a young scholar, "a man whose life is devoted to the study of poetry is as fully a specialist as a man whose life is spent in an effort to find a way of changing sea water into champagne".[4] That is, the reality in which the author of the *Physiologus* was indeed a specialist may not have been the biological reality of Aristotle but another passion altogether. It is that other reality that I would like to explore in this essay.

The *Physiologus* is a collection of fifty-odd chapters, each of which addresses the behavior or "natural activity" (to use the text's own phrase) of a particular animal, plant, or mineral. While there are a few stories devoted to various trees and rocks, most deal with animals, especially wild animals, the beasts of the kingdom. These animals figure realities both theological and psychological, and, fittingly, they frequently give rise to allegories of a most bestial sort, embodying as the stories unfold such activities as mockery, reversal, deadly pretense, trickery, disguise, deception, metamorphosis, and a great deal of devouring and killing.

The structure of the chapters is also noteworthy. Typically, each story is introduced by a quotation from the Old Testament in which the featured animal is mentioned. Then the animal's characteristic behavior is described. The evocation of the nature of the beast is followed by an allegorical appropriation of that nature in a Christian context, and the story closes with a quotation from the New Testament that sometimes also mentions the beast but more often appeals to the spiritual significance of the whole story. Thus in each story there are three and sometimes four groups of images placed in interpretative juxtaposition: an Old Testament quotation, an animal's character and its allegorical significance, and a New Testament quotation. Perhaps not surprisingly, the relation among all these is often asymmetrical, and it is difficult to plot a smooth flow of meaning from one image to the next. What is significant, from our perspective, is that the animal is the "between", the imaginative ground that gives rise not only to connections between two scriptural traditions but also to metaphoric understandings of the divine and human worlds that are related precisely through the realm of the beasts.

It is as though meaning happens between the images, by virtue of their juxtaposition, and that moment of insight has beastly contours. Consider, for example, *Physiologus* 14, "On the Hedgehog", which continues a discussion begun in chapter 13 of Isaiah 13:21: "demons and sirens and hedgehogs will dance in Babylon".

> The *Physiologus* has said that the hedgehog is a small animal, shaped like a ball, completely covered with prickles. It gets food for itself in the following way. It goes into a vineyard and climbs up to a bunch of grapes. It plucks the grapes and throws them down on the ground. Then it throws itself down on its back, and the grapes stick on its prickles, and it brings them to its young. It leaves the clusters empty on the vine branches.
> So you, O Christians, stand by the spiritual and true vine [John 15:1], which is Christ the true God. Consider how you have let the evil spirit come into your heart, and how you have destroyed your beautiful order, how you have scattered and so strayed into the prickles of death that you have expanded the order of the opposing powers. You give yourselves up to the desolate way of the cluster, having no branches in you at all.[5]

This appears to be a fairly straightforward piece of psychology. The human heart that harbors an evil spirit is like a hedgehog dancing demonically in Babylon. If Babylon is the vineyard, the vines there have no fruitful clusters, no true spirit. Yet there is something odd here. The quotation from Isaiah, which places the hedgehog in the company of demons and sirens, does not prepare us for the description of the animal's behavior, an ingenious trick for gathering food for its young. Further, Christians are asked to stand by the vine, presumably just as the hedgehog does. However, the hedgehog with its "prickles of death" quickly becomes itself a figure for an evil vineyard where all is scattered. At this point, we begin to feel secure; the hedgehog has been all along a figure for the devil. But the reader is deprived of this interpretation by the last sentence, which forsakes the hedgehog altogether, moving instead to the desolate way of the cluster that has no branches!

If the foregoing is a sample of the psychology of the *Physiologus*, here is one version of its theology. *Physiologus* 1, "On the Lion", reads as follows.

> We shall begin by speaking about the lion, the king of wild beasts, indeed of all animals. For Jacob, praising Judah, said: "Judah is a lion's cub; out of this shoot, my son, you have sprung up. He reclined calmly like a lion and like a cub; who will awaken him"? [Gen. 49:9].
>
> The Physiologus has said about the lion that it has three natures. The first nature is this: when the lion walks and travels about in the desert, and the scent of the hunter comes to it, the lion covers its tracks with its tail, lest the hunter, following its tracks, discover its lair and bear down on it.
>
> Thus also my savior, the victorious spiritual lion out of the tribe of Judah, the root of David, who was sent by the eternal Father, has covered his spiritual tracks, that is, his divine nature. With angels he became an angel, with thrones a throne, with powers a power, with men a man, until, descending, he came into the womb of Mary, the God-bearer, in order that he might save the wandering race of men.
>
> "And the word became flesh and dwelt among us" [John 1:14]. Therefore those who have come down from heaven who fail to understand said: "Who is this king of glory"?. But the Holy Spirit said: "The Lord of hosts, this is the king of glory" [Ps. 23:10].

Here again, the relationships among these images are convoluted, and their labyrinthine entanglements certainly discourage logical analysis and, perhaps, logical theology as well. The metamorphoses of the descending Christ are the erased tracks of the wary lion on the move, which thereby preserves the secrecy of its lair. But the secrecy of the Christ's lair is not preserved but revealed: it is the womb of the God-bearer. Or is it a human body, given the quotation from the gospel of John? And what are we to make of the final passage in which the "king of glory" is declared to be Lord of the very hosts whom he has just erased?

These two chapters are not strange members of the *Physiologus* corpus but representative anecdotes of the whole. I hope it is clear that by evoking the cunning trick of a hedgehog and the deceptive reversal of a lion, these texts have been able to suggest fundamental, if complex, visions of God and the soul. This way of meditating on natural phenomena, so different from the keen observation of Aristotle yet no less acute in its own polymorphic way, is based in a tradition of interpretation stemming ultimately from the speculative physics of the pre-Socratic philosophers. More immediate to its Greco-Roman context, however, were understandings of *phūsiologia* as a divinatory art that was able to uncover dimensions of the divine lying hidden in all things.[6] This view of the natural world as a potentially explosive cache of theological realities was developed in a Christian context by the Alexandrians Clement and Origen, both of whom considered meditations on *phūsis* to be a way of initiation into the sensuous enigmas of the spirit. Nature was a symbolic language, a theological text. A remark of Origen's characterizes well the perspective that I think the *Physiologus* embodies.

> Perhaps just as God made man in his own image and likeness, so also did he make the remaining creatures after certain other heavenly images as a likeness. And perhaps every single thing on earth has something of an image and likeness in heavenly things, to such a degree that even the grain of mustard which is the smallest of all seeds may have something of an image and likeness in heaven.[7]

That the *Physiologus* is Alexandrian in both its allegorical method and its theological orientation has been emphasized by both Perry and Wellmann, although they disagree over the date of the document, Perry placing it in the second century, Wellmann in the fourth.[8] Neither man, however, develops the significance of the *Physiologus's* Alexandrian perspective, Wellman noting the Philonic structure of its biblical exegesis and Perry its "mystical" worldview.[9] I would suggest, however, that the Alexandrian hermeneutic implicit in the text must not be overlooked if we are to see the *Physiologus* with other than scornful, biological eyes. If nature is a text, and if what that text gives to be read are *images* and *likenesses* of *hidden* realities, then of course the reading will yield fantastical creatures. From the perspective that I am suggesting, what is basic to the *Physiologus* is that the world of the beasts does not mirror God literally but imaginally, reflecting in multiple ways a kind of bestial poetry of heaven.

If the *Physiologus* owes its hermeneutic to the Alexandrian tradition, it owes many of its images and stories to quite another tradition, the *Phūsika* literature. This literature has been discussed in some detail by Festugière and in great detail by Wellmann; I want only to mention some of its salient features here insofar as they provide context for the *Physiologus*.[10] Bolos of Mendes, a Hellenistic thinker of the third century B.C., is the man credited with inaugurating the *Phūsika*. Ranked with Aristotle and Theophrastus as an authority on natural sciences, he was widely read, and his *Phūsika dūnamera* was used as a major source-text by such noted naturalists as Pliny the Elder, Plutarch, Aelian, and Galen.[11] His work was also influential in Hermetic circles: the *Kyranides*, which along with the *Physiologus* is the most complete extant member of the *Phūsika*, is described by Festugière as a "medico-magical" treatise that studied birds, fish, plants, and stones in an alphabetical schema, so that, for example, the letter "alpha" would have four entries, one each for bird, fish, plant, stone, and so on for "beta", "gamma", to the end of the alphabet. Similar was the Hermetic *Kyranides,* a bestiary in which animals were studied alphabetically.[12] This coordination of the elements of language with the elements of nature is, it seems to me, rather significant, implying as it does both the textuality of nature as something to be "read" and the "natural" character of language as something alive with feathers, scales, roots, and minerals.

Along with this connection between nature and language, however, is the connection between nature and medicine mentioned by Festugière. For example, one can find in the *Phūsika dūnamera* and the *Kyranides* such passages as the following: "one heals a scorpion sting by saying into the ear of an ass, 'a scorpion stung me', and the hurt passes to the ass".[13] For Bolos as for others in this tradition, discovering the natures of animals and plants involved an uncovering of their secret powers, powers that carried the sympathies and antipathies infused throughout the cosmos as one of its basic structures.[14] As Wellmann has pointed out, this interest in the medicinal properties of animals in particular is found in the *Physiologus*, too: the plover swallows human sickness, for example, and its excrement is a cure for eyesight (*Physiologus* 3); the beaver's genitals are a *therapeia* (*Physiologus* 23); and the baby elephant's hair and bones protect against serpents and demons (*Physiologus* 43).[15]

While it is true that the *Physiologus* preserves traces of the interest in the medicinal qualities of animals, it would be more faithful to the text as a whole to say that the most profound remedy that it offers is not medical but spiritual. And it is heavenly medicine of a most bitter kind, for part of the cure involves an acceptance of violence and real antipathy in the divine world itself. In the theology of the *Physiologus*, what we are cured of is the one-sided vision of God that sees God as only positive, only sympathetic, without scales or the heaviness of a rock. Consider, for example, *Physiologus* 5, "On the Owl", where the signal characteristic of the owl, a figure for Christ, is that it loves the darkness of night better than the day. Then, in *Physiologus* 3, there is the plover, also an image of Christ, which finds its nourishment in human disease. Further, both of these animals are said by the text to be "against the law"; they are unclean and yet, paradoxically, bear Christic likenesses.[16]

Animals indeed seem to be the "shadows of the Gods", as Carl Jung once remarked.[17] Particularly grueling in this regard, yet graphically revealing of God's inner darkness, is the behavior of an Egyptian animal called the ichneumon. According to Aelian, this animal is androgynous, containing both male and female and able both to procreate and to give birth.[18] Completely self-sufficient, the ichneumon is thus a paradoxical beast, holding opposites in creative tension. Hostile to the crocodile, the ichneumon is also a wily beast. In order to set the context for the *Physiologus's* story about it, I would like to give Oppian's report on the animal.

> Against the crocodile, the ichneumon weaves a subtle device. With eyes askance, it watches the huge beast until it is confident that the crocodile is asleep. Then, having rolled itself in mud, it flies with daring heart through the gate of death and passes through the wide throat. The crocodile gasps wildly and rolls in agony, but the ichneumon heeds not but enjoys its sweet repast. Finally it leaps forth and leaves the body of the beast empty. What a task you have undertaken, advancing your body to the very jaws of death![19]

As Oppian and Aelian both report, the ichneumon is also the enemy of the asp and kills it with a similar trick.[20] Perhaps it was for the reason that the ichneumon is hostile to two serpentine animals that the *Physiologus* split its story between two animals; in any case, as we will see, the two stories refer to the same beast.[21]

Physiologus 25, "On the Otter *(enūdris)*", says that this animal, which has the form of a dog, is an enemy of the crocodile.

> When the crocodile sleeps, it holds its mouth open. Then the otter comes up and rubs its whole body with mud. When the mud dries, the otter leaps into the mouth of the crocodile and eats its entrails. The crocodile is like the devil, but the otter is an image of our Savior. For when he received the earthly substance and flesh, he went down into Hades and destroyed the pains of death, and in three days he rose.

This story is followed by *Physiologus* 26, "On the Ichneumon".

> There is an animal called the ichneumon. It is the enemy of the dragon. Whenever it finds a really fierce dragon, as the *Physiologus* says, it goes and rubs itself with mud, and it guards its nostrils with its tail. Thus also our Savior received the substance of earth, that is, the body that he took on, until he killed the spiritual dragon sitting in the river of Egypt [Ezek. 29:3], that is, the devil. For if, while incorporeal, Christ had destroyed the dragon, the dragon would have spoken against him, because he is God and Savior. But the one who is greater than all humbled himself, so that he might save all [Phil. 2:8].

In its Christian context, some of this imagery is fairly obvious. The dragon is, of course, a standard figure for the devil; and jaws, gates of death, and the belly of the beast are typical metaphors of hell.[22] What is not so obvious, however, is that the humble Christ should relish in such a ghastly meal. At this point, a passage from Origen's *On Prayer* may be instructive. Commenting on the various kinds of "bread" that one might eat, Origen remarks,

> He who partakes of the *epiousios* "bread strengthens" his "heart" and becomes a son of God; but he who participates in "the dragon" is none other than "the Ethiopian" spiritually, himself changed into a serpent because of the toils of the dragon.... And David says this concerning the body of the dragon that was feasted upon by the Ethiopians: "Thou brakest the heads of the dragons upon the water: thou didst smite the head of the dragon in pieces; thou gavest him to be meat to the peoples, the Ethiopians".[23]

Origen is commenting on Ps. 73:13-14 (LXX), where Leviathan is a dragon and the people inhabiting the wilderness are the Ethiopians. That the wicked have the devilish dragon for their food is not a belief peculiar to Origen; it is found also in Theophilus of Alexandria and Jerome.[24]

Perhaps what appears in the *Physiologus* is a curious theological twisting of this tradition. For in the two stories about the ichneumon, it is the Christ, not the wicked, who eats the animal. While this image surely suggests the salvific quality of God, it does so in a terrifying way, picturing a negative Eucharist in which Christ is not host but guest at a most bestial banquet. But this is not the only equivocal image in these stories. There is also the picture of the Christ descending to the underworldly interior of the spiritual world, where he does battle by means of a deadly disguise. The hero is released to perform his murderous task precisely when he is clothed with the beast. It is as though the bestial imagery of the text allows the horror basic to spiritual reality to be spoken in a way that no other language can.

This point has been made in a striking and persuasive way in a recent French study of a scene in Homer's *Iliad*, in which Odysseus and his friend Diomedes don animal skins in order to stalk and kill the Trojan spy Dolon, who is similarly disguised.[25] In this scene in which men are animals, an eerily extended night defies the day, and heroic combatants turn into stealthy slayers, "divinity shows its terrible face". The focus is on Diomedes, who, as lion, performs the human sacrifice, breaking the barriers between the human and the divine as well as between the human and the animal. Inspired to act by Athena, Diomedes enters the nocturnal dimension of the gods, and his animality is "at once frontier and place of passage" into the somber, savage violence of an extremely ambiguous reality.[26]

What I am suggesting by way of this analogy from the *Iliad* is that the Christ of the ichneumon stories is similarly ambiguous, oscillating between the divine and bestial worlds, or, better, incarnating them both at once. The message of the *Physiologus* seems to be that the victorious Savior is also a savage figure. Further, not only is it the bestial disguise that allows this other dimension to appear, but also the animality of the text's metaphors, which might themselves be described as the "place of passage" into God's darkness.

The animality of the text itself—its cunning, deceptive character—can be seen in a stunning way in the final story that I will discuss, the story of the panther in *Physiologus* 16.

> The prophet prophesied and said, "I have become like a panther to Ephraim" [Hos. 5:14 (LXX)].
> The *Physiologus* has said that the panther has the following natural activity. It is the friendliest of all living beings, but it hates the serpent. It is many-colored like Joseph's coat [Gen. 37:3]. It is gentle and very tame. When it eats and feeds, it falls asleep in its lair. On the third day, it wakes from its slumber and roars, howling with a mighty voice. Animals both near and far hear this sound. But from the panther's throat comes forth every sweet smell of spices. The animals are guided by the sweet fragrance of the smell of the panther, and they run quickly close to it.
> Just so, Christ, awakening on the third day and rising from the dead, was every sweet fragrance for us peaceful ones both far and near [Eph. 2:17]. Many-colored is the spiritual wisdom of God [Eph. 3:10]. As the Psalmist said [Ps. 44: 10], "The queen stands at your right hand, clothed in a many-colored robe interwoven with gold", which is the church. Many-colored is Christ, he being virginity, self-control, mercy, faith, virtue, patience, oneness of mind, peace [Gal. 5:22].

This is a strikingly beautiful text, and its image of a fragrant, many-colored Christ could be placed in the Pauline context of the "aroma of Christ" or the Origenist context of "the Christ who comes breathing sweet odors".[27] Here is a picture of a gentle, tame, peaceful God whose roar is reassuring. The *Physiologus* indeed seems to have spoken well about the panther.

However, for a reader familiar with the prophetic passage that evokes these lovely images, there is a startling omission. For Hosea goes on to say that the God who will be like a panther to Ephraim will prey upon Ephraim, rending, carrying off, with no hope of rescue. And for a reader familiar with stories about the panther from the naturalists, this tale would be more astonishing still. Such a reader would recognize that the text's message lies as much in what is not reported as in what is told and would see immediately that antipathy lurks insidiously in the shadows of this sympathetic story.

Prominent religiously and mythologically as the animal companion of the god Dionysus, the panther was a much discussed animal in Greco-Roman literature devoted to such topics.[28] Stories about this beast abound in such authors as Theophrastus, Pliny, Philostratus, Aelian, and Oppian. One of its most remarkable features is its appearance. Set in what Pliny describes as its "savage" head are shining eyes, "grey-green at once and red within, flaming as if on fire", and in the mouth "the teeth are pale and venomous". Marked on the shoulder by a crescent moon, its coat is described as *poikilos*, "many-colored".[29]

This adjective, *poikilos*, is a fitting description of the lunar panther, which is one of the supreme embodiments of cunning intelligence in the animal world. As Marcel Detienne and Jean-Pierre Vernant have shown recently in a remarkable study, *mētis*, cunning intelligence, was for the Greeks a way of being in the world, and "its field of application was the world of movement, of multiplicity, and of ambiguity". *Mētis* denoted a way of conniving with shifting reality, with "fluid situations which are constantly changing and which at every moment combine contrary features and forces that are opposed to each other". To be *poikilos*, many-colored, is one of the marks of a *mētis* figure: it refers to "the sheen of a material or the glittering of a weapon, the dappled hide of a fawn, or the shining back of a snake mottled with darker patches. This many-colored sheen or complex of appearances produces an effect of irridescence, shimmering, an interplay of reflections ... ". Indeed, as Detienne and Vernant point out, "Shimmering sheen and shifting movement are so much a part of the nature of *mētis* that when the epithet *poikilos is* applied to an individual it is enough to indicate that he is a wily one, a man of cunning, full of inventive ploys and tricks of every kind".[30]

The *Physiologus* says the panther is *poikilos* and goes on to describe the seductive sweetness of its breath, which attracts other animals to it. What it does not describe, however, is reported by Pliny: animals indeed are attracted by the panther's odor, but they are frightened by the savage appearance of its head, "for which reason panthers catch them by hiding their head and enticing by other attractions".[31] Aelian makes this scene quite explicit. Describing the panther's fragrance as *euōdia thaumastē*, a "marvelous odor", he says that it catches other animals by concealing itself in a dense thicket, and, having thus made itself invisible, "it just breathes".[32] Animals are drawn by the magic of its fragrance, here defined as *iugks,* an erotic spell or charm. The unsuspecting animals close in on the thicket, and the panther springs out and devours them.

The panther's smell, seemingly so sweet, is a *pharmakon,* a deadly trap that gives the hidden animal more presence than the visible ones.[33] But I would like to suggest, further, that the *Physiologus's* story is itself a trap, hiding its savage message with a sweet perfume. Its prophetic introduction, which conceals within it a flesh-rending God; its repetition of the adjective *poikilos,* which suggests the shimmering, shifting qualities of spiritual wisdom; its cunning reversal of the received tradition about the animal—all these suggest that the text itself is a panther, an interpretation that is completely bestial, as the word itself says: *pan-thēr,* all beast.

This bestial poetry of nature, which reflects the divine world in images and likenesses that flame like the panther's inner eye, might be fittingly characterized by a passage from Norman O. Brown's *Closing Time,* which suggests that what is "elemental" is "the hour of the beast", in which one says, "not Pater noster but Panther monster".[34] The beasts that are paraded through our text are indeed monstrous, fantastical, extreme. They never existed in the natural world, and I suspect that the author of the *Physiologus* knew this full well. His latter-day critics notwithstanding, this author had not perverted the Aristotelian view of reality. In fact, he was not interested in that view at all. His passion was nourished in another reality, the reality of nature as a poetic text.

Notes

1   Stevens to Simons, 10 August 1940, in *Letters of Wallace Stevens,* p. 364.
2   Festugière, *La Révélation d'Hermès Trismégiste,* vol. 1, pp. 195, 196; Perry, "Physiologos", *PW* 20, cols. 1098, 1075; Wellmann, "Der *Physiologos:* Eine religionsgeschichtlich-naturwissenschaftliche Untersuchung", p. 1.
3   Wellmann, "Der *Physiologos",* p. 1.
4   Stevens to Peter H. Lee, 17 February 1955, in *Letters of Wallace Stevens,* p. 873.
5   All translations from the *Physiologus* are mine. For convenience and brevity, I have used the critical edition of the text by Lauchert, *Geschichte des Physiologus,* pp. 229-279. For an exhaustive compilation and discussion of all extant Greek texts of the *Physiologus,* see F. Sbordone, *Physiologus* (Milan, 1936).
6   Curley (trans), *Physiologus,* x-xii. In his translation of the Latin *Physiologus,* Curley provides a brief but excellent introduction to this literature, stemming from pre-Socratic ancestry to Greco-Roman developments.
7   Origen, *Comm. in Cant.* 3.12, quoted and discussed by Curley, xiii-xiv. For an extended discussion, see Cox, "Origen and the Bestial Soul: A Poetics of Nature".

8 Perry, "Physiologos", *PW* 20, cols.1101-1104; Wellmann, "Der *Physiologos*", pp. 11-13,112-113.
9 Wellmann, "Der *Physiologos*", p. 3; Perry, "Physiologos", *PW* 20, cols. 1097-1098, 1100, 1104.
10 See Festugière, *La Révélation d'Hèrmes Trismégiste*, vol. 1, pp.187-216, and Wellmann, "Der *Physiologos*", pp. 18-81, and especially idem, "Die Phūsika des Bolos Demokritos und der Magier Anaxilaos aus Larissa".
11 Festugière, *La Révélation d'Hèrmes Trismégiste*, vol. 1, pp. 198-200; Wellmann, "Der *Physiologus*", pp. 18-20.
12 Festugière, *La Révélation d'Hèrmes Trismégiste*, vol. 1, pp. 202, 208.
13 Bolos, *Phūsika dūnamera* 15=*Koiranides 11*, 70.8, quoted in Festugière, *La Révélation d'Hèrmes Trismégiste*, vol. 1, p. 198.
14 Note that the alternate title of Bolos's work *is Peri sūmpatheiōn kai antipatheiōn*. For discussions of sympathy and antipathy as a cosmic structure, see Festugière, *La Révélation d'Hèrmes Trismégiste*, vol. 1, pp. 196-98, and Wellmann, "Die Phūsika des Bolos", pp. 3-4.
15 Wellmann, "Der *Physiologus*", p. 19.
16 This kind of reversal is found in the *Physiologus*'s psychology also. In chapter 11, for example, the serpent, traditional enemy of humankind from the Judeo-Christian perspective, becomes the model for good Christian behavior.
17 Jung, *Memories, Dreams, Reflections*, pp. 215-16.
18 Aelian, *On the Characteristics of Animals* 10.47. I have followed the English translation of Scholfield, *Aelian: On the Characteristics of Animals*.
19 Oppian, *Cynegetica* 3.414. I have followed the English translation of Mair, *Oppian Colluthus Tryphiodorus*. See also Cherniss, Harold and Helmbold, Williams C. (trans), Plutarch, *De sollertia animalium* 966D, in *Plutarch's Moralia*, vol. 12.
20 Oppian, *Cynegetica* 3.432; Aelian 3.22.
21 See Tardieu, *Trois Mythes Gnostiques*, pp. 262-274, for a detailed discussion of the relation between the *enūdris* and the ichneumon.
22 For an extended discussion, with sources, of such bestial metaphors of hell, see Miller, "The Two Sandals of Christ: Descent into History and into Hell", pp. 173-178.
23 Origen, *On Prayer* 27.12, in Oulton, J.E.L, and Chadwick, Henry (trans), *Alexandrian Christianity*, p. 301.
24 See Oulton, J.E.L. and Chadwick, Henry (trans), *Alexandrian Christianity*, p.368n; and *TDNT*, s.v. *drakōn*.
25 Schnapp-Gourbeillion, *Lions, Héroes, Masques*, pp. 95-131. The basic point in her discussion of *Iliad* 10 is that the animal disguises allow the hidden complexities of those so disguised to appear. "Les désguisements animaux ... exprime enfin une polysémie normalement proscrite" (p.129).
26 Ibid., pp. 128-131, 203.
27 2 Cor. 2:14-16; Origen, *Hom.in Cant.* 1.3 (trans. Lawson, p. 271).
28 See Otto, *Dionysus, Myth and Cult*, pp. 110-112; for artistic evidence, see Kerenyi, *Dionysos*, pp. 266, 271, 376-377, and plates 66D, 70; and Detienne, *Dionysos mis à mort*, especially pp. 93-94. Oppian's story is most interesting in this regard: in *Cynegetica* 4.235-311, he reports that panthers were once the maenads and nurses of Dionysus, who changed them into their present animal form so that they could attack Pentheus; their Dionysiac character survives in panthers' love of wine.

29 Pliny, *Natural History* 8.62 (Rackham); Oppian, *Cynegetica* 3.63-80; Aesop, *Fables* 37 and 119, cited and discussed by Detienne and Vernant, *Cunning Intelligence in Greek Culture and Society*, pp. 19, 35-36. The term for "many-colored" used by the *Physiologus* is *pampoikilos*, an intensification of an already intense word.
30 Detienne and Vernant, *Cunning Intelligence in Greek Culture and Society*, pp. 18-21.
31 Pliny, *Natural History* 8.62.
32 Aelian 5.40; see also Plutarch, *De sollertia animalium* 976D, and Pliny, *Natural History* 8.62.
33 See Detienne, *Dionysos mis à mort*, p.124, n. 115. Also interesting in this regard is the evidence given by Detienne (pp. 96-97) from Aristophanes, *Lysistrata* 1014-1015: courtesans, with their perfumed bodies as snares, were called panthers.
34 Brown, *Closing Time*, p. 61.

Chapter Four

Jerome's Centaur:
A Hyper-icon of the Desert

Introduction: From Nature To Landscape

In his recent book entitled *Landscape and Memory,* the historian Simon Schama has observed that, "although we are accustomed to separate nature and human perception into two realms, they are, in fact, indivisible. Before it can ever be a repose for the senses, landscape is the work of the mind".[1] For an example of what he means by the transformation of nature into landscape by way of human perception, he draws on a remark by the noted contemporary photographer, Ansel Adams. Adams is well known for his photographs of natural formations in Yosemite National Park in the American West, and he had this to say about a particular rock formation named Half Dome: "In the last analysis Half Dome is just a piece of rock ... [But] there is some deep personal distillation of spirit and concept which moulds these earthly facts into some transcendental emotional and spiritual experience".[2] Nature neither locates nor names itself; rather, it is we, as perceivers, who change nature into landscape by infusing it with emotion, with memory and desire, and indeed, as Adams says, with religion. As Schama remarks, there is a "craving to find in nature a consolation for our mortality".[3]

Schama's precise observation, that "it is our shaping perception that makes the difference between raw matter and landscape",[4] has particular relevance for the function of the desert in early Christian asceticism. As Peter Brown has noted, the desert was "the outer space of the ascetic world", a "measureless imaginative distance".[5] The "nature" of the desert was transformed into a variety of "landscapes", most notably the civic landscape offered by Athanasius' exclamation that the monks had made the desert a city,[6] and the Biblical landscape offered by observers of desert ascetics, who characterized the place as Paradise and its inhabitants as angels.[7] Despite these positive perceptual transformations, however, the desert-as-landscape was not a univocal construct. Enticing *and* forbidding, the desert was a place both of refuge and temptation, where the howling of wild beasts was heard along with prayers of the monks. Angels might dwell there, but so also did demonic forces.[8] As a metaphor for the most basic makeup of the human, the desert exposed both angelic and demonic tendencies. The desert was thus a landscape charged with ambivalence and, unlike the Yosemite of Ansel Adams' desire, it not only offered consolation for our mortality but also judgment: if, as Guillaumont argues, ascetics sought in the desert a therapy of the soul, it was because the soul needed healing.[9]

The Desert As Landscape: Jerome's Letters

The particular landscape with which this essay is concerned is the desert as it was perceived by Jerome, both in his reported experience of it and his writing about it. With what Schama calls "the organizing move of the artist",[10] Jerome transformed the "raw matter" of the desert—its dust, heat, and caves—into a landscape charged with the sensibilities of his particular religious vision.

Jerome's most famous portrait of the desert was written some ten years subsequent to his two-year sojourn there.[11] The frame for this portrait was Jerome's theory of the body as a boiling cauldron of *libido,* a theory that he included in a letter to Eustochium, a young Roman woman, in order to alert her to the kind of vigilance she would have to maintain to preserve her virginity.[12] Remembering his experiences in the desert in this letter, Jerome transforms its raw materiality in two ways. He apostrophizes his cave as though it were a sentient being: "I feared my cell as though it knew my thoughts"—thoughts charged, no doubt, with the "sweet heat" of the "seductive fire of sensual pleasure" about which he has been warning Eustochium.[13] Here Jerome has offered an anthropomorphic image of the desert; it is a landscape that functions religiously as the conscience of the ascetically-minded Christian. Even more striking is Jerome's transformation of the sunshine and heat of the desert into a torrid landscape of the suffering ascetic's psyche:

> When I was living in the desert, in that vast solitude ... inflamed by the burning heat of the sun, how many times did I imagine myself amid the delights of Rome! ... Although in my fear of Hell I had condemned

myself to this prison, with scorpions and wild beasts as my only companions, I was often surrounded by troupes of dancing girls. My skin was pale with fasting but, though my frame was chilled, my mind was burning with desire, and the fires of lust bubbled up while my flesh was barely alive.[14]

Clearly this landscape offered Jerome no consolation for his mortality but rather a searing judgment; the "raw matter" of the desert has become a negative embodiment of psychic torment, a landscape eerily conscious of human desire. In both these instances, nature has been infused with emotion, and the resulting portrait of the desert presents a landscape that has a religious understanding of the human being as its inseparable double.

If Jerome's memory of the desert represents the negative pole of this ambivalent landscape, his fantasies about the desert before he went there, and even many of his thoughts about it while he *was* there, represent the positive pole. Shortly before he finally made the decision to go to the desert, Jerome identified himself with "the sick sheep that strays from the rest of the flock" of Luke's parable of the lost sheep (Lk. 15:3-6).[15] Unable as yet to resist what he calls "the charms of my previous riotous living", Jerome writes effusively to a group of anchorites about how wonderful it would be could he only make the decision to join their company. In a mood rather like Augustine's "Give me chastity—but not yet",[16] Jerome idealizes what seems like a deliciously impossible dwelling-place to attain, calling the desert "the loveliest city of all", "like paradise".[17] This desert of his desire thus emerges as a landscape that is both civic and Biblical at once. These tropes for transforming desert into landscape seem to have captured Jerome's imagination at this point in his life, for in a letter written shortly after this one, he describes his friend Bonosus, who had recently taken up the solitary ascetic life on an island, as "a new inhabitant of Paradise" now "enrolled as a citizen of a new City".[18]

Once in the desert, Jerome continued to write letters, many of which betray his intense loneliness there.[19] One of these, written to encourage his friend Heliodorus to join him, shows how Jerome could incorporate even negative aspects of life in the desert into his idealistic landscape. Referring to the effects of ascetic practices on the body and the soul, Jerome supplies positive religious values to them all:

Do you fear poverty? But Christ calls the poor blessed. Does work terrify you? But no athlete is crowned without sweat. Are you thinking about food? But faith does not fear famine. Are you afraid of bruising on the bare ground your limbs eaten up by fasting? But the Lord lies by your side. Are you afraid of a dirty head bristling with uncombed hair?

> But Christ is your head. Does the boundless immensity of the desert terrify you? But you may walk in Paradise in your mind. Is your skin scabrous without baths? But he who has washed once in Christ does not need to wash again.[20]

Here Jerome gives a positive view of what would, from the commonsense perspective of the uninitiate, seem to be among the privations of the desert. But he colors these terrors and physical discomforts with an enthusiasm that his later memory of them, at least as he expressed it to Eustochium, does not convey.

In the same mood, he also extends the Biblical trope of the desert, and this time he contrasts the civic and Biblical tropes of the desert rather than combining them. Thus he now writes that "the prison of cities full of smoke" is a negative counterpart to the "desert rejoicing in intimacy with God".[21] Further, extending the implied metaphor of Paradise as a garden, Jerome exclaims, "O desert, lush with the flowers of Christ".[22] The desert has become an organic landscape in which ascetic "nature"—in the form of life and practice in the desert—is opposed to civic "culture"—in the form of ties to family and to the ecclesiastical institutions of the city.[23] Indeed, arguing that "it is not possible for a monk to be perfect in his own country",[24] Jerome writes to Heliodorus that, in the desert, he "sees more light" and even takes pleasure in "casting off the burden of the flesh to fly to the pure brightness of the ether".[25]

Such paeans of praise were not to last, as Jerome's portrait of the desert changed according to shifts in his own circumstances and feelings. As landscape, in other words, the desert took on the colorations of Jerome's religious and emotional sensibilities. As it happened, the desert was not immune to theological controversy, and neither was Jerome. At some point during his desert sojourn, probably in the year C.E. 376, his fellow monks began to pester Jerome to accept what was for him an odd-sounding formula for the persons of the Trinity, which seemed to him to replace the Nicene Creed's understanding either with an Arianizing or with a tritheistic formulation.[26] Writing to Pope Damasus for advice, Jerome now sees himself not as a desert flower but as an exile in a desert negatively characterized as "barbarous".[27] Things got worse. In his next letter to the Pope, Jerome repeats his description of his surroundings as "a barbarian land" and, in what may have been his final letter from the desert, he writes to a fellow monk there in a spirit of bitterness, suggesting that his sackcloth and ashes, sweat, chains, and dirty hair have gotten him nothing but condemnations as a heretic.[28] Jerome was being hounded out of the desert—"not one corner of the desert is granted to me"—and, as he was about to depart, he wrote (quoting others who had also departed), "it is better to live among wild beasts than with such Christians".²⁹ As Kelly has observed, "all his starry-eyed illusions about monks dropped from him", and, I would add, his use of the word "barbarous" more than once to describe the desert in this letter suggests that his starry-eyed illusions about a paradisal desert had dropped away also.³⁰

The Desert As Landscape: Jerome's *Vita Sancti Pauli*

Thus theological controversy clouded Jerome's perception of the desert as he swung in his shaping of this ambivalent landscape from its positive to its negative pole. Yet, despite these expressions of alienation from his earlier, radiant landscape, the desert remained rooted in Jerome's imagination. While he was still in the desert, or, more probably, just after he had returned from the desert to Antioch, Jerome wrote his *Vita Sancti Pauli Primi Eremitae*, the *Life of Saint Paul, the First Hermit*.³¹ As several commentators have noted, Jerome wrote this biography with Athanasius' *Life of Saint Antony* in mind and, whether his hero Paul was fictional or not, Jerome presents him not as an imitator of Antony but as his precursor; as Rousseau remarks, "Jerome may have wished to rival the achievement of Athanasius" and so presented a monk superior to Antony in ascetic practice and piety.³² Literary aspirations aside, Jerome may also have wished to provide support, by means of this beguiling portrait, to Western Christians with ascetic leanings.³³ It would not have been the first time, as evidenced by his letter to Heliodorus, that Jerome constructed the desert as a landscape intended to provide a compelling statement of his own view of asceticism as the highest form of Christian life.

The Egyptian desert that Jerome's *Life of Saint Paul* offers seems indeed very beguiling. Unlike the desert of Athanasius' *Life of Saint Antony*, there are no demons in this desert, nor is Paul shown doing nightly battle with libidinous thoughts in the form of lascivious phantom-women. This desert is nothing if not paradisally hospitable: Paul's cave, open to the sky, harbors a stream flowing from a spring and a palm tree that provides shade as well as food and clothing.³⁴ Wild beasts do not pose a threat, either; Paul does not have to face down a pack of menacing hyenas as Saint Antony does in Athanasius' biography.³⁵ Indeed, aside from Paul and Antony, only animals seem to inhabit this desert, and they are, in Guillaumont's felicitous phrasing, "quelque peu étranges, mais fort sympathiques".³⁶

Animals are introduced into Jerome's narrative as part of his figuration of Paul as Antony's precursor in the eremitic life. At the behest of a dream, Antony sets off into the desert to find Paul, "another and better monk than he".[37] Along the way he encounters two hybrid creatures, a centaur and a satyr, who helpfully point out the way to Paul; additional helpers are the she-wolf who alerts Antony to the location of Paul's cave, as well as the raven that provides dinner for the two when they meet, and the lions, whom Antony faces "as though they were doves", that help bury Paul when he dies.[38] Given this beatific landscape, in which "even mute animals perceive that God exists", it is no wonder that Jerome has Antony exclaim, "I have seen Paul in Paradise".[39] As Guillaumont remarks, "how could one not be seduced by such a desert?".[40]

Contemporary commentators have indeed been seduced by this desert. Or rather, they have been seduced by their conviction that the *Life of Saint Paul* reflects Jerome's romance with the desert. Seen as a biography that is more novel than history, it has been described as "a romantic idealisation of monastic withdrawal, as full of wonders and fabulous creatures as a fairy-tale".[41] Kelly and Rousseau are agreed that the biography reflects Jerome's understanding of asceticism as a life based on poverty, withdrawal, and self-denial.[42] But Kelly sees this work as "a masterpiece of storytelling" and comments in particular on Jerome's "eye for detail, his feeling for the beauties of nature, his credulity and fascination for the marvellous, the ecstatic nature of his piety", whereas Rousseau finds the biography to be "a short and muddled collection of anecdotes—bizarre stories of visions in particular".[43] Yet another commentator found that the fanciful elements of the biography were so inimical to its presumed historical character that he criticizes Jerome for being "unable to draw a definitive line between reality and legend", although he too finds the biography to be "delightful in romantic charm", however faulty its historical methods.[44]

Wild Men In The Desert: Centaurs

Perhaps because of their conviction that many of the images in the *Life of Saint Paul* stem from Jerome's romantic fancy and credulity, these commentators have not asked what seems to me to be an obvious question: What is a centaur doing in the middle of a Christian desert?

It is true that there are touches of some features of the eremitic idyll that would later become so familiar from collections such as the *Apophthegmata Patrum* and the *Historia monachorum in Aegypto*. Stories of miraculous feedings, like that concerning Paul and Antony, were common, although it was more usual for sustenance to be provided by angels than by ravens; there were monks like Theon, who kept company with wild animals, though they are not reported to have been hybrid creatures from Greek mythology; and there were helpful animals, including lions.[45] In the late fourth century, the desert was producing its own romance.

But there is nothing romantic about a centaur. The centaur, or "hippocentaur", as Jerome calls it, half-man and half-horse, is a discordant image in his text, and it is an image with a distinctive style that is not innocent, despite its romanticized or idyllic setting. In Greek myth as reflected in poetry, art, and drama, centaurs were hybrid, cross-species creatures that were noted for two traits in particular: their hyper-masculine and violent sexuality, and their hostility to what ancient Greeks saw as foundational norms of culture, especially relations of guest-friendship and hospitality and the institution of marriage.[46]

As Page duBois has argued with regard to their sexuality, centaurs were liminal characters: "They are not simply nature spirits, or river creatures, but also hybrid monsters whose existence in myth permitted speculation about boundaries and kinds. The Centaurs formed an asymmetrical, overly masculine, violently bestial alternative to the norm of what was seen by the Greeks as human culture ...The violence and sexuality of horses was super-added to human virility in their bodies".[47] Centaurs' rejection of marriage also marked them as liminal creatures whose existence permitted speculation about difference and limits; they had no need of marriage "because they were creatures of a lost past, before sexual difference".[48] Similarly, their refusal of the conventions of gift-exchange showed them to be both "greedy and incapable of receiving guests".[49]

DuBois concludes about centaurs that they functioned to facilitate "speculation about difference to define the cultural norm, the human Greek male who was set in opposition to the strange, half-human creatures". Further, they were connected by analogy with barbarians as the "other" through which properly civilized individuals knew themselves to be such.[50] In other words, as figurations of wildness and animal appetite, centaurs were opposed to culture—and yet, it is important to emphasize, it was only through them that civilized society recognized itself as civilized. Centaurs were a strange mixture of the animal and the human, of bestiality and civilization; negatively, they figured not only a literal "other" but also an intimate other, the wildness within the human. But there was another dimension to the centaur as well, one which accented a positive aspect of this union of animal and human.

The myth of the centaur had two poles: "one as a wild man who was humanoid and the other as a wise and just man who was bestial".[51] Chiron the centaur, who had learned medicine, music, and divination from the Gods and was the teacher of heroes, represented the latter, positive pole of the centaur as a blend of nature and culture.[52] Roger Bartra has observed that it was possible for "a human with wild characteristics (Chiron) [to] represent wisdom and culture" due to "the superhuman qualities of nature itself". "Not only did nature savagely assault civilized man, but nature also communicated the signs and symbols of a profound knowledge, forging an odd link between a wild nature and a prophetic "knowledge".[53]

DuBois' perspective adds to this portrait when she argues that Chiron's positive character further accentuates the liminal quality of centaurs: "they lived in nature both as violent, uncivilized beasts, and as characters from a lost past, before the necessity for a separation between gods and men, before work, cooking, death, all the evils that culture brings. They demonstrate the Greeks' fundamental ambivalence about nature and about the prehistory of mankind. The world before culture was viewed with nostalgia as well as loathing".[54] Indeed, as Hayden White has observed about the long tradition of speculation about the wild man in ancient, medieval, and early modern European thought, a tradition in which the centaur figured prominently, the wild man held in a tensive balance two contrary views of the relation of the human to nature and the animal: on the one hand, identifying with the wild man signified a regressive return to bestiality, while on the other, sympathizing with him signalled a radical rejection of the values, norms, and institutions of a civilization now viewed as cramping and corrupt.[55] The wild man could be an idealized metaphor used to rebel against culture as well as a corrupt image of all that civilization had rejected in constituting itself *as* culture.

As wild man, then, the centaur can best be conceptualized not as a romantic, fairy-tale figure but rather, following the poet Ezra Pound's definition of an image, as "that which presents an intellectual and emotional complex in an instant of time"—"a cluster of fused ideas endowed with energy".[56] Jerome seems to have realized that his introduction of such an image into the desert needed some explaining. Following his narration of Antony's encounter with this creature, he says: "Whether the devil himself took on the shape of this creature, thus to terrify Antony, or whether the desert, typically capable of engendering monsters, also gave birth to this beast, we know not".[57] Here Jerome seems to accent the negative dimension of the centaur, noting its terrifying and monstrous qualities. Yet, in the preceeding section, another, positive dimension of the centaur is presented. I will quote the whole passage in which Antony, having dreamed that he ought to seek out that monk who is better than he, sets out to find him, though he has no idea where to go.

> By midday, the sun blazed overhead, but [Antony] did not falter and stayed his course, saying, "I trust in my God that he will show me that servant of his whom he promised". No sooner had he said this than Antony spied a man horse [*hominem equo mixtum*]. (The fancy of poets name this creature a "hippocentaur".) At the sight of this creature, Antony protected himself by making upon his forehead the sign of the cross. "Hey, you!", said Antony, "where does this servant of God dwell?". The beast gnashed its teeth and tried to speak clearly, but only ground out from a mouth shaking with bristles some kind of barbarous sounds rather than lucid speech; the creature indicated the sought-for route by extending its right hand and then, as Antony watched in amazement, it fled swiftly over the open ground and vanished.[58]

In this scenario, the centaur embodies the monk's trust in God; it is a religious figure of the highest order. Moreover, despite its barbarous speech, it knows where the holiest monk of all dwells and so exhibits the profound knowledge that was associated with such wild men as the centaur Chiron.

Jerome's use of the centaur in his biography of Paul is a clear indication that his presentation of the desert is not an imitation of reality but rather a construction that embodies a vision of a new form of human identity that, as I will argue, has a great deal to do with the passionate physicality of the animal, and with this hybrid animal in particular. The "numinous grossness" of the centaur—its combination of bestiality and superhuman knowledge—disrupts the aesthetic completeness of the desert as Arcadian garden with its welling springs and shady palm trees and thus advertises its metaphoricity.[59] At the same time, the centaur also indicates the ambivalence of the desert-as-landscape, since it pictures a wildness that the ascetic ideal of the human unleashed at the same time as it tried to control it (a phenomenon for which Jerome's visions of dancing girls provide ample testimony).

It is important to underscore the artfulness of Jerome's crafting of the nature of the desert, particularly in regard to the centaur. In the first place, by putting a centaur in the desert, Jerome has engaged in a very basic form of imagination since, as contemporary theorists have argued, "the first function of the imagination is to create animal forms".[60] Further, by introducing the centaur into the desert and by asserting the appropriateness of its presence there (recall that, in Jerome's view, the desert is "typically capable of engendering monsters"), Jerome has intensified the significance of the desert by giving it an imaginative dimension drawn from myth. Jerome, then, does not approach the desert as a naturalist; rather, he uses it as the medium *through which* to offer a picture of a religious sensibility.[61] By using fiction—the mythic centaur—instead of naturalistic descriptions, Jerome has produced a figurative desert that is strongly charged with meaning.

If Jerome's representational strategy toward the desert is viewed as that of an imaginative artist rather than a muddle-headed *naïf,* the status of the desert as a dynamic concept of place emerges clearly. I emphasize the concept of place in the context of Jerome's transformation of desert into landscape because, as Jonathan Smith has observed, a total world-view is implied in an individual's (or a culture's) imagination of place; indeed, "it is through an understanding and symbolization of place that a society or individual creates itself".[62] This is the conceptual framework that best fits Jerome's metaphorical recreation of the desert in his biography of Paul.

Wild Men In The Desert: Satyrs

The desert was so charged with significance that no literal description could capture it; from this perspective, Jerome's task was to find an iconic idiom to convey the essence of the place. Given the idyllic setting that he first constructs for Paul in the biography, his choice of a centaur as the figure that is pivotal to the forward motion of the story seems odd, even uncanny. Wildness, however, seems to have captured Jerome's imagination as an appropriate vehicle for his vision of the desert. In the *Life of Saint Paul,* a centaur shows Antony the correct route toward his destined meeting with Paul.[63] Immediately following this scene, Antony is described as being in wonderment about what had just happened but continues on his journey nonetheless:

> In a brief time he came to a rocky valley and saw there a dwarf [*homunculus*], whose nostrils were joined together, with horns growing out of his forehead, and with the legs and feet of a goat ...The creature I have just described offered to Antony, as pledges of peace, dates to sustain him on his journey. Antony perceived the creature's intent, stepped forward, and, after asking it what it was, he received this reply: "I am a mortal being, one of the inhabitants of the desert, whom

the pagan race, confused by various errors, worship and call fauns, satyrs, and incubi. I come as the ambassador from my herd. We beseech that you pray for us to our common Lord, whom we acknowledge came for the salvation of the world, and his sound has spread among the lands".[64]

Now a satyr shows Antony the way. In the figure of the satyr, Jerome has reduplicated the centaur as animal-human cross-species, such that the hybrid character of the inhabitants indigenous to the desert is highlighted.

The satyr, like the centaur, was an ambivalent creature. A combination of goat and human, the satyr was the generic form of which the most famous specific instance in Greek lore was the god Pan. Jerome, indeed, preserves the connection to Pan when he indicates that his homunculus was called a *faunus*, one of the Latin translations of Pan.[65] Described as "aggressively ithyphallic", Pan also, like the centaur, was hyper-masculine and signified both "erotic threat" and "estranging fear", as Borgeaud describes him.[66]

So prominent was Pan's aggressive sexuality that one recent commentator has described fauns and satyrs as "imagistic representations of libidinal impulses which could not be expressed or released directly ... They are little more than ambulatory genitalia".[67] Despite the intense *libido* of the satyr-figure, however, its sexuality was finally sterile. Further, like the centaurs, Pan inhabited an all-male world; as Borgeaud notes, "the isolated haunts of Pan ... are in principle closed to women",[68] suggesting that satyrs also harked back to a world before sexual differentiation, at least as one dimension of their nature. Inclined to violence and attempted rape like the centaurs, Pan functioned to thwart marriage; his sexuality was "by definition nonfamilial and wild".[69] Thus the figure of the satyr, again like the centaur, also functioned in a system of speculation about the limits of culture.

Threatening but frustrated masculine sexuality was only one dimension of Pan, however. On the positive side, Pan's erotic impulsiveness was crucial for the fertility of animals and, in the hands of Latin poets like one of Jerome's favorites, Virgil, Pan presides over a bucolic Arcadia that "dramatizes an original happiness prior to the city's foundation".[70] Further, Pan's sexuality was connected with music; as Borgeaud explains, "the ancients thought that panic sexuality, so violent and unstable, could end in music and become an initiatory theme", as it does, for example, in Longus' novel *Daphnis and Chloe*.[71] Finally, through the connection with the incubus that Jerome knows of and supplies in his description of the homunculus that speaks with Antony, the satyr was, like the centaur, a guardian of undeciphered secrets since, as Harvey has pointed out, "an Italic tradition conceived of the incubus as a leprechaunlike creature: he guarded a treasure obtainable by the human who acquired control over the incubus".[72]

The satyr was thus, like the centaur, an ambivalent figure: "music and noise, longing and animality, correspond",[73] as do seduction and repulsion, sterility and fertility, bestiality and humanity. Jerome was familiar with this ambivalence, and he exploits it in his portrait of the homunculus in the *Life of Saint Paul*. On the one hand, he seems to emphasize the human aspect of this hybrid creature. The homunculus says, "I am a mortal being" (*mortalis ego sum*). The word *mortalis* refers not simply to a being subject to death, in which case it would refer to all animals, but specifies humankind in particular, often by contrast with the immortal gods.[74] Further, the creature communicates in a way that is more recognizably linguistic than the centaur's sign language (even though Antony "marveled that he could comprehend the dwarf's speech"[75]—a suggestion that the homunculus' language may be bestial after all).[76]

On the other hand, the bestiality of the creature is accented by Jerome's string of categories—fauns, satyrs, and incubi—which carry the homunculus' wild, goatlike dimension, and by the homunculus itself, which announces that it is acting as an ambassador for its herd (*legatione fungor gregis mei*). While Jerome does not here accentuate the savage dimension of this satyr-like figure, he shows elsewhere that he knew of the satyr's wild aspect. This knowledge is evident from Jerome's Vulgate, his translation of the Bible from Hebrew into Latin. Isaiah 13:21, part of God's condemnation of Babylon, reads in part, "And satyrs will dance there" (RSV). Jerome's translation, *"et pilosi saltabunt ibi"*, "and the hairy ones will dance there", renders the Hebrew *se'irim* as "hairy ones".

The term *se'irim* literally designates he-goats, and was understood in ancient Hebrew folklore to refer to some type of desert demon.[77] Jerome's translation of the term as "hairy ones" provided the precedent for understanding the *se'irim* as satyrs.[78] Jerome's own commentary on this passage from Isaiah is instructive. He says, "When in the following it is said that 'the hairy ones will dance there' we must understand this to mean either incubi or satyrs or a certain kind of wild men [*silvestres quosdam homines*] whom some call *fatui ficarii* and understand to belong to the race of demons".[79] As Bernheimer has pointed out, "*fatui ficarii* were satyrs known for their insatiable lasciviousness and thus closely akin to incubi, the professional ravishers of mortal women".[80] Thus Jerome has associated the incubus and the satyr with a demonic complex of the *homo sylvestris*, the Latin version of the wild man with unrestrained libidinous animality.[81]

Jerome does not make this negative set of associations explicit in his presentation of the homunculus in the *Life of Saint Paul* (though he can hardly rid this image of its wildness). On the contrary, the bestiality of the satyr-like creature is affirmed. When the creature makes its declaration of Christian faith, Antony "rejoice[s] in the glory of Christ and the defeat of Satan", and then addresses the city of Alexandria with the following apostrophe: "Alas for you, Alexandria, you who worship monstrosities instead of God. Alas, city of whores, where have gathered all the demonic powers of the world. What now will you say? Beasts speak of Christ and you worship monstrosities instead of God".[82] In this passage the beast has true religious knowledge, whereas those in the city do not. Here Jerome may be inverting the negative aspect of the satyr-incubus figure so that, as Harvey observes, in the *Life of Saint Paul* "the incubus represents uncorrupted nature, receptive to the gospel, while corrupt urban society is not".[83] One is reminded of Jerome's remark as he was being hounded out of the desert by theologically-minded ascetics: "It is better to live among wild beasts than with such Christians".[84]

Wild Men In The Desert: Ascetics

In Jerome's *Life of Saint Paul*, animal wildness and authentic religious understanding are brought together in the hybrid images of the centaur and the satyr. In what follows, I will refer primarily to the centaur, since the satyr functions mainly as a repetitive duplication of the cross-species image that extends and intensifies its function in Jerome's imagination of the desert. As I have already suggested, centaurs were early instances of "wild men"—those hairy creatures, human and bestial at once, who haunted the European imagination for hundreds of years, from Greek antiquity through the Renaissance.[85] The image of the wild man was supremely ambivalent, since it could signify an idealized state of existence, a rejection of all the corrupting features of civilization, or it could signify a degraded state of existence, an unleashing of bestial desires that civilization exists to control. Furthermore, the animal and human aspects of the wild man were not neatly aligned respectively with the degraded and the idealized dimensions of life; the animal could carry either, as could the human. In the case of the centaur, for example, the "animal" aspect could connect the human aspect with a lost Arcadian world still present in a latent way in corrupt human culture, or it could connect the human with its own barbarous longings, particularly regarding sexual desire. Likewise, the "human" aspect could either tame the beast or corrupt its profound "natural" knowledge with the trappings of civilization's social controls. Bartra sees in the figure of the wild man "the ancient horror and fascination for wildness", but this figure has also functioned to define and protect the limits of civilization.[86] In this uncanny hybrid, both the animal and the human carry both negative and positive metaphorical charges.

The wild man was thus a paradoxical image in which animal and human forms were conjoined *and* in which contrary or different readings co-existed in a single figure. As Hayden White has suggested, these different readings have tended to be either primitivist or archaizing. Primitivism, as he explains, "seeks to idealize any group as yet unbroken to civilizational discipline ... I]t sets the savage over against the civilized as model and ideal; but instead of stressing the qualitative differences between them, [it] makes of these differences a purely quantitative matter, a difference in degree of corruption rather than in kind". From the primitivist perspective, what is envisaged is not "a reconstitution or reconstruction of an original, but subsequently lost, human perfection", but rather "a throwing off of a burden [the restraints of civilization] that has become too ponderous".[87]

Archaism, by contrast, "tends toward the idealization of real or legendary remote ancestors, either wild or civilized ... It can be used to produce enabling myths which may serve to inspire pride in group membership ... or may be used in traditional society to help present a revolution as a *revival* or *reformation* rather than as an innovation". However, "archaism usually contains within it a recognition that the men of the idealized early age were inherently superior to the men of the present .... And thus the appeal to the golden age in the past can serve just as often to reconcile men to the hardships of the present as to inspire revolt in the interest of a better future".[88]

A final feature of these two perspectival frames within which the wild man has appeared is their view of nature, and it is in this regard in particular that we shall see that Jerome has adopted features of both these views by using the centaur as icon of the desert. Again, as White has observed, "The archaist's image of nature is shot through with violence and turbulence ... animal nature 'red in tooth and claw'". By contrast, the primitivist's view of nature is "Arcadian, peaceful, a place where the lion lies down with the lamb.... [I]t is the world of the enclosed garden ... the world of the picnic. Only in this second kind of nature can the Wild Man take on the aspect of the Noble Savage".[89]

Whether the image of the wild man was used to express primitivist or archaizing perspectives, its primary function was to provide a means to meditate on the human condition. It was, in other words, an anthropological image, a picture of human identity. Such summary images, in which different readings inhere, have been called "hyper-icons" by the contemporary literary theorist W. J. T. Mitchell.[90] Hyper-icons—like Plato's cave—are pictorial images in which theories of knowledge are condensed. In particular, they play a central role in figurations of theories of the self and human identity. As Mitchell remarks, "In their strongest forms, [hyper-icons] don't merely serve as illustrations to theory; they picture theory".[91]

My thesis is that Jerome's centaur is such a hyper-icon, and that it pictures his fundamentally ambivalent standpoint toward the desert and its role in the development of Christian anthropology. If Jerome had been looking for an image that could contain in itself both the negative and the positive poles of the desert as ambivalent landscape of ascetic identity, he could hardly have found a better one than the centaur, because this image encapsulates both the hopes and the fears that centered on the person of the monk as he confronted that inner wildness that was the source of the ascetic's strength, and also his weakness.

Living in the desert "in close identification with an animal kingdom that stood, in the imagination of contemporaries, for the opposite pole of all human society", as Peter Brown has written, the ascetic hoped to achieve thereby a new humanity.[92] It is significant that, in asceticism, Christian anthropology became complex: "the great divide was no longer between soul and body as representing lofty spirit and base matter but cut right through the subject itself".[93] This newly "reflexive" self in which body and soul were seen as an integrated whole was nonetheless accompanied by what Brown calls an "insistent physicality",[94] and it is this emerging awareness of the religious importance of materiality that comes to expression in Jerome's use of the centaur as a marker of ascetic identity.

Jerome And The Primitivist View Of The Wild Man

What is most immediately striking about Jerome's *Life of Saint Paul* is the presence of a primitivist understanding of the centaur and its native habitat. Although it is repeatedly described as a monster, the centaur does not seem to belong to "nature red in tooth and claw" but rather to the idyllic construct described by White, where the lion lies down with the lamb. Indeed, the desert in which the centaur is placed even coheres with the primitivist's view of nature as a "world of the picnic", for this is precisely what the helpful raven provides in bringing a loaf of bread for Antony and Paul's meal. Furthermore, even though the centaur's speech is barbarously unintelligible to the human ear, it communicates nonetheless, and it does so in the tradition of the wild man as described by Bartra:

> The wild man did not have language, but took words by storm in order to express the murmurings of another world, the signals that nature gave to society. The wild man spoke words that did not have literal meaning, but were eloquent in communicating sensations that civilized language could not express. His words were devoid of sense, but expressed feelings ... It was] a form of language shared by the wild beasts, a secret network of passionate messages emitted from the deep wells of nature.[95]

There are two features of the centaur's mode of communication that are important for understanding how the centaur functions in Jerome's biography as a marker of the true ascetic. First, it is a language of the *body*—the centaur shows Antony the way to Paul by pointing his hand; and second, it is a language that is countercultural, stemming not from civilization but from the nature of the desert.

If the centaur is seen as a picture of human identity that conveys an ascetic sensibility, it is the prominence of the animal that is most striking. By Jerome's time, it was a philosophical truism that the human body was closely linked with nature, and particularly with irrational animal nature. Jerome was fully versed in this line of thinking and later exploited it in his quarrel with Jovinian regarding the superiority of ascetic practice in reining in the animal wildness of the bodily appetites.[96] Yet in his *Life of Saint Paul,* Jerome, writing during a time in his life when his own ascetic experience of the body was very much on his mind, it is a "wild man" with an accentuated animal nature that points the way to the founder of asceticism. Significantly, the founder, Paul, is himself described as a wild man: his body, decayed with age, is covered with unkempt hair *(putridis senectute membris operit inculta canities).*[97] He is one of the "wild and hairy anchorites" whose stories were to proliferate in the medieval period.[98]

As hyper-icon of the desert, then, Jerome's centaur contains an important ingredient of ascetic theory concerning the importance of the human body in the eremite's attempt to regain a lost Paradise still latently present within him. Even Jerome's letter to Heliodorus, written from the desert, contains this essential alignment of the body with spiritual attainment (and incidentally also contains the motif of the monk's shaggy appearance): "Are you afraid of a dirty head bristling with uncombed hair? But Christ is your head ... Is your skin scabrous without baths? But he who has washed once in Christ does not need to wash again".[99] Many years later, Jerome would again insist on the integrity of the human body, arguing in the context of the Origenist controversy that every part and particle of it, right down to teeth, genitals, and intestines, would be resurrected.[100] As Caroline Walker Bynum observes, "To Jerome, the body is valuable because it is where salvation happens".[101]

The desert assumed such great imaginative significance because it was there that the transformative implications of the Incarnation for the body were put into practice. As Brown has observed, "Through the Incarnation of Christ, the Highest God had reached down to make even the body capable of transformation".[102] As a theory of human identity, asceticism can be defined as an attempt to reimagine the role of the body, now seen as an essential component of the constitution of the person.[103] The "messages emitted from the deep wells of nature"—the human body itself—were messages that the ascetic could not ignore.

The other primitivist aspect of Jerome's hybrid hyper-icon is its countercultural character. Centaurs and satyrs did not belong in civilization but in uncivilized regions, like the "wild" ascetics of the desert. From the primitivist point of view, the wild man did not represent a regression to an animal state but rather a positive return to "nature" understood as a landscape where the trappings of civilization were no longer present. As indicated earlier in this essay, the centaur functioned for ancient Greeks to enable speculation about difference and boundaries, particularly boundaries between a positively valenced human culture and a negatively valenced wilderness. For Jerome and other eremites, however, these valences were reversed: it was civilization that was corrupt, and it was the liminal space of the desert that offered possibilities of an original happiness prior to the establishment of society and its evils, as in Virgil's treatment of Arcadia. In this context, the centaur functions as a picture of a theory of human destiny when the human is released from a society viewed as obstructing the pursuit of religious transformation.

Jerome's inversion of the usually savage figure of the satyr in order to contrast corrupt urban society with an uncorrupt and authentically Christian natural world has already been noted. In the *Life of Saint Paul*, the beast in a desert described as Paradise (recall Antony's exclamation, "I have seen Paul in Paradise") acts in concert with the eremites Antony and Paul to express the ascetic confession of Christ. Further, at the end of the biography, Jerome as narrator addresses his readers directly with a barbed attack on one feature of civilized society that is particularly corrupting, wealth. He contrasts Paul, "this barely clothed old man" who never lacked for anything, with those "who clothe their homes with marble, who string on a single thread the cost of villas",[104] thus playing once again on the motif of wildness as a positive picture of ascetic virtue when contrasted with the misplaced values of rich urban Christians.

Their religion, too, it is implied, is a sham: Paul has earned "merits" but the others, "the punishments they deserve".[105] Finally, playing on the motif of resurrection so central to ascetic theory, Jerome pictures Paul, who at this point in the biography has just died, as lying "covered with ordinary dirt; he will be resurrected in glory". And then he asks: "Why do you wrap your dead in garments of gold? Is it because you think the corpses of the rich know not how to decay unless wrapped in silk?".[106] By implication, the city and its corruptions are linked with decay, while the desert with its "ordinary dirt" is the locus of resurrection.

Jerome struck a countercultural note also in the letters from this period of his life. He described the desert as a new form of city that appears paradisal when compared to actual cities, which he condemns as "smoky prisons", as indicated earlier.[107] Even more pointed is his strategy in the letter he sent to his friend Heliodorus in an attempt to convince him to come to the desert. There Jerome contrasts the intimacy with God that is possible in "the desert blooming with flowers of Christ" with the flaws and temptations of life as a priest in the city. Indeed, Jerome implies that those ascetics "who remain in their cities" are flirting with vice: "But if the pious and flattering words of the brothers induce you to be ordained to the priesthood, I shall rejoice at your elevation, but I shall fear a fall". This is because "a monk cannot be perfect in his own country", for his true country is the desert; "what are you, a solitary, doing in a crowd?", Jerome asks.[108]

Jerome And The Archaizing View Of The Wild Man

The foregoing primitivist reading of the ascetic as wild man seems to lead the *Life of Saint Paul* in the direction of the romantic idyll. As a hyper-icon for the desert as a landscape within which ascetics created a new human identity, the centaur has been seen to embody many of the positive qualities that Jerome and other ascetics associated with the desert. Its profound knowledge of animality—the body—as a clue to salvation and its liberation from the burdens of human culture make it a potent sign of ascetic ideals. Further, its liminal character as a creature from a lost (but, for the ascetic, recuperable) past before the establishment of culture and all its evils, including sexual differentiation and marriage, also seems fitting for an ascetic understanding of the goals of life in the desert.

As indicated earlier, however, the centaur is not a romantic image, but a paradoxical one. As a species of the wild man, it points not only toward an idealized nature but also toward nature as the archaizing perspective sees it, red in tooth and claw. Existing alongside the nostalgia that the centaur evokes are the loathing and fear of regression to bestiality, which takes the particular form of overly masculine sexual violence and aggression. This is an image, in other words, which offers not only a consolation for mortality, but also a judgment. Jerome was correct when he characterized the centaur as one of the desert's monsters.[109]

As Lawrence Sullivan has pointed out, in the history of religions "critical knowledge of the body is frequently related to critical experiences that are religious. Such critical experiences are envisaged as crises", and these crises were often understood in terms of mythical monsters.[110] In desert asceticism, critical knowledge of the body, through the rigors of ascetic practice, was crucial, for this was the body that would "register with satisfying precision the essential, preliminary stages of the long return of the human person, body and soul together, to an original, natural and uncorrupted state", as Brown has argued.[111] But the ascetic body was a body in crisis, because plumbing its nature revealed a wildness that was both physical and psychological.

One of the features of desert life that anchorites feared most was a literal regression to bestiality. Brown's description is succinct: "This was the dire state of *adiaphoria* [indifference]. In it, the boundaries of man and desert, human and beast, collapsed in chilling confusion", as monks wandered like animals, eating the same food as they did.[112] When Jerome remembered this brutalizing aspect of his experience in the desert in his letter to Eustochium, he pictured himself as having only "scorpions and wild beasts" as his companions.[113] But what appears to have been most fearsome to Jerome was not this literal form of reversion to the beast but rather its psychological companion, the unleashing of the passions, especially sexual passions, that accompanied ascetic practice.

As Geoffrey Harpham has observed, "the desert became an empire of feeling", feeling that had to be "constantly beaten into submission, crushed into form through prayer and ritual".[114] Like other ascetics, Jerome wept often in the desert.[115] His tears were tears both of frustration and of remorse, because the more he subdued his body, the livelier and more persistent were his sexual fantasies. Like other ascetics, he had discovered the intimate connection between the body and the soul, for the body's resistance to discipline pointed to unsuspected passionate depths in the soul as well: "what was most enduringly physical about [the monk]—his sexual needs and lingering sexual imagination—seemed most intimately interwoven with the state of his soul".[116]

The radical self-consciousness that was demanded of the eremite as part of desert asceticism's experiment in human transformation was thus accompanied by a searing experience of a passionate physicality that was not only of the body but also of the soul. It would be difficult to find a more appropriate image for picturing this form of self-knowledge than the centaur, whose wild animal appetites threatened the integrity of human culture. Jerome's wild man thus advertises not only the ideal nature of ascetic experience but also the savagery—the barbarism within—that was its enduring and painful companion.

What, then, is a centaur doing in the middle of a Christian desert? It serves as a summary image for the remarkable complexity of ascetic theory and practice. In the image of the centaur, Jerome affirmed the coarse materiality of the desert—its "numinous grossness"—while at the same time he indicated its dangers. This wild man is an imaginatively honest icon of the desert and its inhabitants.

Notes

1 Schama, *Landscape and Memory*, pp. 6-7.
2 Ibid., p. 9.
3 Ibid., p. 15.
4 Ibid., p. 10.
5 Brown, *The Body and Society*, p. 215.
6 Athanasius, *Vita Antonii* 14 (PG 26.865B).
7 See Miller. "Desert Asceticism and 'The Body from Nowhere'", pp. 137-53, for sources.
8 See the discussion by Guillaumont, "La conception du désert chez les moines d'Égypt".
9 Ibid., p. 20.
10 Ibid., p. 12.
11 The dates of Jerome's stay in the desert near Chalcis are approximate, from Autumn C.E. 374 o early 375 until sometime in 376 or 377 (see Kelly, *Jerome*, pp. 46, 57).
12 See especially *Ep.* 22.6.4 (CSEL 54.151) and, for discussion, Miller "The Blazing Body: Ascetic Desire in Jerome's Letter to Eustochium".
13 *Ep.* 22.7.4; 22.6.4 (CSEL 54.154, 151).

14 *Ep.* 22.7.1-3 (CSEL 54.152-53).
15 *Ep.* 2.3 (PL 22.331). For the dating of this letter to Autumn 374, see Cavallera, *Saint Jérome*, vol. 2, p. 153.
16 Augustine, *Conf.* 8.7.17.
17 *Ep.* 2.3 (PL 22.332): "riotous living"; *Ep.* 2.1 (PL 22.331): desert as city and paradise.
18 *Ep.* 3.4.2 (PL 22.334); for the dating of this letter to C.E. 375, see Cavallera, *St. Jérome*, vol. 2, p. 154.
19 See Kelly, *Jerome*, pp. 51-52.
20 *Ep.* 14.10.3 (PL 22.354).
21 *Ep.* 14.10.2 (PL 22.354).
22 *Ep.* 14.10.2 (PL 22.353).
23 See *Ep.* 14, sections 2.1, 3.2-6, 6.1 for Jerome's exhortations against being bound by family ties, and sections 6.4, 8.1 ("the case of monks is different from that of the clergy"); 8.2-6; 9.1 ("Not all bishops are bishops"); 9.2; and 9.3 ("If a monk falls, a priest will pray for him; but who will pray over a fallen priest?"), for Jerome's thinly veiled critique of clergy in the city (PL 22.348-353); see Rousseau, *Ascetics, Authority, and the Church*, pp. 103-4, for a discussion of this letter.
24 *Ep.* 14.7.2 (PL 22.352).
25 *Ep.* 14.10.2 (PL 22.354).
26 See *Ep.* 15 (PL 22.355-358). Jerome was being asked to adopt the phrase "three hypostases" to describe the three persons of the Trinity, a phrase that appealed to Eastern theologians as a way of avoiding confusing the persons with each other. However, as Kelly explains, "Since Latins regarded 'hypostasis' as the Greek equivalent of 'substance', and in the Nicene Creed 'hypostasis' and 'essence' or 'substance' had been treated as synonymous, to speak of 'three hypostases' seemed to verge on tritheism, or at least on Arian subordinationism" *(Jerome*, p. 38; see also 52-55). For the dating of *Ep.* 15, addressed to Pope Damasus and appealing to him for theological advice, see Cavallera, *Saint Jérome*, vol. 2, p. 16.
27 *Ep.* 15.2 (PL 22.355-356).
28 *Ep.* 16.2 (PL 22.358); *Ep.* 17.2.3-4 (PL 22.359-360).
29 *Ep.* 17.3.1-2 (PL 22.360).
30 Kelly, *Jerome*, p. 55; Jerome, *Ep.* 17.1.2 (PL 22.359): "I am compelled to speak out against the barbarousness of that place of yours [the desert of Chalcis] with the well-known verses: 'What race of men is this? Or what country permits such a barbarous custom?'" [Virgil, *Aen.* 1.539ff.].
31 This biography is difficult to date. Cavallera, *Saint Jérome*, vol. 2, pp. 16, 154, dates it between C.E. 377 and 379, and Kelly, *Jerome*, pp. 60-61, also supports a date following Jerome's stay in the desert, as does Rousseau, *Ascetics, Authority, and the Church*, p.106. Text (hereafter cited as *VP*) in Oldfather, William Abbott (ed), *Studies in the Text Tradition of St. Jerome's Vitae Patrum*, (Urbana: University of Illinois Press, 1943), pp. 36-42; English translation and intro. by Harvey, Paul B. Jr., in Wimbush, Vincent L. (ed), *Ascetic Behavior in Greco-Roman Antiquity: A Sourcebook*, (Minneapolis: Fortress Press, 1990), pp. 357-69.
32 For Jerome's rivalry with Athanasius, see Kelly, *Jerome*, p. 60; Harvey, *Ascetic Behavior*, p. 358; Rousseau, *Ascetics, Authority, and the Church*, p. 133. For the debate among scholars regarding the historicity of Paul of Thebes, see Kelly, *Jerome*, p. 61 and Rousseau, *Ascetics, Authority and the Church*, pp. 132-33; as the first section of his *Life of Hilarion* attests, even Jerome's contemporaries doubted whether Paul had ever existed (see *Vita Sancti Hilarionis* 1, in Oldfather (ed), *Studies in the Text*

Tradition of St. Jerome's Vitae Patrum, p. 42). For a careful study of Jerome's treatment of the characters of Antony and Paul, as well as a demonstration of the negative metamorphosis that Antony undergoes in Jerome's work as compared with that of Athanasius, see Leclerc, "Antoine et Paul: métamorphose d'un héros", pp. 257-65.

33 See Rousseau, *Ascetics, Authority, and the Church*, pp.134-35, and Harvey, *Ascetic Behavior*, p. 358.
34 Jerome, *VP* 5. On this point, see Leclerc, "Antoine et Paul", p. 261: "Paul devient un héros de roman, il vit dans une retraite dont la description reprend le thème conventionel du *"locus amoenus'* où la nature s'organise pour l'accueil du héros. Nous sommes loin des sinistres grottes remplies de démons qu'Antoine habite successivement".
35 Athanasius, *VA* 52 (PG 26.917C).
36 Guillaumont, "La conception du désert", p. 10.
37 Jerome, *VP* 7.
38 See Jerome, *VP* 7, 8, 9, 10, 16.
39 Ibid., 16; 13.
40 Guillaumont, "La conception du désert," p. 10.
41 Kelly, *Jerome*, p. 60. See also Guillaumont, "La conception du désert", p. 10, and Johannes Bauer, "Novellistisches bei Hieronymous Vita Pauli 3", pp. 130-37.
42 Kelly, *Jerome*, p. 61; Rousseau, *Ascetics, Authority, and the Church*, p. 134.
43 Kelly, *Jerome*, p. 61; Rousseau, *Ascetics, Authority, and the Church*, p. 134.
44 Coleiro, "St. Jerome's Lives of the Hermits", pp. 161-78, especially 163-64, 171, 178.
45 For miraculous feedings, see *Apophthegmata Patrum*, Bessarion 12 and *Historia monachorum* 2.9, 8.6, and 11.5; for the story of Theon, see *HM* 6.1; for animals, see *HM* 9.6, 12.5, and 12.7-8; another tale about a helpful lion is in *Life of St. Mary of Egypt* 26-27 (I am grateful to one of the anonymous readers of this essay for pointing out that the hagiographic tradition that developed around the death and burial of Mary the Egyptian was modeled on the death-scene of St. Paul in Jerome's *Vita Pauli* 15-16).
46 See duBois, *Centaurs and Amazons*, pp. 27-48. For sources pertaining to the anti-marriage character of centaurs, see, for example, Pindar, *Pyth.* 2 (the myth of Ixion); Sophocles, *Trach.* 562-65 and *passim* (the centaur Nessos); on their violent and inhospitable behavior, see Apollodorus, *Bibl.* 2.83ff (Heracles and the centaur Pholos) and, for the story of the centaurs and the Lapith women, see the many references in duBois, *Centaurs and Amazons*, p. 43, n. 14.
47 Ibid., p. 31.
48 Ibid., p. 34.
49 Ibid., p. 28.
50 Ibid., p. 71.
51 Bartra, *Wild Men in the Looking Glass*, p. 16.
52 See Bartra, *Wild Men in the Looking Glass*, p. 11, and duBois, *Centaurs and Amazons*, pp. 28-29.
53 Ibid., p. 16.
54 DuBois, *Centaurs and Amazons*, p. 30.
55 White, "The Forms of Wildness: Archaeology of an Idea", pp. 22, 28.
56 In *Ezra Pound: A Critical Anthology*, ed. Sullivan, pp. 41, 57.
57 Jerome, *VP* 7.
58 Ibid.

59 For the phrase "numinous grossness", see Long, "Towards a PostColonial Method in the Study of Religion", p. 5, where it refers to a kind of materiality that does not split matter and spirit.
60 Bachelard, *Lautréamont*, p. 27. See also Mitchell, *Picture Theory*, p. 333: "In his classic essay, 'Why Look at Animals?', John Berger has argued that the relation of humans and animals is deeply inscribed in the mythical origins of both painting and metaphor: "The first subject matter for painting", he notes, "was animal. Probably the first paint was animal blood. Prior to that, it is not unreasonable to suppose that the first metaphor was animal".
61 See the argument of Lévi-Strauss, *The Savage Mind*, p. 95: "The mistake of Mannhardt and the Naturalist School was to think that natural phenomena are *what* myths seek to explain, when they are rather the *medium through which* myths try to explain facts which are themselves not of a natural but a logical order" (emphasis in original).
62 Smith, *Map Is Not Territory*, p. 143.
63 *VP* 7.
64 *VP* 8.
65 See Borgeaud, *The Cult of Pan in Ancient Greece*, p. 223, n.21. See also *The Oxford Classical Dictionary*, s.v. *faunus*.
66 Borgeaud, *The Cult of Pan*, p. 74.
67 White, "The Forms of Wildness", p. 24.
68 Borgeaud, *The Cult of Pan*, p. 77.
69 Ibid., p. 77: "Aphrodite's powers, when mediated by Pan, are thus placed in an environment that negates their ultimate purpose: marriage. Pan's sexuality seizes whatever is available, or becomes perverted. It is by definition nonfamilial and wild".
70 Borgeaud, *The Cult of Pan*, pp. 5-7; this is an Arcadia quite distinct from the stark Arcadia in ancient Greek imagination.
71 Ibid., p. 81; see pp. 74-87 for a full discussion of the connection between sexuality and music.
72 Harvey (trans), "Jerome, Life of Paul, the First Hermit", p. 364, n. 18; see Petronius, *Sat*. 38.8. As Harvey notes, the incubus was commonly associated with Pan and particularly with Pan's association with sexually predatory dream-demons; see also Borgeaud, *The Cult of Pan*, pp. 222, n. 20 and 223, n. 21.
73 Borgeaud, *The Cult of Pan*, p. 121.
74 See Lewis and Short, *A Latin Dictionary*, s.v. *mortalis*.
75 Jerome, *VP* 8.
76 Jerome further emphasizes the human aspect of the homunculus by recounting a story that is very much like Pausanias' account of the discovery of "real" satyrs by sailors who discover islands inhabited by "wild men" with "tails as long as horses" *(Desc. of Greece* 1.23.5-7.117); at the end of *VP* 8, Jerome assures his readers: "No doubt should move anyone to disbelief in this event [Antony's meeting with the homunculus]. It is confirmed by something that happened during the reign of Constantius, when the world was witness. A living man of exactly the sort I have described was brought to Alexandria and exhibited to the populace as a great spectacle. Afterwards the cadaver was preserved in salt (so that the body would not decay in the summer's heat), taken to Antioch, and shown to the emperor". This is an interesting attempt to show the essential concordance between myth and history.
77 On the term *se'irim*, see Bernheimer, *Wild Men in the Middle Ages*, p. 96; see also Bartra, *Wild Men in the Looking Glass*, p. 45.
78 Bartra, *Wild Men in the Looking Glass*, p. 45.

79 Jerome, *Comm. in Isa.* 5, on Isaiah 13:20-22 (PL 24.163).
80 Berheimer, *Wild Men in the Middle Ages*, p. 97.
81 The same set of associations is also mentioned by Augustine, *Civ. Dei* 15.23.1, where *incubi*, Silvans and Pans, are said to prey sexually on mortal women.
82 Jerome, *VP* 8.
83 Harvey (trans), "Jerome, Life of Paul, the First Hermit", p. 364, n. 18.
84 *Ep.* 17.3.2 (PL 22.360).
85 See Bartra, *Wild Men in the Looking Glass*, passim. See also Bernheimer, *Wild Men in the Middle Ages*, esp. pp. 85-120.
86 Bartra, *Wild Men in the Looking Glass*, p. 206; see also pp. 14-18.
87 White, "The Forms of Wildness", pp. 25-26.
88 Ibid. (emphasis in original).
89 Ibid., p. 27.
90 Mitchell, *Picture Theory*, p. 49. (For clarity, I have hyphenated this term, whereas Mitchell does not.) See further pp. 35-82 for a detailed discussion of the "metapicture", another way of designating the hyper-icon; particularly relevant for the present context is Mitchell's observation about "pictorial paradox" (like the centaur in this essay) as the "'wildness' of the metapicture, its resistance to domestication, and its associations with primitivism, savagery, and animal behavior" (p. 57).
91 Ibid., p. 49.
92 Brown, "The Rise and Function of the Holy Man in Late Antiquity", p. 92.
93 Stroumsa, *"Caro salutis cardo"*, p. 30.
94 For a discussion of the Christian development of a reflexive model of the person, see Stroumsa, *"Caro salutis cardo"*, pp. 25-31; for Brown's discussion of the importance of the body in ascetic practice in the desert, see *The Body and Society*, p. 222.
95 Bartra, *Wild Men in the Looking Glass*, p. 124.
96 Jerome, *Contra Jovinianum* 2.8-10 (PL 23.310B-313B).
97 Jerome, *VP* 10.
98 See the work of Williams, "Oriental Affinities of the Legend of the Hairy Anchorite". Another early instance of the hairy eremite is the *Life of St. Mary of Egypt*; see Ward (trans), *Harlots of the Desert*, pp. 35-56.
99 *Ep.* 14.10.3; see above at n. 20 for discussion.
100 See, for example, *Contra Johannem* 25-35 (PL 23.392-405), and see the discussions in Bynum, *The Resurrection of the Body*, pp. 86-94; and Clark, *The Origenist Controversy*, pp. 121-51.
101 Bynum, *The Resurrection of the Body*, p. 92, n. 125.
102 Brown, *The Body and Society*, p. 31.
103 See Stroumsa, *"Caro salutis cardo"*, passim; see also Miller, "Desert Asceticism and 'The Body From Nowhere'", pp. 137-53.
104 Jerome, *VP* 17.
105 Ibid., 18.
106 Ibid., 17.
107 *Ep.* 3.4.2-3 and 14.10.2; see the section entitled "The Desert As Landscape: Jerome's Letters", above.
108 *Ep.* 14, sections 8.4, 7.2, and 6.1 (PL 22.352, 350).
109 *VP* 7.
110 Lawrence Sullivan, "Body Works: Knowledge of the Body in the Study of Religion", pp. 87-88.
111 Brown, *The Body and Society*, p. 223.

112 Ibid., p. 220. See also Williams, "Oriental Affinities of the Legend of the Hairy Anchorite", pp. 71-81, for a discussion of this motif in sections of the *Apophthegmata Patrum*.
113 *Ep.* 22.7.2 (CSEL 54.152).
114 Harpham, *The Ascetic Imperative in Culture and Criticism*, p. 25.
115 *Ep.* 22.7.1-4 (CSEL 54.152-54). On monks and weeping, see Brown, *The Body and Society*, p. 238.
116 Brown, *The Body and Society*, p. 236.

PART II

POETIC IMAGES AND THE BODY

PART II

POETIC IMAGES AND THE BODY

Preface

Late antiquity was a period during which the body and its pleasures were viewed with increasing suspicion. The old Platonic cliché—that the body was the "prison" of the soul—had broken down, or become more complex. Thus it was not enough simply to ignore or debase the body because it had been reconceptualized as an essential part of the self. This reimagining of corporeality, however, did not lessen but rather heightened awareness of the body's dangerous association with the passionate senses and thus with vice. Seen as playing an integral, if ambivalent, role in the well-being of the psyche, the body now drew the anxious gaze of those who sought spiritual and moral improvement.

Practices designed to control the body's perceived tendency to excess, particularly with regard to food and sex, developed along a continuum from moderation in diet and love-life to the more extreme forms of asceticism in desert monasticism. Yet sheer physicality did not exhaust the significance of the human body in late ancient thought. Although medical schools developed therapies of the literal body, in religion and philosophy the body was appropriated as a map of meaning useful for exploring divine and human creativity in a variety of ways. In cosmology, anthropology, and hermeneutics, the body's desires provided a sensuous language for expressing the world's most basic structures and dynamics.

The sensuous idiom of the texts presented in this section was derived primarily from aspects of human sexuality; shifting love-making and giving birth from a literal to an imaginal key, these texts used physical metaphors to express human longing for knowledge of God and the self. When poetized in this way, the body became supremely articulate, capable of signifying both spiritual lack as well as spiritual plenitude.

The prevalence of sexual metaphors in late ancient texts presents something of a paradox given this era's view of the problematic character of the body and its sexual desires. In the context of the various asceticisms that proliferated in late antiquity, the "fiery flesh", as Jerome called it, was viewed as particularly dangerous not only to the body but also to the soul. Yet when used theologically, metaphors of desire were powerful articulations of the soul's longing, whether for union with an ultimate principle of being or for self-transformation.

In many, especially Christian, texts, the denial of literal erotic activities resulted in their figural intensification. Like the body itself, however, erotic metaphors could be ambivalent; that is, they could have both positive and negative valences, sometimes at once. Because eros, desire, was typically construed in the double sense of the word "want", connoting lack and loss as well as desire and longing, erotic images tended to be radical metaphors that collapsed pain and pleasure into a single but complex linguistic expression.

When Plotinus, for example, wanted to convey the anguish—but also the ecstasy—of a writer's attempt to find words adequate to that "love passion of vision" regarding his supreme principle, the One, he used as figure a woman giving birth, her pain nonetheless bringing her "so close to what she seeks" (Ch. 5). Likewise, in his allegory on the Song of Songs, Origen of Alexandria presents the bride, who is a figure for both soul and reader, as "intolerably inflamed with love" (Ch. 6). These are good examples of ancient philosophical and religious uses of the poetic body as a signifier of desire in all its complexity.

In this section, three of the essays pertain to early Christianity, and one to Gnosticism and Plotinian Neoplatonism. Despite the variety of image and tradition that they represent, they all have in common a problematic well expressed by Lawrence Sullivan, who has observed that in the history of religions, "critical knowledge of the body is frequently related to critical experiences that are religious. Such critical experiences are envisaged as crises... " (see Ch. 4, n. 110). The authors of the texts in the essays that follow did not always make explicit the particular "crisis"—whether cosmological, anthropological, or theological—in which they found themselves. My readings as interpreter have often been conducted "against the grain" of a given author's announced or surface intention in order to elicit the underlying fabric of images and metaphors that speak to the critical experiences around which the text is organized.

The crisis addressed in the texts in the first chapter of this section was both cosmological and theological. Meditating on the creative activity of God, these texts objected to conceptions of divine creativity that presented God as a maker of "things". Rejecting such a technological model and the resulting dichotomy between the divine and material realms, both the Gnostic and the Neoplatonic author redefined God and the cosmos by appealing to metaphors of divine making that were organic, feminine and sexual. The cosmic and existential reality that emerged from this crisis of definition—embodied, for example, in the Gnostic *On the Origin of the World* by mythopoetic images of Eros, Psyche, and Aphrodite—was characterized as pleromatic connectedness rather than as a hierarchy of power.

In the chapters on Christian texts that follow, the crises had arisen in the areas of anthropology and hermeneutics. Origen of Alexandria, confronted in the corpus of texts sacred to his tradition with a highly erotic text, the Song of Songs, used allegorical interpretation in order to claim (and tame) the text for Christianity. Yet what resulted was an erotic Christology as well as an "erotics" of reading: the Bridegroom/Christ, described as beguiling and flirtatious, offers words to the Bride/reader that are described as kisses, darts and love-charms. Jerome, also preoccupied with images of the Bride from the Song of Songs, was engaged in anthropological redefinition prompted by a keen sense of the danger of sexuality to Christian holiness. Yet when he used those erotic images to develop, ironically, a theory of asceticism, he produced a theory in which erotic sensibilities were intensified despite his attempt to express desire in a non-carnal way.

The crisis that underlay the texts in the final chapter in this section was perceptual. The phenomenon of desert asceticism in late ancient Christianity was founded, at least in part, on the premise that human holiness could somehow be seen or perceived visually. The body itself could serve as a marker of an ascetic in the process of being transformed into an angelic "man from heaven". Yet, given the ravages that ascetic practice could wreak on the literal body, how could such holiness be perceived? This chapter explores how new conditions of visual perception enabled observers to imagine how the human body could signify both lack and spiritual plenitude.

Overall, the discussions in this section focus on late ancient appropriations of the body and metaphors derived from it. Despite the ascetic tenor of many of these texts, the critical knowledge that emerged from them was sensuous because these "poetic bodies" were signifiers of desire. Eros was a generative concept in late ancient religion.

Chapter Five

"Plenty Sleeps There": The Myth of Eros and Psyche in Plotinus and Gnosticism

> It is proper, then, that I should begin with the first and most important head, that is, God the Creator, who made the heaven and the earth, and all things that are therein (whom these men blasphemously style the fruit of a defect), and to demonstrate that there is nothing either above him or after him.[1]

So Irenaeus begins his devastating critique of Gnostic theology, with special emphasis on its attribution of creation to a secondary God. As Rowan Greer has argued, I think persuasively, Irenaeus's theological critique is founded in the doctrine that the one God is to be defined by his creative act; he is the Maker, and all else that one might say about God flows from that primal characterization.[2] From Irenaeus's perspective, his opponents had deprived the One God of the very name that various Biblical texts uphold.[3] It is a perversion of Scripture not to realize that to say "God" is to say "Creator".[4]

My interest, however, is not to discuss Irenaeus's perspective, but rather to engage what I see as a—perhaps the—fundamental theological disagreement between Irenaeus and his opponents: how is God to be named, and what is at stake in that naming?

That "fox", as Irenaeus so scathingly describes the Gnostic creator of the world, is variously imagined by Gnostic texts to be an "arrogant ruler", a "blind chief", foolish Saclas, the erring Samael.[5] This God is the "sinister Ialdabaoth" (to use a phrase of Hans Jonas's);[6] he not only creates the world but makes the "vain claim" that he is the only God who exists, thus revealing his ignorance of the greater divine powers within whose context he actually works.[7]

From Irenaeus's day to the present, readers of Gnostic texts have understood these derogatory names for the Creator-God to indicate a

Gnostic revulsion either against the world that was created by this God or against that God himself. On the one hand, the Gnostics are pictured as a group of people nauseated by the miseries of life in this world; their derisive characterization of the Creator of the world is really an attack on the world itself.[8] On the other hand, the Gnostic revulsion is imagined to be not so much against the created world as against the Biblical monotheistic view of God and in favor of two (or more) divine "powers"; the demotion of the Creator is really an attempt to save the upper echelons of divinity from blasphemous attributes like anger and jealousy, which suggest that the Godhead is the source of evil as well as good.[9] These explanations of the Gnostic portrait of the Creator agree that the portrait is evidence of some sort of alienation, whether existential or theological. Further, both place that alienation in a moral context: the Gnostic depreciation of the Creator and/or his creation is most basically an attempt to draw the line between good and evil more decisively.

While I agree that the Gnostic picture of the Creator-God is evidence of a real revolt, I do not agree that the basis of the Gnostic critique is a moral one, nor do I agree with the conclusion usually drawn from that argument, namely, that Gnostic thinking is dualistic. Such explanations confine the Gnostic view of the Creator and the creation within the very set of assumptions that they were criticizing. The Gnostic thinkers with whom this essay is concerned, the authors of the *Apocryphon of John*, the *Hypostasis of the Archons*, and especially *On the Origin of the World*, have not simply turned Genesis on its head. Rather, they have placed it in an ontological framework whose vision of reality has forced a radical reimagining of this revered picture of God and the world.

My thesis is as follows: when Gnostic texts picture the Creator as blind, arrogant, and foolish, they are not objecting to the world that this God created, nor are they objecting to God as creator; rather, the target of their critique is the reduction of God to a single name, "Creator", and thus to a particular understanding of his creative function. From the Gnostic perspective, the name "Creator" does not exhaust divine being; indeed, to insist upon such a name as the dominant metaphor of one's theology constricts God, binding divinity to a particular model of making. Using the issue of the name "Creator" as a mode of entrée, I propose to explore the Gnostic attitude toward the naming of God and to place that fundamental theological activity within a Plotinian context, which provides a perspective on naming more akin to Gnostic thinking than Irenaeus's perspective does.

The Vain Claim

"Be sure that your theory of God does not lessen God".[10] Precisely in the context of a discussion about how to name God in relation to all else, Plotinus utters this cautionary statement. Strictly speaking, no name is appropriate to this profound reality, although, since "name it we must", Plotinus uses a variety of names, from the numerical "One" through the topological "There" to the familial "Father".[11] More important than any particular name, however, is one's attitude toward naming: unless one realizes that such names are radical metaphors that "sting" one into awareness of overwhelming presence, one will always be cut off from what Plotinus describes as an "erotic passion of vision known to the lover come to rest where he loves".[12] Names, while they are signposts on the path and thus aid one's understanding, do not constitute or in any way circumscribe that Presence: "our teaching is of the road and the travelling".[13]

In the group of texts under consideration here, one of the most notable features of the Creator is his "vain claim", a statement that does indeed "lessen God". After this God makes heaven, earth, and various angelic beings, he "boasts": "I do not need anything. I am god and no other one exists except me".[14] Precisely in the context of creation, the claim that the name "Creator" provides the only access to God's existence is shown to be an arrogant boast, a blind assertion. That assertion has immediate consequences. As the *Apocryphon of John* tells it, the Creator's jealous guarding of his exclusivity provokes, not belief, but disbelief. "But by announcing this he indicated to the angels who attended to him that there exists another God, for if there were no other one, of whom would he be jealous"? The angels are not the only figures to be disturbed. For after the boast, the mother begins to "move to and fro", repenting of the monster she has produced. As recognition of her repentance, the pleroma or fullness of heavenly powers pours holy spirit upon her and she is taken up "above her son". Finally, a voice "from the exalted aeon-heaven" announces the existence of man, who has been given "perfect, complete foreknowledge" by the "holy Mother-Father". This revelation causes the Creator and his minions to tremble and shake, for the man has intelligence "greater than that of the chief archon".[15]

The structure of the consequences of the Creator's arrogant claim is much the same in the *Hypostasis of the Archons* and *On the Origin of the World:* the claim is described as a sin "against the Entirety" or "against all of the immortal ones";[16] a feminine figure (Sophia or Pistis) denounces the claim as a mistake[17] and the existence of the true man is revealed: "An enlightened, immortal man exists before you. This will appear within your molded bodies. He will trample upon you like potter's clay".[18] This latter statement is striking: turning the "potter" metaphor of creation in Genesis back upon itself, it suggests that enlightened human understanding rejects "Creator" as the presiding metaphor of theological reality and shatters the accompanying artistic or plastic model of creating. What the true man sees when he sees through the repressive dominance of "Creator" is a theological reality that is pleromatic—and organic.

The "vain claim" is a sin against "the entirety" of the immortal ones, and that claim is immediately countered by a feminine dimension of deity that is doubled (Pistis-Sophia), tripled (Pistis-Sophia-Zōē), almost endlessly multiplied.[19] The feminine dimension of reality not only appears, but is intensified, underscored, by its multiplied form, setting the masculine world of Ialdabaoth atremble. Accompanied by metaphors of desire, erotic ecstasy, flowing and pouring, and watery reflection, these figures carry a vision of reality that is organic rather than plastic, sexual rather than technological.

This view of theological reality, characterized as authentic human understanding, is offered in the context of the creation story. To be enlightened, in other words, involves coming to terms with metaphors of divine making. Our texts do not deny the pivotal importance of "making" as a theological metaphor; on the contrary, meditation on "making" provides the occasion for reflections on the nature of divine reality as well as on the nature of human speech about that reality. Just as, under the aegis of an explosive name, *nous*, Plotinus sees human language to be a metaphoric fullness and reality to be an assembly of "real beings",[20] so these Gnostic authors, by "exploding" the name "Creator", express a pleromatic vision. The figures who compose the pleroma, like the "real beings" of Plotinus's realm of *nous*, are the metaphors of divine reality; they are the collection of signposts that dot the "road and the travelling" of human attempts to express in language the profound mystery at the heart of things.

Like Plotinus and like Irenaeus, the Gnostic texts under discussion here do arrive at names for this mystery. For the author of *On the Origin of the World*, the name of names is "the boundless one", who is "unbegotten" and dwells in a "kingless realm".[21] For the *Hypostasis of the Archons*, it is the "Father of Truth", also characterized as "Incorruptibility", "Root".[22] Finally, there is the God of the *Apocryphon of John* who, being "illimitable", "unsearchable", "immeasurable", "invisible", and "ineffable", is not surprisingly "unnameable".²³ "Not one of the existing ones", this God who has no name is like Plotinus's God who plays or broods over all that is,²⁴ not incarnating meaning but presiding silently over a flow of meaning, a pleroma of names. The realm of names—the mobile world of language—is plenteous and bountiful, and when one's understanding of reality is "structured" in this way, the ineffable One is a loving and instantaneous presence everywhere.²⁵ This One is "all things and no one of them"; "seeking nothing, possessing nothing, lacking nothing", it "overflows", and what we know is what its "exuberance" has produced.²⁶

The Gnostic pleroma is such an exuberance, and it is revealed to human understanding when exclusive focus on the plastic model of making signified by "Creator" is shown to be a restrictive view of divine making. Gnostic language about God attempts to be faithful to the Gnostic vision of reality, and this dynamic is nowhere more forcefully shown than in the erotic, profusely productive qualities of both its conception of divine making and its language about that process. It is to Eros that we now turn.

Erotic Naming

Gnostic texts about making, which are also about the inner dynamics of the divine world, speak a poetry of the body that has few rivals in late antiquity. Expressed primarily in metaphors of desiring, love-making, and giving birth, Gnostic theological language has sensuous qualities that are striking. This did not escape Irenaeus, who at one point chooses to ridicule Valentinus' sexual vision of making with an equally organic and sensuous language, not from the human but from the vegetative world, envisioning fruit "visible, eatable, and delicious".²⁷ Valentinus's "melons" might be "delirious", but Irenaeus's choice of metaphor is revealing; he seems to have realized that Gnostic thinking about making had placed "the intercourse of Eros" at center stage.²⁸ Of course along with Eros come Psyche and Aphrodite; indeed, as Tardieu has shown, the mythic constellation of Eros and his feminine companions provided a language with which to describe cosmology and anthropology that many Hellenistic and late antique authors used.²⁹ One of the most stunning appropriations of the sensuous imagery of the myth of Eros can be found in the Gnostic text *On the Origin of the World,* which will serve as the focal point of the present investigation of the Gnostic revision of "making".

Although *On the Origin of the World* had "companions" in the work of reimagining the creative process in terms of sexualized, feminized, and organic language, it was in this text that such language was intensified.[30] Pleromatic making is here carried by a group of feminine figures: Pistis, Sophia, Zoē, Pronoia, Psyche, Eve. It is tempting to view the successive appearance of these figures as a progressively articulate and ever more differentiated picture of woman, beginning with the cosmic Pistis and moving to the human Eve. However, the relationships among these figures cannot be plotted along such linear lines. Linear order is confounded in the first place by the fact that the names of these figures tend to flow together; thus in addition to Pistis, Sophia, Zoē, Pronoia, Psyche, and Eve, there are also Pistis Sophia, Sophia Zoē, and Zoē "who is called Eve".[31] The biological or generational notion of successive pairs of mothers and daughters does not work either, since Pistis is the source of both Sophia and Zoē, Sophia is responsible for the "patterning" of Eve, and Psyche is given no mother at all. As we will see, the "order" of making that is set in motion by these feminine figures is a pattern of repetitions, a flow of likenesses, and not a hierarchical structure of fixed entities.

It is significant that the apparently discrete figures of this feminine pleroma tend to flow together, for their stories are variations on a single motif. As Plotinus remarked, myths "must separate in time" things that fundamentally belong together because of the constraints of the narrative form of myths.[32] In the mythic narrative under consideration here, the diverse feminine figures belong together because they express a shared vision of the erotic foundations of creating. Impelled by desire, they are figures in travail, and their making, which is their very being, is described in terms of movement. The "first reality" is a flow,[33] not the work of a potter.

When making is seen from the perspective of the metaphor of the potter, it is an action of forging. The maker shapes a reality other than himself and is related to the objects that he has forged from nothing by power rather than by nature.[34] By contrast, our text envisions making under the banner of desire. It is the kind of desire that is set in motion when God is dead—that is, when God cannot be personified or finally characterized in understandable terms but is rather called "boundless", an unfathomable something that constantly eludes human categories and defies "objective" language that would distance the maker from what is made. The "boundless" cannot be captured, as Plotinus remarks about the "One"; but it can be imagined. Indeed, it imagines itself as it "breaks into speech", unleashing a flow of likenesses, a dynamic "middle" where maker and thing made, knower and known, come together in a bond of love.[35]

It is this erotic "middle" in which the vision of *On the Origin of the World* is situated:

> After the nature of the immortals was completed out of the boundless one, then a likeness called "Sophia" flowed out of Pistis. (She) wished (that) a work (should) come into being which is like the light which first existed, and immediately her wish appeared as a heavenly likeness, which possessed an incomprehensible greatness, which is in the middle between the immortals and those who came into being after them, like what is above, which is a veil which separates men and those belonging to the (sphere) above.[36]

In this text, the "middle" is a realm of likeness that has flowed from the desire of Pistis (or Sophia; the "she" is ambiguous).[37] It is a "veil" that marks the paradoxical nature of the boundless one (the "aeon of truth") whose inside is light and whose outside is darkness.[38] Pistis, Sophia, and the other feminine figures in the text are creatures of this middle realm; neither pure light nor pure darkness, they preside over the watery flowing and pouring that mark the middle. Liquid metaphors are prominent: thus Pistis "pours" light and is herself visible as a watery reflection, a floating image, and Sophia casts a "drop" of light that both floats on and patterns water.[39] Impelled by desire, these figures show making to be a fecund process of watery reflection in which light is poured into receptive darkness.

The "middle" is erotic. The desirous flowing of Pistis is repeated and intensified by a later feminine figure, Pronoia, and it is in the context of her flowing that Eros, who is himself an intensification of the desire of the middle, appears. In one of the many watery appearances of Pistis, a human likeness is reflected.[40] Pronoia falls in love with this reflection and, in her ardor, desires to embrace it but is not able to do so.[41] Like Pistis, whose desire for the boundless one ended, not in a captivating grasp or an embrace but rather in a flow, Pronoia who was "unable to cease her love" "poured out her light upon the earth". At this point the text itself becomes a swirl of liquid metaphors. From the moment of this pouring of light, the human likeness is called "'Light Adam', which is interpreted 'the enlightened bloody (one)'".

> Also at that time, all of the authorities began to honor the blood of the virgin. And the earth was purified because of the blood of the virgin. But especially the water was purified by the likeness of Pistis Sophia ...

> Moreover, with reason have they said, through the waters. Since the holy water gives life to everything, it purifies too.[42]

The watery flow that is the medium of reflection is now imagined as feminine blood. It is out of this blood that Eros appears.

The dynamic character of the "middle" is at this point revealed. It is Eros, love, who "appeared out of the mid-point between light and darkness" where his "intercourse" is "consummated".[43] The desirous making of Pistis and the other figures in the "middle" is founded in love, which, as Eros, is described as "Himeros", a "yearning" that is the "fire" of the light, and as psychic blood ("blood-Soul"). The blood of intercourse, or the flowing of organic connectedness, is what characterizes the erotic making "out of the midpoint between light and darkness".[44] Eros, as the ambiguous uniter of two realms, the fire and the blood, dry and humid, male and female,[45] is a fitting embodiment of the middle. There is, however, another figure or name for this realm, and it is revealed in the course of yet another repetition of feminine flowing.

Following the appearance of Eros there is a description of his gardens, whose plants reinforce the view of erotic movement as a "desire for intercourse" (*epithūmia tes sūnousias*).[46] This most basic desire for "being-with" is then pictured again with yet another trope on the liquid movement so characteristic of this text:

> But the first Psyche loved Eros who was with her, and poured her blood upon him and upon the earth. Then from that blood the rose first sprouted upon the earth out of the thorn bush, for a joy in the light which was to appear in the bramble. After this the beautiful flowers sprouted up on the earth according to (their) kind from (the blood of) each of the virgins of the daughters of Pronoia. When they had become enamored of Eros, they poured out their blood upon him and upon the earth.[47]

This picture bears a striking resemblance to the myth of Psyche and Eros written, in a more detailed form, by Apuleius.[48] The Psyche of Apuleius's tale, who desires to pour light on her unseen lover, loses him (is unable to grasp or capture him), but that moment marks the beginning of her initiation into the realm of Aphrodite, the mother of love and primal mistress of flowing waters.[49]

So also here, Psyche, in love with love itself, pours, and from her flow of blood comes the rose, the Aphroditic dimension of herself. Named after the flood of perfume that pours from it (*rhodos: rheuma tēs odōdes*),[50] the rose was Aphrodite's favorite flower and was said to have originated from the drops of blood that fell from her foot when she pricked it on bramble thorns.[51] An unspoken presence who comes forth in this text in the "likeness" of a rose, Aphrodite is a crucial figure for the erotic "middle" where making is a flow of desire for *sūnousia,* connection, being-with. From the Aphroditic perspective, the picture of the "middle" is not a veil or a mid-point, but a garden full of flowers where the rose presides as a compact image of the bleeding that flows and creates.

The flowing that characterizes this text's view of making might seem to indicate that creating is an irenic process were it not for the fact that flowing is characterized as bleeding as the narrative moves on. That the flowing of Pistis becomes the pouring blood of Pronoia and Psyche is surely an indication that the image is being intensely feminized, but it also suggests that the "desire for intercourse" involves a painful giving of life's very substance. Love is a "sting", as Plotinus remarked,[52] and this sentiment was given graphic, even gruesome, shape in the Great Paris Magical Papyrus, where instructions for engraving an amulet (appropriately, on a magnet!) picture Aphrodite astride Psyche as on a horse, holding her hair as reins in her hands, with Eros underneath burning Psyche with a flaring brand.[53] Aphrodite "rides" on the erotic yearnings of the soul, just as love "stands under" or gives the foundation for the Aphroditic dimension of psychic reality.

Creating as Loving

That there is a flow at the heart of things, rather than a creator set over against a thing created, seems to be the guiding insight of *On the Origin of the World.* The love of "being-with", the desire to connect— the dynamic that *is* the "middle"—provides the basis for all distinction. The essence of making, in other words, is loving. This text, as its modern title aptly states, is concerned with origins. Where do things come from? However, as I have tried to show, by attacking the model of making signified by the name "Creator", this text implies that the question of origins is not to be phrased as above, "where do things come from?". The question of origin is rather a question of the dynamic that empowers the coming-to-be of all things. By rejecting the dichotomy of creator and creation, *On the Origin of the World* has revised the question of origins. The insight that underlines this revision is, it seems to me, a Plotinian one; or, better, it is a perspective on the issue of origins that informs both the Gnostic text and Plotinus, and I would like to move now to a brief consideration of Plotinus's thoughts on this topic.

Generally more discursive than his poetic Gnostic counterpart, Plotinus poses the problem directly: "But this Unoriginating, what is it?".[54] What is this principle, best defined as "undefinable",[55] that we imagine as father and source of all?

> The difficulty this Principle presents to our mind in so far as we can approach to conception of it may be exhibited thus: We begin by posing space, a place, a chaos; into this container, whether conceived in our imagination as created or pre-existent, we introduce God and proceed to inquire: we ask, for example, whence and how He comes to be there; we investigate the presence and quality of this newcomer projected into the midst of things here from some height or depth. But the difficulty disappears if we eliminate all space before we attempt to conceive God.[56]

As Plotinus continues his discussion in this passage, he develops a whole catalogue of terms that may not be used in conceiving of this principle: space, environment, limit, extension, quality, shape, all these lead to erroneous ways of imagining the source. God is not a Being among other beings, nor the Thing of things, but rather their wellspring.[57] Our problem seems to be that we place God within an objective category or frame and then posit God as the "subject" of that object; such a procedure is dualistic from the start and opposes maker to thing made.[58] We should rather conceive of this principle "sheerly as maker; the making must be taken as absolved from all else; no new existence is established; the Act here is not directed to an achievement but is God Himself unalloyed: here is no duality but pure unity".[59] This is an outright rejection of the view of origin that understands the maker in terms of a making of things. From Plotinus's perspective, making "is not directed to an achievement"; making is the very being of God, but it is not to be understood in terms of objects.[60]

What, then, is this "origin"? It is, says Plotinus, "the productive power of all things" (*dūnamis tōn pantōn*);[61] it is the active force present to all things that enables them to witness the spectacle of their own unity, their own self-gathered center.[62] The principle in which "all centers coincide", the "Supreme" contains no otherness; indeed, it might be described as absolute connectedness: "Thus the Supreme as containing no otherness is ever present with us; we with it when we put otherness away".[63] Experienced by the soul as a drunken revel of love, this dynamic "origin" is what makes of desirer and desired, seer and object seen, one: "Here is no duality but a two in one; for, so long as the presence holds, all distinction fades; it is as lover and beloved here, in a copy of that union, long to blend".[64] The One is an "allurer",[65] and its magic is manifested in the experience of the "two in one", the relatedness that allows things to be what they are.

The One is love,[66] and the soul that experiences the relatedness described above becomes love itself.[67] John Rist has argued convincingly the possibility that "Plotinus regarded *Erōs* as an all-embracing term" and has noted what he calls Plotinus' deliberate use of sexual metaphors to describe the relationship between God and the soul.[68]

There are indeed many erotic metaphors in Plotinus' discussions of the dynamic of the One, but what is specially striking in our context is the feminized character of Plotinus' erotic language. In the course of one of his discussions of "the making principle", Plotinus stops to question what he has been doing as an interpreter. As though reading over what he has just written, he asks:

> May we stop, content with that? No: the soul is yet, and even more, in pain. Is she ripe, perhaps, to bring forth, now that in her pangs she has come so close to what she seeks? No: we must call upon yet another spell if anywhere the assuagement is to be found. Perhaps in what has already been uttered, there lies the charm if only we tell it over often? No: we need a new, a further incantation.[69]

Here is a picture of the interpreter himself as a woman in travail, laboring to find a language appropriate to that "love-passion of vision"[70] that he is trying to express. The problem is that the experience of the One as love takes the interpreter beyond discursive knowing and writing: "The vision baffles telling; we cannot detach the Supreme to state it".[71] The interpreter must remember that his teaching is "peregrination"; it is "of the road and the travelling", and to forget that is to make of Love itself a "common story".[72]

Given this perspective on the travailing nature of language,[73] it seems fitting that, when Plotinus names what the soul always is, he turns to a feminine image. That the soul's "good" is with the One

> is shown by the very love inborn with the soul; hence the constant linking of the Love-God with the Psyches in story and picture; the soul, other than God but sprung of Him, must needs love. So long as it is There, it holds the heavenly love; here its love is the baser; There the soul is Aphrodite of the heavens; here, turned harlot, Aphrodite of the public ways; yet the soul is always an Aphrodite. This is the intention of the myth which tells of Aphrodite's birth and Eros born with her.[74]

As in *On the Origin of the World*, Aphrodite appears as image of the soul in love with love, and it is again an agonized picture.

When Plotinus discusses love directly in a treatise devoted exclusively to that topic, he does so in terms of the myth of Eros, Psyche, and Aphrodite. What is significant here for the purpose of the present discussion is that the doubled Aphrodite gives birth to, and presides over, a view of loving that is remarkably similar to the perspective that guides the feminine flowing of *On the Origin of the World*. The first Aphrodite that Plotinus presents is shown as a figure directing her energy toward and feeling affinity with her source. "Filled with passionate love for him", she brings forth love. "Her activity has made a real substance", says Plotinus, and he goes on to describe that love as "a kind of intermediary between desiring and desired".[75] The second Aphrodite is she whose birthday party provides the occasion for another story about the birth of love. The scene is a garden in which Poverty and Plenty make love and give birth to an Eros marked by a simultaneous fullness and emptiness.[76]

In both of these pictures of the loving of the Aphroditic soul, Plotinus emphasizes the dynamic and productive qualities of love. To be in love is to make, and the making is founded in achieving an experience of connectedness, of the "two in one" that is the flow between desiring and desired. There is, of course, an agony here. The "sting" of love is that "he is a mixed thing, having a part of need, in that he wishes to be filled, but not without a share of plenitude, in that he seeks what is wanting to that which he already has".[77] The loving soul is like the interpreter who cannot rest content with a single telling lest he profane the mystery by pretending to have "grasped" what is not "graspable". Like the feminine figures of *On the Origin of the World*, he is condemned to repetition; he must be alive to the Poverty of his Plenty. Yet that awareness makes of his vision a continuous flow that is both source and substance of all making.

That making is a loving that sees through dichotomous structures is the perspective that links the work of Plotinus and our Gnostic author. Creation is not, in this view, a single event that establishes distance between maker and thing made but rather a continuous process of the birth of the boundless One in the soul, and the erotic, sexual imagery of both texts serves, I think, to underscore this point. There is an Aphroditic rose blooming in these gardens.

Notes

1   Irenaeus, *Haer.* 2.1.1.
2   Greer, "The Dog and the Mushrooms", pp. 140, 155-60, 167.
3   See especially *Haer.* 2.2.5.

4   Irenaeus, *Haer.* 2.8.10.
5   A catalogue of these names collected from the *Hypostasis of the Archons*, *On the Origin of the World*, the *Apocryphon of John*, and the *Gospel of the Egyptians* can be found in a convenient collection in Dahl, "The Arrogant Archon", pp 693-94.
6   Jonas, *The Gnostic Religion*, p. 193.
7   For a detailed discussion of the "vain claim", see Dahl, "The Arrogant Archon", pp. 692-701.
8   This is the thesis that guides the interpretation of Jonas in *The Gnostic Religion*; see, more recently, Jonas' article, "Delimitation of the Gnostic Phenomenon—Typological and Historical", p. 96: "This figure of an imperfect, blind, or evil creator is a gnostic symbol of the first order. In his general conception he reflects the gnostic contempt for the world ... ". See also Rudolph, *Gnosis*, pp. 67-84.
9   See Dahl, "The Arrogant Archon", and Segal, *Two Powers in Heaven*.
10 Plotinus, *Enn.* 6.8(39).21,28 (MacKenna).
11 On the issue of the inappropriateness of names, see *Enn.* 6.9(9).5 and 5.3(49).14 (MacKenna).
12 *Enn.* 6.9(9).4 (MacKenna); true expression is, as Plotinus says in *Enn.* 5.5(32).6, an "agony", and "we name, only to indicate for our own use as best we may". Strictly speaking, "we should put neither a This nor a That to it; we hover, as it were, about it, seeking the statement of an experience of our own, sometimes nearing this Reality, sometimes baffled by the enigma in which it dwells" (*Enn.* 6.9[9].3 [MacKenna]). Yet at the same time, the soul "breaking into speech" carries "sounds which labor to express the essential nature of the being produced by the travail of the utterer and so to represent, as far as sounds may, the origin of reality" (*Enn.* 5.5[32].5 [MacKenna]). The point is that we must be "in collusion with" language, "everywhere reading 'so to speak'", that is, reading all words as metaphors (*Enn.* 6.8[39].13: the verb *sūnchōreō*, which MacKenna translates as "have patience with", has a range of meanings including "defer", "concede", "be in collusion with", "connive at").
13 *Enn.* 6.9(9).4 (MacKenna).
14 NHC II, 5, 103 (*On the Origin of the World*, hereafter *OrgWrld*). I have used Robinson, ed., *The Nag Hammadi Library in English*, for all quotations from Gnostic texts.
15 NHC II, 1, 13-15 (*Apocryphon of John*, hereafter *ApocryJn*).
16 NHC II, 4, 86 (*Hypostasis of the Archons*, hereafter *HypArc*); NHC II, 5, 103 (*OrgWrld*).
17 NHC II, 4, 87 (*HypArc*); NHC II, 5, 103 (*OrgWrld*).
18 NHC II, 5, 103 (*OrgWrld*).
19 See especially the multiple feminine figures in NHC II, 5 (*OrgWrld*).
20 See Plotinus's comments on dialectic, which is the language and mode of thinking appropriate to *nous*: "It is not just bare theories and rules; it deals with things and has real beings as a kind of material for its activity" (*Enn.* 1.3[20].5 [Armstrong]). For descriptions of the realm of *nous* see, among others, *Enn.* 5.8(31) and the helpful discussions of Wallis, "NOUS as Experience", pp. 121-53; and Armstrong, "Form, Individual, and Person in Plotinus", pp. 49-68.
21 NHC II, 5, 98 and 127 (*OrgWrld*).
22 NHC II, 4, 86-87 and 93 (*HypArc*).
23 NHC II, 1, 3 (*ApocryJn*).
24 *Enn.* 1.1(53).8 (Armstrong), where the verb *epocheomai* carries the meanings "ride upon", "float upon", "brood", "hover", and "play upon".

25 *Enn.* 5.5(32).11 (MacKenna).
26 *Enn.* 5.3(49).1 (MacKenna).
27 Irenaeus, *Haer.* 1.11.4.
28 *NHC* II, 5, 109 (*OrgWrld*).
29 Tardieu, *Trois Mythes Gnostiques*, pp. 141-214, especially pp. 146-48.
30 On Gnostic use of "biological" metaphors, see Perkins, "*On the Origin of the World (CG II, 5)*: A Gnostic Physics", pp. 36-46, especially pp. 37-38.
31 *NHC* II, 5, 100, 113, and 115 (*OrgWrld*).
32 *Enn.* 3.5(50).9 (Armstrong).
33 *NHC* II, 5, 98 (*OrgWrld*). For an understanding of "first work" as first "reality", see Tardieu, *Trois Mythes Gnostiques*, p. 56.
34 In "The Dog and the Mushrooms", Greer has shown that Irenaeus, arguing on behalf of the Creator, insists that the relationship between God and creation is based on knowledge, not on a community of nature between the two. "The Gnostic understanding that God and the universe (at least the spiritual seeds in it) are related by nature but not by knowledge is contrasted with the orthodox view that the relation is one not of nature but of knowledge" (p. 161).
35 On the One breaking into speech, see *Enn.* 5.5(32).5 (MacKenna); on the One and love, see *Enn.* 6.8(39) (MacKenna).
36 *NHC* II, 5, 98 (*OrgWrld*).
37 See the comments by Tardieu, *Trois Mythes Gnostiques*, pp. 57-58, on the ambiguity of Sophia.
38 *NHC* II, 5, 98 (*OrgWrld*).
39 *NHC* II, 5, 100, 104, 111 (*OrgWrld*).
40 *NHC* II, 5, 107-108 (*OrgWrld*).
41 *NHC* II, 5, 108 (*OrgWrld*).
42 *NHC* II, 5, 108 (*OrgWrld*).
43 *NHC* II, 5, 109 (*OrgWrld*).
44 *NHC* II, 5, 109 (*OrgWrld*).
45 See the comments by Tardieu, *Trois Mythes Gnostiques*, pp. 163-74, on *Erōs* and his ambiguous, doubled functions and powers. From Tardieu's perspective, *Erōs* is marked by "sa duplicité fondamentale" (p. 174).
46 See Tardieu, *Trois Mythes Gnostiques*, pp. 207-8.
47 *NHC* II, 5, 111 (*OrgWrld*).
48 See Tardieu, *Trois Mythes Gnostiques*, pp. 146-48.
49 For valuable discussions of Aphrodite, see Grigson, *The Goddess of Love*; Friedrich, *The Meaning of Aphrodite*.
50 See Detienne, *Dionysus Slain*, p. 50.
51 See Joret, *La Rose dans l'Antiquité et au Moyen Age*, pp. 47-50.
52 *Enn.* 3.5(50).7 (Armstrong).
53 *PGM* IV.1718-45.
54 *Enn.* 6.8(39).11 (MacKenna).
55 *Enn.* 5.5(32).6 (MacKenna).
56 *Enn.* 6.8(39).11 (MacKenna).
57 *Enn.* 6.9(9).9 and 5.3(49).11 (MacKenna).
58 See *Enn.* 6.8(39).13 and 20 (MacKenna).
59 *Enn.* 6.8(39).20 (MacKenna).
60 See the astute discussion of this issue in Plotinus by O'Meara, "Gnosticism and the Making of the World in Plotinus", pp. 365-78.

61 *Enn.* 3.8(30).10 (Armstrong).
62 *Enn.* 3.8(30).10 (Armstrong): oneness; 6.9(9).8 (MacKenna): centering.
63 *Enn.* 6.9(9).8 (MacKenna).
64 *Enn.* 6.7(38).34-35 (MacKenna).
65 *Enn.* 6.6(34).18 (MacKenna).
66 *Enn.* 6.8(39).15 (MacKenna).
67 *Enn.* 6.7(38).22 (MacKenna).
68 Rist, *Eros and Psyche*, pp. 78-79, 99.
69 *Enn.* 5.3(49).17 (MacKenna).
70 *Enn.* 6.9(9).4 (MacKenna).
71 *Enn.* 6.9(9).10 (MacKenna).
72 *Enn.* 5.3(49).17: peregrination; 6.9(9).4: the travelling; 6.9(9).11: the common story (MacKenna).
73 See *Enn.* 5.5(32).5 (MacKenna).
74 *Enn.* 6.9(9).9 (MacKenna).
75 *Enn.* 3.5(50).2 (Armstrong).
76 *Enn.* 3.5(50).6-8 (Armstrong).
77 *Enn.* 3.5(50).9 (Armstrong).

Chapter Six

"Pleasure of the Text, Text of Pleasure": Eros and Language in Origen's *Commentary on the Song of Songs*

One cannot sing "this unique song" of *erōs* that is the Song of Songs until one has first sung a series of songs that take the singer through the whole of Scripture. For the one who would give voice to this song of all songs, there are Moses' song, Deborah's song, David's song, and all the other songs to sing as one passes through Scripture toward the unique song (Origen, *Comm. in Cant.*, pro. 4, 80-83/46-50).[1] To be truly "enflamed towards the word of God", Origen seems to be suggesting that one must lose one's own voice or speech in the song or words of the text (*Comm. in Cant.*, pro. 2, 74/38). But this loss constitutes the maximal plenitude: the Bride, figure for all who would sing the unique song, says, "Let him kiss me with the kisses of his mouth—that is to say, pour the words of his mouth into mine" (*Comm. in Cant.*, 1.1, 90/60). "Intolerably inflamed with love" in the "place of delights" that is the text itself, the Bride experiences the carnal reality of the word: "I have received the word made flesh" (*Comm. in Cant.* 1.1, 90/60; 2.1, 114/93).

Using the *Commentary on the Song of Songs* as the primary text, I wish to explore Origen's understanding of the word "word" not only as a Christological concept but also as a perspective on language. Actually, the Christological dimensions of *logos* and the linguistic possibilities figured by *logos* are intimately connected in the *Commentary*, where Origen typically refers to the Christ as "word" when he wants to suggest how a reader dwells profoundly in the textual reality of Scriptural language. That that profound dwelling is erotic is the thesis of this essay.

The Song of Songs is, in Origen's words, an *epithalamium*, the song sung before a bridal chamber (*Comm. in Cant.*, pro. 1, 89/21). It is also a "drama of love" (*dramatis amatorii*) in which the Bride is described as *sponsa verbi*, "the Bride of the word" (*Comm. in Cant.* 3.9, 195/200; 3.13, 218/231). The word to which she is espoused, the Christ, is a "saving wound", a *philtron,* an erotic presence in language, the factor in every word that pierces and disturbs; yet, for the Bride, "all delights are in the word" (*Comm. in Cant.* 3.8, 194/199). Origen's descriptions of "word" and "words" as kisses, wounds of love, darts, and love-charms are various ways of suggesting how "word" is "flesh", that is, how the Scriptural text can be seen as the erotic "body" of God.

Of course, the text that Origen is interpreting lends itself to such an erotic perspective on reading; yet, for Origen, the excess of pleasure is verbal, not voyeuristic. It is not a question of looking at an erotic text and interpreting it allegorically, nor is it a question of *looking* at a text—any text—erotically; rather, it is to let the text "enter, fill, grant euphoria" with its "*secret* metaphors of love" (*Comm. in Cant.* pro. 3, 78/44).[2] It is the text that is erotically active, not the reader. Origen's achievement was to evoke the painfully loving dimensions of words themselves.

Language, in this view, is actively erotic. It is not an abstract entity, nor is it the sum of words.[3] Rather, language establishes a relationship between a reader and a text that may (or may not) yield a reading that inflames the consciousness of the reader and that unleashes the powers of *erōs* burning in the text. Such reading, as Origen makes quite clear in his descriptions of the condition of the Bride—desire *in extremis*—is both dangerously disturbing and pleasurable: it is erotic.

"I am interested in language because it wounds or seduces me".[4] So the French essayist Roland Barthes wrote, inaugurating what one critic has called "a new age of the licentious reader".[5] I would like to suggest, on the contrary, that there is nothing "new" about Barthes's erotics of textuality; rather, his insightful remarks in his *The Pleasure of the Text* can be read as modern echoes of Origen's position on the relationship between *erōs* and language. Hence I will appeal to Barthes from time to time for expressions, in a more modern idiom, of Origen's "text of pleasure".[6] Such texts are, in Barthes's words, "outside criticism, unless they are reached through another text of bliss: you cannot speak 'on' such a text, you can only speak 'in' it, in its fashion".[7] Let their relation, then, be heard as a kind of antiphony of bliss.

"In the paradise of words", Barthes remarks, "we are gorged with language".[8] In this paradise, "verbal pleasure chokes and reels into bliss".[9] This association of food, words, and bliss is characteristic of Origen's understanding of language in his *Commentary on the Song of Songs;* indeed, it is one of that work's major themes. Origen begins with images of banqueting from Plato's *Symposium.* There is the banquet that provides the frame for the entire dialogue, as well as the particular feast that marked

Aphrodite's birthday and the birth of *Erōs*. Commenting on the framing metaphor, Origen remarks that the banqueters' feast consists of "words and not of meats" (*Comm, in Cant.*, pro. 2, 63/24). Furthermore, "*erōs* holds the highest place at this banquet" (*Comm. in Cant.* 2.8, 165/159). *Erōs*, the name of God as well as the name of the word of God, as Origen argues at length, presides over the feast of words (*Comm. in Cant.*, pro. 2, 68-71/31-35).[10] The delights of this banquet are words, and the place of honor is held by *the word*, language itself. Speaker and lover have been fused, and the reality over which the speaker-lover presides is linguistic. As Origen remarks, the divine words transmit the "order of living" (*in verbis divines ... traditus est ordo vivendi*) (*Comm, in Cant.*, pro. 3, 77/42).

Origen's use of the word *logos* carries this relation between word and life. In the *Commentary on the Song of Songs* and elsewhere, the traditional sense of the Christological title, *logos theou*, is expanded such that it signifies the linguisticality of experience. This is to say that all of reality is presented in words. Origen's expansive understanding of *logos* has been described as the "glissement"—the sliding—of meaning characteristic of Origen's handling of the term.[11] An example of such "glissement" is Origen's reading of Mt. 24:35: "Heaven and earth will pass away, but my words will not pass away". Origen's comment on this passage is Christological, metaphysical, and linguistic at once: "For we know that even if heaven and earth and the things in them pass away, yet the words (*logoi*) about each doctrine, being like parts in a whole or forms in a species, which were uttered by the Logos who was the divine Logos with God in the beginning, will in no wise pass away" (*C. Cels.* 5.22). The *logoi* about which Origen is speaking here are words, but they are also principles of existence as well as principles of knowledge. The word is an embrace of animate being.

Encompassed by *Logos*, which is the scheme of their "rapports", their affinity and connectedness, the *logoi* are also *theōrēmata*, a word that means both "parts of speech" as well as "objects of contemplation".[12] World and text, contemplation and speech, have slipped into each other. In the *Commentary on the Song of Songs*, the reader who understands this slipping, who contemplates the "beauty of the things created in the word", is "pierced", suffers a wound, and is "kindled with the fire of the word's love" (*Comm. in Cant.*, pro. 2, 67/29-30). His "heart is enlarged" by the "stretching out" that "love's language" effects (*Comm. in Cant.*, pro. 3, 77/43; pro. 1, 62/22). Thus the reader is part of that world that has its life in the erotic embrace of the word. Origen is suggesting, with his own "stretching" of *logos,* what Barthes calls a "science of the various blisses of language".[13]

The kind of understanding that Origen both recommends and exemplifies in his *Commentary on the Song of Songs* has traditionally been termed "contemplative" or "mystical".[14] But these translations of the term "enoptic" are too passive and do not adequately convey the active, even impulsive, qualities of contemplating as Origen describes it. For to contemplate is to desire: the name of love is the substance of language itself (*Comm. in Cant.,* pro. 3, 79/46). Further, the desirous longing is painful, not only because the words that stretch the heart are "parables, dark speech, and riddles" but also because language, the Word itself, is beguiling and seductive (*Comm. in Cant.,* pro. 3, 77-8/42-4).[15] As in any love affair, "deep lacerations" are inflicted on the one who would espouse himself to the word in this way.[16] When word and love are fused, and when they become the fact of life itself, language is a "place of delights" —*locus deliciarum*—in which contemplation is voluptuous and active (*Comm. in Cant.,* 1.4, 104/79).[17]

In Origen's writing, the Song of Songs is a text that desires the reader and not the other way around.[18] The reader—the Bride—"is kindled and enflamed towards the word of God ... desiring to be united to the Bridegroom *through the word* so that she may conceive by him ... " (*Comm. in Cant.,* pro. 2, 74/38). The Bride runs toward the fragrance of the Bridegroom (*Comm. in Cant.,* 1.4, 103/77). However, as I have noted, the Bridegroom is elusive and inflicts pain. I would like to turn now to the desiring, seductive, wounding dimensions—the deep lacerations—of "love's language" as Origen portrays them in his *Commentary.*

The text with which Origen is engaged is a love-song in the form of a dialogue between a bride and a bridegroom. It is their words of love to each other, as well as what their dialogue reveals about the character of each, that interests Origen most. Although he comments on the Song verse-by-verse, there are certain thematic images that recur as well as an overall dramatic movement that make his commentary more consistent than a verse-by-verse reading might at first suggest. Rather than charting Origen's versicular strategy, I am going to follow the Bride, the Bridegroom, and the course of their love-affair because they are the elements that give a coherent "body" to Origen's discourse.

Barthes remarks about the text of bliss that it is "the text that imposes a state of loss, the text that discomforts, unsettles the reader's historical, cultural, psychological assumptions, values, memories, brings to a crisis his relation with language".[19] Enter the Bridegroom, the word of God.[20]

Referred to in the Prologue as a "dart" that "smites" with passionate love, the Bridegroom delivers his "wound of love" and departs (*Comm. in Cant.* pro. 2, 67-9/29-32). The Bride first appears in the text in a state of loss: in Origen's words, "she is grieved with longing for his love because the bridegroom delays his coming for so long" (*Comm. in Cant.* 1.1, 89/58). The absent Bridegroom is present as an "inward wound of love" and it is at this point that the Bride says, "Let him kiss me with the kisses of his mouth" (*Comm. in Cant.* 1.1, 89/59). She has been truly discomforted, erotically unsettled, by her encounter with the word, "inflamed beyond all bearing" by desire, as Origen says (*Comm. in Cant.* 1.1, 90/60). Origen describes this crisis of relation in linguistic terms: "When she has begun to discern for herself what was obscure, to unravel what was tangled, to unfold what was involved, to interpret parables and riddles and the sayings of the wise ... then let her believe that she has now received the kisses of the Spouse himself, the Word of God" (*Comm. in Cant.* 1.1, 91/61). Unbearably provoked by the text of bliss that is the word of God, the Bride is unsettled in her relation to words, which are present only by their absence of meaning until she can accept their riddling, parabolic character, the wounding enticements of words themselves.

The word emptied itself, according to Origen, "so that what has been shut in silence might no longer remain unspoken" (*Comm. in Cant.* 1.4, 101/75).[21] This emptying of the unspoken is experienced by the Bride as an "ingrafting" (*insero* in Rufinus's Latin translation), an erotic sowing in the mind (*Comm. in Cant.* 1.4, 102/75). "Thy name is as ointment emptied out". True to the text's aesthetic image, Origen describes the dynamic of emptying and ingrafting further as the word's taking possession of all the senses of the longing soul (*Comm. in Cant.* 1.4, 103/78). When the sensuous self of the reader is possessed in this way by the word, Origen says: "Let us reckon that we have been kissed by the Bridegroom's mouth" (*Comm. in Cant.* 1.1, 92/62).[22] Such a kiss is an "insight", a little flash that lights up the dark speech of the text (*Comm. in Cant.* 1.1, 92/62).[23] The words of the text, of course, do not disappear in that flash of light, nor are they stripped naked. As Origen remarks elsewhere, words are not "bare"; they are rather visible provocations toward the invisible, the unspoken, and they do not pass away.[24] The Bride is "hastening to consummate her union with the Bridegroom", as Origen says, but in the meantime what she experiences is the seduction of the provocative word, which tantalizes her with momentary insight (*Comm. in Cant.* 3.9, 195/200).

Like Origen, Barthes also thinks of the text as an erotic site that seduces with intermittent meaning: "Is not the most erotic portion of a body where the garment gapes? It is this flash which seduces, or rather: the staging of an appearance-as-disappearance. The pleasure of the text is not the pleasure of the corporeal striptease".[25] The phrase "the staging of an appearance-as-disappearance" is a concise statement of Barthes's perspective on language that, like the Oracle at Delphi, neither reveals nor conceals, but signifies.[26] When the language of a text gapes, its surface or obvious meaning disappears and plural possibilities of meaning appear. The tease of the text is this unending allure of multisignification.

So also for Origen, although in a different idiom. He says that the names of the Bridegroom are an "incitement" to those who hear them; "the soul holds the word of God, fast bound and tied to her by the chains of her desire" (*Comm. in Cant.* 2.11, 171/166; 2.10, 170/165-66). Such words are binding because they are "likenesses" and "not in one respect only, but in several" (*Comm. in Cant.* 3.12, 208/219). Words signify, but they do so only as a seductive flash, as gapes in the garment of the text.

Again, enter the Bridegroom. In Book 3 of the *Commentary on the Song of Songs,* Origen considers the following verses (Cant. 2:9-10): "Behold, he stood behind our wall, leaning against the windows, looking through the nets. My Nephew answered, and He says to me: 'Arise, come, my neighbor, my fair one, my dove'" (*Comm. in Cant.* 3.13, 216-23/229-38). The word of God—the Bridegroom—is found "not in the open courtyard but covered over and as it were hiding behind the wall" (*Comm. in Cant.* 3.13, 218/232). He wants his presence to be noticed, says Origen, "though as yet he would not enter the house openly and for all to see but, lover-like (*erōtikōs*) would first look through the windows at the Bride". "With a leap he reaches the windows of the house having in mind to peep in at her" (*Comm. in Cant.* 3.11, 199-200/206).[27] Peeping in, the Bridegroom entices the Bride to come out with descriptions of the place where they will make love, the time when she will unveil her face (*Comm. in Cant.* 3.11, 201/208).[28] Still, the Bridegroom "does not show himself openly and wholly to her yet; rather, ... he encourages and urges her not to sit idle but to go to him outside and try to see him" (*Comm. in Cant.* 3.13, 219/233). However, "because she cannot yet behold him thus, he stands not in front of her, but at her back, and behind the wall" (*Comm. in Cant.* 3.13, 219/233).

A more blatant statement of the seductive flirtation of the word is hardly imaginable, yet Origen carries this scene on.

> The Bridegroom, however, is to be understood as a husband who is not always in the house, nor is he in perpetual attendance on the Bride, who stays in the house. He frequently goes out, and she, yearning for his

love, seeks him when he is absent; yet he himself returns to her from time to time. It seems therefore that all through this little book we must expect to find the Bridegroom sometimes being sought as one who is away, and sometimes speaking to the Bride as being present with her (*Comm. in Cant.* 3.13,217/230).

The word, then, desires the reader, and it visits and forsakes not only to kindle desire but also to display its character.

As I noted earlier, using Barthes' terminology, when words are paradise, there is an excess of verbal pleasure that chokes and reels. "Choking" and "reeling" are appropriate characterizations of Origen's picture of the word leaning on the window sill and enticing the Bride to come out since, in Rufinus's translation, words are "charms" (*venustas*) that "smite" or "beat" (*percutio*) the reader (*Comm. in Cant.*, pro. 2, 67/29). Words have a Venusian or Aphroditic quality that is percussive, sending the one so struck reeling, head-over-heels in love and stricken with a saving wound.

According to a Greek fragment of Origen's *Commentary* preserved by Procopius, Origen's term for the "charm" of the word is *philtron* (*Comm. in Cant.* 3.8, 194/198).[29] The Bride says: "I am wounded with a *philtron*", a love-charm or potion that one might well imagine choking on. That the saving wound delivered by the word is a *philtron* suggests its paradoxical nature: it is a kind of *pharmakon*, a poison that heals. This association of language and love-charm is an old one. In the *Phaedrus*, Plato calls writing a *pharmakon*, "a potion for wisdom"; Pindar remarks that the words of a poet could persuade "as with a *philtron*"; and Gorgias says that the word as charm, "intimately frequenting the fancy of the soul, seduces her, persuades her, transforms her by a sort of sorcery".[30] Wittingly or unwittingly, Origen has allied himself with this tradition, which emphasized the seductive power of words.

According to Origen, to say, "I have been wounded by love", is the same as to say, "I have been wounded by Wisdom" (*Comm. in Cant.* 3.8, 194/199). *Logos* is the connecting factor between love and wisdom, and it is in its character as Wisdom that *logos* appears at its most seductive, where being gorged with words that are philters takes on a decidedly Aphroditic tone. We turn now to the Bride.

"Driven about by language's illusions, seductions ... pivoting on the bliss that binds me to the text ... ": these phrases from Barthes are wonderfully expressive of the condition of the Bride as Origen describes her.[31] "Aflame with longing for wisdom", she is finally conducted into the "king's chamber", a place of feasting and drinking that Origen imagines to be the "House of Wine" where Wisdom "offers the flesh of the word"

(*Comm. in Cant.* 3.8, 194/199; 3.6, 181/184; 181/185). There are two aspects of this scene that Origen is particularly interested in: the furnishings of the king's chamber and the banquet that is taking place there.

First, the king's chamber. Origen is commenting on two passages: *Cant.* 1:11-12, "We will make thee likenesses of gold with silver inlays, till the King recline at his table"; and *Cant.* 1:16, "Behold, Thou are good, my Nephew, behold, Thou art fair indeed. Our bed is shady" (*Comm. in Cant.* 2.8,156-65/148-59; 3.2,174-75/172-74). The focus is on the place of reclining, about which Origen remarks that the advanced soul will "receive 'the King reclining at his table' in herself" (*Comm. in Cant.* 2.8,164/158). The King is the word reclining in the love-sick soul, about whom Origen exclaims, "Blessed is that roomy soul, blessed the couches of her mind!" (*Comm. in Cant.* 2.8, 165/158). Only now does the Bride look closely at the beauty of the Bridegroom. It is at this moment that she "speaks in riddles", as Origen says. The riddle is that "her body is the couch shared by herself and her Bridegroom" (*Comm. in Cant.* 3.2, 175/172).[32] What soul and word, reader and language, have in common is the body, the couch of love, the erotic body of the text. In this ecstatic moment of recognition, the Bride speaks in riddles as seductive as the dark, flirtatious speech of the Word itself.

Meanwhile, there is a feast going on. The Bride says, "Bring ye me into the house of wine", about which Origen remarks, "it is almost as if she said, 'Unite me to the body of Christ'" (*Comm. in Cant.* 3.6, 184/185).[33] The Bride feels herself compelled to enter "the house of pleasure" (*domus laetitiae*), as the feasting room is called. The house of pleasure is the house of wine, the place where "Wisdom has mingled her wine in a bowl" (*Comm. in Cant.* 3.6, 184-85/185-87). Yet Wisdom offers more than wine: "she also supplies plenty of fragrant apples, apples so sweet that they not only yield their luscious taste to mouth and lips but keep their sweetness also when they reach the inner throat" (*Comm. in Cant.* 3.5, 181/181). Wisdom's apples are what Origen has in mind as he interprets *Cant.* 2:3: "As the apple tree among the trees of the wood, so is my Nephew among the sons; in his shadow I desired and sat, and his fruit was sweet in my throat" (*Comm. in Cant.* 3.5, 179-84/179-85). Suddenly the house of pleasure has an apple tree in it! The apple tree is the Bridegroom, "the word", as Origen says, "whose fruit the Bride finds sweet in her throat" (*Comm. in Cant.* 3.5, 180-81/180-81). The Word of God "presents himself as fragrant apples to those who crave delights" (*Comm. in Cant.* 3.8, 194/198).

This is another of Origen's associations of food and word in a markedly blissful erotic context. Eating the apples of the Bridegroom, the Bride is bound to him. As in the *Song of Songs*, so also in the wedding ceremonies of Greek antiquity, apples played a part in the process of erotic binding. As Marcel Detienne has noted, apples were "offered to the young couple and sometimes thrown at the wedding procession ... Freshly-picked apples were poured into the bride's garment, or a young woman accompanying the bride and groom held an apple between two fingers and presented it to them. At Athens, the ritual gesture was even sanctioned by the Solonic Code, which charges the bride to munch an apple of Cydon before crossing the threshold of the bridal chamber".[34] Apple-eating would give the bride sweet words, as Plutarch remarks.[35] Even the pips of the apple were thought to be an aphrodisiac.[36] Mythologically, the apple was Aphrodite's fruit, the irresistible trap of sexual pleasure.[37] "Apple-throwing (*melobolein*) was a proverbial expression that signalled Aphrodite's mode of action: 'render passionate, put into ecstasy, entice with the lure of sex'".[38] There are many attestations of apples as lovers' gifts, like the apple that Philostratus inscribed "*philōse*", and sent to his mistress.[39]

Medicinally, the apple was thought to be an antidote to poison, the sweet fruit that poisons poison.[40] It is fitting, then, that in Origen's text the apple is the fruit of *logos*. Poison and love-charm at once, the apple is the Bride's *pharmakon*. Having tasted the apple and found it sweet, the Bride says: "Encompass me with apples, because I am wounded by love" (*Comm. in Cant.* 3.8, 191/195). Origen explains that "she wants to rest with quantities of apples all around her ... so that she may partake of their richness"—the very richness that she has earlier "escorted into the depths of herself as into a bridal chamber" (*Comm. in Cant.* 3.8, 191/197-8; 3.5, 180/180).[41] Already amply fed, as Origen remarks, the Bride asks to be further sustained by apples, "knowing that all delights are in the word for her; and she discourses (*discurro*) about these especially when she feels that she has been wounded by the darts of *erōs*" (*Comm. in Cant.* 3.8, 194/198, my translation). The apples of the Bridegroom are the words of the Word, language at its most erotic pitch. Lying with apples "rolling around her", as the text literally says, the Bride achieves her discourse, and it is a discourse about apples (*Comm. in Cant.* 3.8, 193/197)![42] Her words have become one with the word. She has received the gift of Wisdom, "the flesh of the word" (*Comm. in Cant.* 3.5, 181/181).

Origen was, of course, a figurative thinker, and never was he more insistently figurative than in his *Commentary on the Song of Songs*. Barthes remarks about figuration that it is "the way in which the erotic body appears in the profile of the text ... The text itself can reveal itself in the form of a body, split into erotic sites".[43] Just as the human being has an anatomical body, so the text has a grammatical body. "But the human being also has a body of bliss consisting solely of erotic relations, utterly distinct from the anatomical body ... ".[44] Thus with the text: its body of bliss "is no more than the open list of the fires of language ... ".[45] For Origen, as for Barthes, the text is an erotic body where word and reader, Bridegroom and Bride, are joined.

Notes

1. For this and other passages, I have followed the English translation of Lawson, *Origen: The Song of Songs*. In the textual citations in the body of the paper, I have given the book and chapter numbers from the *Commentary on the Song of Songs*, followed by the page numbers from the Latin and English texts, in that order. Whenever translations are my own they will be so marked.
2. The first quotation in this sentence is from Sontag, "Writing Itself", p. 445.
3. *Logos*, for Origen, must not be understood as "the sum of God's thoughts," nor is it the sum of Scriptural (God's) words; see Nautin, *Origène: Homélies sur Jérémie*, vol. 2, p. 253, n. 4. On the topic of Origen's understanding of the function of *logos* with respect to language, see especially the fine essay by Harl, "Origène et la Sémantique", pp. 161-67. She discusses at length both the role of *Logos* as interpretative mediator between reader and Scriptural text and what she calls "les 'habitudes' sémantiques" of the *Logos*.
4. Barthes, *Pleasure of the Text*, p. 38.
5. Leitch, *Deconstructive Criticism*, p. 247.
6. It should be noted at this point that Barthes describes the reader's relation with a text with two terms, "pleasure" (*plaisir*) and "bliss" (*jouissance*), which he uses virtually synonymously. "Bliss", the more radical of the two terms, describes the active capability of words to unsettle—even ravage—the reader with an almost terrifying excess of meaning, an excess that is nevertheless experienced as pleasurable. I have followed Barthes in using the two terms interchangeably.
7. Barthes, *Pleasure of the Text*, p. 22.
8. Ibid., p. 8.
9. Ibid.
10. Origen is quite adamant on this point: although *agapē* may be a more "respectable" word morally speaking, *erōs is* the proper word, love's true name. "You must take whatever Scripture says about charity as if it had been said with reference to passionate love, taking no notice of the difference of terms; for the same meaning is conveyed by both" (*Comm. in Cant.*, pro. 2, 70-71/34). See the discussion of Origen's conception of *erōs* by Rist, *Eros and Psyche*, pp. 195-212.
11. Crouzel, *Connaissance Mystique*, p. 58.
12. Ibid., pp. 56-7.
13. Barthes, *Pleasure of the Text*, p. 6.

14 For Origen's discussion of the three branches of learning (physics, ethics, contemplation), see *Comm. in Cant.*, pro. 3,75-79/39-46, as well as my discussion of the issue in Cox, "Origen and the Bestial Soul", pp.118-20 and n. 26.
15 See the detailed discussion by Harl, "Origène et la Sémantique", pp. 334-71). She shows that Origen's theory of Scriptural inspiration and interpretation stemmed in large part from his view of Biblical language as riddling, parabolic, and dark. "Pour Origène ... les tours obscurs du langage, et même les ambiguités ou les incohérences du texte, tout appartient authentiquement au texte original" (p. 359). She shows that such passages as *C. Cels.* 6.17, with its references to darkness as God's hiding-place, to the "great deep" that covers God like a garment, and to "the depth of the knowledge of the Father" refer for Origen not only to the "unknowability" of God but also to Biblical texts that obscure and hide (p. 338 with n. 12 and passim).
16 Barthes, *Pleasure of the Text*, p. 12. The phrase "deep lacerations" is used in a context in which Barthes is discussing a kind of reading that suffers the text's "layering of significance", the "vertical din" of a text's language.
17 Origen is discussing the many sorts of food offered by the "Word of life". The "place of delights" contains an abundance of such foods; there, the one who is with the Word "will taste and see the satisfaction of the Lord". As we will see later in this essay, food is one of Origen's many metaphors in the *Commentary on the Song of Songs* for words/Scriptural texts. Thus the "place of delights" with its many foods is the Scriptural text itself, and the one who "tastes and sees" is the reader able to handle the abundance of Scripture's words without despairing of their metaphoric surplus.
18 Barthes, *Pleasure of the Text*, p. 6.
19 Ibid., p. 14.
20 The Bride and the Bridegroom denote "the soul in her union with the Word of God" (*Comm. in Cant.* 1.1, 89/58)
21 This passage is a fragment from Origen's *Commentary* preserved by Procopius in his *Commentary on the Song of Songs* 1.2. Both the Latin edition and the English translation of Origen's *Commentary* print these fragments.
22 Fragment from Procopius, *Comm. in Cant.* 1.2.
23 See the discussion by Harl, "Origène et la Sémantique", p. 355, on this aspect of Origen's hermeneutic, in which the obscurity of Biblical texts is resolved by an illumination in the heart. Such lighting up of the heart, however, does not wipe out the obscure words from the text.
24 See my discussion of *De principiis* 4.2.2, in Cox, "Origen and the Witch of Endor", p. 146, n. 25. In this passage, Origen exposes the error of those who think that words are *psilos*, "bare", and argues that words are icons, metaphors about to explode with meaning.
25 Barthes, *Pleasure of the Text*, p. 9.
26 The allusion here is to Heraclitus (Diels-Kranz, fr. 93): "The Lord whose oracle is at Delphi neither reveals nor conceals, but signifies [*sēmainei*]". For a discussion of Origen's sense of polysemy in language, see Harl, "Origène et la Sémantique", pp. 164-65.
27 Fragment from Procopius, *Comm. in Cant.* 2.8.
28 Fragment from Procopius, *Comm. in Cant.* 2.8.
29 Fragment from Procopius, *Comm. in Cant.* 2.5.
30 In the *Phaedrus* 274d-e, Theuth (Hermes in Egyptian disguise) offers to the King of Egypt his invention, the alphabet, which he characterizes as a "recipe for wisdom". The word for "recipe" is *pharmakon*, a word that captures the double-edged nature of

language since it is a drug that can both poison and heal. For Pindar, *Nem.* 4.3, 8.48; *Pyth.* 3.64 and Gorgias, *Helen 10*, see de Romilly, *Magic and Rhetoric*, pp. 4-37; see also Lain Entralgo, *Therapy of the Word*, for a discussion of this understanding of language in classical antiquity.
31 Barthes, *Pleasure of the Text*, p. 18.
32 Fragment from Procopius, *Comm. in Cant.* 1.14.
33 Fragment from Procopius, *Comm. in Cant.* 2.4.
34 Detienne, *Dionysos Slain*, p. 43. See also Littlewood, "Symbolism of the Apple", p.154, n.15, who gives Philostratus' description of two *Erōtes* kissing an apple that they toss to each other.
35 *Conj. Precepts* 138D.
36 Littlewood, "Symbolism of the Apple", p. 158.
37 Ibid., pp. 159-60.
38 Detienne, *Dionysos Slain*, p. 44.
39 Littlewood, "Symbolism of the Apple", p. 168.
40 Ibid., p. 167, n. 40.
41 Fragments from Procopius, *Comm. in Cant.* 2.5; 2.3 (my translation).
42 Fragment from Procopius, *Comm. in Cant.* 2.5.
43 Barthes, *Pleasure of the Text*, p. 55.
44 Ibid., p. 16.
45 Ibid.

Chapter Seven

The Blazing Body: Ascetic Desire in Jerome's *Letter to Eustochium*

As a way of introducing the thematic concerns of this essay, I begin with a poem by the contemporary poet Robert Creeley.

LOVE

There are words voluptuous
as the flesh
in its moisture,
its warmth.

Tangible, they tell
the reassurances,
the comforts,
of being human.

Not to speak them
makes abstract
all desire
and its death at last.[1]

In this poem, Creeley expresses the view that words can be as voluptuous as the flesh, and that such words make desire humanly tangible. In the absence of such words, desire becomes abstract, and so dies. In my reading, this poem articulates a paradox of desire, a conundrum that I wish to explore here. The paradox is this: desire finds its voluptuous expression not in the flesh, where one would expect to find it, but in words; the tangible warmth of desire comes alive in language, spoken across the space *between* bodies, where words express the "presence of want".[2]

St. Jerome, lifelong lover of words by his own admission,[3] may seem an unusual, even inappropriate, conversation partner for the poet Creeley, since Jerome's voluptuous words were directed against the voluptuous and for the ascetic cause. Yet, there is in Jerome's writing, as in the poet's, a peculiar net of relationships involving the body, desire, and language. Nowhere is that net more densely intertwined than in his letter to Eustochium, which will be the focus of this analysis.

Jerome wrote this letter in C.E. 384 during his second sojourn in Rome.[4] These were heady days: consultant to Pope Damasus, *Doktorvater* to a circle of talented and wealthy Christian women, Jerome was riding high on the crest of rigorous ascetic doctrine that he was urging on the Roman church.[5] His letter to Eustochium is generally considered to be the finest expression of his ascetic doctrine, a "systematic theory of sexuality".[6]

Eustochium, daughter of Jerome's beloved student and friend Paula, was an adolescent girl who had already dedicated her life to asceticism, and particularly to perpetual virginity.[7] To her Jerome wrote a very long letter characterized by one modern scholar as "the greatest slander of women since Juvenal's sixth satire".[8] Of course Eustochium was not the one so slandered in the letter; on the contrary, her status, described almost entirely in terms of her body and her sexuality, is repeatedly viewed by Jerome in terms of the bridal imagery from the biblical Song of Songs.[9] Her closed virginal body, token of a soul already "laden with gold", is subject only to the highest praise.[10] Yet, as Jerome says, the object of his letter is not praise of virginity. Rather, his goal is that Eustochium should understand that she is "fleeing from Sodom and should be fearful of the example of Lot's wife".[11]

Contemporary scholars have noted the oddity of Jerome's warm friendships with women in the face of his advice to other men to avoid their lascivious, contaminating company.[12] In the case of this particular letter, there is the further incongruity of sending to a woman a portrait of women that is filled with biting ridicule. Yet there is no reason to doubt that Jerome intended this letter to be religiously educational. As Elizabeth Clark has pointed out, "[Jerome's] letters to women are in fact educational devices for Scriptural instruction", and the letter to Eustochium is no exception with its hundreds of references to Biblical texts.[13]

Jerome's stated intention as author was to warn Eustochium about the dangers to spirituality that were posed by the body, and, on its surface, the letter presents itself as an expression of pastoral care for the moral well-being of its recipient. The explicit intentions of an author, however, cannot always control or limit the meanings that arise from the associative movements and configurations of his or her text's tropes and metaphors. Texts can articulate perspectives and bear significations that are quite different

The Blazing Body: Ascetic Desire in Jerome's Letter to Eustochium

from the announced goals of the author.[14] Thus in exploring the relationships among body, language, and desire in Jerome's letter, I am going to follow the metaphorical figurations of the text rather than Jerome's explicit intention of offering avuncular advice to the daughter of his friend. When the letter is read by attending to the figurations that emerge in its constructions of the female body, such metaphors as "the flight from Sodom" take on a life of their own that is different from Jerome's vitriolic cautionary tale. In this letter there is in fact a double "flight": the movement of the letter's "flight" from the literal female body has a parallel in a "flight" toward a metaphorical female body that is a creation of language, a "textual" body that is the object of Jerome's desire. It is this figurative movement that this essay will follow.

In the letter to Eustochium, Jerome describes the body in general as "fragile"; it is bestial, it is voracious, but most of all it is sexual.[15] The "Sodom" of the body is its *libido,* its desire, which "titillates the senses"; even more, "the seductive fire of sensual pleasure floods us with its sweet heat".[16] According to Jerome, the body's major tendency is to be on fire. Speaking against the drinking of wine, he asks, "Why do we throw oil on the flame? Why do we supply kindling-wood to a little body that is already burning with fire?".[17]

This blazing body is burning with the signifiers of desire. For Jerome, the fiery flesh is not only a physical fact; it is also a psychic landscape or, perhaps better, it is a physical alphabet of the inner person's most basic drives.[18] In the letter to Eustochium, it is the texts of the physical bodies of women with which Jerome is seemingly most concerned. The sensuality and lewdness of women is described in terms of their bodies: what they wear, what they eat and drink, the color of their skin, their gestures, their pronunciation of words.[19] From the pompous display of a rich widow distributing alms, to the women who disfigure their faces and lower their voices to a whisper to simulate fasting, women's physicality is presented as both disturbing and disgusting.[20]

Dismayed by the pornographic bodies of women, which he interprets as though they were texts to be inspected for clues to psychic flaws, Jerome proceeds to rewrite those bodies, using Eustochium as his model. The female body, fearful for "its power to articulate itself",[21] is re-articulated by Jerome. This re-articulation is based on what Jerome presents in his letter as social criticism of Roman Christian women, whose behavior he had observed at first hand. However, it has been shown convincingly that Jerome's observations are not straightforward descriptions, but caricatures. He based his portraits on the rhetorical conventions of Roman satire and mimicry.[22] The conceit of the letter is social critique, which disguises the rhetorical indebtedness of the text to a literary technique. But the satirical rhetoric of the text disguises another of the text's figurations, which is Jerome's re-articulation of the too-open body of woman as the closed body of the virgin.

Women's bodies were disturbingly open for Jerome not only because they were obviously open to sexual penetration. Rather, encoded in that openness was the dangerous strength and persistence of that fiery desire that Jerome came to identify with the flesh.[23] The "surface" of the literal body mirrors the "depths" of the psyche, ablaze with sensuous desire. Writing, for example, about good and bad virgins, Jerome argues that virginity is not only a condition of the body, but also of the inner self. Virginity may be lost even by a libidinous thought: such are "evil virgins, virgins in the flesh, not in the spirit".[24] In this instance, however, the non-virginal mind shows that the literal body's virginity is a sham. Jerome appears to be caught in a dilemma: on the one hand, the literal bodies of women are blatant signifiers of psychic *libido* and other moral flaws; but on the other hand, as in the case of the evil virgin, the literal body can lie, presenting a false mirror of the soul.

Because of the semiotic problems presented by the female body, I suggest, Jerome moved away from the literal physicality of women altogether, and he did so by shifting to a figurative mode of interpretation in which the psyche is described with bodily *metaphors*. To return to the "evil virgins": following his statement that their virginal flesh does not reflect a virginal spirit, Jerome then characterizes loss of virginity in the inner self with bodily metaphors drawn from Scripture. Such women will be found with their skirts over their faces, opening their legs to all who pass by.[25] Using images of prostitution from the Biblical prophets Jeremiah and Ezekiel, who had themselves appropriated the female body metaphorically as a sign of spiritual debasement, Jerome moves from the semiotically unstable physical body to a textual body that does not lie.[26]

In his discussion, Jerome has shifted his focus from the actual physicality of women (whose grossness is apparent even, or especially, in his caricatures) to bodily metaphors used to describe psychic states. It is at the level of physical metaphor that Jerome's rewriting of the female body takes place, and it is there that he will construct an erotics of asceticism that will be applicable not only to women but also to men. Curiously, as Jerome distances himself from the libidinal contagion of literal female bodies, the "blaze" of the body burns more brightly in the metaphorical constructions of his text. With regard to Eustochium, whose body will be the sign of

The Blazing Body: Ascetic Desire in Jerome's Letter to Eustochium 139

Jerome's own desire, it is the transmutation of the physical body into a textual—specifically, a Scriptural—body that is most striking, and that engages Jerome's interpretative energy.

Jerome begins by giving Eustochium the usual ascetic advice, encouraging her in the course of action that she had already undertaken. Counseling avoidance of wine and delicate food, he writes Eustochium's body by reducing it to "a rumbling stomach and fevered lungs", both of which are images that he has drawn (rather arbitrarily) from Scriptural passages.[27] Eustochium's literal body is not only reduced to three of its organs, it cannot even be understood apart from textual references. The body's physical needs, like eating and drinking, can corrupt the soul; in order for a soul to flee from its own Sodom, it must have a newly-inscribed body, rewritten in Scriptural metaphors. Much of Jerome's practical advice to Eustochium repeats this movement from the physical to the metaphorical. Oddly, the virginal body is achieved at the expense of the actual physical body; biological femaleness is not overcome or erased but *transformed* by being absorbed into Scriptural texts.[28] Once safely textualized, that body was ready for use as a signifier of theological desire.

It is when Jerome writes Eustochium's virginity as such, as differentiated from advice on how not to lose it, that the displacement of the physical by the metaphorical is most stark and paradoxically most voluptuous. The virginal body breaks the Biblical curse: "Death came through Eve, but life through Mary. For that reason, the gift of virginity comes forth more richly in women because it began from a woman".[29] The virginal body is most essentially a female body, yet it becomes the site for Jerome's drive toward signifying the ideal human body. Although physical woman, as Jerome so satirically shows, is "nothing", her textual body is really "something", and it provides the space for a stunning theological articulation of desire.[30]

Jerome accomplishes the transformation of Eustochium's physical body into a metaphorical body by way of tropes from the Song of Songs. From the many images offered by this Biblical poem, Jerome draws particularly, indeed almost exclusively, on two kinds: images of closure and images of seductive sexual foreplay. Eustochium is, as Jerome often says, God's bride, and as such she lives in a "paradise of virginity". Textually speaking, paradise is found in a Scriptural love poem, where Eustochium is the Shulamite, the Bride, the black but comely one who has been "washed white".[31] The coarse and disturbing physicality of her body, characteristic of all women's bodies, has been "whitewashed" *(dealbata)* in the course of its transformation into a poetic body of Jerome's construction, an imaginal body that becomes a signifier of desire precisely because of its closure.

Practically speaking, Jerome advises Eustochium to stay inside her house.[32] Domestically sequestered, she is doubly closed, and the physical space of her enclosure underscores the psychic significance of her virginity. Jerome's poetic articulation of her enclosed body places her, however, in the king's chamber of the Song of Songs.[33] This is no ordinary room, but a bridal chamber, a space of sexual love. Eustochium's imaginal body is for Jerome "a garden enclosed, a fountain sealed",[34] but this closing of the female body does not end erotic desire. It intensifies it.

Jerome's choice of the king's bridal chamber and the enclosed garden as images that articulate Eustochium's body leads directly to the other set of images from the Song of Songs to which he appeals. The king desires his bride and will lead her into his chamber with his own hand; he will kiss her, and she will seek him by night; he will put his hand through the opening and her inner body will be moved for him.[35] As Jerome remarks, "desire is quenched by desire": the poetic body is an erotic body of the highest degree; it is the text of inner desire.[36]

Interpreters have noted how peculiar it is to find such sensuous language in a text that argues for rigorous asceticism. In his biography of Jerome, J. N. D. Kelly, for example, observes that "it is ironical to reflect that, in urging a young girl like Eustochium to crush the physical yearnings of her nature in the effort to surrender herself the more completely to Christ, he should feed her fantasy with such exciting images".[37] A similar perspective is offered by Geoffrey Galt Harpham in his book *The Ascetic Imperative in Culture and Criticism*. Commenting on Jerome's appropriation of the scene of sexual foreplay, Harpham says, "The difference between the pleasures of the figural bridegroom and those of any literal one is not altogether clear; one cannot say with complete confidence that ascetic 'sport' is altogether non-erotic".[38] To Kelly's sense of the irony of Jerome's use of the Song of Songs in an ascetic context and Harpham's sense of the blurring of boundaries between the literal and the figural, I would add Julia Kristeva's understanding of the Song of Songs, which will help to show the appropriateness of Jerome's use of this love poem in his rewriting of the female body.

Kristeva notices that union is not achieved in the Song of Songs. There is no sexual intercourse. "Conjugal, exclusive, sensuous, jealous—love in the Song of Songs is indeed all of that at the same time, with in addition the unnamable of carnal union".[39] Love in the Song of Songs is "sensuous and deferred"; never fulfilled, the erotic sensibility in this poem is "indissolubly linked with the dominant theme of absence, yearning to merge", such that the poem is "a legitimation of the impossible, an impossibility set up as amatory law".[40] The Song of Songs constructs erotic love in such a way that its climax is always deferred, never quite reached, yet it holds out union as the end toward which the lovers strive. Desire is continuously kindled, but never satisfied.

For Jerome, too, union was the ideal. It was his "amatory law". As he says in the letter to Eustochium, "flesh desires to be what God is" *(cum caro cupit esse, quod deus est).*[41] Like the "unnamable" of the carnal union of the bride and the bridegroom in the Song of Songs, however, the union of flesh with God is perpetually deferred but also tantalizingly seductive in its ongoing appeal. As Harpham has suggested, "asceticism is essentially a meditation on, even an enactment of, desire ... While asceticism recognizes that desire stands between human life and perfection, it also understands that desire is the only means of achieving perfection, and that the movement towards ideality is necessarily a movement of desire".[42]

Jerome chose to move toward ideality by reconfiguring the female body as a text that could mediate between the flesh and God. Eustochium's virginal body, which closes the fearful articulation of women's physical bodies, becomes a poetic text, but the paradox is that her *imaginal* body is still fearfully articulate, having become even stronger in its erotic charge. The female body is still open, but now it is open as a channel of theological desire. In one of his literary-critical essays, the Italian novelist Italo Calvino wrote that "the language of sexuality makes sense only if it is placed at the top of a scale of semantic values. When the musical score needs the highest and the lowest notes, when the canvas requires the most vivid colors: this is when the sign of sex comes into operation ... The positive or negative connotation that accompanies the signs of sex in every single literary production determines how values are assigned within the text".[43] Asceticism was Jerome's musical score, and he used the language of sexuality to hit the highest and lowest notes. This helps to explain how the figuration of women's bodies in Jerome's letter signifies more than social critique or satiric exercise in misogyny. Upon woman's paradisal body he constructed a space for the expression of the erotic desire that asceticism only seemingly denies.[44] When it is textualized, woman's erotic body hits the "high note" of desire for union with God.

Why did Jerome choose the female body for the articulation of his erotics of asceticism? We have already noted that Jerome wrote to Eustochium that virginity, as the gift of Mary, was in a sense engendered as female. Thus the female body is the more appropriate one for ascetic signification. However, in the letter, Jerome's erotics of asceticism is applicable to men as well as to women—indeed, it is applicable particularly to himself! Woman's body has become a text to be read by women *and* men. The erotic ideal of a union that is never consummated—that is to say, the constant desire for what is other-than-oneself—has been encoded as feminine, as woman.[45] What is other to the self, which constitutes the goal of the self's desirous theological yearning, is figured as woman.

Having used his re-articulation of the body of woman to express the paradoxical erotics of asceticism, Jerome is then free to explore his own eroticism. Eroticism is here understood as a desire for what is other to the self. As Anne Carson has explained, "*eros* denotes 'want', 'lack', 'desire for that which is missing'. The lover wants what he does not have".[46] Construing desire as "want" catches nicely the ambiguity inherent in the concept, a simultaneous feeling of yearning and recognition of absence. Desire fulfilled would no longer be desire. This is as true of theological as it is of carnal desire, a fact that makes Jerome's use of the Song of Song's dynamic of unfulfilled, and so continuously present, desire so fitting as a trope of ascetic desire. As he explores his own desire in this letter, Jerome presents the reader with a textualized version of his own body. His body, too, is subject to the kind of imagistic troping that transformed Eustochium's body from a literal to a metaphorical register. Leaving the literal body, the ascetic turns to language, "the true medium of sexuality" for asceticism, as Harpham has argued.[47] However, Jerome's physical presence in the letter is very strong—much stronger, in fact, than Eustochium's—and, as we shall see, he was not able to achieve that metaphorical closure for his body that he accomplished for Eustochium's.

One aspect of Jerome's physical presence in the letter is the fact of the letter itself. It is well known that Jerome was a prolific letter-writer, and that he used the epistolary form not only to send greetings and news but also to provide exegeses of texts and theological reflections on various issues.[48] But it is especially his frequent use of the letter as the form within which he developed his ideas about asceticism that is of interest here.[49] The letter as a form is an erotic construction, as Carson has shown.[50] Her argument is as follows: "Letters are the mechanism of erotic paradox, at once connective and separative, painful and sweet. Letters construct the space of desire and kindle in it those contradictory emotions that keep the lover alert to his own impasse. Letters arrest and complicate an existing two-term situation by conjuring a third person who is not literally there ... ".[51] Part of the paradox of letters is that they would seem to dissolve the boundary that erotic desire erects, that is, "the boundary of flesh and self" between two people.[52] But, as Carson notes, the fact of a letter underscores separation as much as connection. Yet, while a letter betokens the presence of absence, it is itself a kind of presence, a poetic or imaginal presence, a "third" person. In a letter, one fabricates one's own metaphorical body; such was, in a formal way, Jerome's "physical" presence in his letters.

It seems significant that Jerome sent Eustochium his thoughts on asceticism in a letter (he was, after all, literally "just across town" and presumably could have spoken with her in person). It also seems significant that he used the erotic medium of a letter to construct Eustochium's body as a Scriptural body and an erotic text. "Assuming the character of language",[53] Eustochium becomes a pure representation of that which Jerome himself desires. However, she assumes, not the character of language in general, but the character of the Song of Songs in particular. This was not a language that was available to Jerome for the erotic textualization of his own body, because, as Peter Brown has observed, "the language of the Song of Songs ... came, in the course of the fourth century, to settle heavily, almost exclusively, on the body of the virgin woman".[54] While his articulation of the desire on which his ascetic program was founded did enable Jerome to explore his own body in the letter, he did not have available to him the kind of erotically-charged metaphor of desire that he used to construct Eustochium's body as ascetic text.

Interestingly, Jerome made one attempt in the letter to textualize his own body by using a female metaphor from Scripture. Describing to Eustochium his struggles with the "bubbling fires of lust" in the desert, Jerome casts himself in the role of the sinful woman of Luke 7:37-50, who had washed the feet of Jesus with her tears and dried them with her hair. "Helpless", Jerome wrote, "I threw myself at the feet of Jesus, watered them with tears, dried them with my hair, and I subdued my resistant body with weeks of fasting".[55] Sadly, this attempt at encoding his body with a textual metaphor was not theologically satisfying for Jerome. Unlike his troping of Eustochium's body with an ecstatically erotic metaphor of virginity, Jerome troped his own body with an image of prostitution, and it served only to remind him of his own lost virginity: "I do not blush with shame [in the face of] my wretchedness, rather I lament aloud that I am not now what I used to be".[56] This failed attempt at "feminizing" his body with a Scriptural metaphor is suggestive of the difficulty that the encoding of virginity as female presented for Jerome, since the literal male body is not easily metaphorized with images of closure and intactness. This may explain Jerome's obsession with Eustochium's body as the most appropriate field for the cultivation of ascetic virtue: as a paradigm, her body functioned as an erotic allure that fired his ascetic longings as well as his attempts to conceive his own body in an imaginal way.

It appears that Jerome was doubly bound by his physical maleness and loss of virginity and by his inability to find a Scriptural metaphor that would, by textualizing his body, safely remove him from the fiery *libido* of the flesh. Nonetheless, he experimented with languages to use for articulating his desire; these experiments, I will argue, can be seen as steps in Jerome's journey toward the paradigmatic goal that he so forcefully expresses under the sign of "Eustochium".

The space of Jerome's letter to Eustochium consists of oddly juxtaposed passages in which the presentation of Eustochium's idealized body gives way to Jerome's presentation of his own body. These shifts of focus are accompanied by shifts in language, for while the language of Scripture applies most successfully to Eustochium, the languages of memory and dream apply to Jerome. There is an intriguing passage in Aristotle's *Rhetoric* that can provide a helpful interpretive framework for understanding Jerome's presentation of his body in these ways. Aristotle defined desire as "a reaching out for the sweet"; in her discussion of this passage, Carson explains that he goes on to say that "the man who is reaching for some delight, whether in the future as hope or in the past as memory, does so by means of an act of imagination (*phantasia*)".[57] Desire is encoded imaginally, that is, in languages of figural perception. While Jerome did not have the imaginative code of the Song of Songs to use in constructing his erotic body, he did have the languages of memory and dream, or, in Aristotle's terms, languages of the past and the future. It was these that he used "to reach for delight" as he investigated the possibilities for articulating an imaginal body for himself.

There are two places in Jerome's letter where he is bodily present. The first is his memory of his years in the desert, in which he "writes" his remembered body with metaphors of *libido*, picturing himself as a lustful bag of bones, tormented body and soul by physical and psychic heat.[58] The second is his nightmare, a brutal projection of his future should he continue in his Ciceronian reading habits.[59] These two references to his person accord well with Aristotle's sense that desire, the reaching out for delight, is configured imaginatively either as a future hope or as a memory of the past. However much a nightmare experience of the future and a memory of a desert past may not seem to partake of delight, both the dream and the memory are exercises of *phantasia*, of imagination, and, most importantly, both are grounded in *erōs*.[60]

The languages of dream and memory are both erotic because they participate in lack—and here I petition the "wanting" and "lacking" dimensions of *erōs*, discussed earlier, that give the term "erotic" a meaning that is more encompassing than "mere" delight. In memory and dream, the imagination constructs as present objects that are literally absent. "Eros is lack", and, as Freud and many others both ancient and modern have shown, "that which is known, attained, possessed, cannot be an object of desire".[61] What Jerome did not possess was his body, that is, the metaphoric body that would make union with God, the object of his desire, possible. In memory and dream, then, he constructed an imaginal body, a move that, paradoxically, both displaced his literal body and underscored its problems all the more forcefully.

The other of the self that Jerome desired was the ideal face of his soul's divinity, the union of his flesh with God.[62] Such unachievable perfection was tauntingly seductive, and I suggest that it was with a sense of the impossibility of what was nonetheless an "amatory law" that Jerome remembered and dreamed his body. What he found there was lack and an uncomfortable feeling that something was missing, that his body was too "open" and not yet virginally "closed". In this regard, Carson has written that, "reaching for an object that proves to be outside and beyond himself, the lover is provoked to notice that self and its limits. From a new vantage point, which we might call self-consciousness, he looks back and sees a hole ... Desire for an object *that he never knew he lacked* is defined, by a shift of distance, as desire for a necessary part of himself".[63] Having constructed his paradigm in his rewriting of Eustochium's female body, Jerome could explore the "gaps" in his own body as part of his journey to a closed "female" body of his own.

In his letter, Jerome offers both of his personal reminiscences to Eustochium as illustrative warnings about the dangers of the ascetic commitment. Since he presents the memory of his days in the desert in section seven of the letter, and his dream in section thirty, I will deal with the memory first, although in chronological terms it is probable that the dream preceded Jerome's stay in the desert.[64]

Just prior to his account of his experience in the desert, Jerome had been telling Eustochium about the inner heat that attacks the senses: "lust [*libido*] titillates the senses" and "the seductive fire of sensual pleasure floods us with its sweet heat".[65] Such inner heat, for Jerome a phenomenon both physical and psychological, apparently reminded him of the literal heat of the desert sun; it was a libidinal theory of the body that triggered his memory.

> When I was living in the desert, in that vast solitude ... inflamed by the burning heat of the sun, how many times did I imagine myself amid the delights of Rome! ... Although in my fear of hell I had condemned myself to this prison, with scorpions and wild beasts as my only companions, I was often surrounded by troups of dancing girls. My skin was pale with fasting but, though my frame was chilled, my mind was burning with desire, and the fires of lust bubbled up while my flesh was barely alive. Helpless, I threw myself at the feet of Jesus, watered them with my tears, dried them with my hair, and I subdued my resistant body with weeks of fasting. I do not blush with shame in the face of my wretchedness, rather I lament aloud that I am not now what I used to be ... I feared my cell as though it knew my thoughts.[66]

As with Eustochium, Jerome pictures himself as enclosed, he in a cell, she in a garden. Her garden, however, is sealed, while his cell opens on a torrid landscape of psychic fever.

Peter Brown has described this passage as an "artistically brilliant contraposto of the sweltering body of the monk and the untamed sexual drives of his mind".[67] However, apart from the opening reference to the burning desert sun, Jerome describes his body as literally icy cold, his flesh as good as dead. The literal pallor and chill of a body ravaged by ascetic fasting was not matched by a cooling of desire; indeed, Jerome's libidinal imagination was producing dancing girls by the dozen. As with the evil virgin described earlier, Jerome's literal body was not a trustworthy mirror of the condition of his psyche. I suggest that Jerome's opening picture of himself as *exusta solis ardoribus*, "inflamed by the burning heat of the sun", is a portrayal of his *imaginal*, not his literal, body. *Exusta*, from *exuro*, can carry the metaphorical sense of "inflamed" as well as the literal sense of "burned" or "dried up".[68] Whatever one might say about his actual body, it was the "body" of his imagination that was on fire.

It was this kind of passage that led an older generation of scholars to view the basis of asceticism as a dualistic split between body and soul; hatred and therefore punishment of the body were the complement of spiritual devotion.[69] A newer generation of scholars has almost completely reversed this view. In the words of Brown, "Seldom, in ancient thought, had the body been seen as more deeply implicated in the transformation of the soul; and never was it made to bear so heavy a burden ... In the desert tradition, the body was allowed to become the discreet mentor of the proud soul".[70] I agree with this perspective as an overview, but in Jerome's case I think it needs to be qualified. Given his flight from the actual body and his attempts to construct a paradigm of an ideal body in his letter to Eustochium, the question that presents itself is: *which* body served as mentor to the soul? It would appear that only the body-as-metaphor could serve Jerome as psychic tutor.

In his epistolary textualization of himself in this memory-space of desire, Jerome has taken the steps he took when writing women's bodies: he has noted his own gross physicality, and he has then shifted his vision to a bodily metaphor—the chorus of girls—to signal his psychic condition. What he has not yet attained, however, is a poetic body that would allow him to express his erotic drives in a register other than the carnal. The one Scriptural image that he does find in the passage quoted above, the Lukan image of the penitent prostitute, only underscores his dilemma. Lacking, then, a transformative Scriptural body, Jerome remained too open to the fearful articulations of his *libido.* Only by assuming the character of language in the mode of the chaste eroticism of the Eustochium-paradigm could Jerome unite his physical and psychic bodies in that "third" body where erotic expression could be given free rein.

Harpham has written that the man who went to the desert had placed himself "under a virtual obligation to reinvent himself".[71] The self of the ascetic in the desert was an unfinished work of art for whom "the personal is the trivial; it is that which must be sacrificed in the interests of form".[72] This was exactly Jerome's situation in the desert, at least, this was Jerome's situation in his written memorial of his experience in the desert. In this textualization of his memory, he was struggling to banish the personal and, like his view of Eustochium, to become the form of his own imaginal body. That he took a step toward the final chiseling of his self in the desert is not part of his narrative to Eustochium, but we know from elsewhere that he did take that step, and he did it in and by language.

Given the specific Scriptural images that Jerome used to rearticulate Eustochium's body, it is interesting that, while he was in the desert, he asked Rufinus to send him a copy of a then-popular commentary on the Song of Songs.[73] It would seem that, burning with "heat" as he was at that time, he needed textual images of eroticism to gratify his own blazing body. The language of the Song of Songs was not, however, the language that provoked a turn in Jerome's relation with his carnality; rather, that language was Hebrew.

In a letter written some thirty years after his stay in the desert, Jerome wrote:

> When I was a young man walled in by the solitude of the desert, I was unable to resist the allurements of vice and the hot passions of my

nature. Although I tried to crush them with repeated fastings, my mind was in a turmoil with sinful thoughts. To bring it under control, I made myself the pupil of a Christian convert from Judaism. After the subtlety of Quintillian, the flowing eloquence of Cicero, the dignified prose of Fronto, the smooth grace of Pliny, I set myself to learn an alphabet and strove to pronounce hissing, breath -demanding words.[74]

Language—in this case, the Scriptural language of Hebrew—provided Jerome with a refuge from his body. But it also proved itself to be an erotic outlet, with its "hissing words" that made him literally "pant" for breath.[75] Only by submerging his desire in a language that took his breath away could he begin to experience the closure for which he longed. Jerome had discovered that his fasting could not satisfy the voracious hunger of his inner self. Contrary to his ascetic expectations, a hungry body did not make for a chaste *libido*.[76] Like the haiku poet who said,

> I can't eat all this
> Lust

Jerome found another way in which to engage his desire.[77]

Moving from Jerome's memory of the desert to his dream, it will again become apparent that his goal was to cure his body through language. The idea that language might be a therapy of the body is not unique, it would appear, to contemporary psychoanalysis; it was already at work in Jerome's quest for healing.[78] Particularly in his account of his famous dream in the letter to Eustochium, there is explicit evidence of a conviction that a new language, the language of Scripture, could bring Jerome closer to his ideal body.

Jerome recounts his dream to Eustochium in the course of advising her not to be overly eloquent either in her pronunciation of words or in her choice of reading material. He characterizes such trifling with language by using, typically, a sexual metaphor: such trifling is an "adultery of the tongue".[79] He follows this with his well-known paraphrase of Tertullian: "What has Horace to do with the psalter, Virgil with the gospels, Cicero with the Apostle?".[80] As though in direct answer to those questions, Jerome then narrates his dream. He prefaces the narrative of the dream with an account of the beginning of his ascetic practice: unable to give up his beloved library, he would fast—only to be able afterwards to read Cicero as a reward for his labors. So too with Plautus and, by implication, the rest of the secular corpus that he so admired. Sadly, he remembers, the style of the Scriptures seemed "rude and repellent" by comparison.[81] According to

Jerome, "the serpent was sporting [*inluderet*] with" him, just as the Bridegroom will later "sport" (*ludat*) with Eustochium.⁸² However, the serpent's play ensnared Jerome in a clash of forms and a reluctance to reinvent himself; such sporting produced, not a re-made body like Eustochium's, but a deadly fever. In the midst of this illness, Jerome dreamed.

> Suddenly I was caught up in the spirit and dragged up to the tribunal of a judge ... Asked about my identity, I replied, "I am a Christian". And he who sat [behind the tribunal] said, "You are lying; you are a Ciceronian, not a Christian; for where your treasure is, there is where your heart is also". Immediately I became mute, and, amid the floggings—for he had ordered that I be beaten—I was tortured more strongly by the fire of conscience, pondering within myself that verse, "In hell who shall acknowledge you?". Nevertheless I began to cry out and woefully to say: "Have mercy on me, Lord, have mercy on me". Amid the lashings this sound rang out. Finally those who were standing around, falling down on their knees before the one who was presiding, begged that he have mercy on my youth and give me the opportunity for penitence. There would be more torture at a later point if I were ever again to read pagan literary books ... I began to make an oath and, calling on his name as witness, I said: "Lord, if at any time [in the future] I possess pagan writings or read them, I will have denied you". Dismissed after this oath, I returned to the upper world ... This was not an idle dream ... My shoulders were black and blue, and I felt the bruises after I awoke from sleeping. Thenceforth I read the divine books with much more eagerness than I had read the books of human beings".⁸³

The picture of himself that the dream presented to Jerome is very much like his portrayal of himself in the desert. There, determined to forget or somehow beat his body into submission, he was obsessed with images of women's bodies.⁸⁴ Caught between two literalisms—that is, a negative theology of his own carnality, on the one hand, and a possessive sexualization of women, on the other—desire wreaked havoc on him both psychically and physically. Likewise, the dream also presents Jerome to himself as a battleground, and again his body is the locus of the clash, this time a clash of cultures, one secular and the other religious. In both memory and dream, Jerome reveals that he had suffered the delicious return of what he had tried to repress. Cicero and the dancing girls would not give way to Scripture and chastity.

Although Jerome prefaces this dream with a lucid account of the condition that provoked the dream, I think it is the case that he was not conscious of his schizoid swing between denial and gratification until after the dream had occurred. As Aristotle said, the one who is impelled by desire reaches for delight by means of an act of imagination. One cannot know one's desire apart from such acts.

In the dream theory of late antiquity, the dream was a phenomenon of imagination in two particular ways.[85] First, theorists and ordinary dreamers alike thought that dreams were predictive of the future—not "merely" predictive but deeply revelatory of the flow in time of configurations embedded in the present.[86] Jerome's dream, for example, shows him the necessary outcome of his present conflicted condition, and marks that condition on his very body with bruises, the physical tokens of his imaginal experience. A second aspect of late antique culture's understanding of dreams that is important to bring to bear on Jerome's dream is their source. Dreams were not considered to be *personal* acts of imagination originating in the inner self of the dreamer but were rather thought to be presentations to the dreamer by an extra-personal figure, usually divine.[87] Again, Jerome has no doubt about the truth and divinity of this dream, or of others that he mentions elsewhere.[88]

Dreams, then, were thought to deal with the hidden present, a present not accessible to the consciousness of the dreamer until the dream itself appeared. What a dream presents is the "other" of the conventionally constituted self, since the self presented by the dream does not match the dreamer's (prior) self-perception. The dream is a picture of a self that does not yet exist; it is a text of desire, founded on lack. Further, since the source of dreams was located in otherness—in God—the dream presents the dreamer to himself as "written" by what is other to himself. The "I" of the dreamer is estranged from itself, decentered and reformulated.

Harpham notes that St. Anthony urged his desert followers to write down their dreams, thus, in his words, "moving textuality into the undisclosed regions of the self".[89] From this perspective, Jerome's dream is doubly textual and also doubly disclosive. Written in the letter to Eustochium, the dream is a text that is about text, and it reveals not only an undisclosed region of Jerome's self but also an unknown aspect of his body. In Jerome's case, writing down his dream issued in a textualization of the unknown self that he desired; but it also produced a physicalization of his inner self. The unknown self that comes to consciousness in Jerome's dream—the self split between a desire for style and a desire for religious sensibility—is played out entirely on the body of the oneiric Jerome. Like Eustochium's, his body is a space of desire, and it is on his body that his quest for his own imaginal form is pursued.

The dream writes Jerome's body just as Jerome wrote Eustochium's body. In both instances, the language out of which the desired body is constructed is Scriptural language—literally, for Eustochium, in the images of the Song of Songs, and potentially, for Jerome, in the turn from secular to sacred literature. Jerome, waking up with black and blue shoulders, did not quite manage the ideally closed and untouchable body of metaphor that he concocted for Eustochium and, as any reader of the text in which this dream-text is embedded knows, he did not keep the oath he made in the dream even in the letter in which he tells the dream, studded as it is with allusions to the very classical texts that he supposedly foreswore.[90] Still, the idea that drives Jerome's letter, that is, the idea that language can be a therapy of the body, rewriting it in voluptuous imaginal terms, is present in the dream-text's picture of Jerome suffering the forging of a new language in the fabricated body of his imagination.

Encoded in Jerome's bruises were the signifiers of his desire, a desire to reinvent himself in Scriptural terms. Much more so than his memory of the desert, the dream encapsulates and brings to expression the intricate relationships among body, desire, and language that fuel the letter's passion. Although memory too is a desirous act of imagination, it retains the possibility of an historical kernel, a remembered contour of the self from the past. A dream, however, is entirely fictive; as a phantasmatic signifier of what is other to and lacking in the self, it is a pure projection of desire and so was a particularly fitting vehicle for Jerome's rearticulation of the body—his own, and, in fact, Eustochium's as well.

What my discussion has suppressed to this point is that the most heavily eroticized passage in Jerome's letter to Eustochium, the moment when her body is aroused by the sexual foreplay of the bridegroom, is presented by Jerome as a dream! Here are his words: "The secrets of your bedchamber always guard you; your bridegroom always sports with you on the inside. Do you pray?: you speak to the bridegroom. Do you read?: he speaks to you. And, when sleep comes upon you, he will come behind the wall and put his hand through the opening and touch your inner body, and trembling you will rise up and say, 'I am wounded by love'".[91] As a representation of the self's otherness, the dream served Jerome well as a vehicle for the ideal body, wholly external to its own carnality yet voluptuous nonetheless, ephemeral in its poetic composition yet tangible as a textual "magnet for erotic interest".[92]

A written dream is a curious combination of the ephemeral—the dream—and the permanent—the text. It is a paradoxical construction that matches perfectly the erotically chaste body of Jerome's desire. As I have pursued this paradox through Jerome's letter to Eustochium, I have not, of course, been reading Jerome's understanding of the intentionality of his text. I have been following a figuration of the text's imagistic structure. Interestingly, a subsequent exchange between Jerome and Eustochium suggest that she, too, had perceived the erotic underpinnings of her mentor's ascetic advice.

Jerome probably sent his letter to Eustochium in the early Spring of C.E. 384. Some weeks later, at the end of June, Eustochium sent Jerome some presents to mark the feast of St. Peter, a celebratory day for Roman Christians.[93] We know about these presents because Jerome wrote another letter to Eustochium thanking her for the gifts.[94] To the man who had recently configured her as the erotic bride of the Song of Songs, Eustochium sent a letter, bracelets, doves, and a basket of cherries. Unfortunately we do not have Eustochium's letter to Jerome, but it is hard to believe that his earlier letter was not on her mind, since in it Jerome refers so often to the passage in the Song of Songs in which the bridegroom calls his lover a dove.[95] In the form of a gift of doves, Eustochium sent to Jerome a token of her imaginal body.

At the beginning of this second letter, Eustochium's erotic response to him seems to have escaped Jerome, who devotes half of his text to an exploration of the hidden significance of her gifts of a letter, doves, and bracelets. He converts them into a threefold warning: "Take care that you do not abandon the ornaments of good works, which are the true bracelets of the arms. Do not tear the letter written on your heart as the wicked king cut with a penknife the letter brought by Baruch. Do not let Hosea say to you as to Ephraim, 'You are like a silly dove'".[96] The doves, bracelets, and letter are all explained by way of Scriptural passages. Deflecting the gifts from himself, Jerome is again writing Eustochium's body, but this time it is a moralistic, not an erotic, body.

Halfway through this letter, Jerome finally thanks Eustochium for her gifts in a tone that suggests that he realized that his moralizing allegories might seem a rather sharp way to receive presents. He names in particular the cherries, which he has not mentioned to this point. "Still, lest I seem to slight your gifts", he writes, "I accept them, especially the basket filled with cherries so fine and blushing with such virgin modesty".[97] Writing what Kelly calls "an almost skittish reference to the colour of the cherries, which recalls a virgin's blushes",[98] Jerome immediately displaces the cherries, since there are no Scriptural references to them, and speaks of figs instead, also in a moralizing tone. His deferral and displacement of these cherries suggests that Jerome actually did perceive an *erōs* in Eustochium's presents, and it made him "skittish". Why? Why could the man who had so eroticized this young woman's body, transferring it so completely to an imaginal register, not accept the round, red tokens of the space of her desire?

Jerome's attempt to erase the literal body by reimagining it as an assembly of textual metaphors appears not to have worked. Even the poeticized body was dangerous. Despite recent scholarly attempts to view positively the place of the body in asceticism, Jerome was fleeing from the body, even as he constructed seemingly "safe" poeticized versions of it. However erotic that poetic body of metaphor was, and however paradoxical was his figuration of asceticism, Jerome's distaste for carnality (and his pull toward it) was so strong that, instead of achieving a union of flesh and soul in the textual body of his dreams, he produced a split between them that was all the more dangerous because his paradigm was so physically poetic, so appealing as a mirror of desire. Had he accepted the cherries with delight, the end of my story would be different. But the cherries, I think, provoked in him that untamed libidinous fire that is the other side of bodily repression. In fact, unlike the poet with whom this paper began, for whom words are *as* voluptuous *as the flesh*, Jerome displaced all of his desire onto words, leaving the fleshly body prey to the schizoid situation he was trying to overcome.

Jerome's second letter to Eustochium shows that his attempt in his first letter to construct a space of desire in which a union of flesh and spirit could take place ended in a fetishization of language. And his rewriting of the body—woman's body in particular—made *it* a fetish as well. When female sexuality is identified with textuality, as it often has been, the woman's body becomes a "blank page" to be written by men, and its "fearful power to articulate itself" is allowed only the channels of ephemeral virginity or pornographic carnality.[99] Finally, Jerome's vision of an imaginal female body universally available as the goal of religious *erōs* was only a "tragic way of killing a woman", to borrow the title of a recent book.[100] It was also a tragic way of killing a man, as his own biographical sketches in the letter to Eustochium show. He never achieved the poetic closure that he projected as his ideal body because the ideal itself did not take the body seriously, and he remained a slave to sexual lust.[101]

"Desire is quenched by desire" is a dangerous battle cry on the field of the body.[102] It closes the space that *eroōs* needs in order to flourish.

Notes

1 Creeley, "Love", in idem, *Later*, p. 18. *Later* is copyright © 1970 by Robert Creeley. Reprinted by permission of New Directions Publishing Corp.
2 This phrase is taken from Carson, *Eros the Bittersweet*, p. 31.
3 See the discussion of Wiesen, *St. Jerome as a Satirist*, p. 7. Late in his life Jerome still saw his youthful self in his dreams as "curly-headed, dressed in my toga, declaiming a controversial thesis in front of the rhetorician" (*C. Ruf.* 1.30 [PL 23.422B]).
4 For issues of dating Jerome's letters, I have followed the chronology of Kelly, *Jerome*; for the date of the letter to Eustochium *(Ep.* 22), see p. 100.
5 Kelly, *Jerome*, pp. 100-1; see also Cavallera, *Saint Jérome*, vol. 1, pp. 104-13; Wiesen, *St. Jerome*, pp. 68-74.
6 Kelly, *Jerome*, p. 102.
7 For a discussion of Jerome's circle of women friends in Rome, see Clark, *Jerome, Chrysostom, and Friends*, pp. 44-79; Kelly, *Jerome*, pp. 91-103; Rousseau, *Ascetics, Authority, and the Church*, pp. 108-13.
8 Wiesen, *St. Jerome*, p. 164; Clark, *Jerome, Chrysostom, and Friends*, p. 45.
9 *Ep.* 22.1.2-5, 2.1, 6.2, 17.4, 24.1-25.1, 26.2, 35.3 (CSEL 54.144-46, 150-52, 166, 176-79, 181, 198).
10 *Ep.* 22.3.1 (CSEL 54.146).
11 *Ep.* 22.2.1 (CSEL 54.146).
12 Wiesen, *St. Jerome*, p. 164; Clark, *Jerome, Chrysostom, and Friends*, p. 45.
13 Clark, *Jerome, Chrysostom, and Friends*, pp. 47, 75-76.
14 For discussions of these issues of authorial and textual intentionality, see Foucault, "What is an Author?"; Barthes, "The Death of the Author".
15 *Ep.* 22.4.1 (CSEL 54.148) and throughout the letter. See the discussion by Brown, *The Body and Society*, pp. 376-77, who remarks that, for Jerome, "the human body remained a darkened forest, filled with the roaring of wild beasts, that could be controlled only by rigid codes of diet and by the strict avoidance of occasions for sexual attraction ... Men and women were irreducibly sexual beings" (p. 376).
16 *Ep.* 22.6.4 (CSEL 54.151).
17 *Ep.* 22.8.2-3 (CSEL 54.154-55). On the medical view of the body as a "little fiery universe", see Brown, *The Body and Society*, pp. 17-20; on Jerome's reliance on medical advice concerning avoidance of foods, including wine, that might increase the body's heat, see Rousselle, *Porneia*, p. 174. Doctors recommended a dietary regimen of cool and dry food for reducing sexual desire (Rouselle, *Porneia*, p. 19).
18 Brown, *The Body and Society*, pp. 223-37, and Rousselle, *Porneia*, pp. 141-59, for ascetics' use of the body to articulate the desires of the soul.
19 *Ep.* 22.8 (CSEL 54.154-56), wine and food; 22.10-11 (CSEL 54.157-59), gluttony, luxury, dainty food; 22.13-14 (CSEL 54.160-62), false virgins with swelling wombs, clothing; 22.16 (CSEL 54.163-64), clothes as signifiers of inner disposition; 22.17 (CSEL 54.164-66), skin color; 22.27 (CSEL 54.182-84), physical gestures of false humility; 22.29 (CSEL54.186-89), affected speech. See Wiesen, *St. Jerome*, pp. 119-65.
20 *Ep.* 22.32 (CSEL 54.193-95), the rich widow; 22.27 (CSEL 54.184), simulation of fasting.

21	This phrase is from Gubar, "'The Blank Page' and the Issues of Female Creativity", p. 76. Gubar traces the history, in Western culture, of woman's body as a "blank page" written on by men, with an emphasis on the nineteenth and twentieth centuries.
22	Wiesen, *St. Jerome*, pp. 7-15, 119-28 on the satirical elements in *Ep.* 22.
23	Brown, *The Body and Society*, pp. 376-77, discusses Jerome's "definitive sexualization of Paul's notion of *the flesh*" (emphasis in original).
24	*Ep.* 22.5.3 (CSEL 54.150).
25	*Ep.* 22.6.2-3 (CSEL 54.150-51).
26	*Ep.* 22.6.2-3 (CSEL 54.151). The Biblical quotations are from Jer. 13:26 ("I myself will lift up your skirts over your face, and your shame will be seen") and Ezek. 16:25 ("At the head of every street you built your lofty place and prostituted your beauty, offering yourself to any passerby, and multiplying your harlotry").
27	*Ep.* 22.11.1 (CSEL 54.158). Jerome supports this image with a concatenation of verses from Job, Ps., Gen., Ex., Matt., Lk., and Ezek.
28	For a discussion of other ways in which Jerome attempted to transform the femaleness of his friends, see Clark, *Jerome, Chrysostom, and Friends*, pp. 48-59.
29	*Ep.* 22.21.7 (CSEL 54.173).
30	I owe this play on the words "something" and "nothing" to D. Miller, "Why Men Are Mad!", pp. 71-79.
31	*Ep.* 22.2.1, 6.2, 8.1, 16.1, 20.2, 25.1-26.4 (CSEL 54.145, 151, 154, 163, 170-71, 178-82): "God's bride"; *Ep.* 22.18.2 (CSEL 54.167): "paradise of virginity"; *Ep.* 22.1.5 (CSEL 54.145): "washed white".
32	*Ep.* 22.17.1, 25.2 (CSEL 54.164-65, 179).
33	*Ep.* 22.1.5, 6.2, 25.1 (CSEL 54.145, 151, 178-79).
34	*Ep.* 22.25.1-5 (CSEL 54.178-80); this is the most extended passage in the letter in which Jerome eroticizes Eustochium's body with imagery from the Song of Songs.
35	*Ep.* 22.25.1 (CSEL 54.179). Song of Songs 5.4 is translated by the RSV as "My beloved put his hand to the latch, and my *heart* was thrilled within me". Translations of Jerome's *Ep.* 22.25.1 render Jerome's quotation of this verse as follows: "He will come behind and put his hand through the hole of the door, and your *heart* shall be moved for him" *(NPNF*, 2nd ser., vol. 3, p. 498); "He 'will put his hand through the opening and will touch your body'" *(ACW* 33, vol. 1, p. 152). My own translation ("He will put his hand through the opening and your *inner body* will be moved for him") attempts to be more faithful to Jerome's use of the Latin *venter* to translate the Greek *koilia* and the Hebrew *ma'im*. The Hebrew *ma'im* does not mean either "heart" or "body", as the translations above would have it. It means, rather, "internal organs", "inward parts", "belly", "womb" (see Brown, Driver, Briggs, *Hebrew and English Lexicon of the Old Testament*, s.v. *mah*). Similarly, the Greek *koilia*, used by the Septuagint to translate the Hebrew *ma'im*, means "cavity of the body", especially the intestines, bowels, and womb (Liddell, Scott, Jones, A *Greek-English Lexicon*, s.v. *koilia*). The word *venter* carries the same meanings (Lewis and Short, *A Latin Dictionary*, s.v. *venter)*. My translation of this term as "inner body" attempts to be more faithful both to etymology and to the erotic suggestiveness of the verse.
36	*Ep.* 22.17.4 (CSEL 54.166).
37	Kelly, *Jerome*, p. 103.
38	Harpham, *Ascetic Imperative*, p. 46.
39	Kristeva, *Tales of Love*, p. 97.
40	Ibid., pp. 96, 94, 97.
41	*Ep.* 22.40.5 (CSEL 54.209).

42 Harpham, *Ascetic Imperative*, 45.
43 Calvino, *Uses of Literature*, pp. 67-68.
44 See the remarks of Harpham, *Ascetic Imperative*, pp. 70-71: "We may recall how Jerome's formula, 'Desire is quenched by desire', offers a rhetorical and figural substitute for the gratifications of the senses that the ascetic denies himself. Such a strategy permits the entry of desire, even of lust and wantonness, into the arena of denial that constitutes the official program of asceticism ... In figurality ascetic writers discovered an element in language that enabled them to recover and, in a sense, control the world they had renounced".
45 See Jardine, *Gynesis*, p. 25 and passim, for a statement in terms of modern literature of a phenomenon that also occurred in antiquity, namely, that what is other to the self is "coded as *feminine*, as *woman*" (italics in original).
46 Carson, *Eros the Bittersweet*, p. 10.
47 Harpharn, *Ascetic Imperative*, p. 132.
48 See Kelly, *Jerome*, pp. 210-20; Clark, *Jerome, Chrysostom, and Friends*, p. 47.
49 In addition to *Ep.* 22, see also *Ep.* 54 (CSEL 54.466-85 [to Furia]), *Ep.* 107 (CSEL 55.290-305 [to Laeta]), and *Ep.* 125 (CSEL 56.118-42 [to Rusticus]).
50 Carson, *Eros the Bittersweet*, p. 91-110.
51 Ibid., p. 92.
52 Ibid., p. 30.
53 Harpham, *Ascetic Imperative*, p. 20, describes asceticism as "an attempt by human beings to stand 'outside the world' by assuming the character of language". Also, " ... asceticism is an application to the self of certain insights into language: to be ascetic is to make oneself representable" (p. 27).
54 Brown, *The Body and Society*, p. 274; see also Clark, "The Uses of the Song of Songs", an essay that shows in detail how Latin authors, especially Jerome, appropriated the Song of Songs for ascetic purposes.
55 *Ep.* 22.7.3 (CSEL 54.153); my thanks are due to Elizabeth A. Clark for calling this passage to my attention.
56 *Ep.* 22.7.3 (CSEL 54.153); for discussion of the identity of the Lukan woman as a prostitute, see Schüssler Fiorenza, *In Memory of Her*, pp. 127-29; on Jerome's reference to his loss of virginity in *Ep.* 49.20.2 (CSEL 54.385), see Kelly, *Jerome*, p. 21.
57 Aristotle, *Rhet.* 1370a6, quoted and translated in Carson, *Eros the Bittersweet*, p. 63.
58 *Ep.* 22.7.1-4 (CSEL 54.152-54).
59 *Ep.* 22.30.3-6 (CSEL 54.190-91).
60 For discussion by Jerome's contemporaries on these issues, see Augustine, *Conf.* 10, where memory is discussed as a storehouse of images, and Synesius of Cyrene, *De som.* 3-5, on the connection between dreams and imagination.
61 Carson, *Eros the Bittersweet*, p. 65.
62 *Ep.* 22.40.5 (CSEL 54.209).
63 Carson, *Eros the Bittersweet*, pp. 32-33 (italics in original).
64 Kelly, *Jerome*, p. 41.
65 *Ep.* 22.6.4 (CSEL 54.151); Jerome again discusses the topic of "innate heat" in *Ep.* 54.9 (CSEL 54.475), appealing for authority to the Greek physician Galen. For the evidence from ancient medical writings on this and related topics, see Rousselle, *Porneia*, pp. 5-23.
66 *Ep.* 22.7.1-4 (CSEL 54.152-54).
67 Brown, *The Body and Society*, p. 376.

68	Lewis and Short, *A Latin Dictionary*, s.v. *exuro*.
69	Emblematic of this generation is Dodds, *Pagan and Christian in an Age of Anxiety* pp. 29-36: "[C]ontempt for the human condition and hatred of the body was a disease endemic in the entire culture of the period" (p. 35). See Brown, *The Body and Society*, p. 235, nn. 103-104, for further examples.
70	Brown, *The Body and Society*, pp. 235, 237.
71	Harpham, *Ascetic Imperative*, p. 24.
72	Ibid., p. 25.
73	*Ep.* 5.2.2 (CSEL 54.22); see Kelly, *Jerome*, p. 48.
74	*Ep.* 125.12 (CSEL 56.13 1), trans. by Kelly, *Jerome*, p. 50.
75	See Kelly, *Jerome*, p. 50, n. 17: "The participle *anhelantia* (lit. 'panting') refers to the drawing of breath required for pronouncing certain aspirate or guttural sounds in Hebrew". Such forceful drawing-in of the breath would require a correlatively forceful exhalation.
76	On the relation between food and sexuality in ascetic thinking, see Rousselle, *Porneia*, pp. 160-78. Both doctors and ascetics subscribed to the idea that a severely restricted diet would reduce sexual urges, and Jerome was no exception (see n. 65 above); in his case, however, the diet didn't work.
77	This haiku is by Morimoto Norio and is quoted in Sato, *One Hundred Frogs*, p. 143.
78	For a good contemporary discussion of Freud's "talking cure" and its therapeutic effects on the body, especially on the bodies of hysterics, see Hunter, "Hysteria, Psychoanalysis, and Feminism".
79	*Ep.* 22.29.6 (CSEL 54.188).
80	*Ep.* 22.29.7 (CSEL 54.189); for Tertullian's famous exclamation, "What has Athens to do with Jerusalem, or what has the Academy in common with the church?", see *Praescr. haer.* 7 (CSEL 70. 10).
81	*Ep.* 22.30.2 (CSEL 54.189).
82	*Ep.* 22.30.3, 25.1 (CSEL 54.190, 178).
83	*Ep.* 22.30.3-5 (CSEL 54.190-91).
84	This was a frequent occurrence among the ascetics of the desert. See Rousselle, Porneia, p. 153; Brown, *The Body and Society*, pp. 230-37.
85	See n. 56 above; for discussion, see Miller, "Re-imagining the Self in Dreams", pp. 40-42.
86	For a discussion of the relation of dreams to the future, see Miller, "A Dubious Twilight", p. 158; see also Steiner, "The Historicity of Dreams", p. 13, and Price, "The Future of Dreams", for discussions that differentiate late antiquity's orientation of dreams toward the future from Freud's reading of dreams in terms of the past.
87	On the divinity and autonomy of dreams in ancient theory, see Miller, "A Dubious Twilight", pp. 157, 160-61.
88	Jerome remarks in *Ep.* 22.30.6 (CSEL 54.191) that his was not a *vana somnia*, an "idle dream". See also *Ep.* 107.5 (CSEL 55.295), in which Jerome narrates the fulfillment of a dream in real life with no doubt about the causal connection between the dream and the event. In his *C. Ruf.* 1.30-31 (PL 23.421B-424A), Jerome later reversed himself on this topic, calling dreams "vague fancies". But in this case his back was against the wall, since Rufinus, in his *Apol.* 2.6-8 (CCL 20.87-90), had accused Jerome of failing the dream and his oath never to read secular literature again. In self-defense, Jerome objects to being taunted with a "mere dream" and says that the promise made in the dream pertained to the future; if he still quotes secular literature, it is from memory, which he can't erase, not from his post-oneiric reading

practices. Thus Jerome both retains and denies the authenticity of the dream in *C. Ruf.*

89   Harpham, *Ascetic Imperative*, p. 14.
90   Wiesen, *St. Jerome*, pp. 119-27, esp. p. 126; see also Kelly, *Jerome*, p. 43.
91   Ep. 22.25.1 (CSEL 54.178-79).
92   This phrase is from Harpham, *Ascetic Imperative*, p. 51.
93   Kelly, *Jerome*, p. 100.
94   *Ep.* 31 (CSEL 54.249-51).
95   *Ep.* 22.24.6, 26.2, 35.3 (CSEL 54.178, 181, 198).
96   *Ep.* 31.2 (CSEL 54.250); the Scriptural references are to 1 Tim 2:10; 2 Cor 3:2; Jer. 36:23; Hos 7:11.
97   *Ep.* 31.3 (CSEL 54.251).
98   Kelly, *Jerome*, p. 100.
99   See Gubar, "The Blank Page", p. 89, for a discussion of how "woman has been defined symbolically in the patriarchy as a tabula rasa, a lack, a negation, an absence". For a discussion of the movement in Western culture between repression and promiscuity and pornography, see Paris, *Pagan Meditations*, pp. 11-78, esp. pp. 71-78.
100 Loraux, *Tragic Ways of Killing a Woman*. This is a study of the manner in which the heroines of Greek tragedy were put to death; in his comments on the jacket of the book, John Winkler summed up its import succinctly: "In studying the reasons and methods of death, Loraux elicits the code or syntax of female honor from the language of male tragedy. Among other things she shows how the spectacle itself, with its various etiquettes of death, is an act of cultural violence to the mythological heroines it portrays".
101 See Kelly, *Jerome*, p. 295, who discusses a passage from Jerome's *Comm. Amos* 2, pro. (CCL 76.263-64); written when he was in his mid-seventies, this passage "lays bare his guilt-ridden psychology". It shows that, in his old age, Jerome was still bothered by, in his words, "that uniquely burdensome tyrant, sexual desire", which he continues to describe with metaphors of fire: "When one is old, the spark now and then glows among the burnt out ashes and tries to come to life, but it cannot get the blaze going".
102 *Ep.* 22.17.4 (CSEL 54.166).

Chapter Eight

Desert Asceticism and "The Body from Nowhere"

In the closing pages of his *Lausiac History*, Palladius exhorts his reader to "take the lives and labors" of the ascetics whose stories he has told as "a sufficient proof of the resurrection".[1] What can this possibly mean? How can a human life still being lived be proof of that drastic transformation from a physical body to a spiritual body so stunningly envisioned by Paul? What were the conditions of visual perception that made it possible for Palladius to see the "man of dust" as a "man of heaven" (1 Cor. 15:48)?

It may be that such conventional descriptions of ascetic persons as leading "heavenly" or "angelic" or "resurrected" lives were not mere metaphors of pious behavior but rather real indicators of a perceptual construct embedded within ascetic discourse. This perceptual construct enabled observers to "see" ascetic persons as performance artists, enacting the spiritual body in the here-and-now. This perceptual construct, moreover, was immensely satisfying—why else would a person like Palladius have undertaken such arduous journeys in the heat and expanse of the desert to observe these ascetic spectacles?[2] It may seem strange that the boringly repetitive and painfully self-mutilating practices of the desert ascetics provided a feast for the eyes; yet scopophilia—Freud's term for visual pleasure—appears to have been an important feature of perceptions of ascetic activity. What I wish to investigate are the conditions of this visual organization of meaning.

We know that Palladius was a voyeur. He himself tells us that he had "looked into every cave and hut of the monks of the desert with accuracy and pious intent".[3] This insistence on looking, together with its interesting defense of the motive for looking, is characteristic of what might be called desert reportage. Actually, petitioning the gaze may have been one of the premises of ascetic activity itself. Peter Brown, Geoffrey Harpham, and Edith Wyschogrod have all, in their various ways, noted that ascetic activity and visibility form a pair.[4] Ascetic behavior was a performance that petitioned an audience. As Harpham has noted, the ascetic was, "in his very solitude, constantly on display"; further, "we owe to asceticism the notion that the exemplary self is observable".[5]

I would like to add to this discussion a consideration of a curious feature of what Theodoret called "drawing benefit with the eyes".[6] This curious feature of the specular economy of desert reportage is that what those "eyes" claimed to "see" were practices that are frequently said in this literature to have been done in secret. For example, the author of the *Historia monachorum in Aegypto* notes about Ammon and the Tabbenisiots that "each one practices his own asceticism in secret"—and then goes on to relate those supposedly secret practices.[7] There are the stories of the solitary vagabonds, living lives like birds or fish or animals and fed by no human hand but by angels.[8] And there is the intriguing story of Theon, who "used to go out of his cell at night and keep company with wild animals"; according to the *Historia monachorum,* Theon had practiced silence for thirty years, communing with visitors by his gaze.[9] *He* did not tell the secret of his nocturnal socializing, being, as the text says, silent, and our author-observer does not reveal the source of his information.

It seems to me, however, that to ask about the desert reporters, "How did they know?", is to ask the wrong question. The kind of secret about which they were speaking was not the conventional kind of secret. The conventional kind of secret designates a thing not known or hidden from human apprehension; but desert reportage is filled with statements that affirm both the reliability of what has been seen and the "stereoscopic" quality of the observing gaze that penetrated the solitude of ascetic practices. I would rephrase this issue of the gaze as follows: ascetic practice enabled the observer to see something heretofore "secret", where secrecy is a code-word for an "other" kind of seeing. The secret in this secrecy is not hiddenness but another condition of visibility and thus of perception. Further, the ascetics' manipulation of their bodies was integral to this form of perception and cannot, I suggest, be understood apart from it.

It is obvious that ascetic practice was geared toward reshaping the body, but it is not so obvious how this reshaping could be viewed positively rather than negatively, for how, really, could desert reporters look at emaciated bodies, pustulated feet and torsos, bodies seared by red-hot irons, and say, "I saw many fathers living the angelic life"?[10] In an attempt to see as the author of the *Historia monachorum,* and many others, saw, I suggest that such reshapings can be viewed positively, not as acts directed in hatred and disgust against the body *per se,* but rather as acts directed against a way of perceiving the body.

A recent essay by Jean-Pierre Vernant will help toward understanding the perceptual construct embedded in the specular economy of desert reportage that allowed for a positive viewing of ascetic practices of the body. In this essay, entitled "Dim Body, Dazzling Body", Vernant argues that for Greeks of the archaic period the human body was conceptualized as a "dim" version of the "dazzling" bodies of the gods.[11] The human body was perceived by means of a comparative method in which the human was discerned by "deciphering all the signs that mark the human body with the seal of limitation, deficiency, incompleteness, and that make it a sub-body". Further, "this sub-body cannot be understood except in reference to what it presupposes: corporeal plenitude, a super-body, the body of the gods".[12] Judged according to the standards of this divine super-body, the human body is perceived as "ephemeral", "inconstant", "vulnerable to the vicissitudes of time flowing without return", with death as "a witness to its fragility".[13]

This perception of the body as the sign of human misfortune does not, however, conform to the Platonic, and later Cartesian, dichotomous model of human composition that splits the person into a positive soul or mind housed in a negative body construed as a prison or as a mechanistic object in space. As Vernant says, "man's misfortune is not that a divine and immortal soul finds itself imprisoned in the envelope of a material and perishable body, but that his body is not fully one"—that is, for the archaic Greeks, the problem is that the human body is not fully a body.[14]

It seems to me that this archaic employment of a comparative standard for perceiving human identity, as well as this model's use of the image of a divine, "dazzling" body as the privileged signifying ground of that "dim" human identity, was characteristic of early Christian desert asceticism as well. I would like to entertain the idea that, in desert asceticism, the body was perceived to be problematic, not because it was a body, but because it was not a body of plenitude. Although Christian theologians contemporary with desert asceticism, for example Gregory of Nyssa, had embraced the dichotomous Platonic view of the composition of the human person, they could not devalue the body to the level of prison completely if they were to affirm the positive valuation of the created world in Genesis, whose story of the paradisal Adam continued to be a central text for anthropological speculation.[15] By contrast, however, the insistent physicality of the phenomenon of desert asceticism, from the gangrenous leg of Symeon the Stylite to the blackened body of St. Mary of the desert, suggests that it was in the desert that the transformative implications of the Incarnation were put into practice. As Peter Brown has observed, "Through the Incarnation of Christ, the Highest God had reached down to make even the body capable of transformation".[16]

Thus when the body was viewed with despair and disgust, when it was altered by various practices of mutilation, this was not because of its sheer materiality as part of the physical world but rather because it functioned as a signifier of a lack that was not only spiritual but also corporeal. As Harpham has argued, the ascetic body was a disfigured body and, in his view, "the disfigured was figured as desirable" in opposition to classical canons of beauty now conceptualized by Christian ascetics as pagan demonism.[17] I agree with Harpham, but in my view there is more to the positive valuation of disfiguration than opposition to a cultural aesthetic: more importantly, the disfigured was figured as desirable as an act of defiance against the muted speech of the "sub-body". In this way asceticism can be understood as an attempt to manipulate the "dim" body so as to drive it as close as possible toward that corporeal vitality that is the mark of its exemplar. Asceticism, that is, attempts to control the play of the body as signifier; it attempts to reimagine how the body can be read, and what it can say.

The body of plenitude signified an existence that would defy the constraints of time and space. Hence desert reporters typically used metaphors of light to convey how this exemplary embodied self looked. According to the *Apophthegmata Patrum*, for example, the face of Abba Pambo shone like lightning, and Abba Sisoes' face shone like the sun.[18] The author of the *Historia monachorum* observed that Abba Or "looked just like an angel, and his face was so radiant that the sight of him alone filled one with awe".[19] Again in the *Apophthegmata*, the gazing eye saw the entire body of Abba Silvanus shining like an angel, while another old man appeared "entirely like a flame".[20] In the glare of such brilliance as that in the face of Abba Pambo, the observer saw "the image of the glory of Adam".[21] Theologians like Gregory of Nyssa, too, constructed Adam as a dazzling plenitude: Adam, exemplar of an original humanity once lost but retrieved by the incarnate Christ as the sign of human destiny. Totally lacking in the shadows that give perceptual contour to the dim bodies of historical existence, Adam's body "had been unimaginably different from our own", as Brown has explained. "It had been a faithful mirror of a soul which, itself, mirrored the utterly undivided, untouched simplicity of God. It was like the diaphanous radiance of a still midday sky".[22]

Urging the dim body toward the flash of its corporeal plenitude, ascetics "lived perched between particularity and grandeur", in Brown's phrase.[23] I would extend this statement concerning the perch between particularity and grandeur by suggesting that the ascetic view of the human body oscillated between two modes of visual perception that can be aligned with the two views of the body, one that marks its dimness or particularity and the other, its dazzle or grandeur. In her recent book *Saints and Postmodernism*, Edith Wyschogrod has described Maurice Merleau-Ponty's analysis of the two ways in which objects are constructed in visual perception. In a book entitled *Phenomenology of Perception*, Merleau-Ponty "claims that two primary factors govern perceiving, first, the horizon factor, the idea that objects are not seen by themselves but are picked out against a background, and, second, the wholeness factor, the idea that each object is perceptually discriminated as a totality".[24] Merleau-Ponty discussed these two modes of perceiving by using the example of looking at a house. From the perspective of the horizon factor, "I see the house next door from a certain angle, but it would be seen differently from the right bank of the Seine, or from the inside or from an airplane. The house is given against a backdrop which both stations and limits it, a visual horizon against which it comes forward or recedes and can be distinguished from other objects".[25] The second factor governing perception, the wholeness factor, is abstract in that it "suspends the actual spatial and temporal conditions of perception".[26] In this way of perceiving, the focus is not on "the figure-and-ground character of the visual field" but on the object itself. The house is not given all at once, yet the observer claims to see the whole by an act of "visual inference". This claim to see the whole by an act of visual inference is what Merleau-Ponty described as "the house seen from nowhere".[27]

Wyschogrod concludes by observing that "the phenomenon of the horizon as well as the multifaceted character of entities is integral to perception because human beings *are* their bodies. The view from nowhere and the inference to wholeness reflect perception's attempt to transcend the limitations of embodiment".[28] The problem, however, is that the human body is not a visible object like a house: "the body is not an object like others because one cannot distance oneself from one's own body so that it can give itself as a totality. I myself am that body".[29]

Viewed from the perspective of Merleau-Ponty's description of the two operations of visual perception, the ascetic imagination of the angelic super-body is precisely an attempt to view the body from nowhere, to give the body a totality by a paradoxical act of visual inference, paradoxical because the ascetic *is* the body that he is trying to see. When ascetics deride the body, they are viewing it from the perceptual perspective of the horizon; the dim body is the body seen in relation to its background or context—the context of historical time, the context of a body that seems fragmented into a congeries of its own needs and desires. Thus when a desert ascetic says about his body, "It kills me, I will kill it",[30] he is speaking not about the body *per se* but about the body perceived from the perspective of the horizon, whereas when a desert reporter looks at that same body and sees it shining like an angel, he is operating out of the perceptual perspective that infers wholeness, vision in the surround.

What I am suggesting is that asceticism constitutes an attempt to abandon the horizon and to "see from nowhere". Metaphors of light as evocations of the "true" body were so useful because one cannot "see" light, just as one cannot "see" one's own body whole. The lightning flash in the face of a desert ascetic marks the point of turning in what Brown described as the perch between particularity and grandeur, in which foreground and background are dissolved in a change to the perceptual mode that suspends space and time in an inference of wholeness.

The narrative enterprise of the desert reporters was actually a difficult one, for they were trying to show or describe something that is "inherently refractory to representation",[31] an Adamic body in the here-and-now, a living "man from heaven". In part they accomplished the task of representing unrepresentability by their use of metaphors of light, and in part by their straightforward naming as angels those bodies that they perceived as the super-bodies of paradisal plenitude. But the formal structure of their texts was also touched by the perceptual construct out of which they worked. R. M. Price has observed about Theodoret's *Historia religiosa*, a collection of stories about desert ascetics similar to the collections of Palladius and the *Historia monachorum*, that it is "magnificent as a series of stories, but feeble as a series of portraits. Theodoret's holy men are insufficiently differentiated, to the point where most of the stories, accidental details aside, would equally fit most of his holy men".[32] This observation is also characteristic of the other collections and, while the repetitive monotony that one experiences in reading such literature may well mar its standing as great literature, as Price feels, it is the so-to-speak "feebleness" of this literature in terms of historical portraiture that I think is more significant.

Anyone who has read these collections knows that the stories of individual desert ascetics are not presented as biographies that follow a linear line of narration from beginning to end, nor are the subjects of these stories situated in densely detailed or richly thickened socio-cultural contexts. Rather, these collections situate their subjects in an extended "middle" that subverts conventional biographical narrativity. Taking the form of snapshots endlessly repeated, these collections not only deprive their ascetic characters of history—that is, of the perceptual construct from the horizon that emphasizes the figure-and-ground character of the visual field—they also deprive the reader of the horizonal perspective. By their spareness of form in narrative historical terms, these stories invite the reader to share the visual pleasure of the inference to wholeness that structures the perceptual gaze of the reporters themselves. Thus the texts themselves are, as it were, bodies from nowhere that mimic the repetitive performative gestures of the subjects of their gaze. Textual monotony—or, put more positively, textual repetition—serves the ascetic cause by suspending constraints of space and time in order to induce another form of awareness.

I suggested earlier that the ascetics' manipulation of their bodies was integral to the form of perception that produced "the body from nowhere", and I will turn now to consider the role that ascetic practices themselves played in coaxing the body toward plenitude. In recent scholarship on desert asceticism, it has become conventional to view the body as a "map of social meaning" as well as "a site for religious self-formation".[33] This perspective attempts to avoid a dualistic construction of ascetic views of the body by noting that, far from being merely a repression of the body, ascetic practice involves an "interwovenness of spirituality and embodiedness".[34]

While I agree that asceticism can fruitfully be conceptualized as a bodily practice that has self- or spiritual formation as its context, I am wary of treatments of asceticism that, by viewing the body as the ground for the spirit, court the danger of bypassing the body in the very act of trying to bring it forward for consideration. Consider the case of Symeon the Stylite. For his ancient biographers and contemporary interpreters as well, one of the most striking of Symeon's ascetic actions was his constant standing with arms outstretched.[35] Ancient interpreters were particularly taken with the performative aspect of Symeon's standing as a spectacle that enticed the gaze of bystanders. These bystanders became themselves so involved in this activity that, as the *Syriac Life* reports, "his peers began watching him to see if he moved his feet or changed his position".[36]

Many contemporary interpreters, by contrast, have tried to make theological sense of Symeon's standing. For example, one theory proposes that Symeon's standing with arms outstretched was cruciform, that is, that his action was an imitation of Christ on the cross.[37] This theory depends on an assumption that later iconographic depictions of stylites that were theologically motivated in this way can be used to understand Symeon's own motivation. Yet, as David Frankfurter has observed, "whether or not some later sculptors gave such theological reassessment to their local brand of holy man, there is no evidence that Symeon himself was inspired by Jesus' crucifixion".[38] In Frankfurter's view, this interpretive position has associated "one of the least comprehensible forms of ascetic display with a most orthodox Christian theology of the cross".[39]

Another example of contemporary theory is the association of Symeon with "the Platonic-Gnostic idea of the perfected being as 'motionless'".[40] As Frankfurter, again, observes, this interpretive attempt does not theologize Symeon but philosophizes him on the basis of "the diverse interests and ideals of the contemporary Academy".[41] I would add to Frankfurter's critique that such perspectives both tame and domesticate Symeon's action, and, by making this practice of the body a cipher for theological and philosophical ideas, the tangible physicality of the practice tends to recede in importance, if not to disappear altogether.

This is not to say that one should avoid interpretation when addressing issues pertaining to ascetic practices of the body, nor is it to say that ancient biographers of Symeon did not attempt to understand the meaning of his ascetic practices; indeed, as Susan Ashbrook Harvey has shown, each of the three extant biographies constructs its portrait of Symeon within a distinctive ideational framework.[42] What I am pointing to is a question of emphasis. The ancient writers had their eyes fixed squarely on Symeon's body as a valuable phenomenon in itself; even the Platonizing text of Theodoret is unflinchingly corporeal in its presentation of Symeon. As R. M. Price has aptly observed, bodily gestures like those of the stylite "were seen not merely to have psychological effects but to possess intrinsic meaning and value in their visible reality".[43]

Performative visibility was so characteristic of Symeon's ascetic practice, particularly his standing on a pillar, that Theodoret saw him as the successor of Biblical performers: Isaiah walking naked and barefoot for three years, Jeremiah wearing an iron yoke around his neck, Hosea marrying a prostitute.[44] Ordinary onlookers, too, were struck by the performative quality of Symeon's use of his body. One of Theodoret's attendants tried counting the prostrations that Symeon did as part of his daily routine, and lost count after one thousand, two hundred and forty-four.[45] Performing "the body from nowhere" was hard work, and it had devastating effects on Symeon's body—ulcerated feet, a tumorous thigh infested with worms, a dislocated spine, and so on.[46] Yet despite these gross physical deformations, or perhaps because of them, Theodoret could say, "He beautifies the world", while another man, according to the report of the biographer Antonius, picked up one of the worms that had fallen from Symeon's thigh and saw it as a priceless pearl.[47] These are both good examples of the way in which ascetic performance induced the perceptual perspective "from nowhere" that I suggest is operative here.

It is important to emphasize that the perception "from nowhere" did not function to dehumanize the body so perceived. Although I agree with Peter Brown's construction of what he calls "histrionic feats of self-mortification" as "a long, drawn-out ritual of dissociation—of becoming the total stranger", I would add that in ascetic practice, the strange was a ritual form of the familiar—of the familiarly human.[48] Again with regard to Symeon, Theodoret and Antonius both report occasions when Symeon's performances provoked such questions from onlookers as, "Are you some kind of spirit?", "Are you human?"—in response to which Symeon invites the questioner to look at his foot oozing with pus and is forced to show the putrified flesh of his torso that had been wrapped with rope.[49] He is woefully human, but that does not alter the ability of others to see in his humanity a body of plenitude.

Symeon presents a particularly striking case of the ascetic practice of representing unrepresentability by using the material at hand, the body. It is certainly true, as Wyschogrod remarks, that the dazzling body was refractory to representation—refractory, but not entirely resistant. As performance artists, ascetic practitioners constructed new conditions of visibility not by destroying all representative coherence but rather by engaging in ritual behaviors that enabled the body to be perceived in a different way. By conceptualizing ascetics like Symeon as performers, I am following certain contemporary theorists of ritual who have emphasized the performative dimensions of ritual activity. Such emphasis on performance aims to underscore the primacy of the body in ritual behavior as well as to guard against a perceived devaluation of action as compared with thought in some forms of ritual theory.[50] Conceptualizing ascetic behavior as a performative practice enables the interpreter to focus on the doing and acting that are creative of meaning in the ascetic context.

As performers, ascetics did not anticipate or petition audiences in the same way as an actor in a drama would, yet as we have seen, people did come to the desert to watch them, and their positive viewing of such "performances" drew on the perceptual capacity to infer wholeness discussed earlier. Now I would suggest further that ascetics themselves, in their various practices of manipulating their bodies, also drew on this inferential perceptual construct. Ascetic practices of the body defied the constraints of time and space—that is, the constraints of perception from the horizon—and they did so by emptying them of conventional meaning, thus creating a ritual time and a ritual space within which the body could be understood. As Catherine Bell has explained, such ritualizing of time and space involves a certain circularity: "[S]pace and time are redefined through the physical movements of bodies projecting organizing schemes on the space-time environment on the one hand while reabsorbing these schemes as the nature of reality on the other".[51] This ritual dynamic of projecting and reabsorbing is what produced the "angels" of desert asceticism.

The term "ritual" is understood here according to its definition by a contemporary director of drama, Richard Schechner: "Rituals are certain behavioral displacements, exaggerations, repetitions, and transformations that communicate and/or symbolize meanings not ordinarily associated with the behavior displayed".[52] In asceticism, time was ritualized by practices of repetition, like Symeon's repeated prostrations, while space was ritualized by practices of exaggerated subtraction, like Symeon's fastings and self-mutilations that altered the "space" of his body. The desert ascetics in Egypt also engaged in these practices of repetition and subtraction, which manipulated the body so as to drive it as close as possible toward that vitality that was the mark of an "other", paradisal plenitude.

Observers of the desert ascetics reported practices of repeated prayer, hymn-singing, and labor as well as the kind of knee-bending and standing engaged in by Symeon. According to Palladius, Moses the Egyptian filled the water jugs of his ascetic companions every night in a kind of ritual walkabout, and Paul, who knew three hundred prayers by heart, "would collect that many pebbles, hold them in his lap, and at each prayer cast out a pebble".[53] According to the *Historia monachorum*, Apollo offered prayers to God throughout the day, and bent his knees a hundred times in the night and as many times in the day, while John "stood under a rock for three years in uninterrupted prayer".[54] The case of John's standing reveals the radical effect of ascetic repetitive practice, for if repetition is repeated often enough, the practitioner achieves a condition of stasis or stillness, a body from nowhere that is so abstract that it does not even move.

Returning to Schechner's definition of ritual, with its observation that behavioral repetitions and displacements convey meanings not usually associated with such behaviors, it is not immediately obvious how, for example, pebble-throwing might symbolize an angelic body. However, a recent essay by the dancer Susan Leigh Foster shows how this might be so. Writing about repetitive exercises in dancing, she observes that such "drilling is necessary because the aim is nothing less than *creating the body*. With repetition, the images used to describe the body and its actions *become* the body".[55] In dance, she argues, there is a perceived body—the body perceived from the horizon—and there is an ideal body—the body from nowhere that is the goal of training. Unfortunately, "the training regimen reveals the perceived body to be horribly deficient in the size and proportion of its parts". Hence the need for constant repetition, which marks both the striving toward the ideal body and the recognition of lack.[56] The dancer, like the ascetic, is constantly perched, as Brown said, between particularity and grandeur, and both sides of this perch are signified by the same set of bodily behaviors, which display the dim body and the dazzling body at once.

The other kind of ascetic practice that brought the body from nowhere to perceptual awareness was what I earlier called a practice of subtraction, which included the ascetics' eating habits (or lack thereof) as well as acts that marked the body by literally removing flesh from it. Although acts of physical mutilation—burning the fingers in the flame of a candle, wrapping the body with chains or ropes that left disfiguring gaps when removed—are attested in ascetic literature, it was the practice of fasting that most drew the gaze of reporters and led them to marvel at the "bodily contentment" of men whose only food was endives, or roots and herbs, or the Eucharist.[57] In fact, and paradoxically so, it was the body produced by fasting that elicited perceptions of the corporeal plenitude of paradise. The *Historia monachorum* reports that Macarius the faster was given fruits of paradise in the deep desert, and there are numerous stories of ascetics who, like Abba Sourous, ate nothing earthly, for angels fed them each day with heavenly food.[58]

Such admiration of the kind of body produced by sustained fasting did not stem from a fashion-induced obsession with thinness. Rather, fasting was one of what Michel de Certeau has called "practices of the infinite or, if one prefers, the actual, a spatial bringing into play" of the Adamic body of plenitude that is made available to perception by such ritual practice.[59] Fasting not only "transforms the natural and anticipated responses of the body to eating", as Elizabeth Castelli has noted;[60] it also produces a body that looks different from conventional bodies, that is, bodies marked by their ties to social and historical contexts. By ritualizing the space of the body, fasting offers to perception a body so different that it can be declared "angelic" and yet still retain its status as human. A short hymn attributed to

Ephrem the Syrian speaks eloquently to this point: "Hunger that eats up your flesh, offers you the bliss of Eden; thirst that drinks your veins, supplies you the sources of life; fasting that dries up your person, illuminates your countenance".[61] Clearly, in the case of fasting, subtraction adds.[62]

The "shriveled up" face and "wasted" limbs of an ascetic like Eusebius of Asikha presented an enticing sight to an observer like Theodoret because his body figured in spatial terms that which eludes figuring: a living "man from heaven".[63] Yet, like the repetitive practices that ritualized time, the practices that ritualized the space of the body had a double valence, oscillating between the perspective from the horizon and the perspective from nowhere. Negatively, fasting was premised on a recognition of the loss of the super-body of Edenic plenitude but, positively, fasting was an act of constructive defiance against that dim body. In this regard, asceticism can be seen as "a taking charge of the other by the body".[64] This performative "taking charge" by means of the ritual practices of the body just discussed was crucial to the engagement of the perceptual "view from nowhere" that I have argued was operative in asceticism.

At several points in the course of this discussion I have used the word "performance" to describe ascetic behavior. In terms of the ritualizing of time by means of repetitive performance, I used a contemporary example from the arts, dance, to suggest how ascetic practices of repetition might be understood. Now, in order to bring into clearer focus the spatial character of ascetic performance, I will use another example from modern arts, this time a painterly one.

In France in the 1950s, a spatial understanding of "the body from nowhere" was alive and well in the work of the artist Yves Klein. Klein did not place frames around his paintings. As Mark Taylor has explained, "frames interrupt the goal of art, which, according to Klein, is the experience of unification for both artist and viewer. Klein is best known for his monochromatic paintings, most of which are a brilliant blue that came to be known as International Klein blue".[65] Writing about his painting in an essay entitled "The Monochromatic Adventure", Klein said: "As soon as there are two colors in a painting, combat begins".[66] To overcome this combat, as Taylor notes, Klein removed figuration from his paintings and painted a single color on a frameless canvas. For Klein, the experience of painting was religious: "My goal", he claimed, "was to restore lost Eden".[67] His goal might well be compared with the goal of those ancient ascetics whose project has been described as the restoration of "the frankly physical exuberance of Adam's Paradise".[68]

As Taylor has observed, Klein's blue paintings "actually represent nothing. The nothingness of Klein's blue is, however, a curious nothing. Rather than the mere absence or negation of being, this blue embodies the plenitude of being's presence ... Klein paints the ineffable by removing every trace of figure and contrast of color".[69] As Klein himself, again, wrote: "By saturating myself with the eternal limitless sensitivity of space, I return to Eden; and this is why, in my art, I refuse more and more emphatically the illusion of personality and the transient psychology of the linear".[70]

Like Klein in his return to Eden, the desert angels of asceticism had also refused what Klein calls "the illusion of personality and the transient psychology of the linear". These two phrases describe well the view from the horizon, which perceives in terms of historical particulars of individual identity and temporal unfolding. Ritualizing the body causes such figure-and-ground concepts to give way to intimations of totality, or what Klein called "the eternal limitless sensitivity of space".[71]

Klein wanted others to experience the oneness with totality that he thought was a common human desire. Similarly, whether consciously or unconsciously, ascetic performers drew their audiences into their performative rituals as participants, at least in terms of an altered perceptual perspective; and sometimes their spectators became part of the act itself, as we have seen in the case of those who watched Symeon's feet and counted his prostrations. Klein, however, was conscious of his aim to include his audience in the work of his artistic religious vision. To accomplish this, as Taylor notes, "he frequently transformed his art into a public performance".[72]

One of the most dramatic instances of Klein's performative art was called the "Exhibition of the Void", which took place on April 28, 1958 at the Galerie Iris Clert in Paris. I follow Taylor's description of this event. "Klein emptied the gallery of everything and painted it entirely white. The only thing in the gallery that was not white was a blue drink offered to guests as they entered. The exhibition created a considerable sensation. When more than two thousand people tried to squeeze into the small gallery, the police and fire department had to be called to avoid a riot. For Klein, the most important moment in the exhibition was the drinking of the blue cocktail, which he explicitly interpreted as an act of communion. 'The blood of the body of sensibility', Klein declared, 'is blue'. What he did not tell the communicants was that the mixture of gin, cointreau, and methylene blue would make them urinate blue for a week—the precise length of time for which the "Exhibition of the Void" was scheduled".[73] In

Klein's view, blue—the color of Eden—had infused them all, making them all performers of a lost plenitude now literally present in the space of their bodies.

While Klein may seem a bit Svengalian in comparison with ascetics fasting in the desert, still his attempt to realize "the body from nowhere" in the here-and-now by a performative use of the body-in-space is strikingly similar to ascetic ritual performances of the Edenic body. In both cases, art and religion coalesce in a performative gesture that elicits an "other" way of perceiving the body. And, while we might prefer the lightning flash in the face of Abba Pambo to the blue urine of Klein's guests, it is the case for both that performative uses of the body both induce and draw upon the perceptual ability to infer wholeness. Particularly in the less obvious instance of asceticism, what emerges is the importance of the gaze in the construction and execution of its practices. As Abba Bessarion, at the point of death, said: "The monk ought to be as the cherubim and the seraphim: all eye".[74]

Notes

1 Palladius, *Historia Lausiaca* 71 (Butler, vol. 2, p. 169) (hereafter *HL*).
2 For a brief history of Palladius' various visits to desert ascetics between the approximate dates of C.E. 388-412, see Butler, *Palladius: Historia Lausiaca*, vol. 1, pp. 2-3.
3 Palladius, *HL*, foreword (Butler, vol. 2, p. 4).
4 Brown, *The Body and Society*, p. 327; Harpham, *The Ascetic Imperative*, pp. 24, 27; Wyschogrod, *Saints and Postmodernism*, p. 13.
5 Harpham, *The Ascetic Imperative*, pp. 24, 27.
6 Theodoret, *Historia religiosa*, prologue 1 (Canivet—Leroy-Molinghen, vol. 1, p. 124; trans. Price,, p. 3) (hereafter *HR*).
7 *Historia monachorum in Aegypto* 3.1 (Festugière, p. 39; trans. Russell, p. 65) (hereafter *HM*).
8 *Apophthegmata patrum* Bessarion 12 (PG 65.141D; trans. Ward, p.42) (hereafter *AP*).
9 *HM* 6.1 (Festugière, pp. 43-44; trans. Russell, p. 68).
10 *HM*, prologue 5 (Festugière, p. 7; trans. Russell, p. 49).
11 Vernant, "Dim Body, Dazzling Body", pp. 18-47.
12 Ibid., p. 23.
13 Ibid., pp. 24-25.
14 Ibid., p. 25.
15 On Gregory of Nyssa's view of the body, see Brown, *The Body and Society*, pp. 291-304.
16 Brown, *The Body and Society*, p. 31.
17 Harpham, *The Ascetic Imperative*, p. 27.
18 *AP*, Pambo 12; Sisoes 14 (PG 65.372A, 395B).
19 *HM* 2.1 (Festugière, p. 35; trans. Russell, p. 63).

20 *AP*, Silvanus 12; Arsenius 27 (PG 65.41 1C; 80D).
21 *AP*, Pambo 12 (PG 65.372A).
22 Brown, *The Body and Society*, p. 294. Note especially Brown's discussion of Gregory of Nyssa's *De hom. op.* 12.9 and *De virg.* 13.1.
23 Brown, "The Saint as Exemplar in Late Antiquity", p. 14.
24 Wyschogrod, *Saints and Postmodernism*, p. 16.
25 Ibid.
26 Ibid., p. 18.
27 Ibid., p. 16.
28 Ibid.
29 Ibid., p. 17.
30 Palladius, *HL* 2 (Butler, vol. 2, p. 17).
31 Wyschogrod, *Saints and Postmodernism*, p. 13.
32 Price (trans), *Theodoret of Cyrrhus*, xv.
33 Castelli, "Mortifying the Body", pp. 134, 136; cf. Brown, *The Body and Society*, pp. 222-23.
34 Castelli, "Mortifying the Body", p. 142.
35 See the many references to Symeon's standing in the collection of biographies of Symeon in Doran (trans), *The Lives of Simeon Stylites*.
36 *The Syriac Life of Saint Simeon Stylites* 8 (trans. Doran, p. 109); see also Theodoret, *HR* 26.12-13, 22 (Canivet—Leroy-Molinghen, vol. 2, pp. 184-90).
37 Drijvers, "Spätantike Parallelen", pp. 54-76, especially pp. 67-75.
38 Frankfurter, "Stylites and *Phallobates*", pp. 173-74.
39 Ibid., p. 174.
40 Ibid., summarizing the argument of Doran, *The Lives of Simeon Stylites*, pp. 33-35.
41 Frankfurter, "Stylites and *Phallobates*", p. 174.
42 Harvey, "The Sense of a Stylite", pp. 376-94.
43 Price (trans), *Theodoret of Cyrrhus*, xxxiv.
44 Theodoret, *HR* 26.12 (Canivet—Leroy-Molinghen, vol. 2, pp. 186-88).
45 Ibid., 26.22 (Canivet—Leroy-Molinghen, vol. 2, pp. 204-6).
46 Ibid., 26.23 (Canivet—Leroy-Molinghen, vol. 2, p. 206): ulcers; Antonius, *The Life and Daily Mode of Living of the Blessed Simeon the Stylite* 17 (trans. Doran, p. 94): infested thigh; *The Syriac Life of Saint Simeon Stylites* 46 (trans. Doran, p. 130): dislocated spine.
47 Theodoret, *HR* 26.28 (Canivet—Leroy-Molinghen, vol. 2, p. 212; trans. Price, p. 83); Antonius, *The Life and Daily Mode of Living of The Blessed Simeon* 18 (trans. Doran, p. 95).
48 Brown, "The Rise and Function of the Holy Man in Late Antiquity", p. 131.
49 Theodoret, *HR* 26.23 (Canivet—Leroy-Molinghen, vol. 2, pp. 206-8); Antonius, *The Life and Daily Mode of Living of the Blessed Simeon the Stylite* 7 (trans. Doran, p. 89).
50 For a discussion of performance theory, see Bell, *Ritual Theory*, pp. 37-46; see especially her discussion of the ritual theory of Stanley Tambiah and Roy Rappaport on pp. 41-43.
51 Bell, *Ritual Theory*, p. 99, extrapolating on the ritual theory of Jonathan Z. Smith in *To Take Place: Toward Theory in Ritual*, pp. 74-96.
52 Schechner, "Magnitudes of Performance", p. 24.
53 Palladius, *HL* 19 (Butler, vol. 2, p. 62): Moses; *HL* 20 (Butler, vol. 2, pp. 62-3; trans. Meyer, p. 71): Paul.

54 *HM* 8.5 (Festugière, p. 48; trans. Russell, p. 70): Apollo; *HM* 13.4 (Festugière, p. 99; trans. Russell, p. 93): John.
55 Susan Leigh Foster, "Dancing Bodies", p. 484.
56 Ibid.
57 *HM* 8.51-52; 2.4; 13.4; 20.17 (Festugière, pp. 67, 36, 99, 123).
58 *HM* 21.5-8; 2.9; 8.6; 11.5 (Festugière, pp. 125, 38, 48-49, 91).
59 De Certeau, *The Mystic Fable*, p. 45.
60 Castelli, "Mortifying the Body, Curing the Soul", p. 143.
61 Ephrem, *Hymni et Sermones* 4, col. 153, (Vööbus, vol. 2, p. 30).
62 I owe the idea of the "subtraction that adds" to Mark Taylor's discussion of works of art in which "art is nothing other than a complex process of disfiguring ... Subtraction adds and erasure inscribes. Rending creates the space in which forms become articulate". See his *Disfiguring*, p. 278. See also the comments on self-mortification in Brown, *The Body and Society*, pp. 330-31.
63 For Theodoret's comments on Eusebius of Asikha, see *HR* 18.1 (Canivet-Leroy—Molinghen, vol. 2, p. 54).
64 De Certeau, *The Mystic Fable*, p. 45.
65 Taylor, "Nothing Ending Nothing", pp. 44-47 on Klein.
66 Klein, "The Monochromatic Adventure", p. 44, quoted in Taylor, "Nothing Ending Nothing", p. 44.
67 Klein, "The Monochromatic Adventure", p. 224, quoted in Taylor "Nothing Ending Nothing", p. 44.
68 Brown, *The Body and Society*, p. 221.
69 Taylor, "Nothing Ending Nothing", p. 44.
70 Klein, "The Monochromatic Adventure", p. 224, quoted in Taylor, "Nothing Ending Nothing", p. 44.
71 Ibid.
72 Taylor, "Nothing Ending Nothing", p. 46.
73 Ibid.
74 *AP*, Bessarion 11 (PG 65.1411; trans. Ward,, p. 42): "all eye" = *óios ophthalmos*.

PART III

POETIC IMAGES AND THEOLOGY

PART III

POETIC IMAGES AND THEOLOGY

Preface

In late antiquity, theology as a discipline was defined straightforwardly as teaching about or naming God. Unlike other systems of explanation, however, theology found itself in the unique position of attempting to account for something that many thought exceeded the categories of human reason. Especially in the philosophically-oriented theologies of Christianity and in Neoplatonism, the contrast between the spirituality and eternity of God and human finitude raised questions about the limitations of theological discourse. Because God was often understood negatively as beyond the realm of being and therefore essentially unknowable, questions about the status of theological language vis-à-vis its referent became so acute that language itself became an object of scrutiny central to the theological enterprise. How was theological language to be understood by those who conceived of theology as an attempt to express the inexpressible?

Many theological thinkers would have agreed with Plotinus that visions of divinity "baffle telling" because any given linguistic formulation was ineluctably partial and incomplete (Ch. 12). As unsettling as such an observation might seem to the success of the theological enterprise, what it reveals is that in this period the distinction between theology and philosophy of language was blurred. When faced with naming the unnameable, theological thinkers were forced to confront the limits as well as the resources of their own practices as writers. In the texts presented in this section, theological inquiry was constituted as an analysis of discourse; authors asked not only *what* words mean in a discourse of transcendence, but also *how* they mean.

When they engaged in talk about God, many late ancient writers knew that theirs was a figurative enterprise. Using words to express the inadequacy of words, theologians like Origen and philosophers like Plotinus recognized that their interpretive structures were ghosted by an ironic "so to speak". This recognition of the gap between theological language and its subject could produce hermeneutical despair when words seemed to defer rather than to secure the presence of the divine. However, many ancient theologians knew that the dissemination of meaning in language could also be understood positively as an indication of semantic richness. Viewing language as evocative rather than as prescriptive, the writers presented in this section developed a hermeneutic that might best be characterized as a poetics of reading.

Thus despite their recognition of the inadequacies of language for theological disclosure, writers in traditions so apparently diverse as Christianity, Gnosticism, and magic developed remarkably similar perspectives on the central role of image and metaphor in human attempts to articulate the enigma of the divine. Keenly aware of the limitations of logic and discursive analysis, these theologians used language to produce intimations of divinity rather than systematic definitions.

Of the writers studied here, no one was more insistent on the importance of figuration for the theological task than Origen of Alexandria, to whom the first three chapters are devoted. He frequently emphasized the metaphorical character of words in his theological commentaries on Biblical texts. Language was not a passive mirror of meaning for Origen; rather, there was an energy in language that actively constructed the world, as the following catalogue of his metaphors for words indicates: seeds, goads, seducers and flirts, shepherds, and springs. These terms are all presented as figures for the creative dynamic that made Biblical language an explosive cache of divine mysteries. Furthermore, Origen's major technique for interpreting the Biblical texts upon which his theology was based, allegory, was itself an affirmation of linguistic polysemy. Described by a modern interpreter as a "lateral dance" involving "incessant movement from one displaced figural point to another" (Ch. 11), allegory led Origen to a view of theology as an endless disclosure of the imaginal depths of the divine in language.

Like Origen, the authors of the magical texts treated in this section approached theological language as a speaking of the unspeakable. Unlike Origen, however, their method of interpretation was not allegory but rather what I have called "nonsense language". Composed of meaningless strings of letters of the alphabet, theirs was an incantatory use of language that scrambled ordinary words in order to elicit dimensions of reality that were normally not available to human perception. Matching the riddle of the divine with an equally riddling form of discourse, the magical texts were more radical than Origen was in terms of their deconstructive manipulations of the alphabet. Yet there is surprising consonance between the two as well, for both Origen and the magicians understood the transgressive aspects of theological language. Origen's use of Christ harrowing hell as a figure for the interpreter is intriguingly paralleled by the magicians' use of language against itself in the service of meaning.

The idea that meaning occurs in the breaking of form arose in Gnostic theologies as well. The final chapter in this section considers two Valentinian Gnostic texts whose concern centered in part on the dangers of literalism in theological discourse. In conversation with these two texts, the discussion in this chapter addresses a particular dilemma of language considered as metaphor. Its very richness can suggest that theology can achieve closure, that is, that the plenitude of language can lure the interpreter into believing that a final, complete telling is possible. Paradoxically, the danger of polyvalence is fixity. Like Origen, for whom allegory was a figure for an endless narrativity in theology, these Gnostic authors resolved the dilemma by conceptualizing theological knowing as a search rather than as a fixed content. In fact, all of the texts in this section seem to have entertained the uncomfortable thought that what theology offers is the promise of referential meaning together with the rhetorical subversion of that promise. Finally, theological words are traces, trajectories of desire.

Chapter Nine

"In My Father's House Are Many Dwelling Places": κτίσμα in Origen's *De principiis*

> There are many dwelling places which lead to the Father; why the soul stops in them, with what profit, what teaching, what light it finds there, is known only by the "Father of the future age", who said of himself, "I am the door". "No one comes to the Father except by me". Without doubt at each of these dwelling places, he becomes for each soul a door: one enters by him, by him "one goes out" and "finds pastures", and from there one enters into another dwelling place, then into still another, until one comes to the Father himself.[1]

In this passage from his *Homilies on Numbers,* Origen has expressed in concise form part of the divine mysteries to which he so often alludes in his writings.[2] The mystery here involves an odyssey of the soul, whose "profit", "teaching", and "light" Origen reveals, at least symbolically, with some precision as the *Homilies* continue, in spite of the journey's apparent unfathomable character.[3] He also reveals the *topos* of the soul's celestial wandering, which he imagines as a cosmic architecture housing dwelling places, the "depths of God". These dwelling places through which the soul journeys, the μοναί of the Johannine verse,[4] have usually been explained by reference to a "geography of the world above", to "celestial nations", and to "hierarchies and degrees".[5] And in his *Homilies on Numbers*, Origen is indeed concerned primarily to provide map-knowledge of this particular mystery.

However, geography or map-knowledge alone did not exhaust Origen's interest in the dwelling places, for in his earlier work, the *De principiis,* Origen focuses not on the geography but on the topography of these regions. The difference is significant. In the later *Homilies,* Origen wrote about what "fills" the dwelling places, that is, the varieties of angels and demons that flourish in each place and what the soul experiences as it passes through each new door.[6] But in his *De principiis,* Origen's revelations center not on what these abodes contain, but rather on what contains them. Here he is concerned to explicate the foundation of the dwelling places, the space or site in which they find a home. Further, he seems less interested in the particulars of the soul's encounters than in the dynamics of the journey; what he suggests is *how* the transforming process of psychic wandering might be envisioned, a process that is intricately bound to the "space" that embraces the dwelling places.

I

Out of these diverse vessels ... one house. Origen, *De prin.* 2.9.6

Recent scholarship on Origen's *De principiis* has noted that the work treats three basic topics: God, rational natures, and the diverse worlds that they inhabit. Like other philosophical treatises of the time, it attempts to establish a network of relations among these first principles.[7] Within this general schema, Origen is especially interested in explaining the gathering of "diversities of minds into the harmony of a single world" *(De prin.* 2.9.6.).[8] How is it that "the entire universe of things that exist, both celestial and supercelestial, earthly and infernal, may be spoken of in a general way as a single perfect world" that contains all the others *(De prin.* 2.3.6)? In other words, what functions to establish and sustain the relational network that Origen sets forth?

Generally, the Son, the second person of the Trinity, has been seen as the key to Origen's ideas about the gathering. Texts that emphasize the close connection between the *Logos*-Wisdom roles of the Son have been cited to support the view that the Son connects, and so gathers, the world to the Father because he contains the θεωρήματα, the λόγοι that animate created beings and link them to the eternal divine realm. In this perspective, the Son is the paradigm, the rational model that mediates between God the Father and the created order; he is the Word through whom the Father speaks, the image that brings into focus an extensive cosmic hierarchy.[9]

This interpretation sees the relating, gathering, harmonizing roles of the Son mainly through the *Logos* aspect of one of the Son's names, Wisdom. There is, however, another way of seeing Origen's picture of the Son as Wisdom that may give the gathering function of the Son in the *De principiis* a broader context, such that he can be seen not only as the *Logos* of the "immense, monstrous animal" that is the universe, but its body and blood as well *(De prin.* 2.1.3).

In the course of a long discussion about what it means to name Christ "Wisdom", Origen states that Wisdom "opens to all other beings, that is, to the whole creation, the meaning of the mysteries and secrets which are contained within the wisdom of God" *(De prin.* 1.2.3). A few paragraphs later he suggests that Christ, the "invisible image", performs this "opening" function by emptying: "When the Son, who was in the form of God, 'emptied himself', his desire was by means of this very emptying to display to us the fullness of the godhead" *(De Prin.* 1.2.8). This is an unusual use of the "emptying" passage from Phil. 2.7, which is generally taken as a reference to the Incarnation. Yet Origen has quoted the verse while discussing the transcendent Christ as he relates to the substance of the Father.[10] What, then, is the invisible Wisdom, whose emptying reveals a pleroma?

The final catalogue of Wisdom names in the *De principiis* provides a clue. It is the name κτίσμα *(De prin.* 4.4.1).[11] Theologically κτίσμα has been translated as "a created thing", and one legacy of the Arian controversy was the disgracing of this word as a subordinationist insult to the Son. However, κτίσμα can also mean "foundation" or "building".[12] When this sense of the Son's name is set within the Wisdom tradition from which it stems, an architectural definition not only seems more faithful to the name's context, but also opens possibilities for fresh insight into Origen's idea of the Son's place among the first principles.

The two Wisdom passages upon which Origen depends most heavily are Wisdom of Solomon 7.17ff. and Proverbs 8.22. The first passage gives Wisdom the following characteristics: she makes and reveals all things, both hidden and manifest, and by her one learns "the structure of the cosmos and the activities of the elements" (7.17-22); she is unique (μονογενές), yet made of many parts (πολυμερές) (7.22); she pervades and permeates all things (7.24); she makes all things new, while she herself dwells, or abides unchanging (μένουσα) (7.27); she spans the world in power from end to end (πέρας) (8.1); she orders ("keeps house": διοικεῖ) all things (8.1); and she is the "image and mirror" of God (7.26). In the Proverbs passage, Wisdom is the one created (ἔκτισεν) as the beginning (ἀρχή) of God's ways for his works. What unites these diverse activities of Wisdom is her foundational nature: she is the structure that is full; she provides the boundaries for the house that she keeps, and within her dwelling a process of transformation occurs. To call the Son κτίσμα, then, is to associate him with Sophia, God's binding structure within which all things are made new.

As κτίσμα, the Son is God's design and pattern. In him are contained "every capacity and form" of the cosmos; he is the "outline", the "beginning" that holds the "beginnings and causes and species of the whole creation" *(De prin.* 1.2.2; 1.4.4).[13] The Father is the "artificer" whose wisdom is his "plan" and the "fullness of his power".[14] The plan is full; there are depths in the outline, such that the artificer's κτίσμα is not a flat blueprint but full-bodied building.

The plan is full, in the most general sense, of divine spirit and matter, for the Son is agent and locus of the Father's eternal creating activity.[15] The creation "in two general natures", the invisible and the visible, the rational and the material, finds its creative joining "in and through" the Son,[16] who provides a kind of intermediate, or mediating, structure within which νοῦς and σῶμα are associated in varying degrees. For Origen, the falling away from God of the equal minds that he originally created resulted in their attachment to bodies, from the aereal to the animal *(De prin.* 1.7.4).[17] These embodied minds are souls, as Origen states explicitly: "When the mind departed from its original condition and dignity it became or was termed a soul" *(De prin.* 2.8.3-4; see also 2.11.5; 4.2.7). The gathering into a house that constituted God's creation of the world was thus an arranging of souls.[18]

As κτίσμα, the Son is the space within which a diverse psychic realm unfolds. What the Son contained in outline, the species of the whole creation, is emptied into the fullness of diverse worlds of souls, whirling about in the space he provides.[19] Ironically, the diversity produced by the withdrawal of minds from God provided the artificer with the "seeds" and "causes" for arranging the souls in the dwelling places that compose the created universe *(De prin.* 2.9.2; 2.1.1; 3.5.5). Thus the souls themselves furnished the impetus for the orderly housekeeping that characterizes Wisdom. In this respect, κτίσμα maybe compared to the Platonic "third nature", space, "which is eternal and provides a home for all created things".[20] It is, like Eros,[21] the realm between, a relational world that links spirit and matter, heaven and earth, the intelligible and the sensible. The dynamic of the metaxy is one of transformation and restoration; it brings the primordial rift to expression in a fullness that works to lead the soul back to its source.[22]

This transforming process is for Origen dependent upon a cosmic diversity or multiplicity that is at the same time a harmony. Thus as κτίσμα the Son is like Wisdom unique yet made of many parts; he is the only-begotten one who is not confined in any place nor absent to any place *(De prin.* 4.4.2). He is the "ray of God's nature", the "impress" or "stamp" of the divine reality that is "everywhere and runs through all things" *(De prin.* 1.1.6; 4.4.1; 2.11.6). The Son is the unique image and mirror, yet the realm that he contains as κτίσμα is "diverse and various" *(De prin.* 2.9.2), like the reflection of a "face seen in many mirrors".[23] Origen expresses this pleromatic character of κτίσμα in the first place as names. These names, whose elucidation is the "first task" of any investigation of the Son, together express what the only-begotten one is.[24] The Son's titles are "derived from his works and powers" and reveal the multifaceted activity of his role as mediating image *(De prin.* 1.2.4).[25] The Son's nature as image actually undergirds all of the other names, since it is his position as image which, as Origen says, "preserves the unity of nature and substance common to a father and son" *(De prin.* 1.2.6). Thus the names are perspectives on *how* the Son is image; they represent the simple oneness of God reflected fully into the fullness of the realm of souls.[26]

The Son is not, however, merely a mirror, for as image he houses all of the divine images. The κτίσμα is a *mundus imaginalis*,[27] an imaginal world whose framework is the whole complement of divine attributes. As the image that houses all the images, the Son is God's likeness *(De prin.* 4.4.1)[28] He is what all other rational beings, "created in the image", strive to attain: the "perfect image", the likeness.[29] It is through an imaginal world that the soul, itself an image, journeys on its own quest for fullness. The divine names of κτίσμα mark the framework of this world; the dwelling places are its depths.

Origen's vision of the dwelling places is extensive: "By the world we now mean all that is above the heavens, or in them, or on the earth, or in what are called the lower regions, or any places that exist anywhere, together with the beings who are said to dwell in them. All this is called the world" *(De prin.* 2.9.3).[30] Places both "celestial and supercelestial, earthly and infernal" are encompassed by this cosmic house, whose rooms constitute an architecture of "spheres" or "globes".[31] They are described as abodes in the air, stages, schools, nations of souls that are "carried round with the whirl of the universe" *(De prin.* 2.11.6; 4.3.10; 1.8.4).

Origen imagined the spherical dwelling places as forming a hierarchy, a series of abodes through which the soul first traveled in descending movements from the "height of heaven" to the "lower regions" *(De prin.* 4.3. 10). The event that brought about the establishment of the dwelling places was the withdrawal of minds from God, a fall, a "sinking", a "loss of wings", a vertical descent whose issue was a vast structure defined by degrees of withdrawal *(De prin.* 1.8.4; 2.8.3-4).[32] The rooms in this cosmic building are characterized by the kind of souls that inhabit them; thus the loftier abodes contain thrones, dominions, principalities, powers, and various angelic ministering spirits, while the lower reaches hold evil spirits, impure demons, princes of this world, rulers of darkness, and, of course, human beings *(De prin.*1.5.1-2).³³ The dwelling places, then, are psychic qualities. What they hold are rational creatures who, because of their negligence, have assumed varying soul states, defined by Origen as the measure of purity or impurity in their relation to God *(De prin.* 2.9.2; 2.9.8). As he says, "these beings, disturbed and drawn away from that state of goodness, and then tossed about by the diverse motions and desires of their souls, have exchanged the one undivided goodness of their original nature for minds that vary in quality according to their different tendencies" *(De prin.* 2.1.1). Although the loss, or falling away, is in the case of some souls severe, they never lose entirely that "share of the divine nature" that is theirs by virtue of the original creation in the image of God *(De prin.* 4.4.9). Thus the dwelling places consist of souls in diverse imaginal situations; their place in the cosmic world is determined by their position as images, that is, by the degree to which they partake of the word of God, the seeds of Wisdom within *(De prin.* 1.3.6).

These seeds of Wisdom are "seeds of restoration and recall to a better state"; because all souls possess them, they are "of one nature and substance with each other" *(De prin.* 4.4.9). The psychic states that are the dwelling places are therefore united by a transforming process through which the "one nature" continually assumes new imaginal faces, experiencing various levels of psychic awareness. The movement through the dwelling places is a round dance of transformation, a whirl of descent and ascent that ultimately leads to an end that is like the beginning *(De prin.* 1.6.2; 1.6.4; 3.6.3). For souls do not dwell in any place permanently; they become "attached" to particular abodes but do not hold the various ranks "essentially". Descent or ascent depends wholly on the strength of their devotion to divine truth *(De prin.*1.8.4). This journey, although it is finally one of restoration and renewal, is a difficult odyssey, because in each dwelling place the soul can either learn the truth of that place and so pass on to the next higher level, or it can acquire vices that provoke a further descent. "Every rational nature can, in the process of passing from one order to another, travel through each order to all the rest, and from all to each, while undergoing various movements of progress or the reverse, in accordance with its own actions" *(De prin.* 1.6.3). Thus the psychic journey is a process of education in which the soul experiences fully the dimensions of its imaginal possibilities, from the demonic to the angelic, a process whose climax is Godlikeness, when "God becomes all things to the soul" *(De prin.* 3.6.1-3).³⁴

It is the Son who provides the space, the *topos*, for this journey, since as κτίσμα he is the godlike framework, the boundary within which the dwelling places unfold. His dwelling, like Wisdom's, is an abiding that does not change; for in the Son "every good quality is essential and can never be altered" (*De prin.* 1.2.10). Yet within his depths, "all things are made new", as souls gain an increasingly full awareness of their nature as images of God. As the space within which the dwelling places are situated, the Son "is everywhere and runs through all things", just as Wisdom pervades and permeates all (*De prin.* 2.11.6). As the framework that contains the depths, however, the Son is a boundary that "binds and holds together all the diversity of the world" and that "gathered the diversities of minds into one house" (*De prin.* 2.1.2; 2.9.6). The gathering is a binding, for Wisdom provides the boundary for her house as she spans the cosmos from end to end.

Origen uses the word for boundary or end, πέρας, to describe the power of God (*De prin.* 2.9.1).[35] His power as the comprehender and maker of all things must be limited, that is, it must have a boundary, for if a thing has no end, no bounds, it also has no beginning and so will be incomprehensible. To deny God a boundary is to suggest that he has no understanding of himself or of his creation (*De prin.* 3.5.2). It is to say that God does not embrace the dwelling places that he arranged (*De prin.* 2.9.1). For Origen, God's binding embrace is his Son, the "beginning of his ways" to whom all things will be subjected in the end (*De prin.* 3.5.6-7; 1.6.2). As κτίσμα, the Son is the boundary that gives the fullness of God's creation space, dwelling places, within which to move toward a "perfect restoration" (*De prin.* 3.5.7). The power of God, his Wisdom, is bounded in a double sense: it is the "end which is like the beginning", in terms of perfection, when the soul once again knows itself as image of God; and it is the building whose unchanging dwelling lets the perfecting process come to expression.[36] In κτίσμα, the beginning and the end are the same; the First Principle is the realm within which souls are bound to divine reality.[37]

II

The soul runs round God. Plotinus, *Enn.* 2.2.2.

In the apocryphal work *Acts of John*, there is a hymn that celebrates a "round dance of Jesus".[38] In this text, Jesus bids the disciples to dance around him in a circle, while he chants a hymn of praise to the Father. Parts of the hymn give commands to those who would understand the mysteries of God. "To each and all it is given to dance, Amen. He who joins not in the dance mistakes the event, Amen". "Now if you follow my dance, see yourself in Me who am speaking". "I danced, but as for you, consider the whole".[39] These verses use the vivid image of a circling dance to depict how the soul moves in its quest for knowledge about God. The idea that the cosmos and the souls within it move in circular fashion was at least as old as the *Timaeus* (34A4), and through the influence of that work it became standard fare in the Platonic tradition. For Plotinus, the whole universe is whirling, and within that whirl "the soul runs round God and embraces him lovingly, and keeps round him as far as it can; for all things depend on him: since it cannot go to him, it goes round him ... If God is in all things, the soul which desires to be with him must move around him; for he is not in any place" (*Enn.* 2.2.1-2). Origen, too, subscribed to a cosmos composed of whirling spherical dwelling places, the nations of souls (*De prin.* 1.8.4).[40] Like Plotinus and the *Acts of John*, he is especially interested in the dynamic process of the soul's round dance. In his *Homilies on Numbers*, Origen likens the soul to the tents of Israel in the desert; the soul's journey is a nomadic wandering in search of Wisdom.[41] The *Homilies*, however, concern themselves more with *what* the soul experiences as it wanders, whereas in the *De principiis* what interests Origen is *how* the soul participates in the nomadic dance. By what process does the soul move toward what Parmenides called "the unshaken heart of well-rounded truth"?[42]

In Origen's vision of the cosmic whirl, the soul's movement is not a smooth circling. For the soul "wavers"; it is "tossed about by diverse motions" and its thoughts "wind" or "twist round" within.[43] This movement, however, is not completely random. The "various motions" of souls do not issue in cosmic chaos, because souls have a guide, and their whirling follows a pattern (*De prin.* 2.1.2).[44] In one of his well-known complaints against Origen's cosmic vision, Jerome says that "he goes to the extreme length of inferring that Christ will also suffer in the air and in the realms above for the salvation of the demons. And although he does not actually say so, yet it must be understood as a logical consequence, that as God was made man for the sake of men, to set them free, so also for the salvation of the demons he will be made what they are, for whose liberation he is then to come".[45] What is actually at stake in Jerome's objection is Origen's idea concerning how the Son, the "leader" of the psychic journey, becomes all things to all (*De prin.* 4.4.4). For Origen, it is the Son's very fullness as the multiple Christ that makes possible the soul's winding dance.

Describing the soul's movement through the dwelling places, Origen says:

> In each of these he will first observe all that happens there, and then learn the reason why it happens; and thus he will proceed in order through each stage, following him who has entered into the heavens, "Jesus the Son of God", and who has said, "I will that, where I am, they also may be with me". Further, he alludes to this diversity of places when he says, "In my Father's house are many dwelling places". He himself, however, is everywhere, and runs through all things (*De prin.* 2.11.6).

The Son patterns the whirl by virtue of his experience; as κτίσμα he holds the dwelling places, while as the soul of the created world (*De prin.* 2.1.3), he has experienced "all that happens" in each place and so can function as the "door" for all of the created images for whom he is Image.[46] The soul of the son is leader because it has already danced the entire round dance. Its loving embrace has "considered the whole". That the dance is a spiraling, winding one is suggested by the Son's nature as ἀρχή, the beginning of a helix[47] whose spiraling motion to the depths leads finally to the heights. Engaging in this round whirl restores the soul "into that fullness from which it had emptied itself" (*De prin.* 4.4.5). The emptying of the minds created in God's image, the withdrawals that resulted in diversities of souls, was thus countered and contained by the emptying of the Son into the fullness of a cosmic house. In each room of this house the journeying soul comes to know one aspect, one face of its true nature as image of God by passing through the door that the Son provides.

According to Origen, the multiple Christ reveals himself in different aspects, different forms, according to the state of the soul. "Christ becomes present in each individual in such a degree as is warranted by the extent of his merits" (*De prin.* 4.4.2).[48] In each dwelling place the soul learns from the aspect of the Son revealed there one further feature of its own nature as image. As Jesus says in the *Acts of John*, if the soul follows his dance, it will see itself in him. Origen characterized the state of the soul before its fall as a "pure and perfect reception of God into itself" (*De prin.* 4.4.9). In the process of restoring this perfect reception, which is the journey through the dwelling places, the soul sees mirrored in itself the divine attributes of the Image of God in whose fullness it lives. In this way it achieves the honor of the likeness, for the "highest good, towards which all rational nature is progressing", is "to become as far as possible like God" (*De prin.* 3.6.1).[49]

Achievement of the likeness is possible because of "a certain affinity", a "blood relationship" between the soul and God (*De prin.* 1.1.7; 4.4.10).[50] To know God is to see him in the heart (*De prin.* 1. 1.9). The medium for the relationship, the seeing in the heart, is the Son, whose wisdom will be "stamped" on us just as he himself bears the "stamp" of the Father (*De prin.* 4.1.7; 4.4.1). Further, the Son is "in the heart"; he is that "share in God" that constitutes the kingdom within (*De prin.* 1.3.6). Origen's metaphors of the blood relationship and the seeing in the heart suggest that the round dance toward likeness is a relational process in which the images provide contexts for each other. As he says, "as soon as it [the soul] has discovered a small fragment of what it is seeking, it again sees other things that must be sought for; and if in turn it comes to know these, it will again see arising out of them many more things which demand investigation" (*De prin.* 4.3.14). Each dwelling place through which the soul passes is related to the next, since the knowledge gained in one suggests the veiled truth of the next. The desire to know the design, the relational network, is a love implanted by God in the soul (*De prin.* 2.11.4). The soul's loving participation of God is its dance through the dwelling places, the imaginal world housed by the Son. By virtue of this participation, the cosmic building without becomes a kingdom within. The dancing soul is a pleroma in the making.

For Origen, the fall was a failure of imagination. It was a failure to use fully the seeds of Wisdom within, a failure to understand how the simple oneness of God is also a fullness of attributes which do not "divide God into parts" but are completely interrelated (*De prin.* 1.2.6). As Origen's discussion of the divine names shows, each one implies all the others.[51] Thus to recover its own pleroma, to be recalled into its own fullness, the soul must learn to see as God sees, through the images to their relational context. The movement through the dwelling places of the κτίσμα is the building of a house of relations within. The climax of this dance comes when the soul "will think God and see God and hold God and God will be the mode and measure of its every movement" (*De prin.* 3.6.3).

As a failure of imagination, the descending dance is an "eager desire for visible things" (*De prin.* 3.5.5). It is an "inclination towards evil" that consists in a literal attachment to images, regarding them only as "things of sense" (*De prin.* 1.8.4; 2.9.2; 4.4.10). Whether a soul has descended completely or only partially,[52] its position is due to what Origen calls its "fixed purpose" (*De prin.* 2.9.6), a refusal to move from the visible to the invisible, from the outward appearance to the mystery within. Origen defines the soul as "an existence possessing imagination and desire" (substantia φανταστική et ὁρμητική) (*De prin.* 2.8.1). Its thinking is of two kinds: a movement from within itself, and a movement through itself (*De prin.* 3.1.2).[53] The thinking from within occurs when an image (φαντασία) stimulates a desire (ὁρμή), an impulse to act. The thinking through occurs when the soul evaluates the images with the seeds of Wisdom within, its reason (*De prin.* 3.1.3). Images, then, are phantasies, "impressions from without", that stimulate the soul to act (*De prin.* 3.1.4). But when the soul fails to judge the image properly, that is, when it does not see through, the phantasy becomes a "specious attraction" that binds the soul to the body of the image, its flesh (*De prin.* 3.1.4).

The psychology of the soul's spiraling descent, however, contains within it the means for the round dance back to God, for the advance begins with things visible and moves to things invisible (*De prin.* 4.4.10). According to Origen, if the soul "attaches itself to the flesh", that is, if it fails to see through in its judging, "it will be satiated and filled after a time with those very evils which it endures as a result of the vices of the flesh and will be wearied out as it were by the very heavy burdens of luxury and lust, and so may be the more easily and quickly converted from low material desires to a longing for heavenly things and to heavenly grace" (*De prin.* 3.4.3). It is the full burden of the literal, when the soul is satiated with opaque phantasies, that provokes the "eager desire for the reality of things". Again in Origen's words:

> When the soul has gathered within itself a multitude of evil deeds and an abundance of sins, at the requisite time the whole mass of evil boils up into punishment, and is kindled into penalties; at which time also the mind or conscience, bringing to memory through divine power all things the signs and forms of which it had impressed upon itself at the moment of sinning, will see exposed before its eyes a kind of history of its evil deeds ... Then the conscience is harassed and pricked by its own stings, and becomes an accuser and witness against itself (*De prin.* 2.10.4).

The soul's self-accusation consists in its realization that the reality of things, the likeness within the image, cannot be known unless the thinking within is also a thinking through.

The best example that Origen gives for this process, at least for human souls, is the interpretation of Scripture. It is well known that for Origen the letter of the law is a shadow, a veil that conceals hidden splendor within (*De prin.* 4.1.6-7). While the process of interpretation begins with the literal image, which Origen calls "the flesh of the Scripture", it cannot stop there without falling into "irrational", "absurd", "impossible" meanings (*De prin.* 4.2.4; 4.3.4-5). Some of the images, in fact, are intentionally absurd in their literal meaning, lest the interpreter be "so completely drawn away by the sheer attractiveness of the language" that he fails "to learn anything of the more divine element" (*De prin.* 4.2.9). The literal absurdity that prompts a different kind of seeing is like the soul's ability to judge images, which asserts itself when the soul has become satiated with the body of its perception. What the interpreter sees when he "bursts the iron bars" of the literal image are the "hidden treasures of wisdom and knowledge" that lie buried within the image (*De prin.* 4.3.11). The depths of the text reveal the "depths of the wisdom of God" (*De prin.* 4.3.4). When the interpreter thinks by moving from the image to the fullness it conceals, he is able to see the imaginal world of Scripture as a vast network of relationships. As in the imaginal world of the Son, where each name implies all the others, so here seeing through one image provides an entry to the hidden riches of others. The interpretation that sees through the body of the image to its heart provides dwelling places where images are seen as likenesses.

Just as the interpreter who fails to move beyond the literal meaning of Scripture mistakes the true nature of the text, so the soul that fails to join the round dance "mistakes the event". The event is what Origen calls the achievement of "the perfect likeness" (*De prin.* 3.6.1; 4.4.9-10). The dance that achieves this likeness is a particular kind of thinking, which moves through the visible to the invisible, through the object to the relation. As Plotinus said, true reasoning produces a likeness and a partnership between what is outside and what is within (*Enn.* 1.1.9). Likeness is a similitude, a comparison in which a hidden connection is discerned. When one image is likened to another, the relation that is revealed leads to a search for further unveilings. Thus when the soul dances through the dwelling places toward a full knowledge of God, it moves from one image, one "small fragment", to the next. When it has traveled through all of the images it lost in its fall, it will understand the pure relation, the invisible image, the Son. Then it too will dwell as the Son dwells, unchanging. The soul is able to restore its own pleroma because the dwelling places through which it moves constitute a fullness which is by nature God's likeness, his Son. As κτίσμα, the Son is a dwelling that houses and cultivates a way of thinking that turns psychic wandering into a round dance of transformation. The soul gathers images to itself just as the Son gathers the dwelling places into the "harmony of a single world". The harmony is the relational context of the imaginal world of God. The single world is God's κτίσμα, whose space has room for all of the principles because he is the fullness of all the divine images through which God, the "reality of things", is seen. As κτίσμα, the Son is the hidden connection; and the hidden connection is a place in which to dwell.

III

To each and all it is given to dance. Acts of John 95.12

This verse from an early Christian apocryphal text has been used here as a context for reading Origen's vision of the soul's dynamic movement through its experience. It has been a metaphoric reading, for Origen himself thought by way of metaphor. It has often been remarked that Origen was not a truly systematic thinker, and that observation accords well with his propensity for attending to images, especially biblical images, of theological and psychic realities, rather than to abstract formulations of those realities. It also accords with his willingness to follow the spiraling path of the image, as it makes connection with others, to its likeness in metaphor, symbol, and finally in allegory. The idea originally bound in the image is ultimately subject to a rebinding in metaphor, whose work of association unleashes new, often startling, meaning. Origen, then, does not have a system but a *style* of reading; his thinking might well be described as a theological *poiesis*, for in poetry, too, images are tended and nourished until the intensity of their association brings new depth of meaning.

The interpretative conviction that underlies this study is that the reader of a text must let the style of the text itself speak in his own reading and rendering of it. The emphasis on style is intentional, as a brief journey through its linguistic history will suggest. "Style", derived from the Greek στίγμα, comes into English through the intermediary Latin *stiglus* [= *stilus*]; it means "stake", "pale"; sharp pen for engraving letters on wax tablets. Στίγμα, the root word for style, means "tattoo-mark" or "spot", as on a dragon's skin. Cognates of style in English are "stick" and "sting".[54] What this etymology suggests in the present context is that style reveals the places where we are stung into awareness, when we are marked with the spots that distinguish one perspective from others. As Origen says, it is in the dwelling places of soul, the *mundus imaginalis,* where χαρακτήρ (the "stamp" of Wisdom) is revealed. It is here that the impress, the engraving, of God is experienced. Style is character; and Origen's style has something to say about the character of theological thinking, in his time as well as our own.

One of the impressions of Origen's style is the recognition that theology might be the poetic dance of the soul, a following of the spiraling way of religion's images. In its most basic and forceful sense, theology means the "speaking of God". Origen's insistence that the soul's task is to achieve the likeness might be read in context with his metaphor of Scriptural meaning, "the treasure in earthen vessels" (*De prin.* 4.1.7). God's speaking is heard when language, by which we structure the earthen vessel of our reality, is found to be an imaginal realm, a soul world capable of poetic naming, in metaphor, of the divine treasure whose qualities we perceive but cannot name directly. Further, it is important to notice that the theological dance, the speaking of God that paces our experience, takes place in the *soul*. A poetic theology is a call to see that the speaking of God finds its stake, as Origen says, in the soul (the once-rational mind now embodied), that is, in the real-life experience of the soul that comes to its life in the dwelling places of language seen as imaginal.

This study has been an attempt to keep faith with the *poiesis,* the imaginative working, of Origen's thought. In so doing, cosmology and psychology have been read as perspectives within a theology where the speaking of God is heard in the embodied cosmos of psyche. By following the path of a single image, κτίσμα, to its imaginal depth, an intricate world of psychic relations was uncovered, a world bounded by God whose dynamic allows the rebinding of the soul in the style of divine Wisdom. Origen's theology can be read as a soulful dance, a bodying forth in images of the seeds of Wisdom within. It is a dance to which we also are given, if only we will take notice, and allow the figure of the dance to inform the style of our own speaking of God.

Notes

1 Origen, *Hom. on Num.* 27.2 (Méhat, pp. 517-18).
2 For discussions of the meaning of "mystery" in Origen's thought, see Daniélou, *History of Early Christian Doctrine*, vol. 2, pp. 465-69; and Crouzel, *Connaissance Mystique*, pp. 25-31.
3 See *Hom. on Num.* 27.9-13 (Méhat, pp. 532-557) for the journey through the "dwelling places in the desert".
4 John 14.2 (RSV). Note that μονή has the substantive sense of place as well as the verbal sense of abiding, lingering, continuing. See Brown, *The Gospel according to John*, vol. 2, pp. 618-19.
5 Crouzel, *Connaissance Mystique*, p. 69; Daniélou, *History of Early Christian Doctrine*, pp. 469ff.
6 On "celestial families" see *Hom. on Num.* 2.2 (Méhat, pp. 87-88); the soul's experiences are detailed in *Hom.* on *Num.* 27.9-13 (Méhat, pp. 532-57).

7   The following articles are of particular importance: Steidle, "Neue Untersuchungen zu Origenes' *Peri Archon*"; Harl, "Structure et cohérence du Peri Archon"; and Dorival, "Remarques sur la Forme du *Peri Archon*".
8   For this paper, the following editions of Origen's *De principiis* have been consulted: Koetschau, Paul (ed), *Origenes Werke*, 5. Band: *De Principiis*, Die Griechischen Christlichen Schriftsteller, no. 22 (Leipzig: J. C. Hinrichs, 1913); Crouzel, Henri and Simonetti, Manlio (trans and ed), *Origène: Traité de Principes*, 2 vols., Sources chrétiennes 252, 253 (Paris: Les Éditions du Cerf, 1978); and Butterworth, G. W. (trans and ed), *Origen: On First Principles* (New York: Harper and Row, 1966).
9   See Harl, *Origène et la fonction révélatrice du Verbe incarné*, pp. 112-15, 123-28; Harl, "Structure du *Peri Archon*", p. 13, n. 9; Crouzel, *Connaissance Mystique*, pp. 554; Crouzel, *Théologie de l'image de Dieu chez Origène*, pp. 75-142; and Koch, *Pronoia und Paideusis*, pp. 62-78.
10 See the discussion in Crouzel and Simonetti, *Origène: Traité des Principes*, vol. 2, pp. 46-47, n. 48.
11 This Wisdom passage constitutes Koetschau's Fragment 32 and comes from Justinian's *Ep. ad Mennam*. For support for the authenticity of the thinking represented by this passage, see Crouzel, "Grégoire le Thaumaturge et le Dialogue avec Élien", pp. 422-31, who emphasizes the Wisdom context of κτίσμα and discusses the distinctions that Origen draws in other works between κτίσμα and ποίημα.
12 Liddell, Scott, and Jones, *A Greek-English Lexicon*, s.v. κτίσμα.
13 For discussions of the middle-Platonic context of philosophical interpretations of Wisdom, see Grant, "The Book of Wisdom at Alexandria", pp. 462-72, and Crouzel, *Connaissance Mystique*, pp. 55-56.
14 *De prin.* 3.6.7, 3.5.4 (God the artificer); 2.1.2 ("*ratio*") and 1.1.6 ("*ars*"); 2.1.3 (fullness of power). For a discussion of the Son as "power", see *De prin.* 1.2.9.
15 For eternal creation, see *De prin.* 1.4.3-4; and Crouzel, *Théologie de l'image*, p. 125.
16 *De prin.* 3.6.7 (the creation in two general natures); 1.7.1 (the creation in and through Christ).
17 See Origen's Heraclitean consideration of the bodily elements and their transformations in *De prin.* 2.1.4.
18 See *De prin.* 2.9.6 and note that the "harmony of a single world" to which Origen refers here is the harmony of the cosmos and not only the earth.
19 See *De prin.* 1.8.4: "Whole nations of souls are stored away somewhere in a realm of their own, with an existence comparable to our bodily life, but in consequence of the fineness and mobility of their nature they are carried round with the whirl of the universe". Note, in this whole passage, the "rising" and "sinking" language, which suggests that all souls are "whirled", whether up or down, in response to their experiential decisions.
20 Plato, *Timaeus* 52b.
21 Plato, *Symposium* 202a-e.
22 For a discussion of the movement νοῦς-ψυχή-νοῦς, see Crouzel, *Théologie de l'image*, pp. 217-22, 263-64; and Crouzel and Simonetti, *Origène: Traité des Principes*, vol. 2, pp. 201-2, n. 16. Origen discusses God as transformer and restorer in *De prin.* 2.1.2 and 3.6.7. See Daniélou, *History of Early Christian Doctrine*, pp. 421-22.
23 The phrase is Plotinus': *Enn.* 1.1.8 (Armstrong). For the Son as an "unspotted mirror", see *De prin.* 1.2.5.
24 See Daniélou, *Origène*, p. 256; and *De prin.* 1.2.1.

25 See Crouzel, *Théologie de l'image*, p. 127.
26 For the simplicity of God, see *De prin.* 1.1.6. Here Origen also says that "our mind is of itself unable to behold God as he is"; since we are multiple, so too is our beholding of God.
27 For this phrase, and ideas associated with it, I am indebted to Corbin, *Corps spirituel et terre céleste*, pp. 7-19. He uses the word "imaginal" not only as the adjectival form of "image" but also to avoid the pejorative, "imaginary" connotation of the word "imaginative".
28 The statement of the Son's likeness concludes, and brings to a climax, a catalogue of Wisdom names.
29 *De prin.* 1.1.7 (creation in the image); 2.11.4 (the perfect image); 3.6.1 and 4.4.9 (image to likeness). The dynamic of the journey from image to likeness will be discussed in Part II of this article.
30 See *De prin.* 2.3.4-6, and the discussion by Daniélou, *History of Early Christian Doctrine*, pp. 415-25.
31 *De prin.* 2.3.6; 2.11.6.
32 For Origen's view of the Fall, see Koch, *Pronoia und Paideusis*, pp. 36-49.
33 On Origen's angelology and demonology, see Daniélou, *Origène*, pp. 219-42, and *History of Early Christian Doctrine*, pp. 434-41.
34 See Daniélou, *History of Early Christian Doctrine*, p. 423: "Origen's whole system was deduced from two principles, God's love and Man's freedom (*De prin.* 1.8.3; 3.5.6). The point at which these two converge is the final goal".
35 See Crouzel and Simonetti, *Origène: Traité des Principes*, vol. 2, pp. 211-13, n. 2, for a discussion of "limit" and the "infinite". See also *De prin.* 3.5.2 and 4.4.8.
36 For Origen's play on the words τέλος and ἀρχή, see the discussion by Harl, "Structure et cohérence", pp. 28-29 and n. 50.
37 As Harl notes in "Structure et cohérence", p. 22, the title περὶ ἀρχῶν is traditional for a philosophical treatise on God and the world. The Son as both κτίσμα and ἀρχή is thus the foundation for the ἀρχαί considered as the seeds of wisdom in all of the created beings that form the world. The ἀρχαί might be considered as the whole company of created images assembled in the κτίσμα in varying degrees, or dwelling places, of fullness, or their true nature as images. See Crouzel, *Connaissance Mystique*, p. 55, for a discussion of the Son-Wisdom as the receptacle of the λόγοι of the creation.
38 For texts, see Hennecke and Schneemelcher (trans), *New Testament Apocrypha*, vol. 2, pp. 227-32; and Pulver, "Jesus' Round Dance and Crucifixion according to the Acts of John", pp. 178-80.
39 *Acts of John* 95.12 (Pulver, p. 179); *Acts of John* 96.28 (Henneeke-Schneemelcher, vol. 2, p. 230); *Acts of John* 96.49 (Pulver, p. 180).
40 For Plotinus as for Origen, the quality of the soul's dance depends upon the disposition of the soul itself. For Plotinus, the soul whose movement is impelled by wise love (love of the Heavenly Aphrodite) experiences its dance as a joyous round whirl, while the soul whose love is foolish (embracing the Earthly Aphrodite) moves in a deadly dance, for its vision has been partially blinded. See *Enn.* 3.5 "On Love". The circling motion to which Origen and Plotinus both allude has been discussed in this study in context with the metaphor of the dance in the *Acts of John*. For Origen, the dance is, in the first instance, a descent, here described as "spiraling" because of Origen's frequent use of such words as "wavering", "tossed about" and so on (see n. 43). The descent is the negative aspect of the dance of creation.

41 *Hom. on Num.* 27.4 (Méhat, p. 346).
42 Parmenides, fr.1, in *The Presocratics*, Wheelwright (trans), p. 96.
43 *De prin.* 1.8.4 (wavering); 2.1.1 (tossing); 4.4.10 (winding).
44 In *De prin.* 2.1.2, the Son is described as the "plan" that "binds" and "guides the various motions" of souls. Even with the stabilizing aid of bodies, the motions of souls are "fragile" (*De prin.* 1.8.4) and would dissolve in conflict (*De prin.* 2.1.2) were it not for the plan provided by the Son.
45 Jerome, *Ep. ad Avitum* 12 (Butterworth, p. 309, n. 7).
46 See *Hom. on Num.* 27.2 (Méhat, p. 517) for door imagery.
47 See Liddell, Scott and Jones, *A Greek-English Lexicon*, s.v. ἀρχή. In *De Prin.* 1.2.2, the Son is called the ἀρχή of the "ways of God".
48 For a discussion of this issue, see Daniélou, *Origène*, pp. 255-56.
49 While Origen discusses the likeness issue with respect to human beings in particular (due to the convenience of the Biblical quotation), it nevertheless applies to all souls. Human life on earth is, after all, only *one* of the dwelling places.
50 On the issue of "participation" in Origen's thought, see the following: Balas, "The Idea of Participation in the Structure of Origen's Thought", pp. 257-75; Crouzel, *Connaissance Mystique*, pp. 47-84; and Crouzel and Simonetti, *Origène: Traité des Principes*, vol. 2, p. 245, n. 19.
51 See, for example, *De prin.* 1.2.4: "Whatever then we have said of the Wisdom of God will as fitly apply to and be understood of him in his other titles as the Son of God, the life, the word, the truth, the way and the resurrection".
52 Note that Origen is not consistent concerning whether all souls fall away entirely; on the complete falling away, see *De prin.* 3.5.4, 4.3.10, 1.8.4; for the partial fall see 2.8.4.
53 See Butterworth, *Origen: On First Principles*, pp. 158-59, n. 1, for a brief discussion of this dynamic from Origen's *De oratione* 6.1.
54 Lewis and Short, *A Latin Dictionary*, s.v. *stilus*; Liddell, Scott, and Jones, *Greek-English Lexicon*, s.v. στίγμα.

Chapter Ten

Origen and the Witch of Endor: Toward an Iconoclastic Typology

> "No wise fish would go anywhere without a porpoise". "Wouldn't it really?" said Alice, in a tone of great surprise. "Of course not", said the Mock Turtle. "Why, if a fish came to me, and told me he was going on a journey, I should say, 'With what porpoise?'" "Don't you mean 'purpose'?" said Alice. "I mean what I say", the Mock Turtle replied in an offended tone.[1]

The letter of the law is its literal meaning, says the turtle. Or perhaps he meant that the literal meaning of the word at issue here is composed of its letters. In any case, he is offended by Alice's translation, which destroys his pun (if it was a pun) by substituting another word, another group of letters. Alice, meanwhile, is only trying to discern the sense of scripture; but, as interpreter, she offends the text by fixing and laying bare its meaning. However, by suggesting another word, she has entered the play of the text's letters, since after all the text with which she is presented has been composed by a mock turtle. The exegete plays within the play of words.

Origen often proceeds exegetically as though he were Alice and the Mock Turtle rolled into one; that is, his allegorical interpretations grow out of, and find their life in, the literal play of letters. It is this dynamic that I propose to explore.

Commenting on the Song of Songs, Origen remarks:

> Because this little book contains a kind of play, sometimes things are said with reference to a Bridegroom who is present, and sometimes to one absent, and the interchange of characters is so conducted that either sequence seems properly used.[2]

Porpoise or purpose? The questions of meaning and reading are difficult enough when applied to a text that announces itself as poetic and so susceptible by its very nature of multiple meanings and multiple readings. But it may be that these questions are even more difficult when they are brought to a text that presents itself as history. Interpretation of historical texts is difficult because histories seem to be transparent to the realities of which they speak. They are, so to say, "literal", presuming to capture the very fiber of their subject matter. "Records" of "real events", histories defy—even deny—interpretation, since one of the arts of history-writing is to seduce the reader into forgetting that it *is* an art, a literary art that works with words, letters on a page.

The important question that the interpreter must bring to a historical text, as Origen was to argue, is not whether the history "really" happened (modern disclaimers to the contrary), but rather what, and how, such texts mean.[3] Why did God authorize those letters? As Origen makes quite clear, Biblical histories "show reality *through a historical image*" (*dia eikonos historikēs*).[4] Meaning is carried by the words on the page; it is those images that bear divine warrant. As Northrop Frye has recently remarked, "It is the words themselves that have the authority, not the events they describe. The Bible means literally just what it says ... ".[5]

It is unusual to think of Origen as a defender of letters; yet it is precisely the "alphabetical" integrity of the text for which he argues in his *Homily on I Samuel 28*. Indeed, Origen's exegetical strategy in defense of the story of the Witch of Endor is what forced me to consider his interpretative theory in a different light. As we shall see, that story has for Origen the same position as the porpoise for the Mock Turtle: it means what it says.

The text in question, I Samuel 28:5-14 (RSV), reads its follows:

> When Saul saw the army of the Philistines, he was afraid, and his heart trembled greatly. And when Saul inquired of the Lord, the Lord did not answer him, either by dreams, or by Urim, or by prophets. Then Saul said to his servants, "Seek out for one a woman who is a medium, that I may go to her and inquire of her". And his servants said to him, "Behold, there is a medium at Endor".
> So Saul disguised himself, and put on other garments, and went, he and two other men with him; and they came to the woman by night. And he said: "Divine for me by a spirit, and bring up for me whomever I shall name to you". The woman said to him, "Surely you know what Saul has done, how he has cut off the mediums and the wizards from the land. Why then are you laying a snare for my life to bring about my death?". But Saul swore to her by the Lord, "As the Lord lives, no punishment shall come upon you for this thing". Then the woman said, "Whom shall I bring up for you?". He said, "Bring up Samuel for me". When the woman saw Samuel, she cried out with a loud voice; and the woman said to Saul, "Why have you deceived me? You are Saul". The

king said to her, "Have no fear; what do you see?". And the woman said to Saul, "I see a god coming up out of the earth". He said to her, "What is his appearance?". And she said, "An old man is coming up; and he is wrapped in a robe". And Saul knew that it was Samuel. And he bowed with his face to the ground, and did obeisance.

A narrative that has a witch, the ghost of a dead prophet, and a frightened king who breaks his own law is certainly an unusual, if not bizarre, history. Its oddness did not escape Patristic exegetes, who for the most part found themselves affronted by the scene so realistically and economically depicted there.

For a whole tradition of interpreters, including such notables as Tertullian, Jerome, Eustathius, John Chrysostom, and Gregory of Nyssa, the story of Saul, Samuel, and the Witch of Endor was a menacing text, menacing because to read it as the literal history it presumes to be would entail affirming that (1) the prophet Samuel was a shade in Hades; (2) a witch was an appropriate intermediary between the divine and human worlds; and (3) magic works, even on the holy ones of God. It will be obvious that a literal reading of the letters of this text raised too great a specter for the theological imagination of most of the Patristic tradition. Hence they proceeded to undermine the literal text with one of two arguments: either sorcery is just demonic deceit, and what appeared was not really Samuel, but a demon in his guise; or, Samuel was not really in Hades but had been sent by God to announce Saul's fate.[6]

Gregory of Nyssa, for example, supported the view that the witch called up a demon, not Samuel. He arrived at this solution by placing the text within the "frame" of Luke 16:19-31, the parable of Lazarus and Dives, which envisions an impenetrable chasm between heaven and hell. Using this unbridgeable boundary as the guiding metaphor, Gregory argues that, since wizards can only call up the dead in Hades, the witch cannot have brought up Samuel, even had he been willing to go to hell, because of the uncrossable abyss.[7] Augustine, who later changed his mind, at first supported this position by arguing—very much as Erich Auerbach does in his book *Mimesis*—that the sentence "and the woman saw Samuel" is one of many instances of "the Biblical practice to use condensed expressions".[8] Hence the fact that the figure is called simply "Samuel" is biblical shorthand for "a demon that looked like Samuel".[9]

A humorous example of the second kind of argument, that Samuel really did appear but had bent sent by God, not the witch, comes from Theodore bar Konai. As Smelik reports, "In order to prove that Samuel appeared, Theodore points out the fact that the woman shrieked in amazement; and that (in the LXX) Samuel is said to have appeared upright. According to Theodore demons appear lying on their backs during necromancy. Moreover, Samuel was wearing a cloak, and necromancers cannot repair worn clothes, so Samuel must have been sent by the Lord".[10]

Clearly these interpreters felt some necessity to rewrite the letters of this history. Prophets cannot be in Hades, and the nocturnal doings of a disreputable woman cannot be commended. As Eustathius remarked, the appearance of Samuel is best attributed to "the sick imagination of Saul".[11] Augustine and his change of mind excepted, Origen alone among all the major commentators took this text literally. That is, only he resisted the kind of interpretation that actually entails a re-writing of the words that compose the text. Further, only he brought to this story the typological perspective used to find Christic images in the prime movers of other biblical histories. Needless to say, the belly-talking[12] prime mover of the story in I Samuel presents something of a challenge, typologically speaking, especially when compared with such heroic historical actors as Isaac, Moses, and Joshua. As we explore Origen's exegesis of I Samuel 28 as well as its interpretative foundation, we will see him at his most faithful and, perhaps, his most radical.

In one of his *Homilies on Jeremiah,* Origen suggests that Samuel descended into and lived in Hades in order to be instructed in the mysteries of the subterranean realm. Noting, in the same homily, that the Christ had also descended, he then addresses his audience directly: "If you want to understand the word *(logos)* which explains the things above, understand the word which explains the things underneath".[13] This passage of the *Homilies on Jeremiah,* written, according to Nautin's dating, in the same period as the *Homily on I Samuel 28,* strikes one of the keynotes in Origen's discussion of the scene at Endor.[14] He seems to have been much preoccupied at that time both with the underworld and with language. In the passage just quoted, one of the referents of the word *logos* is clearly the Christ; yet the "Christ" to whom the word refers is itself a figure in several scriptural passages that Origen is interpreting. Hence *logos* has here a double valence; it means both the Christ and the language, or the words, in which that figure dwells scripturally. Origen is exhorting his audience to take words seriously.

His treatise on the Witch of Endor opens with the same concerns about language and about the necessity for understanding the chthonic world—not to mention realizing who was in it! "We know", says Origen, "that some of our brothers have looked straight at this text and have said: 'I do not believe in the witch'. 'It says that the witch saw Samuel; it is false'.

'Samuel was not brought up, Samuel did not speak.'".[15] In the face of this kind of attack on the text, Origen adopts a twofold strategy in the first half of his exegesis: he defends the text both formally and materially, using Samuel's location in Hades as the occasion for demonstrating the veracity of the text's words. I will discuss the significance of Samuel's citizenship in hell more fully when I turn to the typological strategy in Origen's treatise; perhaps it will be enough for the moment to note that Origen did not share the theological outrage of his contemporaries on this point because, from his perspective, all of the prophets were in hell until the advent of Christ: "In Hades also Isaiah, and in Hades Jeremiah, in Hades all the prophets, in Hades".[16]

The fact that Origen happens to agree theologically with the vision of this text, however, is far less important than, and even incidental to, his defense of the language of the text. Basically, his argument is that if the text's letters are not secure from tampering, there can be no interpretation. "One must be faithful according to the language (*kata ton logon*)",[17] examining the words well. Again and again he returns to this point: "If so great a man was under the earth and the witch led him up, does she have demonic power over the prophetic soul? What are we to say? It has been written thus. Is it true or is it not true? To say that it is not true urges to unbelief (it will be excluded from the sum of the sayings), but to say that it is true permits us to investigate and raise questions".[18] We must let the language of the text "deafen" us, as Origen says;[19] only then can we hear it.

What, however, do we hear when we affirm the alphabetical integrity of the text, especially when that text is a historical text? Origen himself exclaims in the midst of his exegesis that there is a "great struggle (*agōn*) in the language of God ... ".[20] Biblical texts are agonistic because their words are figural; as Origen says at the outset, the interpreter's task is to "wake up what is useful in all the icons".[21] To make matters more difficult, these icons are inspired. The "narrative person" is the holy spirit, as he argues at length,[22] which gives to the least letter, iota, and dot a virtual "plenitude" of meaning.[23] The literal meaning of a text's letters, then, is not historical, but figural. The letter is not opposed to the spirit; it *is* the spirit.

As the author of a recent book entitled *The Language of Allegory* has observed, "The key to the story's meaning lies in the text's language—its most *literal* aspect—not in a translation of the story's events to a different (metaphorical) set of terms".[24] Translation to a different set of terms was Alice's mistake, and also the error of Origen's fellow exegetes. The heart of the problem, it seems to me, lies in the confusing of "literal" with "historical", a legacy perhaps of the Pauline opposition of "letter" to "spirit" that does not allow a third term. From medieval times to the present, interpreters have tended to think that Origen was guilty of this confusion, too. Yet as Crouzel has pointed out, the "literal" for Origen is the "brute materiality" of the words on the page.[25] Further, as Origen says, those brute words are literally metaphors.

This perspective has far-reaching implications for the interpretation of historical texts, because it implies that history is *not* the base *from which* interpretation takes flight; rather, history is itself one of the tropes (even if it pretends not to be). To interpret a historical text would mean to read its poetic structure rather than to search for some external reality to which the words correspond. To make this point clear, I would like to quote from Northrop Frye's latest book, *The Great Code,* in which Frye suggests that "the only thing that words can do with any real precision or accuracy is hang together".[26] The primary meaning of any text, "which arises simply from the interconnection of the words, is the metaphorical meaning".[27]

In his *Homily on 1 Samuel 28,* Origen's startling exegetical advice is to read, not less, but *more* literally. Only with this kind of reading will a text disclose its poetry of meaning. "Poetry" is not, of course, one of Origen's words; rather the word he uses to describe the process of exploring the plenitude of "letters" is "allegory". As Crouzel and Nautin have both pointed out, "allegory" is not really a precise term in Origen's hands but refers in a general way to the practice of explicating how the spirit dwells in letters.[28] "Allegory", in other words, names an exegetical perspective that affirms what one critic has called "the possibility of an otherness, a polysemy, inherent in the very words on the page; allegory therefore names the fact that language can signify many things at once".[29]

In his literal, which is to say, allegorical reading of the story of the Witch of Endor, Origen isolates the structure that sustains the narrative flow of the story. He then adopts a typological strategy in order to expose the stunning polysemy of this historical text. From mixed metaphor to paradox, allegorical interpretation has many strategies.[30] One of them is typology. I am using the term "typology" to denote that allegorical procedure by which Origen unleashes the polysemantic possibilities of a text by juxtaposing the structure of that text's images with similar structures from other texts. Typology is interpretation by juxtaposition, which allows all of the text's literal figures to retain their own integrity *and at the same time* to reveal their plenitude.

In his treatise on the Witch of Endor, Origen first fixes the letter of the text. Samuel was really in Hades; it was he who was summoned by the witch; the witch had the power to bring him up from the depths; the witch's underworldly power had a transforming effect on Saul, who was brought face-to-face with the life he would lead after death.[31] In the first five chapters of the homily, the process of establishing the literal meaning of the text also reveals the text's structure: it is a poetry of the depths, based on a vertical structure of descending and ascending. Further, the structure of descent and ascent is empowered by a mediating figure who is able to break or transgress the boundary between two normally discrete realms, in this case variously described as the realms of the living and the dead, the human and the ghostly, the earthly and the underwordly.

In Chapter Six Origen introduces the first set of images that will function typologically to suggest the play that is woven into these letters. Having established that Samuel was really in Hades, he can now ask, "Who is greater, Samuel or Jesus Christ? Anyone of those who have already once seen that the Lord Jesus Christ is the one proclaimed by the prophets will not dare to say that Christ is not greater than the prophets. So when you grant that Jesus Christ is greater, was Christ in Hades, or was he not there? Is not the saying in the Psalms true ... that the Savior descended into Hades? The 15th Psalm refers to him: 'For you do not abandon my soul in Hades, nor do you allow your holy one to see destruction'.".[32] Origen goes on at some length in his discussion of the underworldly Christ; the structural similarity of the story of the Christ who descends into Hades but is not abandoned there to the story of Samuel who also descends but rises again to the surface is striking. But there are also curious reversals: Samuel prophesies to Saul above; the Christ prophesies to souls beneath; Samuel ascends to prophesy, while the Christ descends; finally, Samuel's movements are not by choice, whereas those of the Christ are.

These reversals of content, however, do not detract from the typological play that has been set in motion by the juxtaposition of these two sets of images. Indeed, such asymmetry is what gives typology its iconoclastic impact.[33] Samuel does not cease to be Samuel; yet he has become a type of Christ. The image is broken open, but not replaced. As Origen argues from the outset, a text's icons cannot he obliterated if interpretation is to take place. This point is crucial for an understanding of typological interpretation, which is "a specialized form of the repeatability of myth", as one modern critic has put it.[34] Working with distinct images that retain their difference, typology demonstrates their similarity. It is an interpretive strategy that one scholar has named "repetition", and it "arises out of the interplay of the opaquely similar things, opaque in the sense of riddling".[35] The type, then, might be characterized as "the meaning generated by the echoing of two dissimilar things ... ".[36] Typology depends on the troping of one image by another, and it is a process whose repetitions are seemingly endless, as Origen had exclaimed much earlier in his *De principiis*, when he remarked that as soon as the interpreter "has discovered a small fragment of what he is seeking, he again sees other things that must be sought for; and if in turn he comes to know these, he will again see arising out of them many more things that demand investigation".[37]

Given this perspective, it is not surprising that there is a second typological move in Origen's homily on the Witch of Endor. The second move is implicit, not explicit. But I think there *is* a second typology, and I base my reading on a very curious shift in Origen's focus of attention. In Chapters Six through Eight, Origen has established the Christ within the structure of ascent and descent that characterizes Samuel's story. But what of the mediating figure, who makes the movement possible? Samuel is not a candidate for this. In Chapters Nine through Ten, Origen asks, rhetorically, how it is possible to escape from Hades to the place of the tree of life, since "it is impossible to pass by those who are stationed to guard the way to this tree".[38] The cherubim and the flaming sword do not allow passage. Who is able to break through the flaming sword, making passage possible? It is of course the Christ: "The patriarchs and the prophets and everyone were waiting for the arrival of my Lord Jesus Christ, so that he might open the path".[39]

Origen's closing comments indicate that his typologizing of the Christ by Samuel was incomplete, given the literal structure of the biblical text with which he was working. For along with descent and ascent, it has a mediatorial figure who breaks the barrier between the underworld and this world. The witch had the power to bring up the inhabitants of hell, just as the Christ has the power to bring them up and through the flaming sword. The witch is a type of Christ, or so Origen's strange ending implies.

This ending functions as an answer to a question that Origen had asked earlier, in Chapter Six: "What, then, is the witch doing here? What has the witch to do with the bringing up of a righteous soul?".[40] He does not answer the question directly, moving instead to argue that she had really brought up Samuel, who had really been in Hades.

The witch, however, is crucial to the completion of the typology that Origen has been constructing. She is a powerful breaker of boundaries and mediates between the underworld and another realm, just as the Christ does. Again, as with the typology of Samuel, there are curious reversals. The witch is feminine, the Christ is masculine; she calls up into the human world; he calls up into paradise. The iconoclastic force of typological juxtaposition is evident once more.

It seems fitting that Origen's plea for literal reading came in his discussion of a text whose dominant images are those of underworldly depths, whose bounds are transgressed so that prophecy can occur. As Origen says in *De principiis* 4.3.11, interpretation is itself a breaking or transgression. Using a metaphor of hell, he calls the letter a "gate of brass" that must be broken through—but not replaced. That is the literal law of letters, and Origen meant what he said. Typologizing a text about the depths and transgression, he himself broke through to another realm of signification and saved the text at the same time. Like the witch, an *engastrimūthos* speaking from the depths of her own being in order to plumb the depths of the earth, Origen spoke from the literal depths of the text.

Interpreting that "great code", the Bible, is still today a hellish experience in many ways. This essay means to offer Origen's exegetical theories and strategies as ways of passage through the flaming sword. If one of our ways to the word of God is through the words of Scripture, we must give those words the respect they deserve *as words*, not idolizing the icons but entertaining their plenitude. "The squirming facts exceed the squamous mind",[41] yet as Origen insists, it is precisely in that excess of meaning that the interpreter finds his work, "bringing up" the shadows held by the letters.

Notes

1 Carroll, *Alice in Wonderland*, in *The Annotated Alice*, Gardner (ed), p. 137.
2 Origen, *Com. in Cant.* 3.11 (Lawson, p. 210).
3 As Origen argues in *De prin.* 4.3.4, "The passages which are historically true are far more numerous than those which are composed with purely spiritual meanings" (Crouzel and Simonetti, vol. 3, p. 359). Moreover, in *Com. in Ioh.* 5.20, he says that the intention of Biblical authors was "to speak the truth at once spiritually and bodily (*pneumatikōs 'ama kai sōmatikōs*) when that was feasible" (Blanc, vol. 2, p. 395). As he goes on to say, however, the historical dimension is not always present. More important for the interpreter than seeking out historical referents is to investigate *how* the *parts* of a given passage are *connected*, because the connections hold the key to the entire meaning of a given text (*De prin.* 4.3.5 [Crouzel and Simonetti, vol. 3, p. 363]). As Crouzel remarks, Origen "explains the Bible by the Bible" (Crouzel and Simonetti, vol. 4, p. 203, n. 29). Historical facts are there—even "thousands" of them (*De prin.*

4.3.4)—but they are not the basis of interpretation. On these issues see the fine essay by Nautin, "Origène Prédicateur".

4 See, for example, Origen, *Com. in Ioh.* 10.4.17 (Blanc, vol. 2, p. 393). I have discussed this issue at some length in "Origen and the Bestial Soul: A Poetics of Nature", pp. 121-29.

5 Frye, *The Great Code*, p. 60. Frye goes on to give examples (p. 61): "When Jesus says (John 10:9), 'I am the door', the statement means literally just what it says, but there are no doors outside the verse in John to be pointed to. And when the Book of Jonah says that the Lord prepared a great fish to swallow Jonah, there are no great fish outside the Book of Jonah that come into the story. We could almost say that even the existence of God is an inference from the existence of the Bible: in the *beginning* was the Word". As I hope to show, these are thoroughly Origenist statements.

6 Smelik, "The Witch of Endor", pp. 160-79. This article does a thorough job of surveying the spectrum of Patristic commentary on the scene at Endor.

7 Gregory of Nyssa, *De Pythonissa*, discussed by Smelik, "The Witch of Endor", p. 166, n. 24.

8 Smelik, "The Witch of Endor", p. 167.

9 Augustine, *De div. quaes. ad Simpl.* 2.3.2, in Smelik, "The Witch of Endor", p. 167.

10 Smelik, "The Witch of Endor", pp. 171-75, discussing Theodore's *Quaestiones* (*CSCO* 55, p. 222ff.).

11 Eustathius, *De Pythonissa*, in Smelik, "The Witch of Endor", p. 165.

12 The Septuagint translated the Hebrew phrase, "a woman who has an '*ob*'" (underworldly spirit), as *engastrimūthos*, literally "one who speaks in the belly". For a discussion of this phenomenon, see Onians, *The Origins of European Thought*, pp. 488-90; Gaster, *Myth, Legend, and Custom in the Old Testament*, pp. 462-75; and Smith, *Jesus the Magician*, p. 78.

13 Origen, *Hom. in Jer.* 18.2 (Nautin and Husson, vol. 2, pp. 183-85).

14 For the chronology of Origen's Caesarean writings, see Nautin, *Origène*, pp. 401-5, 411.

15 Origen, *De Engastrimūthō* 3. All translations are my own. For information on the form and context of Origen's homiletic preaching, see Nautin, "Origène Prédicateur", pp. 100-12.

16 Origen, *De Engastrimūthō* 3.

17 Ibid., 2.

18 Ibid.

19 Ibid., 4. It is possible that Origen's opponents were not willing to let the text deafen them because, on the basis of Origen's summary of their arguments in *De Engastrimūthō* 3, they seem to have been following the method of rhetorical analysis of historical narratives called *anaskeuē* (refutation), which could prove texts to be improbable, inappropriate, and incredible. Clearly the guide in such analysis would be one's own theological perspective, which would dictate the canons of judgment, and not the text's letters. Origen himself used this method in his exegesis of the gospels but, unlike his opponents here, he used it to disentangle the "literal" from the "historical" and not to rewrite the text itself. In Origen's hands this method left the letters of texts intact and made room for allegorical interpretation. See Grant, *The Earliest Lives of Jesus*, pp. 38-47 and passim.

20 Origen, *De Engastrimūthō* 4.

21 Ibid., 2.

22 Ibid., 4.

23 This point about plenitude comes from Origen's *Hom. in Jer.* 50.11.2 (Nautin and Husson, vol. 2, p. 343), where, as in his *De Engastrimūthō*, he is speaking about the inspiration of scriptural texts: "The Holy Scriptures have not a single dot which is empty of the wisdom of God ... The holy books breathe the spirit of plenitude". See also *Com. in Ps.* 1: "Holy Providence, which made to humankind the gift of a wisdom more than human by means of letters, sowed the oracles of salvation in each letter, so to speak, according to its capacity to receive the imprint of wisdom" (quoted and translated by Nautin, "Origène Prédicateur", p. 137, n. 4).

24 Quilligan, *The Language of Allegory*, p. 68.

25 Crouzel and Simonetti, *Origène: Traité des principes*, vol. 4, p. 184, n. 39. That Origen could and did distinguish the literal from the historical is clear from *De prin.* 4.2.1, where he constantly ridicules those who confuse the two and gives examples of the foolish beliefs with which they then find themselves saddled. Their problem, Origen says in *De prin.* 4.2.2, is that they interpret *pros to psilon gramma*, "according to the bare letter". They think, in other words, that the letter (*gramma*) is bare (*psilon*). It is striking that Origen chose the word *psilos* to characterize the perspective he is criticizing. *Psilos* means "bare" in the sense of being "stripped of feathers and fur". *Logos psilos*, "bare language", refers to language that is abstract and has no rhythm, prose as opposed to poetry, while *poiēsis psilos*, "bare poetry", refers to mere poetry without music (Liddell, Scott, and Jones, *A Greek-English Dictionary*, s.v. *psilos*). Those who think that the letter is bare have not seen that letters are icons, images that contain poetic echoes, the feathers and fur of the Spirit. Origen, however, defends brute letters; they are not *psilos* but carry the rhythm of divine wisdom.

26 Frye, *The Great Code*, p. 60.

27 Ibid., p. 61.

28 Crouzel and Simonetti, *Origène: Traité des principes*, vol. 4, p. 180, n. 31; Nautin, "Origène Prédicateur", p. 145; and Crouzel, *Connaissance Mystique*, passim. There has been a lengthy discussion about how to name Origen's exegetical strategies, the main debate centering on whether "allegory" or "typology" is the correct term. See, inter alia, Daniélou, *Origène*; Hanson, *Allegory and Event*; De Lubac, "Typologie et allégorisme"; and Crouzel, "La distinction de la 'typologie' et de l'allégorie". The discussion has come to a standstill, it seems to me, perhaps because the terms "allegory" and "typology" are not really opposed to each other. I therefore offer in the following paragraph another way of imagining their relation in hopes of provoking renewed discussion.

29 Quilligan, *Language of Allegory*, p. 26.

30 See Frye, *Anatomy of Criticism*, p. 91.

31 Origen, *De Engastrimūthō* 3-5.

32 Ibid., 6.

33 The term "iconoclastic" is used here as I understand its definition by Vahanian, *No Other God*, pp. 37-63. On pp. 42-43, Vahanian argues that "the word is an icon, the image of an imageless reality, which it can equally reveal and conceal ... But the word can open or obstruct the way only if it is *iconoclastic*—if it rebels against freezing reality into an image, a cliché, a slogan, or a dogma ... ". He suggests further that part of the iconoclastic function of the word as icon is that it be able to "inhabit, or receive, another word, only when it calls out the neighborhood of another word, of words" (pp. 58-59). The iconoclasm of Origen's typologizing is situated precisely in this phenomenon of words inhabiting other words.

34 Frye, *The Great Code*, p. 84.

35 Miller, *Fiction and Repetition*, p. 8. Also instructive is Miller's "Ariadne's Thread: Repetition and the Narrative Line".
36 Miller, *Fiction and Repetition*, p. 9.
37 Origen, *De prin.* 4.3.14 (Butterworth, p. 311).
38 Origen, *De Engastrimūthō* 9.
39 Ibid.
40 Ibid., 6.
41 Stevens, "Connoisseur of Chaos", *Collected Poems*, p. 215.

Chapter Eleven

Poetic Words, Abysmal Words: Reflections on Origen's Hermeneutics

In an essay entitled "Is there a Fish in this Text?", the literary critic Robert Scholes reflects upon an anecdote by Ezra Pound that deals with a particular kind of relationship between a writer, writing, and what is written about. Here is the anecdote.

> No man is equipped for modern thinking until he has understood the anecdote of Agassiz and the fish:
> A post-graduate student equipped with honours and diplomas went to Agassiz to receive the final and finishing touches. The great man offered him a small fish and told him to describe it.
> Post-graduate student: "That's only a sunfish".
> Agassiz: "I know that. Write a description of it".
> After a few minutes the student returned with the description of the Ichthus Heliodiplodokus, or whatever term is used to conceal the common sunfish from vulgar knowledge, family of Heliichthinkerus, etc., as found in textbooks of the subject.
> Agassiz again told the student to describe the fish.
> The student produced a four-page essay. Agassiz then told him to look at the fish. At the end of three weeks the fish was in an advanced stage of decomposition, but the student knew something about it.[1]

Underlying this anecdote by Pound are stories by students in the mid-nineteenth century who actually experienced such ritual initiations at the hands of the biologist Louis Agassiz. Into what were they being initiated? Scholes points out that, in the paradigm enshrined by Agassiz, there is a strong presumption that we learn by looking and that, further, we live in "a real and solid world in a perfectly transparent language" that is thus able to communicate that world "as it really is". Yet, as Scholes goes on to remark, "To 'speak the fish' as a biologist or a fisherman or a poet is to speak in a particular discourse".[2] Our post-graduate friend with his rotten fish was being initiated into a specific discourse, a structure within which he could "see" the fish.

Scholes, however, wonders whether the student knew that he was being initiated into a conceptual framework, that nothing can be "'seen' apart from the concept that gives it status". He argues that it is time—indeed, past time—to abandon the uncritical assumption that has informed Western thinking and writing, which is that "a complete self confronts a solid world, perceiving it directly and accurately, always capable of capturing it perfectly in a transparent language".[3] "The way to see the fish and to write the fish", rather, "is first to see how one's discourse writes the fish. And the way to see one discourse is to see more than one. To write the fish in many modes is finally to see that one will never catch the fish in any one discourse".[4]

I have stayed with this fish for some time because I think that, decomposed or not, the fish and structures of perception that one brings to bear upon it may function as figures for one of the focal points of Origen's hermeneutical work. The problem of looking—that is, of interpretation—was central to his writing, and it is that problem that I wish to address.

Scholes' perspective on interpretation is double-edged. To use the terms in the title of this essay, a text offers to an interpreter both abysmal and poetic possibilities, abysmal as in the Greek ἄβυσσος, without bottom, no end to meaning, no chance of catching the fish, yet also poetic as in the Greek ποίησις, a working relationship with words that discloses not only multiple dimensions of the fish but also multiple dimensions of the interpreter's stance toward the fish.

"Abysmal" and "poetic" are not really two different kinds of interpretation; rather these terms indicate how the mood of the interpreter is valenced when faced with "the often problematical process of meaning multiple things simultaneously with one word".[5] Origen's approach to his fish, the Bible, shows awareness of the double-edged quality, the abysmal and poetic dimensions of any interpretative act.

Origen's awareness of ποίησις, of the imaginative working of Biblical words, is evident in the opening sentence of his first *Homily on Exodus*: "I think each word of divine scripture is like a seed whose nature is to multiply diffusely ... Its increase is proportionate to the diligent labor of the skillful farmer or the fertility of the earth".[6] Words are alive, explosive, diffuse, but only if they fall on the fertile ground of a mind alive to multiple meaning. In a change of metaphor, Origen remarks in his *Commentary on Matthew* that words act as goads, prodding the beast, the interpreter, to move in the nuanced world that they offer.[7] In yet another change of metaphor, Origen pictures words in his *Commentary on the Song of Songs* as beguiling and seductive, inflaming their reader with desire.[8] In the *Philocalia,* words are shepherds; in the *Homilies on Genesis* they are springs; in the *Homilies on the Song of Songs* they are, simply, mysteries.[9] Yet under whatever metaphor Origen discusses words—agricultural, erotic, bestial—it seems clear that words are active, that there is a play or an energy packed into language. The interpreter's task is to let words speak, not to perform an exegetical dissection upon them. It is a question of interpretive attitude, as expressed, for example, by the philosopher Martin Heidegger: "Words are not terms, and thus are not like buckets and kegs from which we scoop a content that is there. Words are wellsprings that are found and dug up in the telling, wellsprings that must be found and dug up again and again, that easily cave in, but that at times also well up when least expected".[10]

The interpreter is not, however, merely a passive observer who watches as meaning wells up out of language. There is work to be done. In one of his most extended figures for interpretative labor, Origen shows Isaac dwelling at the wells of vision.[11] As a type of the interpreter as well as a type of Christ, Isaac *digs* the wells of vision and does not merely dwell there. Actually Isaac is re-digging the wells of his father, which had been filled in by envious Philistines.[12] As Heidegger noted, words are well-springs that must be found and dug up again and again because our ability as interpreters to dwell in the mobile realm of figures easily caves in, blocked and choked by the wish for an end, for a word to end all words, for a final truth that will make things clear, for the hope that, as a poet said ironically, "They will get it straight one day at the Sorbonne".[13] Isaac kept on digging—indeed, his digging *was* his dwelling. On this point Origen is uncompromising: just as language is agonistic, so too is interpretative activity.

In his commentary on the story of the Witch of Endor in I Samuel, Origen says that there is "a great struggle (ἀγών) in the language of God".[14] Biblical texts are agonistic because the literal words on the page are figures, icons that hold a plenitude of meaning. Thus the literal quality of every text is metaphoric, and the interpreter's task is to "wake up what is useful" in all the icons.[15] In Origen's view the Bible is a "texte crypté", as Marguerite Harl has put it, and its words are radical metaphors, or catachreses, which are "violent, forced, or abusive" uses of a word "to name something which has no literal name".[16] Words are violent; so also is interpretation.

We have just heard one of Origen's forceful descriptions of interpretative work: to wake up what is useful in the icons, to give a jolt to a slumbering word that will not willingly disclose its dreams, its interior visions. Elsewhere Origen resorts to more violent images. In his *Homilies on Genesis,* Origen takes the Christ of the Gospels as his model interpreter. More specifically, it is the story of the feeding of the five thousand with just a few loaves of bread that engages his interest. "Notice that the Lord in the Gospels breaks a few loaves, and notice how many thousand people he refreshes ... While the loaves are whole, no one is filled, nor do the loaves themselves appear to be increased".[17] As Origen goes on to say, the loaves are the words of Scripture, which must be broken, "crumbled into pieces ... Unless the letter has been discussed and broken into little pieces, its meaning cannot reach everyone".[18] Like the Christ who broke the loaves, the interpreter breaks the word, rending its letters in the service of meaning.

In the *Philocalia,* Origen offers yet another image of the interpretive process. And once again the Christ is the paradigm of the interpreter. Scripture as a whole, says Origen, is "the musical instrument of God, letting a single melody be heard by way of different sounds".[19] The maestro of this symphonic production is the Christ, the Word who can hear harmony in discord, identity in difference. The human interpreter works exactly in this way, playing the discordant notes so that the harmony might become apparent. The presiding figure for all this is astonishingly strong: David playing the lyre to appease the evil spirit of Saul.[20] Although he does not spell out the ramifications of this image, its place in the musical setting is clear: as David, the interpreter appeases evil spirits, the words themselves, since his musical ability consists, according to Origen, in smiting or striking the chords at the appropriate moment.[21] Striking and smiting, the interpreter approaches an equally adversarial text. The musical metaphor would be quite beguiling, lulling one to sleep, had Origen not revealed its foundation in difference and discord.

Finally there is Origen's well-known metaphor of interpretation in *De Principiis,* where words are likened to a field in which treasure is buried. One knows that the treasure is there, but how to expose it? Using a metaphor of hell, Origen says: "These treasures require for their discovery the help of God, who alone is able to 'break in pieces the gates of brass' that conceal them and to burst the iron bars that are upon the gates ... ".[22] "God", in this case, is the descendent Christ harrowing hell, who is in his turn image for the interpreter whose work is one of breaking and transgression.[23] However polysemous their potential, words are gates of brass that must be broken by active interpretation; unless so engaged, they remain like iron bars. The problem, however, is this: how, exactly, does the interpreter go about his violent task while still respecting the depths of meaning in words?

The refusal of words to reveal their depths easily is an agony for the interpreter. Language is not transparent to meaning; on the contrary, as Origen notes often, Biblical language is frequently opaque. The letters—that is, the literal words on the page—are sometimes absurd and they present the reader with conundrums.[24] As Harl has pointed out, for Origen the "semantic habits" of the Christ as Word, as language itself, are obscure, enigmatic, ambiguous, riddling, dark.[25] Words may indeed reveal what Origen calls "the depths of the wisdom of God",[26] but do they not also conceal those depths as well? Is there, in other words, a "bottom", an end to the poetic display of verbal polysemy?

With such a question, we begin to slide into the abysmal aspect of interpretation, with its quandary concerning not only whether one can catch the fish, but whether there is a fish to be caught at all. In his work *Against Celsus,* Origen remarks that "the gospel so desires wise men among believers that, in order to exercise the understanding of hearers, it has expressed certain truths in enigmatic forms, and some in the so-called dark sayings, some by parables, and others by problems".[27] In view of such statements, Harl argues that because it is precisely those obscure passages of the Bible that give access to wisdom, the paradoxical fact is that for Origen wisdom arises from the *silence* of the text.[28] Interpretation is founded on the refusal of speech! Such silence is related to another passage in *Against Celsus* where Origen develops an extended image comparing the unknowability of God with Biblical texts: the obscure words of the Bible are like the "great deep" that covers God like a garment, like the darkness that is God's hiding-place, like the "depth of the knowledge of the Father".[29] Is there a God in this text?

One way to look at this question from Origen's perspective is to examine his famous comment in the first *Homily* on *The Song of Songs.*

> The bride beholds the Bridegroom; and He, as soon as she has seen Him, goes away. He does this frequently throughout the Song; and that is something nobody can understand who has not suffered it himself. God is my witness that I have often perceived the Bridegroom drawing near me and being most intensely present with me; then suddenly He has withdrawn and I could not find Him, though I sought to do so. I long, therefore, for Him to come again, and sometimes He does so. Then, when He has appeared and I lay hold of Him, He slips away once

more; and, when He has so slipped away, my search for Him begins anew.[30]

This statement has typically been used to show Origen as a mystic—or, in Dodds' phrase, a "mystic manqué".[31] The soul is the Bride longing for mystical union with the Christ as Bridegroom. There is, however, another way to understand this statement, for in both the *Commentary* and the *Homilies on the Song of Songs* Origen develops a picture of the Bridegroom as *Logos*—as language—who woos, entices, and seduces the Bride, a figure for a reader or interpreter of texts.[32] In this case, Origen's lament about the disappearing Bridegroom, more present when he is absent, can be read as a hermeneutical comment. The word that slips away at the moment when one thinks that one has "laid hold of it", only to return with promise of renewed meaning, and so on ad infinitum, forms a precise picture of the deferral of final meaning characteristic of the interpreter's abyss. The *Logos*/Bridegroom works to de-center or defer the interpreter's tidy structures of meaning in consonance with the poetic character of words, as we have seen.

Origen wrote in the *Philocalia* that if "'the world is unable to contain the books that would be written' [Jn. 21:25] concerning the divinity of Jesus, it is not because of the number of books but because of the greatness of the realities which cannot be said in human language".[33] Ironically, Origen uses words in order to say that he cannot use words. The irony of this kind of statement has been called in contemporary literary criticism by a French phrase, *mise en abyme*. *Mise en abyme* is a "name for the enigma of the nameless", an "impasse of language which is that however hard one tries to fix a word in a single sense it remains indeterminable, uncannily resisting attempts to end its movement".[34] The paradox of the *mise en abyme* is that "without the production of some schema, some icon, there can be no glimpse of the abyss, no vertigo of the underlying nothingness. Any such schema, however, both opens the chasm, creates it or reveals it, and at the same time fills it up, covers it over by naming it, gives the groundless a ground, the bottomless a bottom".[35] Any word at once creates the "ground" of meaning, names it "properly", so to speak, reveals the ground, and covers it over. What is the interpreter to do in the face of this abysmal paradox?

Origen's response to the silence and the absence at the center of words is allegory, that interpretative strategy most appropriate to his abysmal interpretative consciousness. In a fragment from his exegesis of I Cor. 2:13, he says: "It is by examining together this and that word and by reuniting those that are similar that the sense of Scripture reveals itself, as one might say".[36] Anyone who is familiar with the first book of Origen's *Commentary on John* knows what this procedure is: all the names of the Christ as *Logos* and Wisdom are assembled and become successive metaphors for each other.[37] The "ground", the Christ, is named, but no one name suffices; each in turn becomes the figure for yet another "ground" in a constant displacement of terms that one modern critic has called the "lateral dance of allegory".[38] This lateral dance is "an incessant movement from one displaced figural point to another", an attempt to find the final figure, the trope of tropes.[39] Origen describes allegory's lateral dance thus: as soon as the interpreter "has discovered a small fragment of what he is seeking, he again sees other things that must be sought for, and if in turn he comes to know these, he will again see arising out of them many more things that demand investigation".[40]

In Origen's hands this interpretative strategy is a kind of repetition, an "interplay of opaquely similar things, opaque in the sense of riddling".[41] The "similar words" that Origen unites as he interprets texts are opaquely similar; for how, logically, can one really say that "way", "door", "light", "shepherd", and so on are "similar", except insofar as they are all figures that both cover and reveal the silence and absence of God? Origen's word for this aspect of allegory—this "other-saying"—is μετάληψις: "transposition", "alternation", "succession", "the use of one word for another".[42] Not only does Origen so characterize his work, but such scholars as Crouzel and Harl have noted about his work its operation by *glissement*—the sliding of words into other words characteristic of his handling of a text's meaning.[43] Thus, for example, in the passage from the *Philocalia* concerning the Christ as musician, the maestro is displaced by the peacemaker, who is displaced by the shepherd. Only through such displacement or deferral or discord can meaning appear.

What, then, is allegory? As one critic has suggested, allegory names an exegetical perspective that affirms "the possibility of an otherness, a polysemy, inherent in the very words on the page".[44] But there is more to allegory than this: in the hands of an interpreter like Origen, allegory is the name of interpretation as such, provided that one brings to interpretation the kind of poetic and abysmal recognition that Origen expressed so well. Consciousness of the perceptual structures that one brings to words entails the recognition that all writing is allegory, a fall into a poetic abyss.

The critical stance that allegory names has been well expressed by Vincent Leitch: "Reading uncovers and confronts a language that vacillates uncontrollably between the promise of referential meaning and the rhetorical subversion of that promise. Truth is permanently threatened. A disruptive tropological language endlessly repeats that threat. Whatever wisdom the language of the text offers is undermined through a continuous slide or displacement from figure to substitute figure".[45] Recall the subversive activity of the *Logos*-Bridegroom, endlessly threatening loss of meaning, yet at the same time promising it. Abysmal and poetic at once, the Christ as *logos* is for Origen a figure for allegory itself, both in the Biblical text as well as in texts that displace that text by interpreting it. The *Logos* bestowed on Origen the hermeneutic awareness that we have been exploring here. As Origen's Agassiz, the word initiated him not only into looking, but into consciousness about his *stance toward* looking. The gift of *Logos* to Origen, and his gift to us, is allegory, a poetics of the abyss.

Notes

1 Scholes, "Is There a Fish in this Text?", p. 309.
2 Ibid., p. 310.
3 Ibid.. pp. 315, 310.
4 Ibid., p. 318.
5 Quilligan, *The Language of Allegory*, p. 26.
6 Origen, *Hom. in Ex.* 1.1 (Heine, p. 227).
7 Origen, *Comm. in Matt.* 2 (=*Philocalia* 6.1) (Harl, p. 309). See Harl (trans), *Origène: Philocalie*, p. 316 for a discussion of this passage.
8 In his *Comm. in Cant.*, Origen has offered a sustained figuration of the Bridegroom as word. This word smites with passionate love and flirts with, beguiles, and seduces the Bride, a figure for a text's reader. See the discussion of this figuration in Miller, "Pleasure of the Text, Text of Pleasure".
9 Origen, *Philocalia* 6.1 (Harl, p. 309); *Homilies on Genesis* 13 (Heine, pp. 185-95); *Homilies on the Song of Songs* 1.4 (Rousseau, p. 81).
10 Heidegger, *What Is Called Thinking?*, p. 130.
11 Origen, *Hom. in Gen.* 13 (Heine, pp. 185-95).
12 Ibid., 12.4 (trans. Heine, pp. 180-181).
13 Stevens, "Notes Toward A Supreme Fiction", in *Collected Poems*, p. 406.
14 Origen, *De Engastrimūthō* 4.
15 Ibid., 2.
16 Harl (trans), *Origene: Philocalie*, p. 135; on catachresis, see Miller, "Stevens' Rock and Criticism as Cure", p. 28 and Harl, ibid., p. 129.
17 Origen, *Hom. in Gen.* 12 (Heine, p. 182).
18 Ibid., pp. 182-183.
19 Origen, *Philocalia* 6.2 (Harl, p. 311).
20 Ibid.
21 See the discussion by Harl (trans), *Origène: Philocalie*, p. 321.
22 Origen, *De prin.* 4.3.11 (Butterworth, p. 306).
23 Origen also speaks about Christ as a transgressor of boundaries in *De Engastrimūthō*. For a discussion see Cox, "Origen and the Witch of Endor".

24 On the literal absurdity of some Biblical words, see Origen, *De prin.* 4.3.5 and *Philocalia* 2. In his *Comm. in Ioh.*, Origen remarks that the intention of Biblical authors was "to speak the truth at once spiritually and bodily when that was feasible"; but it was not always possible (Blanc, vol. 2, p. 395). See the discussion of this issue in Harl (trans), *Origène: Philocalie*, pp. 94-100.
25 Harl, "Origène et la Sémantique", pp. 161-87.
26 Origen, *De prin.* 4.3.4 (Butterworth, p. 296).
27 Origen, *Against Celsus* 3.45 (Chadwick, pp. 159-60).
28 Harl (trans), *Origène: Philocalie*, p. 460.
29 Origen, *Against Celsus* 6.17 (Chadwick, pp. 330-31).
30 Origen, *Hom. In Cant.* 1.7 (Lawson, pp. 279-80).
31 Dodds, *Pagan and Christian in an Age of Anxiety*, p. 98.
32 See n. 8 above.
33 Origen, *Philocalia* 15.19 (Harl, pp. 437-38).
34 Miller, "Stevens' Rock and Criticism as Cure", p. 11.
35 Ibid., p. 12.
36 Origen, fragment on I Cor. 2:13, cited in Harl (trans), *Origène Philocalie*, p.143.
37 Origen follows a similar procedure in *De Prin.* 1.2 and 4.4.1-2.
38 Miller, "Fiction and Repetition", p. 68. See also Miller's "Stevens' Rock and Criticism as Cure", pp. 18-19, and the discussion of Miller's concept of "lateral dance" in Leitch, *Deconstructive Criticism*, pp. 190-97.
39 Leitch, *Deconstructive Criticism*, p. 191.
40 Origen, *De prin.* 4.3.14 (Butterworth, p. 311).
41 Miller, *Fiction and Repetition: Seven English Novels*, p. 8.
42 See the discussion of this word, with many texts, by Harl (trans), *Origène: Philocalie*, pp. 133-35.
43 Harl (trans), *Origène: Philocalie*, p. 312; Crouzel, *Connaissance Mystique*, p. 58.
44 Quilligan, *The Language of Allegory*, p. 26.
45 Leitch, *Deconstructive Criticism*, p. 184.

Chapter Twelve

In Praise of Nonsense: A Piety of the Alphabet in Ancient Magic

In a collection of religious texts from late antiquity now known as the Nag Hammadi Library, there is a long poem entitled *Thunder, Perfect Mind*.[1] The poem is the self-revelation of a powerful goddess: she is "perfect mind", and she "thunders". Even a brief glance at this text suggests why the revelations of perfect mind might be connected with the awesome but incomprehensible rumblings of thunder, for Perfect Mind speaks in riddle and paradox, thus subverting the reader's ability to comprehend her in any straightforward or univocal way. Like the elemental "speech" of thunder, her speech cannot be reduced to logical propositions. Indeed, from a rational analytical perspective, the structure of her language *is* nonsense; it offends the ear with its noisy incongruities.

To understand Perfect Mind, one must leave the world of discursive language behind and enter the structure of paradox, where a potentially endless play of opposites is entertained:

> For I am the first and the last.
> I am the honored one and the scorned one.
> I am the whore and the holy one.[2]

How can the first be last? How can Perfect Mind be both whore and holy one? Part of the genius of her language is precisely to force the hearer to ask such questions and thereby to lead that hearer more deeply into her mystery.

Her mystery is, of course, a thunderous silence. As Plotinus once remarked, all visions of divinity "baffle telling" (VI 9 [9], 10-11), and they, frustrate the understandable human desire to tell the story plainly, to capture truth in words at last (VI 9 [9], 11).[3] At the end of words, the mystery still remains, majestically silent:

> I am the hearing which is attainable to everyone
> and the speech which cannot be grasped.
> I am a mute who does not speak,
> and great is my multitude of words.[4]

Words cannot capture truth, but they can carry its resonant echoes. Plotinus goes so far as to say that visions of primal reality "break into speech", whose "sounds labor to express the essential nature of the universe produced by the travail of the utterer and so to represent, as far as sounds may, the origin of reality".[5]

Like Plotinus, Perfect Mind knows that her thundering riddles are the echoes of her reality in words, and it is those words that give her mystery a place in which to dwell in human consciousness. Toward the end of her self-revelatory poem, she says:

> I am the name of the sound
> and the sound of the name.
> I am the sign of the letter
> and the designation of the division.[6]

She identifies herself not only with the paradoxical *images* of language but with *language itself.* Perhaps the ultimate revelation is that this goddess is the very process of speaking that she uses to characterize herself. The structure of her language carries her nature in it: she *is* what she *speaks,* as well as teaching how to speak. In the beginning was the word.

Such is the nature of divinity. There are, of course, many ways of responding to this poetic statement of the linguistic qualities of fundamental reality. In this essay, my interest lies in exploring a particularly (and peculiarly) appropriate linguistic response to linguistic reality in certain religious texts from late antiquity. Designated by scholarly convention as "magical" texts, they embody in a most strident form the *Thunder, Perfect Mind's* perspective on the intimate relationship between being and speaking.[7]

The Sounds of the Spirit

Perfect Mind calls herself "the sign of the letter" and exhorts her followers:

> Hear me, you hearers,
> and learn of my words, you who know me
> I am the hearing that is attainable to everything;
> I am the speech that cannot be grasped.[8]

If one accepts such a conception of deity as the framework for one's own reality, how is it possible to show that one has learned the words of the speech that cannot be grasped? The *Gospel of the Egyptians,* also called "The Holy Book of the Great Invisible Spirit", offers the following reply to our question:

> And the throne of his (glory) was established (in it, this one) on which his unrevealable name (is inscribed), on the tablet (...) one is the word, the (Father of the light) of everything, he (who came) forth from the silence, while he rests in the silence, he whose name (is) in an (invisible) symbol. (A) hidden, (invisible) mystery came forth iiiiiiiiiiiiiiiiiii(iii)   eeeeeeeeeeeeeeeeeee(ee   o) ooooooooooooooooooooo uu(uuu) uuuuuuuuuuuuuuuu eeeeeeeeeeeeeeeeeeee aaaaaaa (aaaa) aaaaaaaaaa oooooooo (oo)oooooooo ooo. And (in this) way the three powers gave praise to the (great), invisible, unnameable, virginal, uncallable Spirit ...[9]

Here is the "sign of the letter" with a vengeance! It would seem that the author of this prayer to the God of silent mystery knew that when language is revealed for what it truly is—a speaking of the unspeakable—it is incomprehensible, not to be resolved in a final word or in words at all. When the God who is "an invisible symbol" breaks into human speech, his sounds are the echoes of the alphabet, the vowels. Elsewhere in this gospel, in an ecstatic invocation of the God that comes near the end of the text, the same kind of "language" appears:

> 0 glorious name, really truly, aion o on, iiii eee eeee oooo uuuu oooo aaaa(a), really truly ei aaaa oooo, O existing one who sees the aeons! Really truly, aee eee iiii uuuuuu ooooooooo, who is eternally eternal, really truly, iea aio, in the heart, who exists, u aei eis aei, ei o ei, ei os ei![10]

A text from the magical papyri, entitled *Monas or the Eighth Book of Moses,* makes the same point more directly:

> Lord, I represent you faithfully by the seven vowels; come and listen to me; a ee eee iiii ooooo uuuuuu ooooooo.[11]

This alphabetical language, which attempts to sound the secret name of God, also gives voice to human reality. In one of the passages from the *Gospel of the Egyptians* quoted above, God's name is "really truly" "in the heart". As the narrative continues, one learns that "this great name of thine is upon me, O self-begotten Perfect one, who art not outside me ... Now that I have known thee, I have mixed myself with the immutable".[12] To say the name is to become mixed with God.

Another document from Nag Hammadi, *The Discourse on the Eighth and the Ninth*, also links the substance of God with the substance of humans through the vowels:

> O grace! After these things I give thanks by singing a hymn to thee. For I have received life from thee when thou madest me wise. I praise thee. I call thy name that is hidden within me: a o ee o ee o eee ooo iii oooo ooooo ooooo uuuuuuu ooooooooooooooooooooooo. Thou art the one who exists with the spirit. I sing a hymn to thee reverently.[13]

Clearly the vowels of the alphabet designate that point at which the human and divine worlds intersect, at least from the perspective of this text. To speak this language is not only to invoke the God; it is also to sound the depths of one's own primal reality. These strings of vowels are hymnic recitations of praise to the God and to human Godlikeness.

Ecstatic though it may be, there is something ominous about this language of the spirit. In the words of a modern poet, we confront

> ... the murderous alphabet:
> The swarm of thoughts, the swarm of dreams
> Of inaccessible Utopia.[14]

Paul of Tarsus agreed. Writing to his unruly congregation in Corinth, some of whom felt that their utopia was not only *not* inaccessible but fully present, Paul felt compelled to warn them about the dangers of the spiritual language that they were speaking. The kingdom was showing itself in Corinthian worship in the form of glossolalia, that speaking "in the tongues of angels" that the "swarms" of alphabetical combinations we have just seen attempt to represent in writing.[15] Christian tradition sometimes attributed such language to Jesus himself, as in the following passage from the Gnostic work *Pistis Sophia:*

> Then Jesus stood with his disciples beside the water of the ocean and pronounced this prayer, saying: "Hear me, my Father, thou father of all fatherhoods, thou infinite Light: aeeiou. iao. aoi. Oia ... ".[16]

So also Paul, in another mood and writing to a different congregation, could say that "the Spirit helps us in our weakness; for we do not know how to pray as we ought, but the Spirit himself intercedes for us with sighs too deep for words".[17] Such "sighs" or "groans" were, as one scholar has pointed out, the "characteristic form of magical utterance"; in writing, they appear as alphabetical combinations by which the devotee "calls the spirit in the spirit's own language".[18] This, for Paul, is how we "ought" to pray. But, if this kind of praying is truly evidence of the spirit speaking through the prayer, why did Paul castigate the Corinthians for their angelic speech, comparing it with "noisy gong and clanging cymbal"?[19]

The problem, says Paul, lies with the impact of such speaking on "outsiders and unbelievers".[20] For them, the "tongues of angels" are not supremely inarticulate, but merely unintelligible, buzzing swarms of letters:

> If even lifeless instruments, such as the flute or the harp, do not give distinct notes, how will anyone know what is played? ... So with yourselves; if you in a tongue utter speech that is not intelligible, how will anyone know what is said?[21]

Paul concludes by saying that the ecstatic praying can continue only if it is interpreted; for the benefit of the understanding of the uninitiate, spirit must be yoked with mind.[22] This concern that spiritual language might be heard and so dismissed as mere gibberish occurs in the magical traditions as well. The *Pistis Sophia,* for example, does what Paul was advising the Corinthians to do:

> And Jesus cried out as he turned to the four corners of the world with his disciples, and ... he said: "iao. iao. iao. This is its interpretation: iota, because the All came forth; alpha, because it will return again; omega, because the completion of all completions will happen.[23]

Whatever we as modern readers may think about the seeming unintelligibility of even the interpretation given here, it is clear that for the ancient writer the inspired language of the alphabet did carry meaning and could be interpreted.

Fully initiate in this language, Paul everywhere shows his respect for it, even in the midst of protests against it: "If the whole church assembles and all speak in tongues, and outsiders or unbelievers enter, will they not say that you are mad?".[24] The verb used in this passage for madness *(mainomai)* is the one used to characterize the oracular utterances of the Delphic priestess and the Sibyls, as well as the rapturous language of the followers of the god Dionysus, all of whom were also said to speak in a tongue.[25] By his use of this verb, Paul has, perhaps in spite of himself, placed glossolalia squarely in a context of sacred utterance.

What are the dimensions of that context? As A.H. Armstrong observed, the spirituality of the hellenized Mediterranean world had an archaic base; it was indebted to "the immemorial observances, always there and underlying all the changes right down to the establishment of Christianity in the Roman Empire, and after".[26] Paul, who *talks about* what the magical papyri *do*, has in his first letter to the Corinthians described basic aspects of alphabetical language. They are aspects that carry the archaic sensibility of that language, especially as it shows itself in the magical papyri where spiritual language is best and most fully preserved. The information from Paul concerns the form and qualities of this language: it is ecstatic prayer that does not sound like normal language but rather like music (as Paul's repeated musical metaphors suggest—gong, cymbal, flute, harp, bugle); it is not intelligible, but it is rhythmic; and it is also powerful, for it brings manifestations of the Spirit. Further, those manifestations take the verbal form not of reasonable words ("For if I pray in a tongue, my spirit prays but my mind is unfruitful") but, as we know from other sources, of strings of letters, particularly of vowels, and these somehow give expression to "mysteries in the Spirit".[27]

In the next sections of this essay, the piety of the alphabet will be discussed as a late antique phase of two much older ways of thinking, one of which connected language with the charm or spell, the other of which identified the letters of the alphabet with the elements of the cosmos.

The Spell of Language and the Language of the Spell

It is curious that modern scholars, if they have studied alphabetical language at all, have tended largely to take precisely the view that Paul had predicted of outsiders and unbelievers: in various ways, it is nonsense. The range of scholarly reaction to such language has run from outright disapproval to a kind of amused fascination. On the negative side, such language has been viewed as compulsive and egotistic, presuming as it does to summon divine presence into the human realm. Establishing a "lien on God" rather than a "means of approach to him", the users of such language mock the true spiritual life with their mutterings of meaningless sounds.[28] On the positive side, such mutterings are transformed into "mystical gibberish", fit to be compared with Rimbaud's "Sonnet to the

In Praise of Nonsense: A Piety of the Alphabet in Ancient Magic   227

Vowels"![29] They are, in other words, symbolic, attempting to reflect in human writing and speaking the "heavenly writing" of the stars. And they are playful, carrying into adult life the alphabetical games of the child learning the letters, reciting them backward, forward, from the ends to the middle, and so on.[30] The child is initiated into the reality of humans, the speaking animals, by playing with the elemental parts of that speech.

A final characterization will serve to locate the perspective of the present essay, which is that alphabetical language is neither mere fancy nor selfish manipulation. It is rather, as Morton Smith has said, "jabberwocky".[31] Anyone who has read Lewis Carroll's famous poem knows that it speaks the language of the Looking-Glass House. It is an enchanted language that reflects a dimension of reality that is normally hidden. The "inside", "other side", or even "underside" of ordinary reality is best spoken in a poetic language that scrambles ordinary words and shows their imaginal potential. When Alice encounters the whiffling and burbling Jabberwock, she remarks, "'It seems very pretty, but it's *rather* hard to understand!'".[32] Alice's comment is insightful: such linguistic play *is* difficult to understand, and that is precisely the point. The idea that words create a meaningful universe is, as a poet said, the "supreme fiction";[33] language is phantasmal, not transparent to whatever "reality" might be. Travailing and laboring, Plotinus said, we speak, and it is jabberwocky, a creation of the world in metaphor: "We must be patient with language", everywhere reading "so to speak".[34]

It is this recognition of the creative and destructive functions of language, which weaves and unweaves meaning with every word, that is so well captured by the alphabetical language under consideration here. Using language against itself by breaking it down into its elemental parts and then reconfiguring those parts in endless permutations and combinations, the magical prayers constitute an iconoclastic piety. Consider, for example, the following passage from *Monas or the Eighth Book of Moses:*

> I invoke you iueuo oaee Iao aee ai ee ae iouo eue Ieou aeo ei oei iae iooue aue uea io ioai ioai oe ee ou io Iao, the great name; be to me (as) lynx, eagle, snake, phoenix, life, strength, necessity, phantoms of gods, aio iou Iao eio aa oui aaaa eiu io oe Iao ai (etc).[35]

Such an invocation clearly breaks the normal forms of language, but the non-sense that then appears bears the "phantoms" (*eidōla*) of the gods! Ultimate meaning dwells in the breaking of form. The "nonsense" prayers are violently reverent.

When ordinary language is scrambled, the "insides" of the great name of God are revealed. It is not surprising, then, that for the texts under consideration here language casts a spell, and its aura is divine. One of the ways in which this conviction appears is in the alphabetical play with a name of God composed only of vowels: *Iaō*, the Greek name of the Hebrew *YHWH*, the holiest name of God. This is the most frequently petitioned God in the magical papyri, and it seems fitting that invocations to *Iaō* should so often consist of staccato-like combinations of the letters of his name (as in *Pistis Sophia* 136, quoted above: "Thou infinite Light aeeiouo iao aoi oia ... "), since this is the God who confused human language, reducing it to babble, as well as the God who gave speech to humanity in the first place, granting the power to name.[36]

God seems to dwell in the making and unmaking of language. This is suggested further by the frequent invocations to Hermes in our texts. The presence of Hermes, second only to *Iaō* in popularity among devotees of alphabetical language, points to one of the dimensions of archaic sensibility that lived on in the magical papyri. It is that the origin of language is divine. Among numerous theories of the origin of language in its written form, the one that captured the imagination of Greek antiquity named the god Hermes as the inventor of the alphabet.[37] Hermes carried into Greek tradition the linguistic genius of the Egyptian god Thoth, with whom he was identified.[38] The *locus classicus* for discussions of these two figures lies in the writings of Plato, whose ideas about writing are fundamental for understanding the alphabetical fantasies of late antiquity.

In Plato's dialogue *Phaedrus*, Socrates tells the story of the god Thoth presenting various arts (number, astronomy, and so on) to the king of Egypt as useful gifts for the people. Last of all, Thoth gives the king writing: "Here, O king, is a branch of learning that will make the people of Egypt wiser and improve their memories; my discovery provides a recipe for memory and wisdom". The king, however, disagrees: "If men learn this, it will implant forgetfulness in their souls; they will cease to exercise memory because they rely on that which is written, calling things to remembrance no longer from within themselves, but by means of external marks".[39] Writing, from the king's perspective, is a mere semblance of wisdom.

Socrates goes on to explore the "strangeness" of writing by using an analogy to painting:

> The painter's products stand before us as though they were alive, but if you question them, they maintain a most majestic silence. It is the same with written words: they seem to talk to you as though they were

intelligent, but if you ask them anything about what they say... they go on telling you just the same thing forever. And once a thing is put in writing, the composition ... drifts all over the place ... [40]

There is something uncanny about writing. It is God-given and, from the perspective of the God, offers a "recipe for wisdom". From the human perspective, however, the written word is a most frustrating crutch: it merely imitates the truth, and when questioned concerning its meaning it "drifts all over the place". Yet, like a painting, its silence is at the same time iconic, bursting with possibility. It is in such a context that the alphabetical words of the magical prayers belong. Attempting to write the ultimate wisdom, the name of God, they imitate that wisdom with explosions of drifting letters, icons of a divine silence. As the Gnostic text *Zostrianos*, which speaks the language of the alphabet, says, "the one who is saved" is "in the word in the way in which he exists".[41] As with the Goddess in *Thunder, Perfect Mind*, so with the human being. Expression and existence form an inseparable pair.

Plato, however, was not comfortable with the kind of writing that is only an "external mark". The discussion in the *Phaedrus* continues as Socrates asks: "But now tell me, is there another sort of discourse, that is brother to the written speech, but of unquestioned legitimacy?". When Phaedrus, his conversation partner, asks what kind of discourse he has in mind, Socrates replies: "The sort that goes together with knowledge and is written in the soul of the learner ... " Phaedrus then says, "Do you mean the discourse of a man who really knows, which is living and animate? Would it be fair to call the written discourse only a kind of ghost of it?". "Precisely", says Socrates.[42] Wisdom is "written" on the soul, and writing in the letters of human language is the "ghost" *(eidōlon)* of that living writing.

The idea that tangible writing is ghostly compared with the invisible writing on the soul is indeed uncanny, but we have seen these ghosts before in an invocation from *Monas or the Eighth Book of Moses,* where strings of vowels are called *eidōla tōn theōn*, ghosts of the Gods who haunt human language. The persistence of the linguistic metaphor for wisdom is striking, yet it is a metaphor from which we cannot escape. As one scholar has argued in a careful and provocative study, "While presenting writing as a false brother—traitor, infidel, simulacrum— Socrates is for the first time led to envision the brother of this brother, the legitimate one, as *another sort of writing*: not merely as a knowing, living, animate discourse, but as an *inscription* of truth in the soul". Further, the living discourse "is described by a 'metaphor' borrowed from the order of the very thing one is trying to exclude from it, the order of its simulacrum".[43]

The "written" character of wisdom is inescapable, even when it is an invisible inscription on the soul.

This conundrum lived on in the texts under consideration here. Recall, for example, *The Discourse on the Eighth and the Ninth,* in which the devotee praises the God who has made him wise by calling the God's name that is hidden within him. In the text, that calling takes the form of writing, and it is alphabetical nonsense. An interesting variant on the same phenomenon is offered in the "Mithras Liturgy", a well-known text in the great Paris magical codex. At the end of this text, there are instructions concerning what the devotee is to do to consecrate himself so that the prayers and requests to which most of the text is devoted will be effective. Part of the ritual describes the devotee's "presentation before the great god": he must write "the eight-letter name" on a leaf and lick off the leaf while showing it to the God; then the God will listen to him. The name is "i ee oo iai", and the text says, "Lick this up, so that you may be protected".[44] The written form of the god's name must be "licked up", eaten, and ingested; to be consecrated is to internalize the written word.

But that written word is an alphabetical fantasia, and it is precisely here that magical language preserves the Platonic conundrum that living language, which cannot be captured by writing, is itself a kind of writing. By writing the name of God, the ultimate form of living discourse, in jumbles of letters that do not make sense, these texts show that it is really ordinary writing that is scrambled and confused, a mere imitation of another kind of inscription. Magical writing takes the form of ordinary writing by using its letters and so is faithful to it, but it betrays that writing by its nonsensical use of those letters and is thus faithful to the writing that is an invisible inscription on the soul. Yet it betrays the invisible inscription as well by writing it in actual letters! Magical language is thus thoroughly paradoxical, betraying and safeguarding with every vowel. It carries forward the Platonic sensibility in a radical way.

Of course Plato also spoke about language under the aegis of Hermes, who is often invoked in the magical papyri as the inventor of letters and as the God with whom the devotee asks to be united. The "inventor of articulate speech" whose name had a hundred letters and who could be approached through "the barbaric names", Hermes was a much-sought-after figure, accompanied in the magical prayers and spells by a great many nonsensical alphabetical formulations.[45] Ancestor to the magical Hermes, the Platonic Hermes is presented in the dialogue entitled *Cratylus*, which is, fittingly, one of the most playful of Plato's writings.

One of the main topics of conversation between Socrates and his companions in the *Cratylus* is the meaning of the names of the gods. What can names tell us about the nature of the gods, and how can the meaning of names be investigated? Socrates proceeds by breaking down the name of each god he considers, finding in the supposed "parts" of each name allusions to two or even several other words. What he offers are highly fanciful etymologies, yet for each name the allusive meanings carried by the etymologies actually reflect the nature of the god. Name after name, Socrates takes the words apart, grouping the syllables now one way, now another, and finds in each case "a hive of wisdom".[46]

Finally his companion Hermogenes asks about the name "Hermes". Socrates says:

> I should imagine that the name Hermes has to do with speech, and signifies that he is the interpreter *(hermēneus)*, or messenger, or thief, or liar, or bargainer; all that sort of thing has a great deal to do with language. As I was telling you, the word *eirein* is expressive of the use of speech, and there is an often-recurring Homeric word *emēsato*, which means "he contrived". Out of these two words, *eirein* and *mēsasthai* the legislator formed the name of the god who invented language and speech.[47]

The name of the inventor of language and speech tells quite a story about his inventions: they interpret and give messages, but they also thieve, lie, and bargain. There is something contrived about language, yet it is divine. As though this were not enough, Socrates goes on to speak about Pan, "the double-formed son of Hermes": "You are aware that speech signifies all things (*pan*= all) and is always turning them round and round, and has two forms, true and false?".[48] The progeny of the divine inventor of language is double-formed; turning things round and round, words are double-edged and, like Pan, perpetually in motion.[49] Hence Socrates shows again and again that if one wants to understand words, one must enter the perpetual motion of their letters.

"Names rightly given", says Socrates, are "the likenesses and images of the things which they name". Further, "imitation of the essence is made by syllables and letters". Thus, the analyst's task is first to distinguish the letters and then to distinguish *among* the letters, dividing them into vowels, consonants, and so on. Entering the flow of words entails, as Socrates says, "taking them to pieces".[50]

When juxtaposed with the magical papyri, the *Cratylus* reads like the manual of instruction out of which the authors of those texts worked, patiently dividing language into letters, letters into vowels, and so on, often invoking the authority of Hermes as they worked. Yet, for the authors of the papyri, Hermes as inventor of the alphabet was not only trickster but also spellbinder. Along with the alphabet, he invented the philter, a charm or spell.[51] This close association of language and the charm through Hermes takes us back to the *Phaedrus*, where Thoth (Hermes in Egyptian disguise) called his invention, the alphabet, a "recipe for wisdom". The word for "recipe" here is *pharmakon*, also a philter, but one that truly captures the double-edged quality of language, for it is a drug that can *both* poison *and* heal.[52] Writing, then, is a *pharmakon*, and the wisdom it offers is a dangerous potion.

The connection between the word and the charm, stated by Plato and put into action by the magical papyri, is a very old one. When, in a prayer for protection against malevolent spirits, *Monas or the Eighth Book of Moses* says, "I invoke you, Lord, with a musical ode I chant your holy power; aeeiouooo", it has petitioned an ancient tradition that one scholar has named the "therapy of the word".[53] Legends about such shamanistic figures as Pythagoras and Orpheus characterize well the therapeutic dimensions of language. Pythagoras, for example, was said to chant his disciples to sleep with soothing and melodic rhythms; his musical words healed sufferings of both soul and body. Orpheus, who accompanied his poems with the music of the lyre, was a master of the *epode*, the incantation; he not only healed the *pathos* of human beings but could also charm beasts and stones and even the hostile spirits of the underworld.[54] When the magical papyri of late antiquity speak their alphabetical words in the context of music, invocation, protection, and healing, they are carrying forward the linguistic sensibility of this shamanistic tradition, for which the musical word or the sung charm was truly enchanting.

Given the transformative powers of such metrical speech, as well as the idea that the rhythmic word can heal, it is not surprising to find in the magical papyri an emphasis on the touching of the *tongue* in spells for healing.[55] Nor is it surprising that there is an insistence on the importance of correct pronunciation of the alphabetical words of power as well as careful reminders of exactly how many letters each string of letters contains.[56] And there is the further conviction that the one who says such words must be divinized—initiated into the nature of the God—because such words of power cannot be spoken with a merely human mouth.[57] Finally, the authors of the magical papyri have also carried on the rhythmic qualities of the spellbinding word. Indeed, so musical is the magical piety of the alphabet that one scholar was led to suggest that "each aeeioueiouo ... must have been a study of scales in a mystical voice-training academy", and another likened it to "hymnenpoesie"![58] We have already seen *Monas or the Eighth Book of Moses* name its magical language explicitly a "musical ode", yet much more frequent in our texts are graphic depictions of the rhythmic character of their alphabetical chants. Typical examples are *PGM* 13.905ff., 17, and 42, which are presented at the end of this essay. As an eminent student of these papyri once noted, such configurations were not "jeux d'esprit". "The letter and the word kept their full potency".[59]

From the archaic shamanistic tradition, the association of word and charm moved into philosophical, rhetorical, and poetic thinking. Xenophon, a contemporary of Plato and a fellow-admirer of Socrates, wrote that Socrates had characterized his own teachings as *philtra* and *epodai*—spells and odes.[60] Plato himself described Socrates' words as "tunes" with a "magic power" that left listeners "absolutely staggered and bewitched", with the "whole soul turned upside down".[61] Further, in his dialogue *Charmides,* Plato connects the *epode*, incantation, with the *pharmakon* and goes on to speak about the curative effect that noble words have on the soul.[62] So also in the poetic tradition: Pindar, for example, said that the words of a poet could persuade "as with a *philtron*, a spell".[63] And in rhetorical circles as well, Gorgias, "the theoretician of the magic spell of words", used whole catalogues of magic-related words to describe the power of language to change reality.[64]

Running through all of these traditions that connect the word with the charm is an emphasis on the power or forcefulness of words. Compulsion, from their perspective, was built into the nature of language.[65] The authors of the magical papyri seem also to have been working out of such a realization. The nonsense words, for example, are often accompanied by imperative commands to the Gods being invoked to "come!" "guard!" "save!" and the spells themselves are frequently closed with the words "now! now! quick! quick!". This compulsive nature of the magical papyri has been repeatedly highlighted by the scholars who have studied them. But scholarly assessment of this compulsion has been negative. Magicians and their spellbinding commands have been seen as arrogant intruders on divine prerogatives.

Yet, from the perspective of the therapeutic, soul-transforming word that we have just discussed, the compulsive nature of magical nonsense words is not arrogant but pious. Such language is both the medium and the message of stark reality. It recognizes precisely the divine power of words, and it uses language in accordance with language's own qualities. Speaking to the gods in the gods' own language, the alphabetical words of the magical papyri expose the inner forcefulness of human language, and they expose that power in a most appropriate way, by placing those words in spells. It has been said that the magic of Socrates' words rested on their "obstinate destruction of all illusions".[66] Such can also be said of the authors of the magical texts: their alphabetical nonsense—rhythmic, incantatory, persuasive—destroys the illusions of language. It is truly a therapy of the word.

The Alphabet and the Cosmos

From the perspective of our fanciers of the alphabet, invoking God shatters human words, breaking them up into their elemental parts. Indeed, language is sometimes so shattered that only its most basic elements, the vowels, remain. Yet these phonetic components of language carry a world: if the vowels offer direct insight into language, they also offer access to the structural components of the cosmos itself. As we will see, the vowels sound a cosmic fullness through the one who speaks—and writes—them.

A striking example of the cosmic dimensions of the letters of the alphabet is given by Zosimus of Panopolis, an alchemist of the fourth century C.E. In a section of one of his treatises in which he is speculating about the proper names of generic man, he comes to the name "Adam", "a name from the speech of the angels". This is a name "with respect to the body", and it is "symbolic, composed of the four elements (*stoicheiōn*) from the whole sphere".[67] Next Zosimus reveals the symbolic meanings of Adam's name by breaking it up into its letters (*stoicheia*):

> For the letter (*stoicheion*) A of his name signifies the ascendant east, and air; the letter D of his name signifies the descendant west, and earth, which sinks down because of its weight; and the letter M of his name signifies the meridian south, and the ripening fire in the midst of these bodies, the fire belonging to the middle, fourth planetary zone.[68]

A, D, M; east, west, south; air, earth, fire: the letters of the name of man (his "body") signify the elements that compose the cosmos. From this perspective, the alphabet is a kind of elemental grammar within which the entire cosmos presents itself in human, earthy terms as the symbolic body of essential human being. By making these associations, Zosimus has not reduced the cosmos to the merely human but has rather divinized the human, since for him as for Greek antiquity generally the cosmos was divine, the visible body of the Gods. Again the alphabet carries a piety, as in one of the briefest of the magical papyri in which the devotee conjures the presence of a God "with the twelve elements *(stoicheiōn)* of heaven and the twenty-four elements *(stoicheiōn)* of the cosmos".[69] The twenty-four letters of the Greek alphabet are cosmic, and they form the exact "double" of the heavenly elements.

These connections between letters and elements can be made because of the multiple meanings of the Greek word *stoicheion,* a word with an interesting history. The basic meaning of the word is "something that belongs to a series". In ancient linguistics, where the enduring meaning of *stoicheion* was first developed, it was used to refer to a sound in a series with other sounds in a word, and so was distinguished from *gramma,* the proper name for the letters of the alphabet that make up a word.[70] Eventually, however, the series of sounds that weave in and out of the letters were identified with the letters themselves, so that *stoicheion* came to be used more or less synonymously with *gramma* and carried into the alphabet a vocal quality like the *Thunder, Perfect Mind*'s "name of the sound and sound of the name". Plato attributed this process to Thoth:

> The unlimited variety of sound was once discerned by some god, or perhaps some godlike man; you know the story that there was some such person in Egypt called Theuth. He it was who originally discerned the existence, in that unlimited variety, of the vowels—not "vowel" in the singular but "vowels" in the plural—and then of other things which though they could not be called articulate sounds, yet were noises of a kind ... In the end he found a number of the things, and affixed to the whole collection, as to each single member of it, the name "letters" *(stoicheia).*[71]

As Plato goes on to say, after dividing all of these *stoicheia* into various groups according to their sounds, the God "realized that none of us could get to know one of the collection all by itself, in isolation from all the rest". Thus "he conceived the 'letter' *(stoicheion)* as a kind of bond of unity uniting as it were all these sounds into one, and so he gave utterance to the expression 'art of letters', implying that there was one art that dealt with the sounds".[72] Plato has done some "weaving" himself here: to the original meaning of "order" or "series" carried by *stoicheion,* he has added "letter" and "sound" and has suggested that understanding this collection is an art given by a god.

To hear the sound of the letter is to be placed in a divine order, according to Plato, and it is particularly noteworthy that he emphasizes the vowels in this context. Later authors not only emphasized the vowels but saw them as first among the *stoicheia.* Thus, Philo of Alexandria, writing in the first century, could call the vowels the best and most powerful of the *stoicheia*, and Plutarch and Zosimus could write, respectively, on why alpha is the first letter, and omega the last letter, of the alphabet.[73] The magical papyri, with their strings of vowels in constantly shifting order, also attest to the power of such *stoicheia;* yet, as we have seen, that power is often extended to include the entire cosmos. That extension is witness to yet another meaning that the word *stoicheion* came to hold.

As one scholar has suggested, "from sound as the original part of a word *stoicheion* probably came to be transferred to the cosmos", and it was used to designate the fundamental principles or constituent elements of the universe.[74] Thus, Philo could write about the heavenly word that places itself between the cosmic elements, thereby preventing them from destroying each other, just as the vocal elements in human words are placed between the silent elements and so perform the same protective function.[75] What is here in Philo an analogy between cosmic elements (*stoicheia*) and alphabetic elements was in the hands of Stoic philosophers an identification. *Stoicheion* came to mean *both* letter *and* element.[76] Thus, the cosmic elements (earth, air, fire, water) and the letters of the alphabet could in some sense be said to mirror each other and, since the human being was thought to be composed of the same elements as the cosmos,[77] a further set of relationships could be added to an already complex phenomenon. It was to such an intricate net of associations that Zosimus was indebted as he took apart the name of Adam and discovered the whole cosmos there.

By the time of late antiquity, *stoicheion* had come to designate not only the constituent components of language and the cosmos but also, with the help of astrologers, the seven planets and even the stars. Astrologers, indeed, found more and more correspondences between human writing and heavenly phenomena; when they contemplated the skies, they saw what one modern scholar has called "Himmelschrift",[78] a celestial text whose lights formed the moving script of divine order.[79] The "Mithras Liturgy" offers one example of how that divine script is mirrored in human writing. During one of this text's ceremonies of invocation, the initiate must invoke "the living, immortal names" that cannot be spoken with mortal sound or speech: eeo oeeo ioo oe eeo eeo oe eo ioo (and so on, for several lines). The initiate is instructed to "say all these things with fire and spirit, until completing the first utterance; then, similarly, begin the second, until you complete the seven immortal gods of the world". When this is accomplished, the "cosmos of the gods" opens.[80] The immortal sounds of the seven vowels of the human alphabet, when they are spoken with "elemental" force ("with fire and spirit") reveal the seven planetary Gods and their realms. It is striking, of course, that such a divine script can be not only spoken but also written in human "language", yet it is here that the overflow of meaning carried by *stoicheion* can best be seen.

The idea that the seven vowels, most potent of the alphabetic *stoicheia*, and the seven planets, divine *stoicheia*, are related is an implicit assumption of the "Mithras Liturgy". This connection was made explicit by Nicomachus of Gerasa, a Neopythagorean thinker of the second century C.E. who carried into late antiquity the old Pythagorean doctrine of the music of the spheres. Pythagoras, who in the sixth century B.C.E. discovered the orderly arrangement of the musical scale, had elevated that order to the heavens. Like the seven notes of the octave, the seven planets moved in a harmonic progression and so made a "music" which, as tradition had it, Pythagoras claimed to have heard on several occasions. For Nichomachus, the vowels sound this mystical music. They are "sounding elements" (*phonēenta stoicheia*) and each vowel rings out the tone appropriate to each planetary sphere.[81] The heavens sing, and the sound is that of the vowels.

In the magical papyri, it is often the case that this Pythagorean music of the spheres is made audible as a human song. One of the most striking of the texts that utter the celestial harmony in earthy tones is the following:

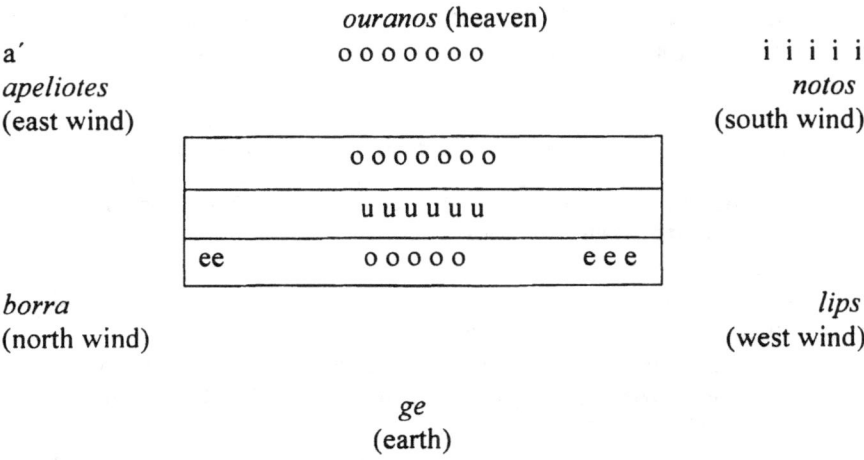

(PGM 13.840)

This diagram, which coordinates seven cosmic elements (heaven, earth, and air plus the east, west, south, and north winds) with the seven vowels of the Greek alphabet, is accompanied by instructions. It is a "picture" of what the initiate is to recite. Samples of the recitations are: "looking to the north wind, with one fist stretched out to the right, say 'e'"; "looking to the heavens, with both hands lying on the head, say 'ō'" and so on through all the elements and vowels in the diagram. Ultimately the initiate says to each of the cosmic elements the whole string of the vowels, and ends by invoking the God "as the cosmos: o uu ooo aaa eeeee eeeeee iiiiiii".[82] The initiate here is called upon to enact with his body and with his voice the entire cosmic scheme, all of which is effected by chanting alphabetical nonsense. It is a song both human and divine and displays fully the multidimensional power that the *stoicheia* had garnered by late antiquity. Archaic speculation lived on in the "elemental" piety of the magical texts.

The Allure of Language

The alphabetical nonsense that I have been discussing in this essay is informed, I would suggest, by a radical philosophy of language best expressed by the Neoplatonist Plotinus, who advised that we must be "in collusion with" language, reading all words as metaphors.[83] That he followed his own advice will be clear from the following passage, in which he is speaking about Being itself, the ultimate reality that underlies everything:

> We cannot think of it as a chance existence; it is not what it chanced to be but what it must be–and yet without a "must" ... Neither thus nor in any mode did it happen to be; There is no happening; There is only a "Thus and no otherwise than Thus". And even "Thus" is false.[84]

We must read metaphorically, letting language do its work of evocation. Strictly speaking, "we should put neither a This nor a That" to reality: "we hover, as it were, about it, seeking the statement of an experience of our own, sometimes nearing this Reality, sometimes baffled by the enigma in which it dwells".[85] Nonetheless, the word for Plotinus is an "outshining" of soul, and discussion, while it cannot capture Being, does call to vision.[86]

Yet the vision baffles telling, perhaps because of the spellbinding character of reality itself. Plotinus had quite a lot to say about magic, most of it negative. "Everything that looks to another is under spell to that ... We move to that only which has wrought a fascination upon us".[87] In this latter statement, Plotinus has used the verb *thelgein* (to "enchant", "bewitch", "charm"), one of the words used by Gorgias long before him to describe the magical charm of words. Yet Plotinus has used it negatively. He is speaking here about the man who is captured by the charm of the external world and so neglects the inner, deeper world of the soul. There is, however, a positive magic: if nature is an allurer, administering as he says a "deceptive philter", Being itself is also beguiling, but beneficently so. In Plotinus' words, "So great is it in power and beauty that it remains the *allurer*, all things of the universe depending from it and rejoicing to hold their trace of it and through that to seek their good".[88] Again the verb *thelgein* appears, but this time it refers to the bewitching allure of reality!

As we saw earlier in this essay, Plotinus thought that attempts to speak and write about this alluring reality were agonistic. Hence, he commends the "wise men of Egypt", who "left aside the writing forms that take in the detail of words and sentences and drew pictures instead". The language most appropriate to reality is hieroglyphic; that is "the mode in which the Supreme goes forth".[89]

Plotinus was not, of course, recommending that we abandon words and draw pictures instead; he wanted to see the "hieroglyphic" quality of all language. So also the authors of the alphabetical nonsense words. They did not abandon language either but formed their hieroglyphs with the letters of the alphabet. That this was not, for them, mere play or a deceptive philter is nowhere more poignantly voiced than in the alphabetical philosophy of Marcus, a Christian teacher of the second century. It is with his thoughts that I will close.

Marcus had taken the first verse of the Gospel of John seriously: "In the beginning was the word". God's creation was linguistic, and the letters of the first potent word that he uttered contained all of the forms of creation, each form presided over by the name of a letter of the alphabet, which is in turn composed of letters, each of which has a name, and so on to infinity. Thus, alpha, the name of the letter *a*, is composed of the letters *a*, *l*, and so on, and these letters have names in their turn, so that, for example, *l*'s name, lambda, contains yet more letters, and more names. Creation, in other words, is eternal and ongoing: "the multitude of letters swells out into infinitude", and "letters are continually generating other letters".[90] The alphabet speaks a divine language, and it does so in a radically generative, metaphoric way, each letter calling up, but never pinning down, the enigmatic nature of reality, the word of God.

Marcus, and his fellow magicians as well, was under spell to the bewitchment of language itself, which had the power to evoke the very heart of being—but it had that power only when broken apart. Shattered in this way, the alphabet was "the body of truth", "the figure of the element, the character of the letter", and it was emblazoned on the body of the human being as well as in the cosmic spheres.[91] Indeed, Marcus describes the human being, who *is* the element that the alphabet figures, as "the mouth" of the silent God, and the song the human sings echoes the elemental sounding of the heavens, each one of which pronounces its own vowel.[92] Marcus's illustration of the sound of this song, which brings letter, element, God, and human being together in one long wail, is the sorrowing cry of a newborn baby. Composed only of vowels, the baby's cry is a hymn of praise, sounding the elemental glory of the heavens and their linguistic creator.[93]

A figure for all attempts to express in language what is ultimately meaningful, Marcus's baby speaks, sorrowing and rejoicing at once. Here is "the murderous alphabet" indeed, and it shows what Plotinus described as the "agony" of speaking in a most wrenching way. As we suggested at the beginning of this essay, the piety of the alphabet is a violent one; its praise is nonsense.

Appendix

Two of the important categories used in this essay are "gnosticism" and "magic". They are typically used by scholars as normative categories that designate philosophical and theological positions. Such usage has recently been questioned, however, and I offer the following remarks both to alert the reader to these issues and to clarify my own use of the two terms.

Most of the texts in the collection called *The Nag Hammadi Library* have been considered by modern scholars to be expressions of gnosticism, which is generally defined as a dualistic, anti-historical religious system with philosophical and mythological elements taken from Platonism and Judaism. The use of the term "gnostic" to describe these texts is, however, highly problematic. The term "gnostic" was used by the second-century Christian heresiologist Irenaeus to describe certain thinkers in the Christianity of his day as heretics whose theology was unsound. Hence the term "gnostic" carried, and tends still to carry, polemical overtones of a decidedly negative sort.

Further, as Morton Smith has pointed out in a ground-breaking essay, most of the thinkers whom Irenaeus branded with the name "gnostic" did not consider themselves to be part of such a "movement" and did not even use the word. In the present essay, use of this term is avoided where possible. Its usefulness is limited to convenient designation of texts and does not extend to descriptions of the contents of such texts. For a pointed discussion of these issues, see Morton Smith, "The History of the Term Gnostikos".

Like the term "gnostic", the term "magical" is problematic because of a negative theological bias that the word still carries from antiquity. What was called "magical" was considered by an earlier generation of scholars to be a debased form of religion in which conjuration replaced contemplation and arrogance toward the Gods replaced humble submission to them, but texts designated as "magical" have more recently been shown to be much more sophisticated and complex. Indeed, the term "magic" itself had in antiquity a very wide range of applicability from true piety to quackery; hence, the reductive use of the term in modern scholarship is not an accurate reflection of the ancient usage or phenomenon. In this essay, "magic" has been used only as a convenient designation of a collection of texts edited by Karl Preisendanz (see bibliography) and as a designation of those portions of texts from the Nag Hammadi Library that share the "alphabetical piety" so common in the magical papyri. For recent discussions of magic in late antiquity, see the excellent studies by Alan F. Segal and Morton Smith listed in the bibliography.

Notes

1   The collection of texts to which *Thunder, Perfect Mind* (hereafter *NHC* VI, 2) belongs was discovered in 1945 in the Naj' Hammadi region of Egypt and has now been translated into English from the Coptic and published as *The Nag Hammadi Library in English* (1977).
2   *NHC* VI, 2, p. 271.
3   *Enn.* 6.9.10-11(MacKenna). See also 5.5.6, where Plotinus describes the attempt to speak about profound reality as an "agony".
4   *NHC* VI, 2, p. 276.
5   *Enn.* 5.5.5.
6   *NHC* VI, 2, p. 277.
7   Most of the magical texts discussed here are located in Preisendanz (ed), *Papyri Graecae Magicae*. Texts from this collection will be cited *PGM*, with papyrus and line numbers following. All translations are my own unless otherwise noted.
8   *NHC* VI, 2, p. 277.
9   *NHC* III, 2, p. 197.
10 *NHC* III, 2, pp. 204.
11 *PGM* 13.206-9.
12 *NHC* III, 2, pp. 204-5.
13 *NHC* VI, 6, p. 296.

242 The Poetry of Thought in Late Antiquity

14 Stevens, "The Man With the Blue Guitar", in *Collected Poems*, p. 179.
15 For the connection between speaking in tongues and alphabetical writing, see Smith, *Clement of Alexandria*, pp. 232-33; and Behm, "glossa", in *TDNT*, vol. 1, pp. 722-23.
16 *Pistis Sophia* 136 (MacDonald, p. 707).
17 Rom. 8:26 (RSV).
18 Smith, *Clement of Alexandria*, p. 232.
19 1 Cor. 13:1 (RSV).
20 1 Cor. 14:16, 23 (RSV).
21 1 Cor. 14:7, 9 (RSV).
22 1 Cor. 14:13-15 (RSV).
23 *Pistis Sophia* 136 (MacDonald, p. 707).
24 1 Cor. 14:23 (RSV).
25 For sources pertaining to mantic speaking in tongues, see Behm, "glossa", *TDNT*, vol. 1, p. 722; and Dodds, *The Greeks and the Irrational*, pp. 64-101.
26 "Introduction", *Classical Mediterranean Spirituality*, xv.
27 1 Cor. 14:2 (RSV).
28 The quotations are from Nock, "Greek Magical Papyri"; see also Festugière, *La Révélation d'Hermès Trismégiste*, vol. 1, pp. 283-309; and Behm, "glossa", *TDNT*, vol. 1, p. 722.
29 Dornseiff, *Das Alphabet*, p. 52 ("mystische Kauderwelsch") and p. 25 (Rimbaud).
30 See Dornseiff, *Das Alphabet*, pp. 18-19; and Dieterich, "ABC-Denkmaeler".
31 Smith, *Clement of Alexandria*, p. 232.
32 Carroll, *Through the Looking Glass*, p. 197.
33 Stevens, "Notes Toward a Supreme Fiction", in *Collected Poems*, pp. 380-407.
34 Plotinus, *Enn.* 6.8.13 (MacKenna).
35 *PGM* 13.876-87.
36 For uses of *Iao*, see Smith, *Clement of Alexandria*, p. 233, n. 10. For the Hebrew *YHWH* who both makes and unmakes language, see Gen. 2:19; 11:1-9.
37 Dornseiff, *Das Alphabet*, pp. 3-8.
38 Ibid., p. 7, n. 4; Festugière, *La Révélation d'Hermès Trismégiste*, vol. 1, pp. 287-93.
39 Plato, *Phaedrus* 274D-275B (Hackforth).
40 Ibid., 275D-E (Hackforth).
41 *NHC* VIII, 1, p. 380.
42 Plato, *Phaedrus* 276A-B (Hackforth).
43 Derrida, *Dissemination*, p. 149 (italics in original).
44 *PGM* 4.785-90 (trans. Meyer, p. 25).
45 See, e.g., *PGM* 8.1-22, 50-53; *PGM* 5.400-423; French translations of many Hermetic magical texts can be found in Festugière, *La Révélation d'Hermès Trismégiste*, vol. 1, pp. 287-96.
46 Plato, *Cratylus* 401E (Jowett).
47 Ibid., 408A-B.
48 Ibid., 408C.
49 Ibid., 408D.
50 Ibid., 439A; 424B-425A.
51 Festugière, *La Révélation d'Hermès Trismégiste*, vol. 1, pp. 287-88.
52 See Derrida, *Dissemination*, pp. 95-117; Lain Entralgo, *The Therapy of the Word in Classical Antiquity*, p. 95; and de Romilly, *Magic and Rhetoric in Ancient Greece*, pp. 34-35.
53 *PGM* 13.630-31; Lain Entralgo, *Therapy of the Word*, passim.

In Praise of Nonsense: A Piety of the Alphabet in Ancient Magic 243

54 Porphyry, *Life of Pythagoras* 30; Iamblichus, *De vita Pythagorica* 15.64-65; for discussion of these figures, see Lain Entralgo, *The Therapy of the Word in Classical Antiquity*, pp. 44-52, 75-86; de Romilly, *Magic and Rhetoric in Ancient Greece*, pp. 14-15; and Burkert, "*Goes*: Zum Griechischen 'Schamanismus'".
55 Smith, *Clement of Alexandria*, p. 223.
56 Betz, "The Formation of Authoritative Tradition in the Greek Magical Papyri", p. 167; Dodds, *The Greeks and the Irrational*, pp. 292-93.
57 Betz, "The Formation of Tradition in the Greek Magical Papyri", p. 167; see Smith, *Clement of Alexandria*, p. 218 for a translation of *PGM* 13.783ff., in which a magician identifies himself with a spirit.
58 Dieterich, *Abraxas*, p. 43; Nilsson, *Geschichte der griechiscben Religion*, vol. 2, p. 668.
59 Nock, "The Vocabulary of the New Testament", p. 346.
60 Xenophon, *Memorabilia* 3.2.16; translated and discussed in Lain Entralgo, *The Therapy of the Word*, p. 122, n. 21.
61 Plato, *Symposium* 215C-E (Joyce). See also *Meno* 80A-B.
62 Plato, *Charmides* 157A (Jowett); for discussion, see de Romilly, *Magic and Rhetoric in Ancient Greece*, pp. 34-37; Lain Entralgo, *The Therapy of the Word in Classical Antiquity*, pp. 121-26.
63 See de Romilly, *Magic and Rhetoric in Ancient Greece*, pp. 4, 7-9 for sources and discussion.
64 See ibid., 3-22, and Lain Entralgo, *Therapy of the Word in Classical Antiquity*, p. 88, for sources and discussion.
65 For discussions of *bia* (force) and *ananke* (necessity), see Lain Entralgo, *The Therapy of the Word in Classical Antiquity*, pp. 89-91.
66 De Romilly, *Magic and Rhetoric in Ancient Greece*, p. 36.
67 Zosimus of Panopolis, *On the Letter Omega* 9 (Jackson, p. 29).
68 Ibid.
69 *PGM* 39.17-18.
70 Delling, "stoicheion", in *TDNT*, vol. 7, pp. 670-71.
71 Plato, *Philebus* 18B-C (Hackforth).
72 Ibid., 18C-D.
73 Philo, *Allegorical Interpretation* 1.14; Plutarch, *Quaestiones convivales* 9.2.2, cited in Delling, "stoicheion", p. 671.
74 Delling, "stoicheion", p. 672.
75 Philo, *On Noah's Work as a Planter* 10, cited in ibid., p. 671.
76 Delling, "stoicheion", pp. 672-75; Dornseiff, *Das Alphabet in Mystik und Magie*, pp. 14-17.
77 See, e.g., the theories of the Greek physician Galen, discussed in Delling, "stoicheion", p. 673.
78 Dornseiff, *Das Alphabet in Mystik und Magie*, p. 89.
79 Ibid., pp. 81-90; see also Delling, "stoicheion", pp. 679-83 for astrology and the elements.
80 *PGM* 4. 605-25 (Meyer, p. 13).
81 See Dieterich, *Eine Mithrasliturgie*, pp. 32-35; Dornseiff, *Das Alphabet in Mystik und Magie*, pp. 82-91.
82 *PGM* 13.824-40.
83 *Enn.* 6.8.13 (MacKenna). The verb *sūnchōreō* has a range of meanings, including to "defer", "concede", "be in collusion with", "connive at".

84 *Enn.* 6.8.9 (MacKenna).
85 Ibid., 6.9.3.
86 Ibid., 3.2.16; 6.9.4.
87 Ibid., 4.4.43.
88 Ibid., 6.6.18.
89 Ibid., 5.8.6.
90 The teachings of Marcus are most fully reported by the Christian heresiologist Irenaeus in *Haer.*, Book 1. On the reliability of Irenaeus's accounts, see Greer, "The Dog and the Mushrooms". The passages cited here are from Irenaeus, *Haer.* 1.14.1-2 (*ANF*, vol. 1, pp. 336-37).
91 Irenaeus, *Haer.* 1.14.3 (*ANF*, vol. 1, p. 337): Truth, who is also human, is described as follows: "Behold, then, her head on high, *Alpha* and *Omega;* her neck, *Beta* and *Psi*, her shoulders with her hands, *Gamma* and *Chi*", and so on through the whole body.
92 Irenaeus, *Haer.* 1.14.3, 7 (*ANF*, vol. 1, p. 337).
93 Ibid., 1.14.8 (*ANF*, vol. 1, p. 338).

Figures

```
            a  a
           ba  ak
          lba  akr                 a a a a a a
         alba  akra                 e e e e e
        nalba  akram                e e e e e e
       analba  akramm             i i i i i i i o o o o
      hanalba  akramma              u u u u u
     thanalba  akrammac             o o o o o
    athanalba  akrammach
   nathanalba  akrammacha           (PGM 42)
  anathanalba  akrammacham
 lanathanalba  akrammachama
blanathanalba  akrammachamar
ablanathanalba akrammachamari
blanathanalba  akrammachamar   aeeiouo    aeeiouoo    aeeiouoouo
 lanathanalba  akrammachama    eeiouoa    eeiouooa    eeiouoouoa
  anathanalba  akrammacham     eiouoae    eiouooae    eiouoouoae
   nathanalba  akrammacha      iouoaee    iouooaee    iouoouoaee
    athanalba  akrammach       ouoaeei    ouooaeei    ouoouoaeei
     thanalba  akrammac        uoaeeio    uooaeeio    uoouoaeeio
      hanalba  akramma         oaeeiou    ooaeeiou    oouoaeeiou
       analba  akramm
        nalba  akram                 (PGM 13.905ff)
         alba  akra
          lba  akr
           ba  ak
            a  a

 (PGM 17)
```

Chapter Thirteen

"Words With An Alien Voice": Gnostics, Scripture and Canon

The title of this article comes from the following passage by Edmond Jabès in *The Book of Questions:* "You, who think I exist, how can I tell you what I know with words which mean more than one thing, with words like me, which change when looked at, words with an alien voice?".[1] Jabès' work can be read as a long meditation on the refusal of words to stay put in the neat canonical—Scriptural—niches to which we assign them. Any text, and any canon defined as a collection of texts, is self-transgressive by virtue of the nature of words themselves: as Jabès remarks, "How can I say what I know with words whose signification is multiple?".[2] If "every word unveils another tie",[3] which requires further words for expression, then the concept of canon as a fixed authority, that is, as a fixed corpus of texts, is mistaken, even delusory.

It is with such a perspective on the nature of writing in relation to a Scriptural canon that this essay explores Gnostic hermeneutics. The focus of attention is not on Gnostic interpretation of isolated passages of Scripture, but rather on Gnostic theories about the qualities of language that contributed to Gnostic use of Scripture and understandings of canon. "Gnostic" here designates the Valentinian tradition as represented by the *Gospel of Truth* and the *Tripartite Tractate*,[4] although the conclusions that this essay will present may have implications for Gnosticism more broadly conceived.

"You try to be free through writing. How wrong. Every word unveils another tie".[5] Jabès seems to suggest that there is something about writing—indeed, about language—that is inherently contradictory, both freeing and alienating. This conundrum at the heart of language was troublesome also to the author of the *Tripartite Tractate*.[6] This text frequently associates the unfathomable origin of all that is with language. On the one hand, "innumerable and invisible are the begettings of his words". This unfathomable one is the fount of language; appropriately, then, "It is possible to speak of him because of the wealth of speech".[7] Seemingly, the wealth of language, with its innumerable words, gives the freedom to speak; speech is freed when there is an abundance of words. However, the same text also says of the unfathomable one that "in silence he himself holds back". "Not one of the names which are conceived, or spoken, seen or grasped, not one of them applies to him ... ".[8] No language can convey him: it would seem that the other side of linguistic plenitude is silence and inadequacy.[9] Words speak with an alien voice.

The *Tripartite Tractate* has intensified the conundrum: how is it possible that the unfathomable one can be both spoken and not spoken? This text does not "solve" the conundrum by siding either with language or with silence; instead, it shifts the ground of the discussion by focusing on language as a quest that both conceals and reveals meaning. The unfathomable one "did not wish that they should know him, since he grants that he be conceived in such a way as to be sought for, while keeping to himself his unsearchable being".[10] The accent here is on the search, for to speak is to search, and that is how the ineffable "origin" can be conceived. What language as search yields, however, is neither the presence nor the absence of the unfathomable one, but rather "traces" of him. All words are traces that mark out the paths of the search.[11]

In order to explicate the idea of word as trace, which is really another way of indicating the liberating-and-alienating character of language, I would like to move briefly to contemporary discussions of the dynamics of the production of meaning in and by texts.[12] In such discussions, what is fundamental to the operations of language has repeatedly been characterized by two concepts: polyvalence and dissemination. Polyvalence refers to the semantic richness of words—to the play of allusion, cross-reference, echo, multiple signification that is unleashed by language. In the *Tripartite Tractate*, the gift of the unnameable one is language: "[I]n order that they might know [what exists] for them, he graciously [granted the] initial form ... he gave them the name 'Father' by means of a voice proclaiming to them that what exists, exists through that name ... ".[13] As what allows the production of meaning, the unnameable one says nothing; rather, he permits saying. "Father" signifies the first linguistic gesture, which is polyvalent, even overdetermined; in it are what the text calls "aeons", which are described as "seeds" and "fetuses" that "Father" begets "like the word".[14] These fledgling words, ready to sprout and take form like seeds and fetuses, have "the sole task of searching for him ... ever wishing to find out what exists".[15] Characterized as having "a love and a longing for the perfect, complete discovery of the Father",[16] the aeons taken collectively are representative of the dynamic of desire in language, the desire to name the unnameable that the polyvalence of words animates.

From the perspective of polyvalence, words are overdetermined, able to operate on several registers of meaning at once. Understandings of the operations of language in terms of polyvalence tend to attribute to language the capability of articulating meaning in all of its fullness: such richness can be present, or so it would appear. However, any single articulation of language—any particular word or text—can only express a fragment of the potential whole. As Italo Calvino has observed, words are "a perpetual pursuit of things, a perpetual adjustment to their infinite variety".[17] In other words, the richness of language is an *"embarras* de richesse": meaning is disseminated, dispersed, in the very attempt to say it, so that to write is to be in perpetual pursuit of the meaningfulness of things.[18] From the perspective of dissemination, to write is not to find but to search. The *Tripartite Tractate* is insistent on this point: "Father" grants that he be conceived of in such a way as to be *sought for*.[19] What is "found" is not some "content", a final naming of the unnameable, since what the aeons know is precisely that what stands behind "Father" as linguistic gesture is unknowable.[20] Hence the "goal" is the search itself, conducted in language, as the aeons—words born of the "first" word—"bear fruit with one another".[21] Words begetting other words, the aeons embody the "places" that mark the path of the dissemination of meaning.[22]

If, from the perspective of dissemination, to write is not to find but to search, it is also characteristic of this dynamic of language that words are entangled in the movement of a "perpetual adjustment to infinite variety". Words are not identical to the things that they name; in thus differing from their referents, words defer meaning. To write is to participate in an infinite deferral of meaning, since each new attempt to articulate meaning repeats the "original" substitution of word for thing.[23] That which allows for the very production of meaning is unnameable and unknowable: it is absent; from this perspective, when one looks at language, one sees defect and loss. If words disseminate meaning, the problematic of writing is "how to express what expression abolishes".[24]

"All letters give form to absence".[25] In an essay on Jabès' work, Jacques Derrida comments on this remark: "Absence is the permission given to letters to spell themselves out and to signify, but it is also, in language's twisting of itself, *what* letters say: they say freedom and a granted emptiness, that which is formed by being enclosed in letters' net".[26] The

Tripartite Tractate dramatizes the disseminative dynamic of language in its narrative about *logos*, one of the aeons. As one of the aeons, *logos*, "word", personifies and so brings to attention the disseminative plight of all the aeon-words that dwell in the depths of language. Like all the aeons, *logos* was "in the Father's thought, that is, in the hidden depth, the depth knew them, but they were unable to know the depth in which they were; nor was it possible for them to know themselves, nor for them to know anything else".[27] Unaware of themselves in the hidden depths of language, the plight of words is their relation to knowledge: how and what do words mean? The drama of *logos* is a drama of the reconciliation of language to its own dissemination, to its entanglement with freedom and emptiness.

The story of *logos* opens with the following recognition: "there is a limit set to speech in the pleroma, so that they are silent about the incomprehensibility of the Father ... ".[28] In the pleroma, the fullness or polyvalence of language, there is a limiting factor, namely, a silence about incomprehensibility. How can words express what expression abolishes? Not knowing this—that is, not knowing the disseminative function of language—*logos* "attempts to grasp the incomprehensibility".[29] As the text says, this attempt was founded in desire, and its intent was good: from the perspective of polyvalence, language longs to express meaning in its fullness.[30] From this act of grasping, that is, from the attempt to use language to fix and so limit the disseminative slide of meaning, comes the drama of *logos*: the "Father and the Totalities drew away from him, so that the limit which the Father had set might be established".[31]

Logos, now cut off from appropriate uses of language, begins nonetheless to create, "but those whom he wished to take hold of firmly he begot in shadows [and] copies and likenesses". "His self-exaltation and his expectation of comprehending the incomprehensible became firm for him and was in him".[32] When there is no recognition that "all letters give form to absence", words lose their freedom to signify and become mere shadows and copies. What *logos* created was literalism, a fixing of words to things such that they signify content rather than the search for meaning. This move is labeled "arrogant" and "deficient", and the text goes on to show how the creations of this mistaken act on the part of *logos* are characterized by ambition, desire for control, lust for power, and so on: such are what the desire for fixation unleashes.[33]

What *logos* did not realize, in its refusal of dissemination, was that the infinite deferral of meaning in and by language entails an endless narrativity. Tragically, it was precisely *logos*' attempt to end the story, an attempt born of the desire to tell the whole story, that produced "little weaklings" that were "hindered by the illnesses by which he too was hindered".[34] Furthermore, *logos* separated itself from the very reality that it was trying to express: Father and Totalities withdrew, and *logos* saw only division.[35] What *logos* did not know has been well expressed as follows: "The other that organizes the text is not the (t)exterior [is not exterior to the text]. It is not an (imaginary) object distinguishable from the movement by which it (Es) is traced. To set it apart, in isolation from the texts that exhaust themselves in the effort to say it, would be to exorcize it by furnishing it with a place of its own and a proper name".[36] Wishing to grasp the incomprehensible in language, *logos* exorcized it.

It is important to note, at this point, that the terms "polyvalence" and "dissemination" do not name two separate dynamics of language; they are rather interrelated moments in the production of meaning. Polyvalence names the fruitful, expressive aspect of dissemination, while dissemination uncovers the dangerous optimism of polyvalence. It is this latter part of the relation that I would like to emphasize. Polyvalence—the richness of language—is dangerous because it holds out the possibility of final naming. It suggests that meaning can, with enough words, be grasped. It also suggests that meaning can be equated with content—with meanings—rather than with the search for meaning. Curiously, the danger of polyvalence is fixity and literalism.[37] This is the lesson that *logos* learned, for his power-hungry creations sickened him and, instead of seeing perfection, he saw defect, division, disturbance and tumult.[38] What the text calls the "conversion" of *logos* originated in a moment of "self-doubt", when the *logos* realized that "he did not reach the attainment of the glories of the Father".[39] Angry at the "apostasy" of his constructions, *logos* underwent *metanoia*, a change of consciousness.[40] "The one who is in the Pleroma was what he first prayed to and remembered; then (he remembered) his brothers individually and (yet) always with one another; then all of them together; but before all of them, the Father".[41] *Logos* remembers first the primal gift, language, and all that it entails with respect to the desire for knowledge. Giving up the dangerous optimism of polyvalence brings restoration to fullness and to the humility of the endless story.

"A blank page is full of paths".[42] If full presence—that which the polyvalence of language seems to promise—is perpetually deferred by the disseminative function of words, still the idea of presence functions as a lure; it is what the text desires. Writing is founded in such desire for the other, for the unnameable that words attempt to articulate.[43] If the articulation of this desire yields texts that are only traces of the unnameable, still *they are traces*; they evoke and allude, yielding ever more paths in the search that constitutes knowledge. Gnostic recognition of the operation of dissemination in language accounts not only for the way in which their own texts are written, but also for the manner in which textual authority is conceived. The Gnostic texts presented here are meditations on the operations of language, and such meditations imply a view of textual authority based on "pursuit" rather than on fixity of content, a view that makes ideas of standards of textual authority (canons) problematic. To explore further how ideas of textual authority are rooted in perspectives on language's production of meaning, especially regarding the problem of canon, I will turn to a discussion of the *Gospel of Truth*.[44]

The *Gospel of Truth* can be read as a text whose primary message is a hermeneutical one. It is a revelation of the linguistic dynamic fundamental to revelation, and its interest is in showing how knowledge is related to language, and how language is related to authority.[45] At the outset, the text declares that its own name, "the name of the gospel", is "discovery for those who search". The text defines itself as "the gospel of the one who is searched for".[46] The *Gospel of Truth* is suggesting that a text that can be called "gospel" is a text that participates in a dynamic of searching and finding.[47] To write is to search, and to search is to write. Further, if "the name of the gospel" is "discovery for those who search", it would seem that what is discovered lies somehow within the text, and not outside it. To look for some extra-textual reality to which the text corresponds is, in the words of this text, to fall into a "fog" concerning knowledge of the Father; it is to be a "material one", a child of error who cannot see "likeness".[48] As in the *Tripartite Tractate*, attempts to grasp what one is ignorant of lead only to an intensification of ignorance, which is negatively aligned with what is solid and fixed. Ignorance yields only a delusory fabrication (*plasma*).[49]

If ignorance in this text is equated with fixed substance, knowledge is understood as a process or dynamic. Best described in its active, verbal form, "knowing" is activated "through the power of the word that came forth from the pleroma".[50] What I want to argue is that the "power of the word" *is* the discovery for those who search; the "power" of the word signifies both the hermeneutic of language that the text defends as well as the hermeneutic principles that the text enacts. These two moments in the hermeneutics of the *Gospel of Truth* are described as the activities of the Son and of Jesus, who represent the two hermeneutical strategies designated by the "power of the word". This doubled figure of the Son/Jesus—doubled since both are described as the hidden mystery within the Father who manifest the Father through language—functions as the hermeneutical process of the search to which the *Gospel of Truth* is devoted.

According to Jabès, "Error is the mournful detour which leads to truth, its base and its threshold".[51] When the "totality" fell into a fog concerning the "unnameable, indescribable" one from whom it had come forth, "it pleased him that his name which is loved should be his Son, and he gave the name to him, that is, him who came forth from the depth, he spoke about his secret things, knowing that the Father is a being without evil. For that very reason he brought him forth in order to speak about the place and his resting-place from which he had came forth, and to glorify the pleroma, the greatness of his name and the sweetness of the Father".[52] As in the *Tripartite Tractate,* error, that "mournful detour", leads to revelation, a change in consciousness that is linguistically defined in terms of speaking and naming. Furthermore, this revelatory speech, which is a revelation about language, is situated in a nexus of pleroma, name, and the "sweetness" of the Father, all of which pertain to the "resting place" from which "Son" comes forth. Elsewhere called the "warm pleroma of love",[53] pleroma here designates the erotic fundament of language, the lure of the linguistic desire to name that characterizes the "fullness" of the polyvalent dimension of words.

In a now famous passage, the *Gospel of Truth* specifies the linguistic conditions of its revelation concerning language:

> Now the name of the Father is the Son. It is he who first gave a name to the one who came forth from him, who was himself, and he begot him as a son. He gave him his name which belonged to him; he is the one to whom belongs all that exists around him, the Father. His is the name; his is the Son. It is possible for him to be seen. The name, however, is invisible because it alone is the mystery of the invisible which comes to ears that are completely filled with it by him. For indeed, the Father's name is not spoken, but it is apparent through a son.[54]

If the Son is "a way for those who were gone astray" and "a support for those who were wavering"—indeed, if the Son is "discovery for those who search"[55]—what does it mean that "the name of the Father is the Son"?

In a landmark essay, Benoit Standaert pointed out that the relation Father, Son, Name is a linguistic relation:

> Parler de Dieu comme Père, c'est le nommer comme tel ... Et le nom de *père* sous lequel on l'invoque, contient en soi, avec l'idée de paternité, une progeniture, un fils. Cette implication linguistique est sous-entendue dans tout le développement et le choix quasi-exclusif du

mot "père" pour désigner Dieu dans *l'Évangile* s'explique peut-être par cette implication ... [56]

"Father" functions here, as in the *Tripartite Tractate*, as a signifier of language, that is, as primal linguistic gesture. What lies before, behind, underneath, or above language cannot be said in words: "The Father's name is not spoken".

The relation of language to the unspeakable is carried in the naming that "Father" represents. Speech is founded on absence; as Joel Fineman has noted, "this is the initiatory gap in language upon which the movement of signification, like the trajectory of desire, depends".[57] If "Father" abolishes the presence of the unnameable in its fullness, it nevertheless expresses the desire of language to name. "Father" as linguistic gesture sets in motion a movement of signification: it produces "Son". The linguistic dynamic designated by the phrase, "the name of the Father is the Son", is a demonstration of how the Son can be "discovery for those who search".

"All letters give form to absence. Hence, God is the child of His Name".[58] What Jabès suggests here is that recognition or consciousness of God comes only after God has been named; thus "God is the child of His Name". However, the entry of God into language brings with it lack and loss; the presence of God is perpetually deferred by the disseminative slide of words.[59] Furthermore, "Father" as a linguistic gesture signifying the presence/absence of that which language wishes to express is itself occluded when "the name of the Father is the Son". In Fineman's terms, "Father" becomes a "hidden signifier" that "is not entirely absent from the chain which it subtends. It is present through its metonymic relationship to the rest of the chain ... Both the Son and the Name of the Father are metonymies of the Father himself (i.e., contiguously related figures of the Father that represent him whole). As such, as metonymies of the Father, they testify to the absence of the Father in that they continually refer to Him whom they replace".[60] This is "the dilemma of original signification": "the metonymic movement of the signifiers of desire, all of them a response to the original metaphoric occultation".[61]

"Father", then, represents the original metaphoric occultation, or what this essay has called the primal linguistic gesture. All writing that attempts to explicate "Father" participates in the same dynamic of dissemination—what Fineman calls the "metonymic movement of the signifiers of desire"—as does the "original" word.[62] The principle operative here, again in Fineman's words, is that "the free play of substitution goes on and on ... in a series that traces the course of Gnostic desire directly back to the displacements and deferments initiated by the origin lost through the Name itself".[63] While this finite free play of substitution might seem to be a despairing view of language, it is important to remember that words are signifiers of *desire:* in the words of the *Tripartite Tractate,* that which comes forth from the linguistic dynamic expressed by the Father-Son relationship does so "like kisses".[64] Language may be disseminative, but it is also polyvalent, such that the search in language for what language abolishes produces an explosive richness in writing. The "other side" of dissemination is polyvalent play: as the *Gospel of Truth* says, "all of the emanations of the Father are pleromas".[65]

This polyvalent play of language that engenders writing—that produces texts—is not sheer or mere play, however. It is not without boundaries. As Fineman has pointed out, it is a free play of substitution, of metonymy, in which the hidden signifier is always somehow present. From this perspective, writers place themselves within the chains of signification established by the words themselves. Authors are responsible not to their own imaginations but to the imagination of words. As Standaert noted, words produce other words: "Father" produces "Son". Hence, according to the *Gospel of Truth,*

> Truth appeared; all its emanations knew it. They greeted the Father in truth with a perfect power that joins them with the Father. For, as for everyone who loves the truth—because the truth is the mouth of the Father; his tongue is the Holy Spirit—he who is joined to the truth is joined to the Father's mouth by his tongue ... [66]

Truth is linguistically defined here: it is the "mouth of the Father". To speak the truth is to engage language under the sign of "Father" as a movement of signification. Furthermore, to be a lover of truth is to be a writer: "he who is joined to the truth is joined to the Father's mouth by his tongue".[67] Since the tongue is that organ of the human body that allows for the production of speech, to be joined to "Father" in this way suggests both that such writers submit themselves to the disseminative and polyvalent play of language and, most importantly, that truth is found in the production of language—in the writing of texts.[68]

While the *Gospel of Truth* conveys its hermeneutics of language in terms of the "Son", it is in terms of "Jesus, the Christ" that this text meditates on writing and on textual production. If the Son signifies the hermeneutical principle of the unnameable, the Christ signifies the hermeneutical principle of the texts that are produced when language is viewed from the perspective of the Son, that is, from the perspective of the dilemma of original signification and the free play of substitution that it entails. It is to the figure of Jesus that we now turn.

The *Gospel of Truth* presents Jesus in close association with a text. This text is called "the living book of the living" and it is further described as "the one written in the thought and mind [of the] Father".[69] The connection of Jesus with this book is premised upon the "invisibility" of the "Father of the totality"; the appearance of Jesus signals the writing or the publication of the book. "For this reason Jesus appeared; he put on that book; he was nailed to a tree; he published the edict of the Father on the cross".[70] The text makes it clear that taking and putting on this book brings death, yet Jesus knows that "his death is life for many".[71] In a passage parallel to this one, Jesus "was nailed to a tree (and) he became a fruit of the knowledge of the Father. It did not, however, cause destruction because it was eaten, but to those who ate it, it gave (cause) to become glad in the discovery, and he discovered them in himself, and they discovered him in themselves".[72]

Again there is a simultaneity or a coincidence of death and knowledge; death brings, not destruction, but an ongoing process of discovery. The first passage describes this process in terms of the book: just before the Jesus who is wrapped in the book is nailed to a tree, the text describes Jesus as a teacher of the "little children to whom the knowledge of the Father belongs"; "they learned about the impressions of the Father"; "they knew, they were known"; "there was manifested in their heart the living book of the living".[73] The publication of the book (and the death of its "author") allows for the rebirth of the book in those who have learned from Jesus. Indeed, the text goes on to say that "those who are to receive teaching [are] the living who are inscribed in the book of the living. It is about themselves that they receive instruction ... ".[74] Just as Jesus put on the book and died into it, so too must those who follow in the path of the living book put it on. They are inscribed in it, and it teaches them about themselves.[75]

The *Gospel of Truth*'s vision of the Jesus who is wrapped in the living book of the living and slain, who is nailed to a tree and becomes a fruit of knowledge of the Father that is eaten, is a complicated one, not least because of its Scriptural allusiveness. If these passages are read together, Jesus is placed both in the Paradisal scene of instruction at the tree of knowledge and in the deadly scene of crucifixion, as though these two scenes implicate each other. Further, the two passages are connected by the appearance in both of the sentence, "he was nailed to a tree". The first passage, which revises the account in Genesis of the tree of knowledge such that its fruit now gives "discovery" rather than "destruction", nonetheless imagines that that discovery grows out of death. The second passage, with its repetition of the death on the tree, expands the imagery of the first passage with the image of the book. The "fruit of the knowledge of the Father",[76] then, is this living book of the living; indeed, this book is the published form of the Father's thought, the textuality of his mind. Why, then, is the emphasis on death continued, even intensified, since the second passage contains an explicit allusion to crucifixion? What is this living book of the living, whose appearance is simultaneous with the death of its author, the one who by putting it on made it manifest?

According to the *Gospel of Truth*, "Jesus, the Christ" came to enlighten those "who were in darkness through oblivion ... he showed them a way, and the way is the truth which he taught them".[77] It is my suggestion that the way is a way of writing, a way of understanding textuality and authorship, and a way of conceptualizing authority with respect to writing. If Jesus embodies the book that is the written form of the Father's thought, then that text—and the texts produced by others who have the living book inscribed in them—is marked by the same dynamics of play, of polyvalence and dissemination, as is language itself.

"Writing unfolds like a game that invariably goes beyond its own rules and transgresses its limits. In writing, the point is not to manifest or exalt the act of writing, nor is it to pin a subject within language; it is rather a question of creating a space into which the writing subject constantly disappears".[78] In this statement, Michel Foucault has situated writing in the dynamic of language's polyvalence and dissemination. Writing is a game—a play—that transgresses its limits, since metonymic movement refuses fixity. Furthermore, by noting the disappearance of the writing subject into the space created by the text, Foucault has emphasized what contemporary critical theory has called "the death of the author". This phrase, "the death of the author", has been most succinctly discussed by Roland Barthes, who argued that an insistence on authorship tends to function as a guarantee of the text's meaning and to restrict a text to its content, thus neglecting the participation of the text, as writing, in the linguistic dynamics as explicated in this essay. "To give a text an Author is to impose a limit on that text, to furnish it with a final signified, to close the writing".[79] Authors do not "own" texts but are themselves a function of the polyvalent and disseminative play of language. As Barthes has said, "a text is not a line of words releasing a single 'theological' meaning (the 'message' of the Author-God) but a multi-dimensional space in which a variety of writings, none of them original [because they are all metonymies], blend and clash".[80]

The death of the author is a sign of the endless narrativity characteristic of language and of textual production. When the author "dies", that is, when the author is no longer considered to be "the subject with the book as predicate",[81] then authority is located in the trajectories of desire that are unleashed by words and by texts. In the *Gospel of Truth*, the "living book of the living" is "the one written in the thought and the mind [of the] Father".[82] This book is a text viewed from the perspective of "Father" as that sign of the initiatory gap in language from which spring the movements of signification characteristic of language in its fullness and emptiness. This is the book "which no one was able to take, since it remains for the one who will take it to be slain".[83] As the hermeneutic of textuality in this text, that is, as the one who "showed a way" with regard to the book, only Jesus can take this book and, in taking it, he is slain. If what is written in the Father's mind is a perspective on textuality and the writing of texts, the one who publishes this edict and who "takes the book", who writes in this way, is pictured as wrapped up in the text. The author dies to the authority of endless narrativity, the story without closure, the desire of texts to express what expression abolishes.

This death, which the *Gospel of Truth* underscores by its repetition of the phrase "he was nailed to a tree" and by its bringing together of the Paradisal scene of instruction with crucifixion, nonetheless unleashes "life for many", a journey of discovery from text to text, endlessly. Texts understood in this way are a *living* book of the living: like words, texts also exist in a metonymous or disseminative relation to each other.[84] They also are subject to "the free play of substitution that goes on and on ... in a series that traces the course of Gnostic desire directly back to the displacements and deferments initiated by the origin lost through the Name itself".[85] In this regard the *Gospel of Truth* says of Jesus, "He draws himself down to death though life eternal clothes him".[86] "Life eternal" marks the way of textuality and writing understood as passage and as traversals of desire.

Texts understood in this way are also a living book of the *living*. Those who follow in the way shown by Jesus are "inscribed in the book of the living. It is about themselves that they receive instruction, receiving it from the Father, turning again to him". These are the ones "whose name the Father has uttered".[87] To be named by "Father" is to be situated in language and in writing under the sign of the death of the author. If the followers of Jesus are also writers who take the book (and Standaert has noted the blurring of distinctions, or the blending of identities, between Jesus and his disciples),[88] then they too are subject to the play of writing where, in Foucault's words, "it is a question of creating a space into which the writing subject constantly disappears".[89] This kind of author "knows in what manner he is called. Having knowledge, he does the will of the one who called him ... ". Furthermore, "He who is to have knowledge in this manner knows where he comes from and where he is going".[90] These "living ones" know that they and their texts are situated in the metonymic slide of meaning; that is where they have come from, and it is where they are going. The life of that journey is the desire in language, the lure of meaning set in motion by words, while the "hope" of the living, "for which they are waiting, is in waiting".[91]

Jabès writes: "Mark the first page of the book with a red marker. For, in the beginning, the wound is invisible".[92] The wound of the book is that no book is final; no book can say "pleroma" at last. The hope lies in waiting, that is, in writing, in tracing the paths that multiply on the blank sheet of paper. The Gnostic texts discussed here view writing under the sign of the trace, the "fingerprints" left by absence.[93] Words are traces engendered by the disseminative dynamic of language, and so too are texts, only on a larger scale. All texts are traces; the disseminative slide of meaning in language will not allow for the privileging of any text as exempt from its dynamic of deferral and loss. Hence to designate any particular text or group of texts as "Scripture" that guarantees the context and limits of meaning, or to conceive of "tradition" in such a way that it becomes an Author who predicates meaning in texts, constitute erroneous views of textuality and language, from the perspective of these Valentinian texts. Such erroneous views have not suffered the wound of the book.

As the concluding portion of this essay, I would like to address briefly a Gnostic revisioning of the idea of "canon" as it pertained to the interpretation and appropriation of "Scripture". The import of my remarks grows out of what has been said thus far concerning language. Now I would like to situate these issues historically, and will again focus on the *Gospel of Truth,* since it was written during the century in which early Christian understandings of canon are said to be rooted.[94]

Harold Attridge, along with many others, has observed that "the author of the *Gospel of Truth* apparently knows and uses a large number of the writings of what came to be the canonical New Testament", although "in no case do we find an explicit citation of a New Testament text as scripture or even as an authoritative source".[95] The *Gospel of Truth* alludes to passages from the Synoptic Gospels, the Johannine literature, and the Pauline corpus, but it "renders no explicit judgment on the authoritative status of the works to which it seemingly alludes".[96] Most recently,

Jacqueline Williams has published a study that "demonstrates conclusively that Valentinus did in fact use many of the writings that would form the New Testament ... ".[97] Williams finds the *Gospel of Truth*'s use of texts, "intriguing" because those texts are never quoted verbatim. Noting "the complete absence of explicit citations" in the text, she remarks that its author "evidently considered the texts that he used to be significant, but there is no overt indication of their importance".[98]

Both of these scholars note the allusive qualities of the *Gospel of Truth*'s style. Attridge, remarking upon the "fluidity and polyvalence of the terminology", argues that the dynamic of the text is a juxtaposition of the familiar with the unfamiliar; familiar images from what would later be canonical texts are juxtaposed with and so reinterpreted by unfamiliar (that is, "unscriptural") metaphors.[99] The bulk of Williams' work details which passages from the nascent New Testament have been used by the *Gospel of Truth* and how those passages have been appropriated by the text. Noting that it is typical of the author's style "to incorporate a melange of allusions", she finds that this style makes identification of precise parallels difficult because "his interpretations are interwoven with his allusions".[100] An example of this allusive, juxtapositional style has already been discussed in this essay (the placing together of Paradise and crucifixion), and Williams offers many more.

The *Gospel of Truth* has been dated in part on the basis of this allusive handling of prior texts. The assumption seems to be that its lack of explicit citation of its precursor texts signals a pre-canonical perspective on the use of texts.[101] Views of the text's allusiveness extend beyond issues of dating, however. Attridge, arguing from the interplay of familiar and unfamiliar images, concludes that "the text becomes a carefully constructed attempt to domesticate the unusual and to minimize the potentially problematic".[102] Further, he argues that "the text conceals major elements of the system which it presupposes", so that "through a careful manipulation of traditional imagery, the text inculcates and reinforces a fundamental theological perspective that stands in some tension with important elements of that traditional material".[103] Allusive style has here become a strategy to insinuate a content into traditional material that alters that material in the direction of what is essentially described by Attridge in terms of an Irenaean view of the Gnostic heresy. Thus the text, in his view, has a "pretext", a content that is concealed by allusion so that ordinary readers might be seduced into the text's hidden agenda. Williams also finds that the *Gospel of Truth*'s style can be explained on the basis of the author's desire to change the content of its percursor texts. On one level, she argues, the author has not been "faithful" to the texts which he interprets: "Valentinus consistently retains enough of a reference to allow a reader to recognize its source while he changes key terms and even ideas".[104] The author thus "alters the theology of the Biblical text" and disregards the context of his sources.[105] Again, there is an assumption that "original meaning" in traditional texts or books has been somehow intentionally changed by the *Gospel of Truth*, and that that change is signaled by the text's style.

There is, I suggest, another way to understand this text's relation to tradition and to the nascent canonical passages to which it alludes without accusing the text of suppressing its own difference in the interest of seduction and without charging the author with a willful misuse of texts. What I want to argue, using Roland Barthes' terminology, is that "the logic that governs the Text is not comprehensive (seeking to define 'what the work means') but metonymic; and the activity of associations, contiguities, and cross-references coincides with a liberation of symbolic energy".[106] The liberation of symbolic energy that happens in the interplay between the *Gospel of Truth* and Biblical texts does not pervert the percursor texts; rather, there is "a *serial* movement of dislocations, overlappings, and variations".[107] It is the *slide* of meaning that is highlighted, as the energy of language is activated. The *Gospel of Truth* does not subscribe to a view of Tradition and Canon (even in its pre-fixed form) as arbiters of original meaning; it subscribes to another view of authority, another view of "canon".

While it is true that the *Gospel of Truth* does not quote explicitly from New Testament texts, this lack of verbatim citation need not mean that those texts were not in some way authoritative. Allusions from one text can live on in another text as touchstones in the continuous desire for meaning that writing sets in motion. There is structure in such a relationship, since the later writer has read the earlier text and has so placed his writing in the chain of significations unleashed by that earlier text. There is structure, but there is also decenteredness and lack of closure: the text that marks the point of origin continues to write and to be written in the texts that follow. Authority here is a process, not a content of meaning.

That the *Gospel of Truth* exemplifies such a sense of authority is not due to the fact that it was written prior to the fixing of the canon of the New Testament. Even though the word "canon" was not used to describe the New Testament as a fixed collection of normative documents until the mid-fourth century,[108] still the *idea* of canon as an authoritative standard was being discussed and enacted in the mid-to-late second century, the very period during which the *Gospel of Truth* was written. Indeed, in Rome in the 140s C.E., the presumed provenance of the *Gospel of Truth*, the Christian writer Marcion proposed a Christian "Scripture", a canon composed of one gospel and several Pauline letters whose intent was to regulate, in fact to close, the contents of Christian meaning.[109] Sacred story had become sacred book. Marcion's sense of authority, rooted as it was in theological content and a conception of "original" or pristine meaning, was adopted some forty years later by Irenaeus of Lyons who, although he did not accept Marcion's version of the New Testament canon, nonetheless did accept the *idea* of canon that Marcion initiated.[110] The point is that the *Gospel of Truth*'s allusive handling of Scriptural texts does not mean that this text was written in ignorance of issues of "canonicity", even though the canon had not been officially fixed; ideas concerning Scripture and Tradition that would eventually be carried in the Church's understanding of canon were already circulating in the period and place in which this text was written.

Irenaeus, who had contacts in Rome but did his writing in Lyons in the 180s C.E., is credited with the definitive statement of a four-gospel canon in direct response to Gnostic, and particularly Valentinian, writing.[111] Irenaeus' critique of his Valentinian opponents is basically that their writings pervert "the Scriptures": "such, then, is their system, which neither the prophets announced, nor the Lord taught, nor the apostles delivered ... ".[112] Their writings are not rooted, in other words, in "tradition", conceived of as an historically-transmitted, discrete body of knowledge.[113] Irenaeus says further,

> They gather their views from other sources than the Scriptures; and ... they weave ropes of sand, while they endeavor to adapt with an air of probability to their own peculiar assertions the parables of the Lord, the sayings of the prophets, and the words of the apostles, in order that their scheme may not seem altogether without support. In doing so, however, they disregard the order and the connection of the Scriptures ... By violently drawing away from their proper connection, words, expressions, and parables whenever found, [they] adapt the oracles of God to their baseless fictions.[114]

As Rowan Greer has explained, for Irenaeus the Valentinian misuse of Scripture "lies in the failure of the Valentinians to use the Rule of Faith as the *hypothesis* in rightly ordering the passages of Scripture. Irenaeus, of course, regards Scripture and the Rule as no more than different aspects of the Apostolic Faith".[115]

As far as Irenaeus was concerned, Gnostic interpretation of Scripture was out of control; he thought that they were using their own rule of faith as a control on the meaning of texts. Because Irenaeus defined Scripture historically and saw its content as an original revelation rooted in the past, he imagined that his opponents shared his understanding of Scripture (the later canon) as equal to its contents; their error lay in their adoption of a different theological model for interpreting Scripture.[116] For Irenaeus, meaning must always come to closure in and by means of a "Rule of Faith". And although he put his finger on some of the *effects* of Gnostic textuality—disregard for the order and connection of Scriptural passages, and so on—he has not understood the *perspective from which* the Valentinians approached interpretation.

Irenaeus understood Scripture and Tradition as an Author; what came to be called canon functioned for him to guarantee, to specify, and to close the contents of meaning. The *Gospel of Truth,* on the other hand, understood what came to be called canon hermeneutically; its concept of authority was rooted not in the past but in the present, and grew out of its understanding of the dynamics of language. For this text, "the author is never more than the instance writing ... The scriptor is born simultaneously with the text, is in no way equipped with a being preceding or exceeding the writing ... ; there is no other time than that of the enunciation and every text is eternally written *here and* now".[117] This is a performative view of textuality, based on dissemination, which makes of canon a very different concept.

When Irenaeus uses the term "the Scriptures", he means by it what later came to be called "canon": a restricted list of books that have a privileged claim to original meaning or divine truth. Implicit in Gnostic theories of language and textuality, however, is a revised understanding of the idea of canon, that is to say, of the notion of Scripture itself. We have already seen the *Gospel of Truth* declaring itself to be "the gospel of the one who is searched for".[118] To write is to search, and to search is to write; such is the dynamic at work in "gospel"—in Scripture. Scripture, or canon, is in this sense a figure for an ongoing quest, not a concept of fixed authority. As one contemporary author has put it, "If canon is what is written, writing itself seems to be unable to take a place in the canon—there is something radically uncanonical about writing itself".[119] Further, "To read the canon as figure of writing is to read the canon against itself because it is to recognize canonicity as inherently deviant from any fixed form which a canon might assume ... The canon functions in a manner that exceeds its content".[120]

A major scholarly assumption is that early Christian understandings of canon developed as a reaction to Gnostic interpretation of Scripture.[121] I would suggest now that the argument was concerned, more basically, with conflicting understandings of Scripture *as canon,* and not with the sudden, reactive appearance of an entity, "the Scriptures", that we now call canon. The definition of canon that the modern world has inherited from the ancient argument is Irenaeus' definition: it is a fixed measure, a ruler, a regulatory principle, an authoritative standard.[122] But this definition has occluded another meaning of the Greek word *kanōn* that might fittingly be applied to the Gnostic sense of Scripture that I have been exploring, namely, that canon is something used to keep a thing straight, like a weaver's rod, the reeds of a wind organ, or the crossbar of a cithara.[123] A canon, in this sense, gives shape, frame, support for weavings and musical fantasias. Here, canon is not identical with its content, since many tapestries can be woven upon the same loom. Rather, canon is a figure for the shaping element within any message; it is the *activity* of weaving (or writing), not the cloth or the exegesis itself. Thus canon is not a content or collection of texts so much as a texture of relationships undergirded by the desire in language signified by both its disseminative and its polyvalent dynamics.[124] "The written canon is undermined by its own writing", and the search goes on.[125]

When Gnostic texts juxtapose the familiar with the unfamiliar, when they open up Scriptural texts with unscriptural figures, they are obeying the "alien voice" of words, of writing, and of textuality. Scripture becomes that blank page full of paths, and the highest respect that one can pay to it is to write on it. The dilemma of original signification is also an opportunity to engage in the endless narrativity signaled by an understanding of canon as figure for the process of textuality. The way in which Gnostic texts relate to Scripture, as well as the theories of language that such texts both expound and enact, exposes their view of literature as a projection of desire. Just as words produce other words, so texts produce other texts in an endless quest. The "living book of the living" is a continuous process of discovering that the book is a lure.

In an essay entitled "Literature as Projection of Desire", Italo Calvino has written a passage that conveys aptly a Gnostic understanding of the relation between canon and texts: "The ideal library that I would like to see is one that gravitates toward the outside, toward the 'apocryphal' books in the etymological sense of the word: that is, 'hidden' books. Literature is a search for the book hidden in the distance that alters the value and meaning of the known books; it is the pull toward the new apocryphal text still to be rediscovered or invented".[126] As the *Gospel of Truth* says, "this is the word of the gospel of the discovery of the pleroma",[127] the library hidden in the book.

Notes

1. Jabès, *The Book of Questions*, p. 40.
2. Jabès, *Je bâtis ma demueure*, p. 41.
3. Jabès, *The Book of Questions*, p. 37.
4. The Valentinian provenance of the *Tripartite Tractate* is discussed by Attridge and Pagels, "The *Tripartite Tractate*: Introduction", pp. 177-90. Concerning the probable authorship of the *Gospel of Truth* by Valentinus himself, I accept the positive conclusions reached by Standaert, "*L'Évangile de Vérité*", pp. 259-65 and, most recently, by Williams, *Biblical Interpretation*, pp. 5, 205-7. Authorship by Valentinus would place the writing of the *Gospel of Truth* in the mid-2nd century C.E.
5. Jabès, *The Book of Questions*, p. 37.
6. I have used the translation of the *Tripartite Tractate* by Attridge and Pagels in Attridge (ed), *Nag Hammadi Codex 1 (The Jung Codex)*, pp. 193-337 (hereafter *NHC* I, 5).
7. *NHC* I, 5.67.24-25; 73.13-14.
8. *NHC* I, 5.55.37; 54.2-6. Attridge and Pagels, "The *Tripartite Tractate*: Notes", remark about "silence" that "apparently to protect the absolute transcendence of the Father, he [the author of the *Tripartite Tractate*] interprets the silence as a quality of the Father's solitary existence" (p. 234). My understanding of silence differs from theirs, in that my focus is on the relation of the unnameable one with language (which the text underscores often). In this context, silence functions not as an indicator of metaphysical status (transcendence) but as a dynamic of language.
9. See *NHC* I, 5.54.16-17.
10. *NHC* I, 5.71.14-19.
11. See *NHC* I, 5.65.39-66.5. This use of the Greek word *ichnos*, "trace", is closely paralleled by Plotinus' understanding of the term, precisely in the context of theological language. See Cox, "'Adam Ate From The Animal Tree'", pp. 179-80.
12. The literature is, of course, immense. I have been most influenced in my own thinking about these issues by Derrida, *Dissemination*, especially Sections I and II ("Plato's Pharmacy"), and idem, *Writing and Difference*, especially Ch. 10, "Structure, Sign, and Play in the Discourse of the Human Sciences"; Barthes, *The Pleasure of the Text*; De Certeau, *Heterologies*, especially Ch. 4, "Lacan: An Ethics of Speech", and Ch. 6, "Mystic Speech".
13. *NHC* I, 5.61.9-17.
14. *NHC* I, 5.60.1-35.
15. *NHC* I, 5.61.24-28.
16. *NHC* I, 5.71.8-9.
17. *Six Memos For the Next Millennium*, p. 26.
18. On dissemination, see especially Derrida, *Dissemination*, passim.
19. *NHC* I, 5.71.14-19.
20. *NHC* I, 5.73.1.
21. *NHC* I, 5.69.19-20.

22 Note that at *NHC* I, 5.70.10, the aeons are called "words of words"; for the connection of aeons and places, see *NHC* I, 5.71.19-21.
23 On the deferral of meaning in language, see especially Barthes, "From Work to Text", and Derrida, *Writing and Difference*, Ch. 7, "Freud and the Scene of Writing".
24 The phrase is from Fineman, "Gnosis and the Piety of Metaphor", p. 299. The whole passage deserves to be quoted: " ... we can specify the problem in very precise terms: how conduct a discourse about the origin of discourse when the origin is structured by the discourse such that it is excluded from it and unspeakable within it—and this precisely because the discourse is conceived and thematized as discourse: how to express what expression abolishes" (298-99).
25 Jabès, *The Book of Questions*, p. 47.
26 *Writing and Difference*, p. 72.
27 *NHC* I, 5.60.16-26.
28 *NHC* I, 5.75.13-15.
29 *NHC* I, 5.75.18-19.
30 *NHC* I, 5.76.1-4.
31 *NHC* I, 5.76.30-34.
32 *NHC* I, 5.77.15-17; 77.25-28.
33 *NHC* I, 5.78.14 (arrogance); 78.30 (deficiency); 79.12-32 (ambition, etc.).
34 *NHC* I, 5.81.1-3.
35 *NHC* I, 5.77.21.
36 De Certeau, *Heterologies*, p. 82.
37 Derrida's remarks are pertinent here: "If there is thus no thematic unity or overall meaning to reappropriate beyond the textual instances, no total message located in some imaginary order, intentionality, or lived experience, then the text is no longer the expression or representation (felicitous or otherwise) of any *truth* that would come to diffract or assemble itself in the polysemy of literature. It is this hermeneutic concept of *polysemy* that must be replaced by *dissemination*" (*Dissemination*, p. 262; italics in the original).
38 *NHC* I, 5.77.29-30; 80.15-19.
39 *NHC* I, 5.77.32-35.
40 *NHC* I, 5.81.19-21. As I have argued in "'All the Words Were Frightful'", the term *metanoia* literally means "change of consciousness" and so has broader implications than its usual translation as "repentance" (p. 328 and passim). According to the *Tripartite Tractate*, "change of consciousness" is also called "conversion", which, as McGuire has shown, need not carry the restrictive moral connotations established by A. D. Nock in *Conversion*. According to McGuire, "It is possible, without setting such narrow restrictions as Nock, to define conversion as the process by which an individual reorients his or her life to any new pattern of attitudes, beliefs, and practices. Freed from Nock's criteria of renunciation of sin and commitment to a specific range of thought and practice, the term conversion can apply to a fuller, more representative range of phenomena of religious change" ("Conversion and Gnosis in the *Gospel of Truth*", p. 342). When the *Tripartite Tractate* says "the conversion which is also called '*metanoia*'", it is pointing in this direction. Conversion can be a turn to another perspective on language.
41 *NHC* I, 5.81.30-35.
42 Jabès, *The Book of Questions*, p. 54.
43 See, for example, de Certeau, *Heterologies*, p. 89, who discusses "the labor of writing which is given birth through the animation of language by the desire of the other".

44 I have used the translation of the *Gospel of Truth* by Attridge and MacRae in Attridge (ed), *Nag Hammadi Codex I (The Jung Codex)*, pp. 83-117 (hereafter *NHC* I, 3).
45 The revelatory function of the *Gospel of Truth* has often been noted, particularly with regard to the movement from ignorance to knowledge, which the text both recommends and exemplifies. However, the text's revelation has typically been understood as a soteriology (Williams, *Biblical Interpretation*, pp. 190-92; Attridge and MacRae, "The *Gospel of Truth*: Introduction", pp. 74-76; Standaert, "*L'Évangile de Vérité*", pp. 269-70; and Ménard, "*L'Évangile de Vérité*", pp. 17-24), rather than as a hermeneutic, although Standaert notes the text's unity "entre la forme et le fond, entre la présentation littéraire, la structure profonde de son langage et le contenu de son message" (p. 269). I base my interpretation here on the *Gospel of Truth*'s insistence on the importance of words and on its characterization of its main figures (Father, Son, and Christ) with phenomena of language—the name and the book.
46 *NHC* I, 3.17.1-4; 18.12.
47 The title of the *Gospel* of *Truth* has occasioned a huge literature, which has focused either on (1) whether this text is the same as that referred to by Irenaeus, *Haer.* 3.11.9; or on (2) the fact that the genre of this "gospel" is not the same as the genre of the canonical gospels, whose genre is defined by virtue of their contents (passion narratives with biographical introductions [Koester, "One Jesus and Four Primitive Gospels"]). Standaert has noted that it was not until the second half of the second century that the word "gospel" came to signify a "text" rather than simply the message of good news, thus denying the generic status of the *Gospel* of *Truth*'s title with an historical rather than a canonical explanation ("'Evangelium Veritatis'," p. 141). The consensus is that the *Gospel of Truth* is best considered a homily or meditation on the gospel message and not a gospel properly (that is, canonically) so called. On this whole issue, see the discussion by Attridge and MacRae, "The *Gospel of Truth*: Introduction", pp. 65-67 and the bibliography appended there. These arguments seem questionable to me. On the one hand, the argument from genre seems unduly protective of the canon; on the other hand, Von Campenhausen's discussion of Marcion's creation of a gospel in a canonical sense before the second half of the second century suggests that the author of the *Gospel* of *Truth*, a contemporary of Marcion's in Rome, was aware of emergent issues regarding the privileging of some texts as solely authoritative (*The Formation of the Christian Bible*, pp. 155ff.). Given the argument that follows in the present essay, it may well be that the use of the title "gospel" by the author of the *Gospel* of *Truth* signified a questioning of the then-developing connection between written gospels and canonical authority.
48 *NHC* I, 3.17.30-31 (fog); 31.1-4 (material one). Attridge and MacRae, "The *Gospel of Truth*: Notes", p. 81, note on this passage that "the source of the 'material ones' is no doubt the 'matter' of Error (17.4-20)".
49 *NHC* I, 5.17.18-19. Although Attridge and MacRae translate *plasma* here as "creation", they note that the term can mean "fiction, pretense, delusion" ("The *Gospel of Truth*: Notes", p. 45), and I here follow that alternative translation.
50 *NHC* I, 3.16.34-35).
51 *The Book of Yukel*, p. 47.
52 *NHC* I, 3.40.16-17; 40.23-41.3.
53 *NHC* I, 3.34.30-31.
54 *NHC* I, 3.38.7-24.
55 *NHC* I, 3.31.28-33.

56 "*L'Évangile de Vérité*", p. 272. With regard to the *Gospel of Truth*'s "quasi-exclusive choice of the word 'Father' to designate God", see now Williams, *Biblical Interpretation*, pp. 193-94, who makes the same point concerning Valentinus' use and citation of Scripture. In the context of this essay's discussion, the change from God to Father is significant, since it serves to underscore the linguistic dynamic, as signified by "Father", to which the *Gospel of Truth is* committed.
57 "Gnosis and the Piety of Metaphor", p. 302.
58 Jabès, *The Book of Questions*, p. 47.
59 See Fineman, "Gnosis and the Piety of Metaphor", p. 302: "In the *Gospel of Truth*, 'lack' is defined as an ignorance of the Father which is eventually redeemed through knowledge of the Father. Here again, the pivotal turn calls up a confusing reflexivity: for the Son through whom knowledge of the Father is revealed is at the same time a representation of the very lack that the revelation is intended to redeem".
60 "Gnosis and the Piety of Metaphor", p. 301.
61 Ibid., p. 299.
62 Ibid.
63 Ibid., p. 304.
64 *NHC* I, 5.58.24.
65 *NHC* I, 3.41.15-16.
66 *NHC* I, 3.26.29-27.3.
67 Attridge and MacRae, "The *Gospel of Truth*: Notes", p. 79, observe that "it is possible that 'tongue' is used here metaphorically for language".
68 In ibid., p. 91, Attridge and MacRae remark that "the imagery of the Book underwent a ... transformation, first referring to what the revealer offers (20.12), then referring to the reality in which the recipients of the revelation are incorporated (21.4), the reality which the recipients in fact are (22.38-23.18)". In other words, the recipients of the book *are* the book, and they too "die" into it.
69 *NHC* I, 3.19.35-20.1.
70 *NHC* I, 3.20.23-27. Attridge discusses *Gospel of Truth* 20.23-27 as an allusion to Col. 2:14 and sees the text's strategy here as the defamiliarization of a familiar image in order to emphasize the revelatory character of the passion ("The *Gospel of Truth* as an Exoteric Text", pp. 246-47); Williams thinks that the passage underscores the salvific quality of the crucifixion (*Biblical Interpretation*, pp. 52-54); and Ménard suggests the Isis mysteries (viz. the priestess dressed in a starry cape) as a context for the Jesus wrapped in the book, and says in any case that the book, whether it signifies the pleroma or heavenly origins, must be interpreted mythically (*L'Évangile de Vérité*, pp. 99-100). See also Blanchette, "Does the Cheirographon of Col. 2, 14 Represent Christ Himself?". To my knowledge, no one has discussed the *Gospel of Truth*'s image of the book *as a book*, as this essay does in the following pages.
71 *NHC* I, 3.20.13.
72 *NHC* I, 3.18.24-31.
73 *NHC* I, 3.19.20-37.
74 *NHC* I, 3.21.3-5.
75 See Williams, *Biblical Interpretation*, pp. 37-41, on the possible Biblical derivation of the idea of a living book from Rev. 13:8.
76 *NHC* I, 3.18.25-26.
77 *NHC* I, 3.18.16-21.
78 Foucault, "What Is an Author?", p. 142.
79 Barthes, "The Death of the Author", p. 147.

80 Ibid., p. 146.
81 Ibid., p. 145.
82 *NHC* I, 3.19.35-20.1.
83 *NHC* I, 3.20.3-6. Attridge ("The *Gospel of Truth* as an Exoteric Text", p. 246), Williams (*Biblical Interpretation*, pp. 41-44), and Ménard (*L'Évangile de Vérité*, p. 96) all see this passage as an allusion to Rev. 5.9, in which only the Lamb is worthy to take God's scroll and "to open its seals". If this passage in the *Gospel of Truth* is indeed an allusion to Rev. 5:9, the Biblical text's emphasis on the opening of the seals is significant to the *Gospel of Truth*'s point about textuality and underscores my reading of this passage as a hermeneutical comment in the text which describes what the text itself is doing hermeneutically.
84 For a discussion of current theories about intertextuality, see Leitch, *Deconstructive Criticism*, pp. 87-122.
85 Fineman, "Gnosis and the Piety of Metaphor", p. 304.
86 *NHC* I, 3.20.29-30.
87 *NHC* I, 3.21.3-8, 29-30.
88 "*L'Évangile de Vérité*", pp. 257-58.
89 "What Is an Author?", p. 142.
90 *NHC* I, 3.22.8-11, 13-15. Typically, this phrase has been understood metaphysically as a statement of celestial origins; see Ménard, *L'Évangile de Vérité*, pp. 107-8.
91 *NHC* I, 3.35.2-4.
92 *The Book of Questions*, p. 13.
93 See ibid., p. 158: "Absence always leaves fingerprints".
94 See above, n. 4.
95 "The *Gospel of Truth* as an Exoteric Text", p. 242.
96 Ibid., p. 243.
97 *Biblical Interpretation*, p. 8.
98 Ibid., pp. 175, 176.
99 "The *Gospel of Truth* as an Exoteric Text", pp. 252, 242; in "*L'Évangile de* Vérité", pp. 258-59, Standaert also has pointed out the "supple and polyvalent" qualities of the *Gospel of Truth*'s use of language.
100 *Biblical Interpretation*, pp. 91, 11.
101 Attridge, "The *Gospel of Truth* as an Exoteric Text", p. 243.
102 Ibid., p. 255.
103 Ibid.
104 *Biblical Interpretation*, pp. 189, 202.
105 Ibid., p. 189.
106 "From Work to Text", p. 76.
107 Ibid. (emphasis added).
108 Grant, "Canon", p. 285.
109 Von Campenhausen, *The Formation of the Christian Bible*, pp. 148-74.
110 Ibid., pp. 182-203.
111 See Irenaeus, *Haer.* 3.11.8, and discussion by Von Campenhausen, *The Formation of the Christian Bible*, pp. 196-99.
112 Irenaeus, *Haer.* 1.8.1.
113 Ibid., 3.2.1-3.5.3.
114 Ibid., 1.8.1.
115 "The Dog and the Mushrooms", pp. 166-67.
116 Irenaeus, *Haer.* 1.9.1-4.

117 Barthes, "The Death of the Author", p. 145.
118 *NHC* I, 3.18.12-13.
119 Readings, "Canon and On", p. 157.
120 Ibid., p. 156.
121 See, most recently, Metzger, *The Canon of the New Testament*, pp. 75-90.
122 Ibid., pp. 282-87, 289-93.
123 Liddell, Scott, Jones, *A Greek-English Lexicon*, s.v. *kanōn*.
124 On relationships between text and texture and their relationship to religion, see the suggestive essay by David Miller, "The Question of the Book: Religion as Texture".
125 Readings, "Canon and On", p. 165.
126 Calvino, "Literature as a Projection of Desire", pp. 60-61.
127 *NHC* I, 3.34.35-37.

Bibliography

Ancient Sources

Acts of John, in Hennecke, Edgar and Schneemelcher, Wilhelm (eds), *New Testament Apocrypha*, Wilson, R. McL. (trans), Westminster Press, Philadelphia, 1965.
Aelian, *On the Characteristics of Animals*, Scholfield, A. F. (trans), *Aelian: On the Characteristics of Animals*, 3 vols., Loeb Classical Library, Harvard University Press, Cambridge 1958-1959.
Antonius, *The Life and Daily Mode of Living of the Blessed Simeon the Stylite*, in Doran, Robert (trans), *The Lives of Simeon Stylites*, Cistercian Publications, Kalamazoo, 1992.
Apocryphon of John, in Robinson, James M. (ed), *The Nag Hammadi Library in English*, Harper and Row, San Francisco, 1977.
Apophthegmata patrum, PG 65.72-440; Ward, Benedicta (trans), *The Sayings of the Desert Fathers*, Cistercian Publications, Kalamazoo, 1975.
Athanasius, *De vita Antonii*, PG 26.837-976.
Augustine, *De civitate Dei*, Dombart, B. and Kalb, A. (eds), CCL 47-48
Augustine, *Confessions*, Chadwick, Henry (trans), Oxford University Press, Oxford, 1991.
Clement of Alexandria, *Stromata*, Mondésert, Claude (ed and trans), *Clément d'Alexandrie: Les Stromates*, vols. 1-2, Sources Chrétiennes 30, 38, Les Éditions du Cerf, Paris, 1951, 1954; Stählin, Otto (ed), *Clemens Alexandrinus*, vol. 2: *Stromata Buch I-VI*, J.C. Hinrichs, Leipzig, 1906.
Corpus Hermeticum, 4 vols., Nock, A. D. and Festugière, A.-J. (eds and trans), Société d'Édition "Les Belles Lettres", Paris, 1945-1954.
Discourse on the Eighth and the Ninth, in Robinson, James M. (ed), *The Nag Hammadi Library in English*, Harper and Row, San Francisco, 1977.
Ephrem, *Hymni et Sermones*, Vööbus, Arthur (trans), *History of Asceticism in the Syrian Orient*, vol. 2: *Early Monasticism in Mesopotamia and Syria*, CSCO 197, Secrétariat du Corpus *SCO*, Louvain, 1960.
Gospel of Philip, in Robinson, James M. (ed), *The Nag Hammadi Library in English*, Harper and Row, San Francisco, 1977.
Gospel of the Egyptians, in Robinson, James M. (ed), *The Nag Hammadi Library in English*, Harper and Row, San Francisco, 1977.
Gospel of Thomas, in *The Nag Hammadi Library in English*, in Robinson, James M. (ed), Harper and Row, San Francisco, 1977.

Gospel of Truth, in Attridge, Harold W. (ed and trans), *Nag Hammadi Codex I (The Jung Codex): Introductions, Texts, Translations, Indices*, E. J. Brill, Leiden, 1985.

Hippolytus, *Refutation of All Heresies*, in Roberts, Alexander and Donaldson, James (eds), MacMahon, J. H. (trans), *Ante-Nicene Fathers*, vol. 5, Wm. B. Eerdmans, Grand Rapids, repr. ed., 1978.

Historia monachorum in Aegypto, Festugière, A.-J. (ed), Subsidia Hagiographica 34, Société des Bollandistes, Brussels, 1961; Russell, Norman (trans), *The Lives of the Desert Fathers*, Cistercian Publications, Kalamazoo, 1981.

Iamblichus, *De vita Pythagorica*, Deubner, Ludovicus (ed), Teubner, Leipzig 1937.

Irenaeus, *Adversus Haereses [Against Heresies]*, in Roberts, Alexander and Donaldson, James (eds), Roberts, Alexander and Rambaut, W. H. (trans), *Ante-Nicene Fathers*, vol. 1, Wm. B. Eerdmans, Grand Rapids, repr. ed., 1979.

Jerome, *Adversus Jovinianum*, PL 23.221-352.

Jerome, *Apologia contra Rufinum*, PL 23.415-514.

Jerome, *Commentariorum in Isaiam Prophetam*, PL 24.17-678.

Jerome, *Contra Johannem*, PL 23.371-412.

Jerome, *Epistolae*, Hilberg, I. (ed), CSEL 54-56 (1910, 1912); English translations of *Ep.* 22: Schaff, Philip and Wace, Henry (eds), *Nicene and Post-Nicene Fathers*, 2nd series, vol. 6, The Christian Literature Co., New York, 1893; Mierow, Charles Christopher (trans), *The Letters of Jerome*, Ancient Christian Writers 33, Westminster Press, Philadelphia, 1953.

Jerome, *Vita sancti Pauli*, in *Studies in the Text Tradition of St. Jerome's Vitae Patrum*, Oldfather, William Abbott (ed), University of Illinois Press, Urbana, 1943, pp. 536-42. English translation by Harvey, Paul B. Jr., "Jerome: *Life of Paul, the First Hermit*", in Wimbush, Vincent L. (ed), *Ascetic Behavior in Greco-Roman Antiquity: A Sourcebook*, Fortress Press, Minneapolis, 1990, pp. 357-69.

Life of St. Mary of Egypt, in Ward, Benedicta (trans), *Harlots of the Desert*, Cistercian Publications, 1987.

Marcus Aurelius, *Meditations*, Staniforth, Maxwell (trans), Penguin Books, Baltimore, 1964.

Mithras Liturgy, Meyer, Marvin W. (ed and trans), Scholars Press, Missoula, Montana, 1976.

Oppian, *Cynegetica*, Mair, A. W. (trans), *Oppian Colluthus Tryphiodorus*, Loeb Classical Library, William Heinemann, London, 1928.

Origen, *Commentarius in Canticum Canticorum*, Baehrens, W. A. (ed), *Die Griechischen Christlichen Schriftsteller der Ersten Drei Jahrhunderte, Origenes Werke*, vol. 8, J. C. Hinrichs, Leipzig, 1925; English translation by Lawson, R. P., *Origen: The Song of Songs, Commentary and Homilies*, Ancient Christian Writers 26, Newman Press, New York, 1956.

Origen, *Commentarii in Iohannem*, in Blanc, Cécile (ed and trans), *Origène: Commentaire sur S. Jean*, 4 vols., Sources chrétiennes 120, 157, 222, 290, Les Éditions du Cerf, Paris, 1966-1982.

Origen, *Contra Celsum*, in *Origen: Contra Celsum*, Chadwick, Henry (trans), Cambridge University Press, Cambridge, 1965.
Origen, *De Engastrimūthō*, Klostermann, Erich (ed), in *Kleine Texte 83: Origenes, Eustathius von Antiochien und Gregor von Nyssa über die Hexe von Endor*, A. Marcus and E. Weber Verlag, Bonn, 1912.
Origen, *De Oratione [On Prayer]*, in Oulton, J.E. L and Chadwick, Henry (trans), *Library of Christian Classics*, vol. 2: *Alexandrian Christianity*, Westminster Press, Philadelphia, 1954.
Origen, *De principiis*, Koetschau, Paul (ed), *Origenes Werke, 5. Band: De Principiis*, Die Griechischen Christlichen Schriftsteller 22, J.C. Hinrichs, Leipzig, 1913; *Origène: Traité des Principes*, Crouzel, Henri and Simonetti, Manlio (ed and trans), Sources Chrétiennes 252, 253, 268, 269, Les Éditions du Cerf, Paris, 1978-1980; English translation by Butterworth, G. W., *Origen: On First Principles*, Harper and Row, New York, 1966.
Origen, *Dialogue with Heraclides*, Scherer, Jean (ed and trans), *Entretien d'Origène avec Héraclide*, Sources chrétiennes 67, Les Éditions du Cerf, Paris 1960.
Origen, *Homilies on Exodus*, Heine, Ronald E. (trans), *Origen: Homilies on Genesis and Exodus*, The Fathers of the Church 71, The Catholic University of America Press, Washington, D.C., 1982.
Origen, *Homiliae in Canticum Canticorum*, Rousseau, Dom Olivier (ed and trans), *Origène: Homélies sur le Cantique des Cantiques*, Sources chrétiennes 37, Les Éditions du Cerf, Paris 1966; English translation by Lawson, R. P., *Origen: The Song of Songs, Commentary and Homilies*, Ancient Christian Writers 26, Newman Press, New York, 1956.
Origen, *Homiliae in Genesim*, Doutreleau, Louis (ed and trans), *Origène: Homélies sur la Genèse*, Sources chrétiennes 7, Les Éditions du Cerf, Paris 1976.
Origen, *Homiliae in Ieremiam*, Nautin, Pierre and Husson, Pierre (ed and trans), *Origène: Homilies sur Jérémie*, 2 vols., Sources chrétiennes 232, 238, Les Éditions du Cerf, Paris, 1976-1977.
Origen, *Homiliae in Jesu Nave*, Jaubert, Annie (ed and trans), *Origène: Homilies sur Josué*, Sources chrétiennes 71, Les Éditions du Cerf, Paris, 1960.
Origen, *Homiliae in Leviticum*, Baehrens, W. A. (ed), *Origenes: Homilien zum hexateuch in Rufins Übersetzung, Die Homilien zu Genesis, Exodus, und Leviticus*, Die griechischen christlichen Schriftsteller der ersten drei Jahrhunderte, Origenes Werke, vol. 6, J. C. Hinrichs, Leipzig, 1920.
Origen, *Homiliae in Lucam*, Crouzel, Henri, Fournier, François and Périchon, Pierre (ed and trans), *Origène: Homelies sur S. Luc*, Sources chrétiennes 87, Les Éditions du Cerf, Paris, 1962.
Origen, *Homilae in Numeros*, Méhat, André (ed and trans), *Origène: Homélies sur les Nombres*, Sources chrétiennes 29, Les Éditions du Cerf, Paris, 1951.
Origen, *Philocalia (1-20)*, Harl, Marguerite (ed and trans), *Origène: Philocalie, 1-20, Sur Les Écritures*, Sources chrétiennes 302, Les Éditions du Cerf, Paris, 1983.

Origen, *Philocalia* (21-27), Junod, Eric (ed and trans), *Origène: Philocalie 21-27, Sur le Libre Arbitre,* Sources chrétiennes 226, Les Éditions du Cerf, Paris, 1976.
Palladius, *Historia Lausiaca,* Butler, Cuthbert (ed), *Palladius: Historia Lausiaca,* 2 vols., Cambridge University Press, Cambridge, 1898, 1904; English translation by Meyer, Robert T., Ancient Christian Writers 34, The Newman Press, Westminster, Maryland, 1965.
Papyri Graecae Magicae, Preisendanz, Karl (ed), 2nd ed. rev. by Albert Henrichs, Teubner, Stuttgart, 1973-1974; English translation by Betz, Hans Dieter, *The Greek Magical Papyri in Translation,* University of Chicago Press, Chicago, 1986.
Parmenides, *Fragments,* in Wheelwright, Philip (trans), *The Presocratics,* Bobbs-Merrill Co., Indianapolis, 1960.
Physiologus, Lauchert, Friedrich (ed), *Geschichte des Physiologus,* K. J. Trübner, Strasbourg, 1889, pp. 229-279. English translation and introduction by Curley, Michael, *Physiologus,* University of Texas Press, Austin, 1979.
Pistis Sophia, Schmidt, Carl (ed), MacDermot, Violet (trans), Nag Hammadi Studies 9, E. J. Brill, Leiden, 1978.
Plato, *Dialogues,* in Hamilton, Edith and Cairns, Huntington (eds), *The Collected Dialogues of Plato,* Princeton University Press, Princeton, 1961.
Pliny, *Natural History,* Rackham, H. (trans), *Pliny: Natural History,* Loeb Classical Library, William Heinemann, London, 1967.
Plotinus, *Enneads,* Armstrong, A. H. (trans), *Plotinus,* 7 vols., Loeb Classical Library, Harvard University Press, Cambridge, 1966-1988; MacKenna, Stephen (trans), *Enneads,* 4th rev. ed. by B. S. Page, Faber & Faber, London, 1962.
Plutarch, *Conjugal Precepts,* Babbitt, Frank Cole (trans), in *Plutarch's Moralia,* vol. 2, Loeb Classical Library, William Heinemann, London, 1928.
Plutarch, *On Isis and Osiris,* Babbitt, Frank Cole (trans), in *Plutarch's Moralia,* vol. 5, Loeb Classical Library, Harvard University Press, Cambridge, 1936.
Plutarch, *De pythiae oraculis,* Babbitt, Frank Cole (trans), in *Plutarch's Moralia,* vol. 5, Loeb Classical Library, Harvard University Press, Cambridge, 1936.
Plutarch, *De sollertia animalium,* Cherniss, Harold and Helmbold, William C. (trans), in *Plutarch's Moralia,* vol. 12, Loeb Classical Library, Harvard University Press, Cambridge, 1957.
Porphyry, *De vita Pythagorae,* Nauck, A. (ed), *Porphyrii philosophi platonici opuscula selecta,* Teubner, Leipzig, 1886.
Rufinus, *Apologia contra Hieronymum,* Simonetti, M. (ed), CCL 20, 1961.
Synesius of Cyrene, *De insomniis,* PG 66.1281-1320; English translation by Fitzgerald, Augustine, *The Essays and Hymns of Synesius of Cyrene,* Oxford University Press, Oxford, 1930.
Syriac Life of Saint Simeon Stylites, Doran, Robert (trans), in *The Lives of Simeon Stylites,* Cistercian Publications, Kalamazoo, 1992.
Tertullian, *De praescriptione haereticorum,* Kroymann, A. (ed), CSEL 70, 1942.

Theodoret, *Historia religiosa*, Canivet, Pierre and Leroy-Molinghen, Alice (ed and trans), 2 vols., Sources Chrétiennes 234, 257, Les Éditions du Cerf, 1977, 1979; English translation by Price, R. M., *Theodoret of Cyrrhus: A History of the Monks of Syria*, Cistercian Publications, Kalamazoo, 1985.
Thunder, Perfect Mind, in Robinson, James M. (ed), *The Nag Hammadi Library in English*, Harper and Row, San Francisco, 1977.
Tripartite Tractate, Attridge, Harold W. (ed and trans), *Nag Hammadi Codex 1 (The Jung Codex): Introductions, Texts, Translations, Indices*, E. J. Brill, Leiden, 1985.
Zosimus of Panopolis, *On the Letter Omega*, Jackson, Howard M. (ed and trans), Scholars Press, Missoula, Montana, 1978.

Modern Sources

A Latin Dictionary (1879), Lewis, Charlton T. and Short, Charles (eds), The Clarendon Press, Oxford.
Armstrong, A. H. (1977), "Form, Individual, and Person in Plotinus", *Dionysius*, vol. 1, pp. 49-68.
Armstrong, A. H. (1986), "Introduction", in idem (ed), *Classical Mediterranean Spirituality*, Crossroad, New York, xiii-xxi.
Attridge, Harold W. (ed) (1985), *Nag Hammadi Codex 1 (The Jung Codex): Introductions, Texts, Translations, Indices*, E. J. Brill, Leiden.
Attridge, Harold W. (1986), "The *Gospel of Truth* as an Exoteric Text", in *Nag Hammadi, Gnosticism, and Early Christianity*, Hedrick, Charles W. and Hodgson, Robert Jr. (eds), Hendrickson Publishers, Peabody, Massachusetts, pp. 239-255.
Attridge, Harold W. and MacRae, George W. (1985), "The *Gospel of Truth*: Notes", in Attridge, Harold W. (ed) (1985), *Nag Hammadi Codex 1 (The Jung Codex): Notes*, E. J. Brill, Leiden, pp. 39-135.
Attridge, Harold W. and MacRae, George W. (1985), "The *Gospel of Truth*: Introduction", in Attridge, Harold W. (1985), *Nag Hammadi Codex 1 (The Jung Codex): Introductions, Texts, Translations, Indices*, E.J. Brill, Leiden, pp. 55-81.
Attridge, Harold W. and Pagels, Elaine H. (1985), "The *Tripartite Tractate*: Introduction", in Attridge, Harold W. (ed) (1985), *Nag Hammadi Codex 1 (The Jung Codex): Introductions, Texts, Translations, Indices*, E. J. Brill, Leiden, pp. 159-90.
Attridge, Harold W. and Pagels, Elaine H. (1985),"The *Tripartite Tractate*: Notes", in Attridge, Harold W. (1985), *Nag Hammadi Codex 1 (The Jung Codex): Notes*, E. J. Brill, Leiden, pp. 217-497.
Bachelard, Gaston (1986), *Lautréamont*, Dupree, Robert S. (trans), The Pegasus Foundation, Dallas.
Bachelard, Gaston (1988), *Air and Dreams*, Farrell, Edith R. and Farrell, C. Frederick (trans), Dallas Institute Publications, Dallas.

Balas, David (1975), "The Idea of Participation in the Structure of Origen's Thought: Christian transposition of a theme of the Platonic tradition", in Crouzel, Henri, Lomiento, Gennaro, and Rius-Camps, Josep (eds), *Origeniana*, Istituto Di Letteratura Cristiana Antica, Università di Bari, pp. 257-275.

Barthes, Roland (1975), *The Pleasure of the Text*, Miller, Richard (trans), Hill and Wang, New York.

Barthes, Roland (1975), *The Pleasure of the Text*, Miller, Richard (trans), Hill and Wang, New York.

Barthes, Roland (1977), "The Death of the Author", in idem, *Image, Music, Text*, Heath, Stephen (trans), Hill and Wang, New York, pp. 142-48.

Barthes, Roland (1977), "The Death of the Author", in idem, *Image, Music, Text*, Heath, Stephen (trans), Hill and Wang, New York, pp. 142-48

Barthes, Roland (1979), "From Work to Text", in *Textual Strategies: Perspectives in Post-Structuralist Criticism*, Harari, Josué (ed), Cornell University Press, Ithaca, pp. 73-81.

Barthes, Roland (1981), *Camera Lucida*, Howard, Richard (trans), Hill and Wang, New York.

Bartra, Roger (1994), *Wild Men in the Looking Glass: The Mythic Origins of European Otherness*, Berrisford, Carl T. (trans), University of Michigan Press, Ann Arbor.

Bauer, Johannes (1961), "Novellistisches bei Hieronymous Vita Pauli 3", *Wiener Studien*, vol. 74, pp. 130-37.

Behm, Johannes (1964), "glossa", in Kittel, Gerhard (ed), Bromiley, Geoffrey M. (trans), *Theological Dictionary of the New Testament*, Eerdmans, Grand Rapids, vol. 1, pp. 719-27.

Bell, Catherine (1992), *Ritual Theory, Ritual Practice*, Oxford University Press, New York.

Bernheimer, Richard (1952), *Wild Men in the Middle Ages: A Study in Art, Sentiment, And Demonology*, Harvard University Press, Cambridge; repr. ed. 1979, Octagon Books, New York.

Betz, Hans Dieter (1982), "The Formation of Authoritative Tradition in the Greek Magical Papyri", in Meyer, Ben F. and Sanders, E. P. (eds), *Jewish and Christian Self-Definition*, vol. 3: *Self-Definition in the Greco-Roman World*, Fortress Press, Philadelphia, pp. 161-70.

Black, Max (1977), "More About Metaphor", *Dialectica*, vol. 31, pp. 431-57.

Blanchette, 0. (1961), "Does the Cheirographon of Col. 2,14 Represent Christ Himself?", *Catholic Biblical Quarterly*, vol. 23, pp. 306-12.

Borgeaud, Philippe (1988), *The Cult of Pan in Ancient Greece*, Atlass, Kathleen and Redfield, James (trans), University of Chicago Press, Chicago.

Brown, Francis, Driver, S. R., and Briggs, C. A. (eds), *A Hebrew and English Lexicon of the Old Testament*, The Clarendon Press, Oxford, 1968.

Brown, Norman 0. (1959), *Life Against Death*, Random House, New York.

Brown, Norman 0. (1966), *Love's Body*, Vintage Books, New York.

Brown, Peter (1971), "The Rise and Function of the Holy Man in Late Antiquity", *Journal of Roman Studies*, vol. 61, pp. 80-101; also in idem (1982), *Society and the Holy in Late Antiquity*, University of California Press, Berkeley, pp. 103-52.
Brown, ·Peter (1978), *The Making of Late Antiquity*, Harvard University Press, Cambridge.
Brown, Peter (1987), "The Saint as Exemplar in Late Antiquity", in *Saints and Virtues*, Hawley, John Stratton (ed), University of California Press, Berkeley, pp. 3-14.
Brown, Peter (1988), *The Body and Society: Men, Women and Sexual Renunciation in Early Christianity*, Columbia University Press, New York.
Brown, Raymond E. (1970), *The Gospel according to John*, 2 vols., Garden City, New York, Doubleday.
Burkert, Walter (1962), "*Goes*: Zum Griechischen 'Schamianismus'", *Rheinisches Museum für Philologie*, vol. 105, pp. 36-55.
Bynum, Caroline Walker (1995), *The Resurrection of the Body in Western Christianity, 200-1336*, Columbia University Press, New York.
Calvino, Italo (1986), "Literature as Projection of Desire", in idem, *The Uses of Literature*, Creagh, Patrick (trans), Harcourt, Brace, Jovanovich, San Diego, pp. 50-61.
Calvino, Italo (1986), *The Uses of Literature*, Creagh, Patrick (trans), Harcourt, Brace, Jovanovich, San Diego.
Calvino, Italo (1988), *Six Memos for the Next Millennium*, Creagh, Patrick (trans), Harvard University Press, Cambridge.
Cameron, Averil (1986), "Redrawing the Map: Early Christian Territory After Foucault", *Journal of Roman Studies*, vol. 76, pp. 266-71.
Cameron, Averil (1991), *Christianity and the Rhetoric of Empire: The Development of Christian Discourse*, Berkeley, University of California Press.
Carroll, Lewis (1960), *Alice in Wonderland*, in Gardner, Martin (ed), *The Annotated Alice*, Clarkson N. Potter, New York.
Carroll, Lewis (1960), *Through the Looking Glass*, in Gardner, Martin (ed), *The Annotated Alice,* Clarkson N. Potter, New York.
Carruthers, Mary (1990), *The Book of Memory: A Study of Memory in Medieval Culture*, Cambridge Studies in Medieval Culture, vol. 10, Cambridge University Press, Cambridge.
Carson, Anne (1986), *Eros the Bittersweet: An Essay*, Princeton University Press, Princeton.
Castelli, Elizabeth A. (1992), "Mortifying the Body, Curing the Soul: Beyond Ascetic Dualism in *The Life of Saint Syncletica*", *differences*, vol. 4, pp. 134-53.
Cavallera, Franchi (1922), *Saint Jérome: Sa vie et son oeuvre*, 2 vols., Spicilegium Sacrum Lovaniense Bureaux, Louvain.
Clark, Elizabeth A. (1979), *Jerome, Chrysostom, and Friends: Essays and Translations*, Edwin Mellen Press, Lewiston, New York.

Clark, Elizabeth A. (1986), "The Uses of the Song of Songs: Origen and the Later Latin Fathers", in *Ascetic Piety and Women's Faith: Essays on Late Ancient Christianity*, Edwin Mellen Press, Lewiston, New York, pp. 386-427.

Clark, Elizabeth A. (1992), *The Origenist Controversy: The Cultural Construction of an Early Christian Debate*, Princeton University Press, Princeton.

Clark, Elizabeth A. (1998), "The Lady Vanishes: Dilemmas of a Feminist Historian after the 'Linguistic Turn'", *Church History*, vol. 67, pp. 1-31.

Coleiro, E. (1957), "St. Jerome's Lives of the Hermits", *Vigiliae Christianae*, vol. 11, pp. 161-78.

Corbin, Henry (1979), *Corps spirituel et terre céleste*, Editions Buchet/Chastel, Paris.

Cox, Patricia (1980), "'In My Father's House Are Many Dwelling Places': *ktisma* in Origen's *De Principiis*", *Anglican Theological Review*, vol. 62, pp. 322-37.

Cox, Patricia (1981), "'Adam Ate From the Animal Tree': A Bestial Poetry of Soul", *Dionysius*, vol. 5, pp. 165-80.

Cox, Patricia (1982), "Origen and the Bestial Soul: A Poetics of Nature", *Vigiliae Christianae*, vol. 36, pp. 115-40.

Cox, Patricia (1984), "Origen and the Witch of Endor: Toward an Iconoclastic Typology", *Anglican Theological Review*, vol. 66, pp. 137-147.

Creeley, Robert (1970), "Love", in idem, *Later,* New Directions, New York. *Later* is copyright © 1970 by Robert Creeley. Reprinted by permission of New Directions Publishing Corp.

Crouzel, Henri (1956), *Théologie de l'image de Dieu chez Origène*, Aubier, Paris.

Crouzel, Henri (1961), *Origène et la "Connaissance Mystique"*, Desclée de Brouwer, Paris.

Crouzel, Henri (1963), "Grégoire le Thaumaturge et le Dialogue avec Élien", *Recherches des Sciences Religieuses,* vol. 51, pp. 422-31.

Crouzel, Henri (1964), "La distinction de la 'typologie' et de l'allégorie'", *Bulletin de Littérature Ecclésiastique*, vol. 65, pp. 161-74.

Dahl, Nils A. (1980), "The Arrogant Archon and the Lewd Sophia: Jewish Traditions in Gnostic Revolt", in Layton, Bentley (ed), *The Rediscovery of Gnosticism*, vol. 2: *Sethian Gnosticism*, E. J. Brill, Leiden, pp. 689-712.

Daniélou, Jean (1948), *Origène*, La Table Ronde, Paris.

Daniélou, Jean (1973), *A History of Early Christian Doctrine*, vol. 2: *Gospel Message And Hellenistic Culture*, Baker, John Austin (trans), Darton, Longman & Todd, London.

De Certeau, Michel (1986), *Heterologies: Discourse on the Other*, Massumi, Brian (trans), Theory and History of Literature, vol. 17, University of Minnesota Press, Minneapolis.

De Certeau, Michel (1992), *The Mystic Fable,* Smith, Michael B. (trans), University of Chicago Press, Chicago.

De Lubac, Henri (1947), "Typologie et allégorisme", *Recherches des sciences Religieuses*, vol. 34 , pp. 180-226.

De Romilly, Jacqueline (1975), *Magic and Rhetoric in Ancient Greece*, Harvard University Press, Cambridge.

Delling, Gerhard (1964-), "stoicheion", in Kittel, Gerhard (ed), Bromiley, Geoffrey W. (trans), *Theological Dictionary of the New Testament*, Eerdmans, Grand Rapids, vol. 3, pp. 670-87.
Derrida, Jacques (1978), *Writing and Difference*, Bass, Alan (trans), University of Chicago Press, Chicago.
Derrida, Jacques (1981), *Dissemination*, Johnson, Barbara (trans), University of Chicago Press, Chicago.
Detienne, Marcel (1979), *Dionysus Slain*, Muellner, Mireille and Muellner, Leonard (trans), Johns Hopkins University Press, Baltimore.
Detienne, Marcel and Vernant, Jean-Pierre (1978), *Cunning Intelligence in Greek Culture and Society*, trans. Janet Lloyd, The Harvester Press Limited, Sussex.
Diels, Hermann (ed and trans) (1934), *Die Fragmente der Vorsokratiker*, Kranz, Walter (rev), Weidmann, Berlin.
Dieterich, Albrecht (1901), "ABC-Denkmaeler", *Rheinisches Museum für Philologie*, vol. 56, pp. 77-105.
Dieterich, Albrecht (1891), *Abraxas*, Teubner, Leipzig.
Dieterich, Albrecht, (1923), *Eine Mithrasliturgie*, 3rd ed. (1966), Teubner, Stuttgart.
Dodds, E. R. (1966), *The Greeks and the Irrational*, University of California Press, Berkeley.
Dodds, E. R. (1970), *Pagan and Christian in an Age of Anxiety*, W. W. Norton, New York.
Dorival, Gilles (1975), "Remarques sur la Forme du *Peri Archon*", in Crouzel, Henri, Lomiento, Gennaro, and Rius-Camps, Josep (eds), *Origeniana*, Instituto di Letteratura Cristiana Antica, Università di Bari, pp. 33-45.
Dornseiff, Franz (1922), *Das Alphabet in Mystik und Magie*, Teubner, Leipzig.
Driivers, H. J. W. (1997), "Spätantike Parallelen zur altchristlichen Heiligenverehrung unter besonderer Berucksichtigung des syrischen Styliten kultes", in *Oikonomia: Quellen und Studien zur ortbodoxen Tbeologie*, vol. 6, Lilienfeld, Fairy v., Bryner, Erich, Felmy, Karl Christian, and Weismann, Werner (eds), Erlangen, pp. 54-76.
DuBois, Page (1982), *Centaurs and Amazons: Women and the Pre-History of the Great Chain of Being*, University of Michigan Press, Ann Arbor.
Duncan, Robert (1963), "Narrative Bridges for *Adam's Way*", in idem, *Bending the Bow*, New Directions, New York.
Eliade, Mircea (1963), *Patterns in Comparative Religion*, Meridian Books, New York.
Eliade, Mircea (1972), *Shamanism*, Princeton University Press, Princeton.
Emerson, Ralph Waldo (1903), "The Poet", in *Essays*, 2nd series, *The Complete Works of Ralph Waldo Emerson*, Houghton Mifflin Company, Boston, vol. 3, pp. 3-42.
Festugière, André-Jean (1944), *La Révélation d'Hermès Trismégiste*, vol. 1: *L'Astrologie et les Sciences Occultes*, Librairie Lecoffre, Paris.

Fineman, Joel (1980), "Gnosis and the Piety of Metaphor: The *Gospel of Truth*", in Layton, Bentley (ed), *The Rediscovery of Gnosticism*, vol. 1: *Valentinian Gnosticism*, E. J. Brill, Leiden, pp. 289-318.

Foster, Susan Leigh (1992), "Dancing Bodies", in *Incorporations (Zone 6)*, Crary, Jonathan and Kwinter, Sanford (eds), Urzone, Inc., New York, pp. 480-95.

Foucault, Michel (1979), "What is an Author?", in *Textual Strategies: Perspectives in Post-Structuralist Criticism*, Harari, Josué V. (ed), Cornell University Press, Ithaca, pp. 141-60.

Frankfurter, David T. M. (1990), "Stylites and *Phallobates*: Pillar Religions in Late Antique Syria", *Vigiliae Christianae*, vol. 44.

Friedrich, Paul (1978), *The Meaning of Aphrodite*, University of Chicago Press, Chicago.

Frye, Northrop (1957), *Anatomy of Criticism*, Princeton University Press, Princeton.

Frye, Northrop (1982), *The Great Code: The Bible and Literature*, Harcourt, Brace, Jovanovich, New York.

Funk, Robert W. (1966), *Language, Hermeneutic, and Word of God: The Problem of Language in the New Testament and Contemporary Theology*, Harper and Row, New York.

Gaster, Theodore (1969), *Myth, Legend, and Custom in the Old Testament*, Harper and Row, New York.

Goldhill, Simon (1994), "The naïve and knowing eye: ecphrasis and the culture of viewing in the Hellenistic world", in Goldhill, Simon and Osborne, Robin (eds), *Art and text in ancient Greek Culture*, Cambridge University Press, Cambridge, pp. 197-223.

Grant, Robert M. (1952), *Miracle and Natural Law in Graeco-Roman and Early Christian Thought*, North Holland Publishing Company, Amsterdam.

Grant, R. M. (1961), *The Earliest Lives of Jesus*, SPCK, London.

Grant, R. M. (1966), "The Book of Wisdom at Alexandria", *Studia Patristica*, vol. 7, pp. 462-72.

Grant, R.M. (1970), "Canon", in Ackroyd, P. R. and Evans, C. F. (eds), *The Cambridge History of the Bible*, vol. 1: *From the Beginnings to Jerome*, Cambridge University Press, Cambridge.

Greer, Rowan (1980), "The Dog and the Mushrooms: Irenaeus' View of the Valentinians Assessed", in Layton, Bentley (ed), *The Rediscovery of Gnosticism*, vol. 1: *Valentinian Gnosticism*, E. J. Brill, Leiden, pp. 146-75.

Grigson, Geoffrey (1976), *The Goddess of Love*, Constable, London.

Gubar, Susan (1982), "'The Blank Page' and the Issues of Female Creativity", in *Writing and Sexual Difference*, Abel, Elizabeth (ed), University of Chicago Press, Chicago.

Guillaumont, Antoine (1975), "La conception du désert chez les moines d'Égypt", *Recherches de l'Histoire Religieuse*, vol. 188, pp. 3-21.

Hanson, R.P.C. (1959), *Allegory and Event*, John Knox Press, London.

Harl, Marguerite (1958), *Origène et la fonction révélatrice du Verbe incarné*, Éditions du Seuil, Paris.

Harl, Marguerite (1972), "Origène et la Sémantique du Langage Biblique", *Vigiliae Christianae*, vol. 26, pp.161-87.
Harl, Marguerite (1975), "Structure et cohérence du Peri Archon", in Crouzel, Henri, Lomiento, Gennaro, and Rius-Camps, Josep (eds), *Origeniana*, Istituto di Letteratura Cristiana Antica, Università di Bari, pp. 11-32.
Harl, Marguerite (1982), "Origène et les Interprétations Patristiques Grecques de l'Obscurité Biblique", *Vigiliae Christianae*, vol. 36, pp. 334-71.
Harpham, Geoffrey Galt (1987), *The Ascetic Imperative in Culture and Criticism*, University of Chicago Press, Chicago.
Harvey, Susan Ashbrook (1988), "The Sense of a Stylite: Perspectives on Simeon the Elder", *Vigiliae Christianae*, vol. 42, pp. 376-94.
Heidegger, Martin (1968), *What Is Called Thinking?*, Gray, J. Glenn (trans), Harper and Row, New York.
Hillman, James (1975), *Re-Visioning Psychology*, Harper and Row, New York.
Hopper, Stanley Romaine (1979), "The Bucket As It Is", in Lombard, Mark D. (ed), *Metaphor and Beyond: Conversations with Stanley Romaine Hopper*, Syracuse University Department of Religion, Syracuse, pp. 5-48.
Hunter, Dianne (1985), "Hysteria, Psychoanalysis, and Feminism: The Case of Anna O.", in *The (M)other Tongue: Essays in Feminist Psychoanalytic Interpretation*, Garner, Shirley Nelson, Kahane, Claire, and Sprengnether, Madelon (eds), Cornell University Press, Ithaca, pp. 89-115.
Irvine, Martin (1994), *The Making of Textual Culture: 'Grammatica' and Literary Theory, 350-1100*, Cambridge University Press, Cambridge.
Jabès, Edmond (1959), *Je bâtis ma derneure: Poèmes, 1943-1957*, Gallimard, Paris.
Jabès, Edmond, (1972), *The Book of Questions*, Waldrop, Rosmarie (trans), Wesleyan University Press, Middletown, Connecticut.
Jabès, Edmond (1973), *The Book of Yukel and Return to the Book*, Waldrop, Rosmarie (trans), Wesleyan University Press, Middletown, Connecticut.
James, Liz and Webb, Ruth (1991), "'To Understand Ultimate Things and Enter Secret Places': Ekphrasis and Art in Byzantium", *Art History*, vol. 14, pp. 1-17.
Jardine, Alice A. (1985), *Gynesis: Configurations of Woman and Modernity*, Cornell University Press, Ithaca.
Jonas, Hans (1963), *The Gnostic Religion*, 2nd rev. ed., Beacon Press, Boston.
Jonas, Hans (1967), "Delimitation of the Gnostic Phenomenon—Typological and Historical", in Bianchi, Ugo (ed), *Le Origini dello Gnosticismo*, E. J. Brill, Leiden, pp. 90-108.
Joret, Charles (1892), *La Rose dans l'Antiquité et au Moyen Age*, Émile Bouillon, Paris.
Jung, C. G. (1965), *Memories, Dreams, Reflections*, Jaffé, Aniela (ed), Winston, Richard and Clara (trans), Random House (Vintage Books), New York.
Jung, C. G. (1967), *Alchemical Studies*, Hull, R.F.C. (trans), *The Collected Works of C. G. Jung*, vol. 13, Princeton University Press, Princeton.

Kelly, J. N. D. (1975), *Jerome: His Life, Writings, and Controversies*, Harper and Row, New York.
Kerenyi, Karl (1960), "Man and Mask", in *Spiritual Disciplines: Papers from the Eranos Yearbooks*, Manheim, Ralph (trans), Bollingen Foundation, New York, pp. 151-67.
Kerenyi, Karl (1976), *Dionysos*, Manheim, Ralph (trans), Princeton University Press, Princeton.
Kingston, Maxine (1984), *The Woman Warrior*, Alfred A. Knopf, New York.
Klein, Yves, "The Monochromatic Adventure", in *Yves Klein, 1928-1962: A Retrospective*, Institute for the Arts, Rice University, Houston; see Taylor, Mark C., "Nothing Ending Nothing", below.
Koch, Hal (1932), *Pronoia und Paideusis: Studien über Origenes und sein Verhältnis Zum Platonismus*, Walter de Gruyter, Berlin.
Koester, Helmut (1968), "One Jesus and Four Primitive Gospels", *Harvard Theological Review*, vol. 61, pp. 203-47.
Kristeva, Julia (1987), *Tales of Love*, Roudiez, Leon S. (trans), Columbia University Press, New York.
Lain Entralgo, Pedro (1970), *The Therapy of the Word in Classical Antiquity*, Rather, L. J. and Sharp, John M. (trans), Yale University Press, New Haven.
Leclerc, Pierre (1988), "Antoine et Paul: métamorphose d'un héros", in Duval, Yves-Marie (ed), *Jérôme entre l'occident et l'orient*, Études Augustiniennes, Paris, pp. 257-65.
Leitch, Vincent (1983), *Deconstructive Criticism*, Columbia University Press, New York.
Lévi-Strauss, Claude (1966), *The Savage Mind*, University of Chicago Press, Chicago.
Lewis, Charlton T. and Short, Charles (eds), A *Latin Dictionary*, The Clarendon Press, Oxford, 1969.
Liddell, Henry George, Scott, Robert and Jones, Sir Henry Stuart (eds) (1968), *A Greek-English Lexicon*, The Clarendon Press, Oxford.
Littlewood, A. R. (1968), "The Symbolism of the Apple in Greek and Roman Literature", *Harvard Studies in Classical Philology*, vol. 72, pp. 147-81.
Long, Charles H. (1995), "Towards a PostColonial Method in the Study of Religion", *Religious Studies News*, vol. 10, no. 2, pp. 3-8.
Loraux, Nicole (1987), *Tragic Ways of Killing a Woman*, Forster, Anthony (trans), Harvard University Press, Cambridge.
McGuire, Anne (1986), "Conversion and Gnosis in the *Gospel of Truth*", *Novum Testamentum*, vol. 28, pp. 338-55.
Ménard, Jacques-É (1972), *L'Évangile de Vérité*, Nag Hammadi Studies 2, E. J. Brill, Leiden.
Metzger, Bruce M. (1987), *The Canon of the New Testament: Its Origins, Development, and Significance*, The Clarendon Press, Oxford.
Miller, David L. (1981), *Christs: Meditations on Archetypal Images in Christian Theology*, Seabury Press, New York.

Miller, David L. (1982), "The Two Sandals of Christ: Descent into History and into Hell", *Eranos Jahrbuch* 50, Insel Verlag, Frankfort am Main, 1982, pp. 147-221.
Miller, David L. (1987), "The Question of the Book: Religion as Texture", in Winquist, Charles (ed), *Text and Textuality (Semeia*, vol. 40), Scholars Press, Atlanta, pp. 53-64.
Miller, David L. (1991), "Why Men Are Mad! Nothing-Envy and the Fascration Complex", *Spring*, vol. 51, pp. 71-79.
Miller, J. Hillis (1972), "Tradition and Difference", *Diacritics*, vol. 2, pp. 6-13.
Miller, J. Hillis (1975), "Deconstructing the Deconstructers", *Diacritics*, vol. 5, pp. 24-31.
Miller, J. Hillis (1975), "Fiction and Repetition: *Tess of the d'Urbervilles*", in *Forms of Modern British Fiction*, Friedman, Alan Warren (ed), University of Texas Press, Austin, pp. 43-71.
Miller, J. Hillis (1976), "Stevens' Rock and Criticism as Cure, II", *Georgia Review*, vol. 30, pp. 333-48.
Miller, J. Hillis (1976), "Ariadne's Thread: Repetition and the Narrative Line", *Critical Inquiry*, vol. 3, pp. 57-77.
Miller, J. Hillis (1979), "The Critic as Host", in Bloom, Harold, De Man, Paul, and Derrida, Jacques, et al., *Deconstruction and Criticism*, Seabury Press, New York, pp. 217-53.
Miller, J. Hillis (1982), *Fiction and Repetition: Seven English Novels*, Harvard University Press, Cambridge.
Miller, Patricia Cox (1986), "'A Dubious Twilight': Reflections on Dreams in Patristic Literature", *Church History*, vol. 55, pp. 153-64.
Miller, Patricia Cox (1986), "'Pleasure of the Text, Text of Pleasure': Eros and Language in Origen's *Commentary on the Song of Songs*", *Journal of the American Academy of Religion*, vol. 54 (1986), pp. 241-53.
Miller, Patricia Cox (1988), "'All the Words Were Frightful': Salvation by Dreams in the *Shepherd of Hermas*", *Vigiliae Christianae*, vol. 42, pp. 327-38.
Miller, Patricia Cox (1991), "Re-imagining the Self in Dreams", *Continuum*, vol. 1, pp. 35-53.
Miller, Patricia Cox (1993), "The Blazing Body: Ascetic Desire in Jerome's Letter to Eustochium", *Journal of Early Christian Studies*, vol. 1, pp. 21-45.
Miller, Patricia Cox (1994), "Desert Asceticism and 'The Body from Nowhere'", *Journal of Early Christian Studies*, vol. 2, pp. 137-53.
Mitchell, W.J.T. (1986), *Iconology: Image, Text, Ideology*, University of Chicago Press, Chicago.
Mitchell, W.J.T. (1994), *Picture Theory: Essays on Verbal and Visual Representation*, University of Chicago Press, Chicago.
Montaigne, *Essays*, Frame, Donald M. (trans), Doubleday, Garden City, New York, 1960.
Moore, Marianne (958), "Poetry", in *A College Book of Modern Verse*, Robinson, James K. and Rideout, Walter B. (eds), Harper and Row, New York, p. 325.

Nautin, Pierre (1976), "Origène Prédicateur", in Nautin, Pierre and Husson, Pierre (eds and trans), *Origène: Homélies sur Jérémie*, vol. 1, Les Éditions du Cerf, Paris, pp. 136-151.
Nautin, Pierre (1977), *Origène: Sa vie et son oeuvre*, Éditions Beauchesne, Paris.
Nemerov, Howard (1972), "On Metaphor", in idem, *Reflexions on Poetry and Poetics*, Rutgers University Press, New Brunswick, pp. 33-45.
Nilsson, M. P. (1950), *Geschichte der griechischen Religion*, vol. 2: *Die hellenistische und römische Zeit*, Beck, Munich.
Nock, Arthur Darby (1972), "The Vocabulary of the New Testament", in Stewart, Zeph (ed), *Arthur Darby Nock: Essays on Religion and the Ancient World*, Harvard University Press, Cambridge, vol. 1, pp. 341-47.
Nock, Arthur Darby (1972), "Greek Magical Papyri", in Stewart, Zeph (ed), *Arthur Darby Nock: Essays on Religion and the Ancient World*, Harvard University Press, Cambridge, vol. 1, pp. 176-94.
Norio, Morimoto (1983), in Sato, Hiroaki (ed), *One Hundred Frogs: From Renga to Haiku to English*, Weatherhill, New York.
O'Meara, Dominic J. (1980), "Gnosticism and the Making of the World in Plotinus", in Layton, Bentley (ed), *The Rediscovery of Gnosticism*, vol. 1: *Valentinian Gnosticism*, E. J. Brill, Leiden, pp. 365-78.
Onians, Richard Broxton (1973; repr. of 1951 ed.), *The Origins of European Thought*, Arno Press, New York.
Otto, Walter F. (1965), *Dionysus, Myth and Cult*, trans. Robert B. Palmer, Indiana University Press, Bloomington.
Paris, Ginette (1986), *Pagan Meditations*, Moore, Gwendolyn (trans), Spring Publications, Dallas.
Pépin, Jean, (1976), *Mythe et Allégorie: Les origins grecques et les contestations judéo-chrétiennes*, 2nd ed., Études Augustiniennes, Paris.
Perkins, Pheme (1980), "*On the Origin of the World (CG II, 5)*: A Gnostic Physics", *Vigiliae Christianae*, vol. 34, pp. 36-46.
Perry, B. E. (1941), "Physiologos", *Pauly-Wissowa Real-Encyclopädie der Classischen Altertumswissenschaft* 20, Part 1, cols. 1074-1129.
Pound, Ezra (1970), *Ezra Pound: A Critical Anthology*, Sullivan, J. P. (ed), Harmondsworth, Baltimore.
Preisendanz, Karl (ed) (1973-1974), *Papyri Graecae magicae*, 2 vols., 2nd ed. revised by Albert Hinrichs, Teubner, Stuttgart.
Price, R. M. (1985), "Introduction", *Theodoret of Cyrrhus: A History of the Monks of Syria*, Cistercian Publications, Kalamazoo, ix-xxxvii.
Price, S. R. F. (1986), "The Future of Dreams: From Freud to Artemidorus", *Past and Present*, vol. 113, pp. 3-37.
Pulver, Max (1978), "Jesus' Round Dance and Crucifixion according to the Acts of John", in Campbell, Joseph (ed), *The Mysteries*, Princeton University Press, Princeton.
Quilligan, Maureen (1979), *The Language of Allegory: Defining the Genre*, Cornell University Press, Ithaca.

Rappe, Sara (1995), "Metaphor in Plotinus' *Enneads* v 8.9", *Ancient Philosophy*, vol. 15 (1995), pp. 155-72.
Readings, William (1989), "Canon And On: From Concept to Figure", *Journal of the American Academy of Religion*, vol. 57, pp. 149-172.
Rilke, Rainer Maria (1949), *Notebooks of Malte Laurids Brigge*, Norton, M. D. Herter (trans), W. W. Norton, New York.
Rilke, Rainer Maria, (1962), *Sonnets to Orpheus*, Norton, M. D. Herter (trans), W. W. Norton, New York.
Rist, John (1964), *Eros and Psyche: Studies in Plato, Plotinus, and Origen*, University of Toronto Press, Toronto.
Rorty, Richard (ed) (1967), *The Linguistic Turn*, University of Chicago Press, Chicago.
Rousseau, Philip (1978), *Ascetics, Authority, and the Church in the Age of Jerome and Cassian*, Oxford University Press, Oxford.
Rousselle, Aline (1988), *Porneia: On Desire and the Body in Antiquity*, Pheasant, Felicia (trans), Basil Blackwell, Oxford.
Rudolph, Kurt (1983), *Gnosis*, Wilson, Robert McLachlan (ed), Harper and Row, New York.
Schama, Simon (1995), *Landscape and Memory*, Alfred A. Knopf, New York.
Schechner, Richard (1990), "Magnitudes of Performance", in *By Means of Performance: Intercultural Studies of Theatre and Ritual*, Schechner, Richard and Appel, Willa (eds), Cambridge University Press, Cambridge.
Schnapp-Gourbeillion, Annie (1981), *Lions, Héroes, Masques: Les représentations de l'animal chez Homère*, Librairie François Maspero, Paris.
Scholes, Robert (1985), "Is There a Fish in this Text?", in Blonsky, Marshall (ed), *On Signs*, The Johns Hopkins University Press, Baltimore, pp. 308-20.
Schüssler Fiorenza, Elisabeth (1983), *In Memory of Her: A Feminist Theological Reconstruction of Christian Origins*, Crossroad, New York.
Segal, Alan (1977), *Two Powers in Heaven: Early Rabbinic Reports about Christianity and Gnosticism*, E. J. Brill, Leiden.
Segal, Alan F. (1981), "Hellenistic Magic: Some Questions of Definition", in Van Den Broek, R. and Vermaseren, M. J. (eds), *Studies in Gnosticism and Hellenistic Religions*, E. J. Brill, Leiden, pp. 349-75.
Sells, Michael (1994), *Mystical Languages of Unsaying*, University of Chicago Press, Chicago.
Singer, Charles (1950), *History of Biology*, rev. ed., Oxford University Press, Oxford.
Smelik, K.A.D. (1977), "The Witch of Endor: I Samuel 28 in Rabbinic and Christian Exegesis till 800 A.D.", *Vigiliae Christianae*, vol. 33, pp. 160-179.
Smith, Jonathan Z. (1982), *Imagining Religion: From Babylon to Jonestown*, University of Chicago Press, Chicago.
Smith, Jonathan Z. (1987), *To Take Place: Toward Theory in Ritual*, University of Chicago Press, Chicago.

Smith, Jonathan Z. (1993), *Map Is Not Territory: Studies in the History of Religions*, University of Chicago Press, Chicago.
Smith, Morton (1973), *Clement of Alexandria and a Secret Gospel of Mark*, Harvard University Press, Cambridge.
Smith, Morton (1978), *Jesus the Magician*, Harper and Row, San Francisco.
Smith, Morton (1980), "The History of the Term Gnostikos", in Layton, Bentley (ed), *The Rediscovery of Gnosticism*, vol. 2: *Sethian Gnosticism*, E. J. Brill, Leiden, pp. 796-807.
Sontag, Susan (1983), "Writing Itself: On Roland Barthes", in *A Susan Sontag Reader*, Farrar, Straus, Giroux, New York, pp. 425-46.
Standaert, Benoit (1976), "'Evangelium Veritatis' et 'Veritatis Evangelium': La Question du Titre et les Témoins Patristiques", *Vigiliae Christianae*, vol. 30, pp. 138-50.
Standaert, Benoit (1976), "*L'Évangile de Vérité*: Critique et Lecture", *New Testament Studies*, vol. 22, pp. 243-75.
Steidle, B. (1941), "Neue Untersuchungen zu Origenes' *Peri Archon*", *Zeitschrift für die Neutestamentlisches Wissenschaft*, vol. 40, pp. 236-43.
Steiner, George (1983), "The Historicity of Dreams (Two Questions to Freud)", *Salmagundi*, vol. 61, pp. 6-21.
Stevens, Wallace (1977), *The Collected Poems of Wallace Stevens*, Alfred A. Knopf, New York.
Stevens, Wallace (1977), *Letters of Wallace Stevens*, Stevens, Holly (ed), Alfred A. Knopf, New York.
Stevens, Wallace (1977), *Opus Posthumous*, Morse, Samuel French (ed), Alfred A. Knopf, New York.
Stroumsa, Gedaliahu G. (1990), "*Caro salutis cardo:* Shaping the Person in Early Christian Thought", *History of Religions*, vol. 30, pp. 25-50.
Sullivan, Lawrence (1990), "Body Works: Knowledge of the Body in the Study of Religion", *History of Religions*, vol. 30, pp. 86-99.
Tardieu, Michel (1974), *Trois Mythes Gnostiques: Adam, Éros et les animaux d'Égypte dans un écrit de Nag Hammadi (II, 5)*, Études Augustiniennes, Paris.
Taylor, Mark C. (1984), *Erring: A Postmodern A/theology*, University of Chicago Press, Chicago.
Taylor, Mark C. (1990), "Nothing Ending Nothing", in Scharlemann, Robert P. (ed), *Theology at the End of the Century: A Dialogue on the Postmodern*, University Press of Virginia, Charlottesville, pp. 41-75.
Taylor, Mark C. (1992), *Disfiguring: Art, Architecture, Religion*, University of Chicago Press, Chicago.
Taylor, Mark (1998), "Introduction", in idem (ed), *Critical Terms for Religious Studies*, University of Chicago Press, Chicago, pp. 1-19.
The Oxford Classical Dictionary, 2nd ed. (1970), Hammond, N. G. L. and Scullard, H. H. (eds), The Clarendon Press, Oxford.
Vahanian, Gabriel (1966), *No Other God*, George Braziller, New York.

Vernant, Jean-Pierre (1989), "Dim Body, Dazzling Body", in Feher, Michel (ed), *Fragments for a History of the Human Body*, Part One *(Zone 3)*, Urzone, Inc., New York, pp. 18-47.
Von Campenhausen, Hans (1972), *The Formation of the Christian Bible*, Baker, J. A. (trans), Fortress Press, Philadelphia.
Wallace-Hadrill, D. S. (1968), *The Greek Patristic View of Nature*, Manchester University Press, Manchester.
Wallis, Richard T. (1976), "NOUS as Experience", in Harris, R. Baine (ed), *The Significance of Neoplatonism*, Old Dominion University Research Foundation, Norfolk, Virginia, pp. 121-53.
Warren, E. W. (1966), "Imagination in Plotinus", *Classical Quarterly*, vol. 16, pp. 277-85.
Wellmann, Max (1928), "Die *Phūsika* des Bolos Demokritos und der Magier Anaxilaos aus Larissa", *Abhandlungen der Preussischen Akademie der Wissenschaften*, Phil.-Hist. Classe, no. 7.
Wellmann, Max (1930), "Der *Physiologos:* Eine religionsgeschichtlich-naturwissenschaftliche Untersuchung", *Philologus*, Supplementband 22, Heft 1, pp. 1-116.
White, Hayden (1972), "The Forms of Wildness: Archaeology of an Idea", in Dudley, Edward and Novak, Maximillian E. (eds), *The Wild Man Within: An Image in Western Thought from the Renaissance to Romanticism*, University of Pittsburgh Press, Pittsburgh.
Wiesen, David S. (1964), *St. Jerome as a Satirist,* Cornell Studies in Classical Philology 34, Cornell University Press, Ithaca.
Williams, Charles Allyn (1925-26), "Oriental Affinities of the Legend of the Hairy Anchorite", *Illinois Studies in Language and Literature*, vol. 10, no. 2; vol. 11, no. 4.
Williams, Jacqueline (1988), *Biblical Interpretation in the Gnostic Gospel of Truth From Nag Hammadi*, SBL Dissertation Series 79, Scholars Press, Atlanta.
Wyschogrod, Edith (1990), *Saints and Postmodernism: Revisioning Moral Philosophy*, University of Chicago Press, Chicago.
Zeitlin, Froma (1994), "The artful eye: vision, ecphrasis and spectacle in Euripidean theatre", in Goldhill, Simon and Osborne, Robin (eds), *Art and text in ancient Greek culture*, Cambridge University Press, Cambridge, pp. 138-96.

For Product Safety Concerns and Information please contact our EU
representative GPSR@taylorandfrancis.com
Taylor & Francis Verlag GmbH, Kaufingerstraße 24, 80331 München, Germany

www.ingramcontent.com/pod-product-compliance
Lightning Source LLC
Chambersburg PA
CBHW071808300426
44116CB00009B/1233